Jambands

The complete guide to the players, music & scene

Jambands

The complete guide to the players, music & scene

by Dean Budnick

Backbeat
Books
San Francisco

Published by Backbeat Books
600 Harrison Street, San Francisco, CA 94107
www.backbeatbooks.com
email: books@musicplayer.com

An imprint of the Music Player Network
Publishers of *Guitar Player*, *Bass Player*, *Keyboard*, and other magazines
United Entertainment Media, Inc.
A CMP Information company

CMP
United Business Media

Distributed to the book trade in the US and Canada by
Publishers Group West, 1700 Fourth Street, Berkeley, CA 94710

Distributed to the music trade in the US and Canada by
Hal Leonard Publishing, P.O. Box 13819, Milwaukee, WI 53213

Cover design by Damien Castaneda
Text design by Michael Cutter
Front cover photo by Jay Blakesberg
Back cover photos by Dean Budnick

Library of Congress Cataloging-in-Publication Data

Budnick, Dean.
    Jambands : the complete guide to the players, music & scene /
    by Dean Budnick.
        p. cm.
    Includes index.
    ISBN 0-87930-745-5 (alk. paper)
        1. Jam bands—Bio–bibliography. 2. Jam bands—Discography. 3. Popular music—
Bibliography. I. Title: Jam bands. II. Title.

ML 102.P66.B88 2003
781.64—dc22

                                                                    2003059572

Printed in the United States of America

03 04 05 06 07   5 4 3 2 1

*To the brainy and beautiful Leanne Carole Barrett
and the beautiful and brainy Caroline Barrett Budnick.*

TABLE OF CONTENTS

GUIDE TO CD RATINGS

★★★★★ An essential part of the canon

★★★★ A fine release that you should have in your collection

★★★ Solid—decent performance, production, song selection/composition; good for light car rotation

★★ Fair—useful for sampling what a band has going on, or for a version of a song or two

★ C & C—for coasters and completists (I receive quite a few of these each week, but most of the bands producing such efforts did not meet the threshold to appear in these pages.)

FOREWORD

As publisher of *Relix* magazine, I have the good fortune to hear about new bands that are making waves in the jamband scene. What defines these bands and their ultimate success is not the number of tickets sold or the number of CDs purchased. Sure, the money helps pay the bills, and no one likes to be poor, but these musicians' yardsticks are not monetary. They measure success by the quality of the music. They embody a new individuality in music. The art of collaborating, playing without a net—a willingness to take chances musically and perhaps to fail—is what separates these artists from those of other genres. The annual Jammy Awards show is a case in point. Stepping onto the stage, musicians often meet their collaborators for the first time in front of thousands of listeners. It's this kind of exposed, raw energy on which these artists thrive.

Jamband fans "get it." They are not easily manipulated into listening to the flavor-of-the-month band pushed by the major record labels. They seek out quality and originality. True devotees, they encourage the bands they love to experiment, to stretch their boundaries and take their fans on a musical journey. When it works, the trip is magic; when it doesn't, it was fun trying.

I often hear people say they are surprised at how fast the jamband scene is exploding. It is growing exponentially and will continue to expand because the growth is for all the right reasons. Unlike pop music that is competitive, style-obsessed, and status-conscious, jambands are inclusive. Live improvisational music embraces many forms. Its influences are diverse: Electronica, blues, bluegrass, newgrass, reggae, jazz, and funk have all sewn seeds in our scene. Preeminent is the music, good music. A talented musician will always be welcomed and often asked to sit in, to challenge, to offer something new.

Fans expect more from these bands. They want four-hour shows, they want something new and fresh every time, and they want it often. Following a favorite band and often traveling many miles to see them has become an essential part of the jamband culture. There is nothing better than hooking up with friends hundreds of miles from home and sharing a great musical experience. The fan-band relationship is symbiotic in the healthiest sense, as fan participation and support is critical for bands that make most of their hard-earned dollars by touring.

This book is meant to be both listened to and read. It is the ultimate guide to jambands, and no one is more qualified to put it together than Dean Budnick—editor-in-chief of Jambands.com, senior editor of *Relix* magazine, co-host of the top-rated "Jam Nation" radio show, and a Harvard Ph.D. to boot. Sit back, relax, and let Dean lay out for you the intricacies of an ever-changing musical landscape.

Steve Bernstein
Publisher
Relix

INTRODUCTION

Come mothers and fathers
Throughout the land
And don't criticize
What you can't understand
Your sons and your daughters
Are beyond your command
Your old road is
Rapidly agin'.
Please get out of the new one
If you can't lend your hand
For the times they are a-changin'.
—Bob Dylan

Seems like the more things change the more they stay the same. The verse from Bob Dylan comes from the very beginning of the "revolution" that my generation was going to spawn. We did not spawn the revolution that many of my peers expected, but we did spawn, as do all new generations, our own revolutions.

The revolution closest to me was in music. As a member of the Allman Brothers Band from its inception in 1969, I saw the music of the young go from silly little songs about teenage angst of all types to serious music about social change crafted by musicians capable of really playing their instruments. We created "true art" rather than cute songs, using rock, pop, and more as its base. We added elements of jazz, blues, and classical music—and something very intense happened. This was new. This was exciting. This took rock music from a pop song idiom aimed at preteen girls to an art form capable of creating moments bordering on religious experiences.

As I said, we started in 1969. That's 34 years ago! Today we are still playing that music, and I am writing this on February 27, 2003—two days away from the start of the Allman Brothers Band Tour 2003. I can truthfully say the feelings I get playing with the ABB now are every bit as intense as they were 34 years ago.

About four years ago, Oteil Burbridge (bass player with the ABB) and I spent almost two weeks following the Jambands.com tour. This was my first full exposure to the new generation of bands that have picked up the torch passed along by groups like the Allman Brothers Band. I was blown away. I was on the tour to find bands for a record label I was starting, and the level of musicianship was astounding. My first night on the tour, I was introduced to a nervous little guy in baggy shorts who also blew me away. You're about to read his book. "Dr. Dean," as I call him, impressed me immediately with his profound love for and knowledge of the jamband scene.

Of course, you will find that there is probably not a band out there that will admit to being a "jamband." That doesn't change the fact one iota that they *are* a jamband. We must have labels. Gregg Allman has solved his dislike of the Allman Brothers Band being called a jamband by stating that we are a band that jams. Semantics. Let us say that what these bands share is: *an ability to play and a seriousness about their music that maximizes musicianship and minimizes showmanship.* That's Butch's "definition of jam music in 15 words." Dr. Dean is the preeminent authority on these bands.

Dean Budnick recently received his Ph.D. in American History from Harvard. I'm still trying to tie this in with his love of jam music and his continuing dedication to compiling all the information available about this genre. I'll let you speculate on that, if you wish. But you don't need to in order to benefit from this book. This is THE definitive book about the bands and musicians playing jam music today. You can read it cover to cover. You can use it as a reference when you want info about a band you may want to explore live or on CD. Or you can just use it to get caught up on who's doing what in the jamband scene. Dr. Dean's essays on everyone from the Allman Brothers Band to Medeski Martin and Wood to Vinyl will give you enough insight into the nature of jam music to decide whether or not it interests you.

If you are a real lover of this type of music, then this book is required reading. Nothing else like it exists and will not again until the Good Doctor writes his next one. Dean Budnick is a unique individual. (Did I tell you he is on the board of directors of my label, Flying Frog Records? I ain't stupid.) There is not another person around with such intelligence, knowledge, and ability to communicate coupled with so deep a passion for this music.

Back to my opening Dylan lyric: I now find myself on the "mothers and fathers" side, but I do my best to "lend my hand." I am not gonna "get out of the new one"—I had a part in creating it. What I find in the new generation of players that Dean writes about here is the same love of music played with skill and intensity, that my generation has had since the '60s. Dr. Dean's gonna tell you a lot about those who are doing it, how well they are doing it, and maybe even give you some insight into why. Enjoy.

Butch Trucks
Drummer, the Allman Brothers Band
President, Flying Frog Records
Palm Beach, Florida

A

A440

www.a440.com

Since the jamband realm is marked by its denizens' propensity for bridging genres, A440's "alternative improvisational groove" was inevitable. This is not to say this space is altogether novel—Lake Trout certainly synthesizes many such influences into its darker tones, and the indie rockers in Rana have jamband roots. But New York's A440 is a bellwether, given the means by which it has melded modern rock vocal stylings and song structures with free-form improvisational rock and funk.

This Long Island quintet, named for Adam Bendy's zeal in tuning his bass to A440 during rehearsal, began gigging in mid-2000. Founders Rob Salzer (guitar, violin) and Fil Bonsignore (guitar) first collaborated as teenagers, but it wasn't until a few years after high school that they assembled the current group, adding Bendy, drummer Dino Foggan, and singer Dave Jensen. While the band writes solid, melodic alterna-pop compositions, it is Jensen's emotive vocals, often reminiscent of Tool's Maynard James Keenan, that animate them. Still, this is not to suggest that the execution always meets the intent, as at times the results are not cohesive—it can feel like A440 is tacking relatively customary guitar-driven improv onto modern rock fare. Plus, one hopes the band will expand its range of covers beyond the normative ("Eyes of the World" and "In Memory of Elizabeth Reed" are staples) to offer expansive takes on the music of, say, Tool or Soundgarden. Nonetheless, A440 is legitimately at the vanguard even if it is still formulating its ideas and some listeners will remain unengaged by the concept.

A440 (2002) ★★ ½

An intriguing document of a band aspiring to innovation, though not always a successful fusion of disparate elements (some of the songs can feel cobbled together). Still, Dave Jensen's vocals impress, there are some decent hooks, and A440 can stretch it out persuasively.

AARON KATZ BAND

www.aaronzkatz.com

Although Aaron Katz first garnered recognition through his drumming with Percy Hill, he has long placed his primary musical focus on his songwriting. Indeed, Katz's linear, melodic compositions were one of the reasons Nate Wilson and Joe Farrell invited him to join Percy Hill in 1998 when the band refashioned its lineup. Many examples appear on Percy's 1999 album, *Colour in Bloom*, which took home the inaugural Jammy Award for Studio Release of the Year. However, in the fall of 2000, when it became clear that Percy Hill would cut back on its gigs, Katz began recording his solo album, which he released the following year. The Aaron Katz Band became a national touring act in 2002.

Katz's music and mindset are well suited for the studio. Here he can layer instrumental tracks and harmonies beneath his own smooth vocals, in the mode of Steely Dan and Paul Simon (artists heralded by Katz). His lyrics often use evocative imagery to relate accounts of fictional characters and romantic musings, with some environmental messages incorporated as well. There is a pop-rock feel to his sound that some deem too light or mainstream but others find warm and engaging.

When he performs with the AKB, Katz is up front on acoustic guitar, enabling him to lean into the vocals (he has drafted a number of talented players for the drummer's chair, including Dave Dincenso and Andy Herrick). Katz also rearranges many of the songs he wrote for Percy Hill ("Ammonium Maze" often receives an expansive reading). The band stays a bit closer to the song structures than Percy, with electric guitarist Josh Pryor adding colors, but while the Aaron Katz Band very much emphasize its namesake's compositions, it still offers the songs room to breathe.

Simplest Warrior (2001) ★ ★ ★

Katz uses the studio to good effect. Still, while his songwriting is often pleasing, the production does render a number of cuts that are a bit too similar in feel. This becomes all the more apparent with "Soul Sister," a lively hidden track with a stark acoustic guitar that closes out the disc and offers a welcome juxtaposition to all that preceded it.

ADDISON GROOVE PROJECT

www.addisongroove.com

It was a long time coming. Addison Groove Project formed in 1997 and released four albums between the spring of 1998 and the spring of 2003, but there was always something holding it back. That something was school, as AGP formed while its members

were teens. During its first six years the group toured and recorded on weekends and vacations. By the summer of 2003, however, the last members of this Massachusetts-based group had graduated, and Addison was finally ready to cut loose.

While the word groove has become ubiquitous (so much so, frankly, that some feel it currently carries little cachet), this was not the case when five Wellesley High School students founded AGP. They selected a moniker that both conveyed their intent (to deliver horn-imbued funk) and also invoked bass player John Hall's father, Addison. (One of AGP's earlier songs, "The Reverend," was written in his honor, as he serves in such a capacity.) While its members were still juniors, the group finished first at Boston radio station WBCN's High School Battle of the Bands. Rob Marscher, a native of nearby Framingham whose group was the runner-up, deemed that the victor's spoils should include a keyboard player, and he joined the group within a month. Addison (the band, not the man) started gigging out in December 1997, securing its initial club date as an opening act for ViperHouse and the Pat McGee Band at Cambridge's Middle East. A few months later the group used studio time it had been awarded at the Battle and successfully lobbied Wellesley High School for "senior project" status to record its eponymous debut.

By the next fall the six musicians were scattered throughout the Northeast. One has to appreciate their work ethic, as Addison remained an active entity despite the challenges brought on by geography. The band performed whenever possible, including a month-long 2000 summer tour with Uncle

Sammy, and a second extended foray a year later. (One notable moment took place at the end of 2001: After opening for Macco Parker at New York's Irving Plaza, AGP saxophone players Dave Adams [alto] and Ben Groppe [tenor] were invited to sit in with the headliner.) The group continued to write new music as well, delving deeper into jazz, dub, and hip-hop. Brendan McGinn, who alternates between guitar and trumpet and also contributes the band's occasional lead vocals, explained in October 2002, "We'll do stuff like lay down tracks on workstations, have cheesy little synth parts and burn them onto a CD, and you can play them to someone. Or you can actually e-mail computer files that have sheet music...the wonders of technology. I imagine we'll eventually be doing virtual rehearsals." Before it came to that, commencement arrived.

The band's sound still embodies its name. While the music certainly has become more sophisticated, AGP continues working towards its original resolve to keep things moving. (McGinn notes, "We like our horn lines tight and our bass loud.") As Addison Groove Project develops into a full-time concern with additional opportunities to write and rehearse, one wonders if the band will introduce more challenging elements, addi-

Addison Groove Project.

tional angular or dissonant aspects. Then again, maybe not, as the group has been doing well for itself thus far with a steady following, particularly in the Northeast. Nonetheless after six years of anticipation, many individuals, band members included, are eager to hear what the future will yield.

Wicked Live 2 (2003) ★★★

Drawn from two nights at Boston's Paradise in October 2002, this disc demonstrates that AGP continues to introduce modes and textures, especially through Rob Marscher's keys. Overall, the results are engaging if not astonishing.

Allophone (2002) ★★ ½

The band does a fine job of opening its sound in the studio, adding wrinkles and additional instrumentation (turntables, flute, percussion). The intent is certainly there, though the core compositions do not always command specific attention.

Also:

Wicked Live (2001)
Addison Groove Project (1998)

ALLMAN BROTHERS BAND

www.allmanbrothersband.com
Let's give the opening words to band namesake and icon Mr. Gregory Lenoir Allman: "We're not one of those jambands, we're a band that jams. We are a progressive blues jazz fusion band, now that there's no more country."

A most respectful dissent must follow here. Allman's initial distinction is a valid one, and not mere sophistry. However, when followed by the descriptive list of genres, it does indeed

place the Allman Brothers Band soundly within the jamband milieu (this atmosphere is animated by the ABB on a sub-molecular level, though, so Gregg should take comfort in the clime).

Allman's comment on the dearth of country is a reference to the departure of Dickey Betts in May 2000, which comprises another lively chapter within the epic tome that is the ABB (and speaking of epic—make that Epic—part of that story relates to the band's ongoing tribulations with record companies, which go all the way back to a sour deal they struck with Phil Walden and Capricorn in 1969, on through Arista's attempts to milk a pop hit from them during the disco era, and to the Epic contract they were finally able to fulfill or at least settle with the release of *Peakin' at the Beacon* in 2000). And as for those passages best suited for tabloid excerpts, founding drummer Butch Trucks reflects, "What's that Clinton said, 'It's the economy, stupid'? Well it's the music. Like too many other rock 'n' rollers we lost sight of that and got caught up in the sex, drugs, and fame and glad-handing and the partying and all that crap. By '76 I realized it had all become a joke. The thing we thought we wanted, fame and fortune, just turned into a nightmare. It took us some time, but eventually we turned all that around, which is why I am so damn proud of the fact that we're out here today, still hitting the note." (That last phrase, which supplies the title to the band's 2003 release, has long been its jargon for those instances when, as Trucks explains, "you get into a place where you can't make a mistake. You're absolutely in the moment with no thought of yesterday or what's coming next.")

More than three decades after the ABB's formation and also since Duane Allman's death in a motorcycle accident on October 29, 1971, the guitarist still towers at the group's center. His innovations on the instrument are well documented (his work on Wilson Pickett's version of "Hey Jude" first turned ears in 1968, including those of Eric Clapton, who was eager to meet Allman two years later when producer Tom Dowd brought them together in the studio while Clapton recorded with Derek and the Dominoes. Allman's achievements during those sessions included the combustive signature notes at the beginning of "Layla" that ensured his participation on the entire album). However, current ABB guitarist (and nephew of Butch) Derek Trucks, whose technique builds on an early immersion in Allman's slide playing, also singles out Duane's other roles, emphasizing, "A significant part of his legacy is the ability to keep the Allman Brothers going for this long. Without him being there at the beginning and whipping everyone into shape I seriously doubt that the band would still be rolling along. Someone with that strong a personality and that much musical vision and fire is an inspiration."

One extraordinary, oft-overlooked fact is that the original lineup performed for only two and a half years. But during that period, the group created songs that remain an essential part of our current musical lexicon, recorded what some have described as the definitive live rock album, and headlined the final nights of a storied venue, the Fillmore East. (The last show was an industry-only affair, so the ABB really cut loose on the penultimate evening.

Butch Trucks recalls, "It was probably the greatest night of music in my life. A whole night of hitting the note and hitting it with everything you can imagine. Every time I would go to play something two or three other guys were already doing it; we were definitely all in the same place at the same time. We played until the sun came up. We finished playing, and there was dead silence, the audience was as completely wasted as we were, sitting there with shit-eating grins on their faces. And I remember Duane getting up, walking by, dragging his guitar behind him going, 'Goddamn, it's like leaving church.'")

Another tragedy followed a year after Duane's death when bassist Berry Oakley also suffered a fatal motorcycle accident, but still the group pushed on. Betts came into his own

Gregg Allman steps forward and strums.

as a songwriter and guitarist, and the group wisely opted to forgo comparisons with the original roster by changing the dynamic with an additional lead instrument, Chuck Leavell's piano. While there were many moments of excess during this period, there were also some celebrated performances, resulting in the ABB's appearance before 600,000 people at the Watkins Glen Superjam (with the Grateful Dead and the Band) on July 28, 1973. (BTW, Cameron Crowe based Stillwater's tour in *Almost Famous* on an actual stretch of Allman Brothers Band shows during this era that he covered as a teenage music journalist, and the film includes the character of real-life ABB roadie Joseph "Red Dog" Campbell.)

From the mid-'70s into the late '80s, the band sputtered through periods of disunion, disfavor, and disservice until guitarist Warren Haynes joined and ultimately spearheaded two separate resurgences of the Brothers. In 1989, Haynes, along with fellow future Gov't Mule member Allen Woody, became part of the reformed ABB that toured in support of the *Dreams* box set and entered the studio to record an album nearly a decade after its preceding efforts. Haynes, who had moved from David Allan Coe's group to the Dickey Betts Band and then on to the Brothers, merited a triple crown for proficiencies in voice, guitar, and songcraft. However, Haynes and Woody left in 1997 to focus on the Mule and also because of stagnancy in the band, with little new material introduced following *Where It All Begins*. Five years later, the dismissal of Dickey Betts, the death of Allen Woody, and the departure of Betts's immediate successor, Jimmy Herring, led Gregg

Allman and Butch Trucks to induce Haynes's return. Initially billed as a special guest during the Beacon shows, he was soon back in the fold, composing the set lists, writing new tunes with Allman, and ultimately co-producing the band's *Hittin' the Note* disc. (Gregg reveals, "I'm so glad to have him back because if we didn't have him within our reach we might have just said to hell with it.")

Some feel that pound-for-pound the players who recorded *Hittin' the Note* rival any ABB roster from the band's career. The elder Trucks doesn't equivocate: "I don't think there's any doubt about it, this band technically blows away any band that has had the name the Allman Brothers Band." (The boldest of assertions, yet one can at least make a case for its validity in emphasizing the callow rawness of the original lineup.) Three of the original six members remain with the group: Allman, Trucks, and Trucks's lifelong drumming partner Jaimoe (née Johnny Lee Johnson—Duane had tapped the pair to mirror the Jabo Starks/Clyde Stubblefield combo at the heart of James Brown's band). The trio is now joined by former Aquarium Rescue Unit bassist Oteil Burbridge (who not only moved from a six-string to a four-string and grabbed a pick to evoke the band's earlier sound, but also secured a mushroom tattoo on his calf, as sported by the group's founders), percussionist Marc Quiñones (Spro Gyra), Haynes, and the long-beyond-prodigy Derek Trucks (named among the 100 Greatest Guitarists of All Time in a *Rolling Stone* cover story, sliding in at No. 81, with Haynes at No. 23, Betts somewhat splitting the difference at No. 58, and Duane Allman finishing second to Hendrix). The departure of Betts has alienated certain fans who miss his guitar tone along with his compositions, few of which remain in rotation. The current guitar tandem no longer fashions itself in particular roles, which alters the nature of the music at times, taking it further away from the familiar. This again has distanced some audience members, though all in all the music certainly remains true to the spirit of the original group. Indeed, Derek observes that "anyone from Wynton Marsalis to Béla Fleck to others who have never seen the band and have the impression of it as a southern rock band, when they actually see us, it freaks them out. I don't think there is any other comparable surviving rock group with that integrity so other musicians will be freaked out by what's going on. It's definitely a living, breathing entity. It's not one of those things where people leave thinking it's a nostalgia act." His uncle adds, "If I didn't know we were out there kicking ass and playing with the same intensity we played with in '69 and '70 then I just wouldn't be doing it."

Alas, name-calling must ensue, as one should expect no less of the world's longstanding, ever-stirring, once-and-future, magisterial jamband. (Sorry, Gregg.)

Hittin' the Note (2003) ★★★★½

A return to form, as a revitalized band delivers a collection of songs that retain the classic ABB feel yet remain bracing and new.

American University 12/13/70 (2002) ★★★★½

Recorded three months prior to the landmark *At Fillmore East* live release, this show is also a part of ABB lore, as the group appeared at the university through the efforts of then-student/future manager Bert Holman.

Peakin' at the Beacon (2000) ★★★

This live disc is drawn from Dickey Betts's final run at New York's Beacon Theater. The performance is not as ragged as some members later suggested, though apart from a few tracks, such as the closing "Highs Falls," it is oomph-deficient.

An Evening with the Allman Brothers Band: 2nd Set (1995) ★★★★

Recorded five years into the band's renaissance, *2nd Set* showcases the strenuous interplay and dynamic between Betts and Haynes, which reaches its apex during the acoustic moments.

Where It All Begins (1994) ★★★★

The final studio disc from the Haynes/Woody incarnation presents a number of songs that would contribute to the latter-day canon, including "Soulshine," "No One to Run With," and Betts's soaring "Back Where It All Begins."

An Evening with the Allman Brothers Band: First Set (1992) ★★★½

Drawn from the spring 1992 tour, this album presents some newer compositions ("Nobody Knows" is the standout) as well as some solid runs through familiar material (including "Blue Sky" and "Dreams") empowered by a propulsive rhythm section.

Shades of Two Worlds (1991) ★★★½

The second disc from the latter-day ABB advances the sound both in terms of songwriting and collective performance, especially on "End of the Line," "Nobody Knows," and an acoustic reading of Robert Johnson's "Come on in My Kitchen."

Supernova" on December 29, 1996, and the Proclaimers' "I'm Gonna Be (500 Miles)" on December 30, 1997. The lure of the stage persisted, eventually leading Marshall to assemble Amfibian.

Amfibian's genesis began with UTALK, a band that Marshall and Phish songwriting partner and guitarist Trey Anastasio intended to assemble for a run of dates. Marshall began to rehearse with bassist Matt Kohut and drummer Peter Cotton, but the group ultimately dissolved before playing a public gig. The seed had been planted, though, and the trio began drawing additional Princeton, New Jersey-area musicians into the fold. Marshall named the band spontaneously, shortly before an early gig. By the spring of 2001 Amfibian toured as a septet with drummer JP Wasicko and three guitarists: future RANA members Scott Metzger and Andrew Southern as well as singer/songwriter Chris Harford. Harford, who began his career with mid-'80s rock trio Three Colors with Hub Moore and Dana Colley (Morphine), elevated the group by adding another assertive presence into the mix (his "Leaf of Fall" became one of the highlights of Amfibian's live sets).

Some fans have been drawn to the band's live gigs to see Marshall interpret some of the songs he has written with Anastasio ("The Wedge" has become an Amfibian staple, and the band offers an extended take on it). Others have attended with the hope that Anastasio himself might make an appearance (as he did at Vermont's Higher Ground on March 31, 2001, the show that marked the public debut of UTALK; at one point during the set Anastasio, Marshall, Kohut, and Cotton performed "Wading in the Velvet Sea"). However, those people who come out solely for the Phish connection may be somewhat flummoxed by Amfibian's sound, which certainly reflects Marshall's other association but owes more to Pavement or Ween (Dean and Gene Ween have guested with the group).

While Amfibian is Marshall's project, he remains a diffident bandleader and performer. Typically he contributes lead vocals on only a limited number of songs per night. In addition, his work on keyboards is rather tentative, and he often lays out. Still, the group offers some of Marshall's most personal songwriting as interpreted by a collection of gifted players, who refine and define its sound with each show. The future of Amfibian as constituted in spring 2001 remains uncertain due to its players' other commitments. Nonetheless it is likely that "Tom Marshall and Co." will resurface.

Amfibian Tales (2000) ★★★

While credited to Tom Marshall and Co., this disc features all of Amfibian except for Harford. *Amfibian Tales* offers concise, often-gentle interpretations of Marshall's music (one exception being Kohut and Metzger's instrumental "Salamander Spread"). Some obvious reference points are the Beatles and Velvet Underground, although songs like "Dream Satellite" and "Mud" are refracted through modern indie rock sensibilities. Phish fans may be intrigued by "Nothing," which sounds a bit like one of the band's late-era tunes as interpreted by the Indigo Girls (in this case the Saras).

www.furrythug.com—the music production company that Marshall founded with Andy Navarro, home to some members of Amfibian's extended family.

TREY ANASTASIO

www.treyanastasio.com

There are a number of fans who hope that Trey Anastasio's group will remain the modern-day analogue to the Jerry Garcia Band. No, these folks don't want Anastasio to take it sloooow (the latter-day JGB shows could be exceedingly so). Instead they hope that since Anastasio will be performing in a different context, delivering a modicum of Phish material, that the venues will remain relatively small and the crowds manageable. Plus, who knows, maybe down the road, akin to Garcia, Anastasio will dig in for an 18-night run at the Lunt-Fontanne Theater (and what the hey, maybe offer up a matinee or two).

Given the professed ardor that so many Phish enthusiasts hold for the guitarist, the hostility they directed at Anastasio during the Phish hiatus was somewhat boggling. Particularly after he assembled a new touring outfit, many fans vociferously blamed him for Phish's self-imposed suspension. Some went so far as to use Anastasio's own mythology

Trey Anastasio Band at Chicago's UIC Pavillion, June 2002.

against him, donning "Trey Is Wilson" shirts referencing the dictator in his Gamehendge song-cycle who had imprisoned a mockingbird. (Anastasio picked up on this and in a jesting, jousting spirit began wearing Wilson-emblazoned athletic gear. Also, when accepting an award for the Trey Anastasio Band's Tour of the Year at the 2002 Jammys, he offered up a song that included the lyrics, "We've tested all your patience, yet you've been tried and true, you're sick of Pork Tornado, you're sick of Vida Blue. If I would just stop talking, you would get your wish: Stop this shit and give us back our Phish.")

Anastasio's solo touring preceded Phish's hiatus. In May 1999 he embarked on 12 dates in which he performed solo acoustic followed by an electric set. In the latter portion of each show, he played in a trio with bassist Tony Markelis and drummer Russ Lawton, who would become the core of the group to follow. ("I asked Tony to be in the band first because he was one guy I knew I wanted to play with as soon as the opportunity arose. I talked to him about drummers and I wanted him to be linked to a drummer that he really liked playing with, so Russ was really his suggestion. Right off the bat I knew you needed to have a happy rhythm section.")

The year 2000 was a year for Phish, but by the summer of 2001, when Anastasio took to the road again with his own project, he did so with a big band, expanding to an eight-piece group with keyboards and four horns (vocalist/ trumpet/tuba player Jennifer Hartswick often served as his dance partner/fencing opponent). A year later, he toured with a bigger band, as the roster expanded by two with the addition of percussionist Cyro Baptista and

Peter Apfelbaum (tenor sax, flute) in support of the *Trey Anastasio* disc. (Speaking of *Trey Anastasio* and Trey Anastasio, while some refer to the group as the Trey Anastasio Band, often using the acronym TAB, the guitarist has opted to forgo any official designation, not even adding the word "band" after his name to reflect the mutable nature of the group and its music.)

By the time of the group's May 2003 tour in support of the double live *Plasma* release, its sound elicited comparisons from King Sunny Ade to the swing bands of the '30s and '40s to Miles Davis's fusion efforts. Anastasio links all three antecedents through their players' interaction, explaining, "The highest level of music, the thing that it has in common is communication among musicians." Thus, when listening to King Sunny Ade's 22-piece group, "You just trance out, and the whole thing is these tiny little bits and pieces where everybody is speaking together. The same thing happens when I hear *Bitches Brew*. What's interesting about it is the interplay, the conversation."

While Anastasio's dectet is engaged in such a conversation, not everyone has deemed the dialogue captivating. One early criticism arose from the similarity between set lists, which finally achieved variance by summer 2002 through the introduction of additional original material. (Prior to this point Anastasio observed, "What I worry about and what I really wonder is at what point are you sacrificing the quality of one show for the ability to tour around and see different stuff every night?") Some listeners still find the approach repetitive, suggesting that Anastasio's guitar leads fail to showcase his full range. Others remain drawn to the energy and ebullience of the group, reveling in the nuances that elude others as well as the environment in which they arise.

Plasma (2003) ★ ★ ★ ½

There are plenty of robust, rousing moments on this double-disc set. One can also appreciate the decision to offer up 20-minute versions of "Night Speaks to a Woman" and "Inner Tube" on side two. Still, some of the ideas recur a bit too often for this to be the altogether celebratory statement that one might expect from the band.

Trey Anastasio (2002) ★ ★ ★ ★

Winner of the 2002 Jammy Award for Studio Album of the Year. A balance of winsome melodies and abstractions as Anastasio's big band fires it down the middle and paints the corners as well.

Trampled by Lambs and Pecked by the Doves (2000) ★ ★ ½

Like *One Man's Trash*, an opportunity to peer through the window (no garbage metaphor needed here). While one is not likely to return to these multitracked demos with much regularity, they do possess an immediacy and charm.

One Man's Trash (1998) ★ ½

Yes, there may be a treasure or two found here—the affable "Happy Coffee Song" as well as early takes on "Mister Completely" and "Quantegy." Even so, as a whole, this is an album for Anastasiophiles (who may well take interest in the atonal horns and electronic abstractions). For most others, this disc will feel more like scraps than sustenance.

ANCIENT HARMONY
www.ancientharmony.com

The name Ancient Harmony carries some vague new age connotations, suggesting druids, monoliths, and possibly a pan flute. Thankfully the reality is far from this, as the group carries blues and boogie to the fringe with a propensity for improv approaching genetically programmed internal mandate. (For example, when given the opportunity to contribute a few tracks to the Lauan Records *Three Sets Vol. 2* compilation, the band delivered a 26-minute version of its song "Memory.") Former keyboard player Hal Month captured AH's essence when he described the group as "southadelic."

Guitarist/vocalist Shell Stamps grew up in Albany, Georgia, with bass player Steve Patton and former drummer Mike Cansler. The three formalized their musical relationship in 1992, soon adding keyboardist Leif Ragnaldsen, who was stationed in the city with the Marine Corps Logistics Base. This lineup began to tour regionally and in 1996 worked, albeit briefly, with Paul Hornsby on the debut disc, *Skywater*. (Hornsby, an early collaborator with Duane Allman, went on to produce the Marshall Tucker Band as well as Charlie Daniels.) As Ancient Harmony's popularity grew, it soon pulled up stakes and moved to Atlanta, changing keyboard players in the process and eventually working with Month, who added a jazz lexicon along with four or five instruments at his fingertips. This version of the band became a staple on Jeff and Maria Dunhams's weekly radio show on Atlanta's Z93 and began national touring. However, the harmony abated in 2002, first with the departure of Cansler and later that of his replacement, Chad Ardnt, along with Month, causing the group to cancel its late fall 2002 tour. Stamps and Patton regrouped, initially performing acoustic duo shows and then performing dates with drummer Jay Hoots. With more than a decade of perseverance (not quite Ancient status, but given the vagaries of the music business, fast-approaching that realm), it is reasonable to suppose that AH will endure in some form.

Live at the Warehouse (2001) ★★★

This disc presents five tracks recorded at the Tallahassee club in August 2000. The songs typically provide little more than a framework for improvisation, as this disc captures both the energy and excess contained in Ancient Harmony's shuffles, boogies, and all-out southern guitar sprees.

Skywater (1996) ★★

The initial quartet is represented on this release, which does a decent job of translating the band's vivacity in the studio. However, some of the material itself echoes too closely that of the band's pantheon—from the Allman Brothers Band to the Grateful Dead, Little Feat, and on through Panic.

B

BAREFOOT MANNER

www.barefootmanner.com

The four musicians in Barefoot Manner take their name seriously. They make manifest this moniker by...well, taking the stage without footwear. This behavior is not prompted by a particular antipathy for shoes and socks but is rather something of a mnemonic device, as it "helps remind the group we can all live in the present moment and collectively experience the beauty of being alive." It also hints at the bluegrass origins of this North Carolina-based quartet.

Barefoot Manner first came together as an acoustic trio in the winter of 2000. Shawn Chase (mandolin), Dave Kleiss (guitar), and Walter Hensey (bass) met for informal yet extended sessions, mostly working up their bluegrass chops. That fall they met percussionist Jeff Garland, whose addition ultimately led them to gig out, debuting as Barefoot Manner in January of 2001. The group began to build a following relatively quickly by introducing original music that often propounded positive messages (as suggested by the band's quote above) through bluegrass-inflected grooves. At the same time, it strived to maintain the high spirits of its audience not only through the music, but through such special events as the Mannerland Festival and a Dr. Seuss-themed show. From the outset, Barefoot Manner has sought to meld other styles into its sound (the band opened its first gig with a cover of "One Way Out"). While it initially introduced reggae vibes, (mostly) acoustic funk, and some jazzier elements, today it's still working to integrate these more fully to create a cohesive amalgam.

Centered (2002) ★★★

Here the band is often successful at referencing bluegrass yet doing so in its own context with an undercurrent of buoyant groove. Such moments include the fluid opener,

"Roots," the graceful "Things," and "The Outlaw," which effectively integrates narrative with improvisation.

Mannerisms (2001) ★ ★ ½

A pleasing debut that doesn't stray too dramatically from traditional bluegrass idioms with percussion (although "Madfunk" lives up to its billing, and "Caribea" hints at the same). One doesn't get to hear the players pick up steam all that often, but the band does build a gentle vibe that permeates.

BÉLA FLECK & THE FLECKTONES
www.flecktones.com

Whoever said television was bad for you? (Well, okay, Gil Scott-Heron, for one.) But "the Box" has not had deleterious effects on Béla Fleck & the Flecktones. Fleck's interest in the banjo was first piqued in his youth when he heard Lester Flatt and Earl Scruggs perform "The Ballad of Jed Clampett" on television's *Beverly Hillbillies* (while the two former members of Bill Monroe's Bluegrass Boys recorded the song, it was written by Paul Henning, the show's creator, who in the mid-'60s also brought *Petticoat Junction* and *Green Acres* to a grateful American public).

Not only did TV play an initial role in Fleck's selection of an instrument (an interest revitalized through "Dueling Banjos" from the 1972 film *Deliverance*), it had a direct impact on the formation of the Flecktones. In 1988, Richard Van Kleeck asked Fleck if he would like to assemble some players to perform on his *Lonesome Pine* TV series that aired nationally on PBS. Fleck called up Howard Levy (harmonica, keyboards) and Victor Wooten (bass), who suggested his brother Roy-El (drumitar), aka "Future Man," for this one-time gig that would soon yield more than 125 shows per annum.

One of the most overused terms employed to describe musicians is "unique." Still, it's a fitting term for a band that has won Grammys for Contemporary Jazz Performance (*Outbound*, 2000), Instrumental Composition Other than Jazz ("Almost 12" from *Left of Cool*, 1998), and Pop Instrumental Performance ("Sinister Minister" from *Live Art*, 1996), while the bandleader has been nominated in the bluegrass, classical, country, spoken word, and world categories, beginning in 1986 for his composition "Seven by Seven." Indeed, Béla Fleck has helped to redefine perceptions of the banjo, drawing on the legacy of traditional bluegrass icons but also the heroes of the jazz world, such as Charlie Parker and Chick Corea, along with progressive bluegrass innovator Tony Trischka, one of Fleck's early teachers.

Trischka recommended Fleck for his first steady professional gig at age 19 with Boston's Tasty Licks, a relatively traditional folk/bluegrass outfit. From there Fleck moved to Kentucky and co-founded the group Spectrum before Sam Bush called, inviting him to join New Grass Revival. Fleck performed with these newgrass pioneers in a lineup that also included John Cowan and Pat Flynn, contributing to five releases before the band members officially moved on to other endeavors after an opening gig for the Grateful Dead at Oakland Coliseum on December 31, 1989. (The Flecktones would open for the Dead two years later for the final GD New Year's Eve show—final due to the death of promoter Bill Graham a few months earlier.)

Flecktones bassist Victor Lemonte Wooten, renowned for his agility and flair, took home three Bass Player of the Year honors from *Bass Player* during the 1990s (the only multiple winner), and the magazine named him one of the Top 10 Bass Innovators of the Decade. Victor, the youngest of the Brothers Wooten, began performing with his siblings as a prepubescent in the Williamsburg, VA, area. The group opened tours for Curtis Mayfield and War before releasing an eponymous disc on Arista in 1985. (Quick quiz: Can you name Victor's four brothers/band mates? Rudy (sax), Roy-El (gravy), Regi (a guitarist who has worked with many artists, including Oteil Burbridge), and Joseph (now on keys with the Steve Miller Band). In 1988, through the initiative of a studio engineer, Victor introduced himself to Béla via a phone call, performed a few basslines, and received an invitation to a jam session at Béla's place. The *Lonesome Pine* TV special soon followed, as did the Flecktones, sparing Wooten the discomfort of causing future band mates to require medical attention, which did occur when a drummer hyperventilated during a Jonell Mosser gig. (As Wooten told Jeff Waful in a Jambands.com interview, "The first night that I played with Jonell, who's an amazing vocalist and an amazing person, I did some things during the show that I hadn't done during the rehearsal. You know, there was one place where she gave me an extended solo and during the rehearsal, I wouldn't do a whole lot, because there was no need to, but during the show I went ahead and let loose. So some people just flipped out, just literally flipped out. That was the night that our drummer got sick, and we ended up having to get another drummer out of the audience to finish the show.")

"Future Man" traveled back from the year 2050 to join the Flecktones (and presumably to bet on Super Bowls). At least that was his story for many years, even if he did bear a curious resemblance to Roy-El Wooten, one of the aforementioned Brothers W. Still, Futch's account did seem plausible due to his primary instrument, the SyntheAxe drumitar, which he slings over his shoulder like a guitar to summon an array of synthesized drum tones through buttons and pedals. (Wooten designed the drumitar himself, gutting a SyntheAxe once owned by Lee Ritenour and adding controls to trigger percussion samples. He also recently devised "The Roy-El," a variant shaped like a piano and modeled after the table of the periodic elements because he "sees the piano like a drum set and the drum set like a piano.") While Wooten elicits a gamut of sounds from the drumitar, when he supplements these by simultaneously moving behind a kit or adding some hand drums, the results can be stunning.

It's easy to fathom why the group named their fifth album *Three Flew Over the Cuckoo's Nest*, but for much of the Flecktones' existence the band has been a quartet. Levy, who departed in December 1992, has carried the harmonica into new planes, performing and recording with classical orchestras as well as with Sandip Burman, Styx, and the Stranger's Hand (to name but three projects starting with the letter S. The latter group includes Oteil Burbridge, Steve Smith, and Jerry Goodman). Following some initial collaboration, Jeff Coffin officially joined the band on saxophone in 1997. Coffin, who studied with Joe Lovano, is a brash player in the mode of Sonny Rollins with a penchant for Ornette Coleman's free jazz expressions and who will bust out the dual saxes as a nod to Rahsaan Roland Kirk. Over the years, the Flecktones have also expanded the roster for particular shows or tours with many other artists, including Sam Bush, Paul McCandless, Bruce Hornsby, Branford Marsalis, Paul Hanson, and Andy Narell (Levy has returned on occasion as well).

A Béla Fleck & the Flecktones performance is outlandish. The group's song "Blu-Bop," from *Flight of the Cosmic Hippo*, only begins to describe the music, which at times feels reminiscent of Corea yet also cascades into world music terrain, introduces classical elements, bounds into R&B, and incorporates some stirring individual displays (the evening is often capped by an informal meet-and-greet at the lip of the stage). Audience members who take in a single show often leave astounded, though some recommend attending only a handful of shows per tour at most (for those so inclined) because the set lists historically have not varied significantly from night to night (the solos certainly do, however, and there are any number of additional nuances and variants). Nonetheless, the Flecktones remain a commanding, tantalizing presence that has drawn invitations to Mongolia, Korea, Thailand, the Czech Republic, and venues throughout Europe, as well as bills with Phish and the Dave Matthews Band. In the years since its debut, the group has also made numerous television appearances on such shows as *Today* and *The Tonight Show*, and Fleck himself is a steady presence on *Sesame Street*, allowing the musician first introduced to the banjo as a

Béla Fleck with Bill Nershi, Stanton Moore, Robert Randolph, and Edgar Meyer, Bonnaroo SuperJam 2002.

TV tyke to perform with the Muppets and turn on the moppets.

Live at the Quick (2002) ★★★★

This live performance from the Quick Center on November 17, 2000, in Fairfield, CT, builds on many ideas introduced in *Outbound* with guests Paul McCandless, Sandip Burman, Paul Hanson, and Andy Narell. The release contains some robust solos from the 'Tones and a sturdy collage of sounds throughout.

Outbound (2000) ★★★ ½

This disc continues the band's engagement with other musical cultures, aided in part by Sandip Burman's tabla, Andy Narrell's steel drum, and Tuvan throat singer Ondar. The music seems better suited to vocals than the previous effort, with additional support from Shawn Colvin and Jon Anderson (though the group offers a number of its signature instrumentals along with a resourceful opening take on Aaron Copland's "Hoedown").

Left of Cool (1998) ★★★

Left of Cool is the first studio recording with Jeff Coffin (and the band's first in five years). Following the bright, intricate "Throwdown at the Hoedown," the disc adds some novel elements such as Middle Eastern seasonings, plus the most significant alteration: vocals, with contributions from Dave Matthews and Amy Grant, but most often from Future Man (whose efforts are competent, though by the end of this release do seem to constrain rather than liberate).

Live Art (1996) ★★★★★

This double live effort encapsulates the inge-nuity and prowess of the Flecktones, drawn from performances over the preceding five-year span. Howard Levy appears, as does Chick Corea, Branford Marsalis, and Bruce Hornsby.

Also

Little Worlds (2003)
Three Flew Over the Cuckoo's Nest (1993)
UFO Tofu (1992)
Béla Fleck & the Flecktones (1990)

Related sites:

Jeff Coffin—*www.jeffcoffin.com*
Future Man—*www.futuremanmusic.com*
Victor Wooten—*www.victorwooten.com*

BEMBE ORISHA

www.mickeyhart.net

During a "Jam Nation" radio appearance in the summer of 2002, Mickey Hart referred to Bembe Orisha as the best band he's ever been in—a bold statement for sure from someone who spent three decades as one of the Grateful Dead's Rhythm Devils. One may assume that he meant the best group outside of the Dead. Yet without question, Bembe is comprised of gifted players steeped in a wider range of musical traditions than any of Hart's recent collectives. To this end, Bembe Orisha is a culmination of the drummer's engagement with the world's music.

Hart describes Bembe's sound as "the roots of the roots." The group draws from Caribbean, Haitian, Cuban, Puerto Rican, African, and even Persian traditions, all of which played some role in the formation of America's musical idioms: blues, jazz, and rock. Yet, by design, this is not an abstract exercise in global fusion. "It's dance music.

Bembe means 'party' and Orisha, is 'of the spirits, of the saints' of West Africa. It's a party for the spirits," Hart says.

While Hart has a history of drawing together the sounds of the globe, he suggests that on certain levels "music isn't really universal." By this he means, "You've got to pick the right musicians with the right spirit and, of course, with the right music. It's not like taking a little bit from here, from there. It's difficult to mix. It's like spices. Some spices just don't go together. It's taken many years to get the blend that you hear."

Bembe Orisha strikes this balance with a number of players who have worked with Hart over the years, yielding a multi-tongued mélange that can move from haunting to ecstatic within the course of a few passages. As one might imagine, the band is percussion-driven, with Hart joined by Cuban-born Nengue Hernandez; Greg Ellis, who often lends Middle Eastern textures; Azam Ali, who also adds a Persian element on vocals and hammered dulcimer; and Siriku Adepoju, "the Paganini of the talking drum." In addition, the roster includes Afro-Cuban vocalist Bobi Cespedes, South African bassist Bakithi Kumalo, who first garnered acclaim in this country through his work on Paul Simon's *Graceland*, and guitarist Barney Doyle, a rock player with some echoes of Garcia in his tone.

Following some initial touring in the fall of 2001, the band picked up steam during the summer of 2002 on its first extended run of dates, which included a performance at the Grateful Dead Family Reunion. While at first blush the octet's sound may be too "foreign" for some listeners, in some respects Bembe Orisha's raison d'être is to challenge this per-ception, not only because of its relation to the fundament of American music but also because Hart views the band as "a great metaphor for what's going on in the world right now. You have to understand each other, that's what this is all based on. All of these cultures can get together and have a marvelous time, an uplifting time, and this is one way it can happen. I think now more than ever these multi-cultural congregations are very important. They take on a different light with the recent situation. I believe music can be an antidote to the hatred."

Note: Hart has stated that he wants Bembe Orisha to evolve on the road before the band enters the studio to record its debut.

DICKEY BETTS
www.dickeybetts.com

Dickey Betts is scary. No, not necessarily his bearing (though, come to think of it, he can have that scowl on his face when he's playing, and on occasion his temper may have had the best of him). Instead, it is his animated and at times purposefully reckless approach to the guitar that elicits this description. Yet Betts also emphasizes discipline, often utilizing a protracted rehearsal regimen to help get across his ideas with precision. It is this balance that has sustained him over the course of a career more than 30 years in the making.

It was the spring of 1969 when Duane Allman persuaded bass player Berry Oakley to bring along fellow Second Coming member Betts to join in a jam session that marked the inception of the Allman Brothers Band. Throughout the subsequent decades of ruckus, reconciliation, and multiple reunions,

Betts's signature leads on his Gibson Les Paul helped define the sound of the ABB. His songwriting served an equally significant role, from "Revival" and "In Memory of Elizabeth Reed" on through "Blue Sky" and "Jessica" and the later "Seven Turns" and "Back Where It All Begins."

During the Brothers' regular inactive periods from the mid-'70s through 1989, Betts created music that differed from his work in the ABB. Initially this sound delved into country with a bit of Bob Willis's Western swing. Following his heralded Highway Call solo debut, which featured some incisive contributions from fiddler Vassar Clements, Betts formed Great Southern, adding blues tonalities through guitarist Dan Toler (who would later join Betts in the reconstituted ABB of the late '70s). Another intriguing project was 1982-83's BHLT, a collaboration with Jimmy Hall, Chuck Leavell, and Butch Trucks that drew on all of the aforementioned genres along with R&B. (Alas, we were still in the disco era, and BHLT never quite caught on—there's no album to document the music, though scarce tapes do float....) By the late '80s, Betts introduced a heavier sound with a new incarnation of the Dickey Betts Band (which he called his group off and on during the '70s and '80s), driven by drummer Matt Abts as well as guitarist Warren Haynes.

The Allman Brothers Band returned in 1989, and Betts focused his efforts on the group until his dismissal via fax in May 2000. The ABB founders cited irregularities in his playing, which Betts denied. Following a brief period of recrimination via the media, he assembled a new band in an avowed effort to prove these charges unfounded. The reformulated Dickey Betts Band was a septet that included Mark May (guitar) and saxophone player Kris Jensen, who added a pronounced jazz element. (One of Betts's influences and enthusiasms remains Charlie Parker—the Betts/Haynes instrumental "Kind of Bird" from *Shades of Two Worlds* earned a 1991 Grammy nomination.)

The next year Betts reunited with Dan Toler, lauding Toler's development on guitar during the years since they had last performed, and rechristened the group Great Southern (while May returned to his solo career). At present Dickey Betts and Great Southern are working their way back through the clubs, and at any given show will present some of Betts's classic compositions (often rearranged) along with a hefty portion of newer material. The latter songs may not yet have the resonance of his earlier ones, but Betts continues to write some affecting music, particularly instrumentals. Moreover, his willingness to return to the clubs and recast his sound as he enters his sixties is a challenge to other musicians to remain active and vigorous, one that some artists may deem scary enough in its own right.

The Collectors #1 (2002) ★★★

Betts fans in particular will savor the opportunity to hear him in this context, interpreting some of his more recent material along with a few standards. There is a Celtic feel that enlivens some of these tracks while others are solid takes from Betts and Great Southern, who emphasize "no instrument has been 'doubled' on this album."

Let's Get Together (2001) ★ ★ ★ ½

Mark May joins Betts on guitar, and the dynamic is a bit like the Allman Brothers Band with Kris Jensen's sax adding punch. In fact, Betts first performed a number of these songs with ABB, and here they receive an enthusiastic reading from this initial incarnation of Dickey's post-Brothers band.

Pattern Disruptive (1988) ★ ★ ★

A pre-ABB Warren Haynes joins Dickey as a guitar foil and songwriting partner for many of these songs suffused with a heavier, late-'80s guitar rock sound. Matt Abts carries some authority here as well, with Johnny Neel playing keys (and Butch Trucks on board for guest percussion).

Atlanta's Burning Down (1978) ★ ★ ★ ½

This one has a classic cover (much more satisfying over vinyl than the shrunken CD) featuring a tight shot of Dickey as sunglasses-bedecked badass (a look Billy Crudup certainly appropriated for the film *Almost Famous*). With the ABB broken up during this period, Betts strives for boogies and blues closer to that band's sound than his previous efforts.

Dickey Betts and Great Southern (1977) ★ ★ ★

This is the first incarnation of Great Southern with Dan Toler joining on guitar. There is some studio gloss along with heavier tones that color this collection of soulful country songs.

Highway Call (1974) ★ ★ ★ ★

Vassar Clements is a presence on fiddle for this disc, which is far more country than the blues that most people associate with Betts.

Aside from the 14-minute instrumental "Hand Picked" that melds bluegrass and honky-tonk with a jazz aesthetic, the remaining five songs are more concise, emotional pastorals.

BIG BLOCK DODGE

www.bigblockdodge.com

Looking for another descriptive term you can employ to characterize the music of your favorite genre-busting, improv-based group? Well, Big Block Dodge, a trio from Asheville, North Carolina, respectfully submits groosion. Frankly, the submission may not be all that respectful, but it's succinct, evocative, and has flow. Of course, one should expect no less—drummer Robin Tolleson is also a journalist whose work appears regularly in *Downbeat*, *Mix*, *Modern Drummer*, and other publications.

In addition to his gig as music scribe, Tolleson is also a crackling kit player whose return to North Carolina in 1999 after a number of years in San Francisco resulted in the formation of Big Block Dodge. Tolleson, who studied under Narada Michael Walden and founded the Bay Area trio Hip Bones (an interesting group in its own right with instrumentation that features drums, bass, and flute), soon met guitarist Bill Altman. Altman had played in a number of local bands over the preceding decade, including the Crystal Zoo. Along with bass player Jeff Hinkle, a staple of the local jazz and blues scene since his mid-teens, the three began writing original instrumentals that bridged collective interests including bebop, Jeff Beck's mid-'70s efforts, Joe Satriani, and the Aquarium Rescue Unit. A BBD opening slot for Project Z (an apt pairing) resulted in Ricky Keller's invitation to record at his Southern Living at Its Finest Studios. Though by no means as "broken" as the sounds of the Z, Big Block Dodge's songs do incorporate some unconventional time signatures and passages, but they are never too dissonant and often return to groove-laden territory. Altman has described the band's music as "Gov't Mule meets Scofield." Until "Sco-Mule" becomes jargon rather than just a Grammy-nominated instrumental, groosion should well suffice.

Manifold Destiny (2002) ★ ★ ★ ½

A fine sampling of the group's instrumentals that proves...manifold. Here Big Block Dodge develops some deceptively complex jazz and blues themes while also often working a robust groove.

THE BIG WU

www.thebigwu.com

On November 2, 2002, the Minneapolis Historic State Theater was the site of a collective big "Whooh!" This vociferation accompanied the CD release party for the Big Wu's *Spring Reverb* after more than a year's postponement. It also marked the return of the Minnesota band from a six-week tour, its first as a quartet following the departure of guitarist Jason Fladager.

The preceding twelve months had been a difficult stretch for the band. In 2001 the group's label, the Phoenix Media Group, shut its doors yet asserted ownership of the Wu's recording contract, making it difficult for the band to satisfy demands for its back catalog and release any new material. It was not until the summer of 2002 that the group received a definitive legal pronouncement to restore its free-agent status. Soon afterwards, Fladager opted to leave the band, as the rigors of the road had become overwhelming and he longed to be closer to his family and especially his young children.

Fladager had been in the initial incarnation of the Wu, which began in 1992 as a cover band at Minnesota's St. Olaf College. Current members Chris Castino (guitar) and drummer Terry VanDeWalker also were in the roster, with VanDeWalker serving solely as a vocalist. (As for the band's name, it references the titular magma-spewing mountain in the film *Joe Versus the Volcano*—hint: not Joe—a film that features Tom Hanks and Meg Ryan in their first on-screen pairing.)

In 1995 the group started performing regular weekly gigs at Minneapolis' Terminal Bar, and while it slowly began to integrate original songs, the Wu primarily performed Grateful Dead material with the occasional Allman Brothers Band selection. Bassist Andy Miller and keyboard player Al Oikari completed the lineup when the band moved its residency to the Cabooze the following year and began a transition towards its own music, achieved in 1998. That year was doubly significant, not only because national touring ended the band's regular Cabooze dates, but for the debut of the Big Wu Family Reunion—now an annual multiday festival that draws thousands of "First Cousins" and "Extended Family" members who contribute tons of canned foods to its food drive. Following the Memorial Day Weekend event, the band moves from host to participant at other national fests, which have included the inaugural Bonnaroo, where the Wu played the initial notes and offered up a modified version of its song "Kangaroo" with Bonnaroo-specific lyrics that became an anthem for some over the weekend. (Jambands.com readers have been able to trace the group's journey; two band members have served as columnists, beginning with Jason Fladager's "Tao of Wu" from 1998 through 2000, and Andy Miller picking up in late 2002 with "Real True Confessions with Padre Pienbique.")

One interesting dichotomy is that while in its home state the Big Wu has long carried the stigma of being a Dead cover band, it has built a national following of listeners familiar only with the group's original material. One can certainly hear the Dead influence, particularly in the tincts and tones that predominate on the debut release, *Tracking Buffalo Through the Bathtub*. Still, the core songs have consistently carried a poppier side with rich harmonies and hooks. The Big Wu's challenge of late has been to rearrange this material written for two guitars while crafting new compositions specifically for the four-piece group. The group's recent tours suggest that this process is ongoing; to some degree the Wu is a new band, yet one that is able to build on more than 1,000 shows of shared history.

Spring Reverb (2002) ★★★

This disc boasts the best production of the group's three studio efforts, and the Wu has more instrumental command than in the past. However, on the whole, the songs themselves don't hold the listener with the vim of their antecedents.

3/13/98—Cedar Cultural Centre (2001) ★★ ½

This was one of the most-requested live shows in the Wu canon, featuring an acoustic set and two electric sets. It is certainly an interesting document of the band's origins that steady supporters will want to own, but others may find it drags a bit occasionally.

Folktales (2000) ★★★★

The strongest overall studio effort in terms of core compositions and performance, with "Minnesota Moon," "Two Person Chair," and "Oxygen" among the standout tracks.

Live at the Fitzgerald (2000) ★★★

A solid offering from the original quintet performing for their St. Paul faithful on April 21, 2000.

Tracking Buffalo Through the Bathtub (1997) ★★★

A disc from a young band, with a Grateful Dead imprint still prominent. Nonetheless, the energy and hooks hold sway, especially in the 9-minute take on "Red Sky" and the catchy "Silcantunitova" opener, something of a poppy curveball.

Fan site:
www.thebigwu.net

BLUE QUARTER
www.bluequarter.com
The prevailing comparisons between Blue Quarter and the New Deal are apt in the broadest sense. Both groups are instrumental trios fluent in drum & bass and techno rhythms, hailing from the fine nation of

Canada. However, while a bounty of keyboards often propels the New Deal, Blue Quarter offers an enhanced Chapman Stick (namesake Emmett Chapman created the Stick as a means to play bass, chords, and melody simultaneously, first producing it commercially in 1974). In addition, BQ is more inclined to moderate the pace and interject the jazz modes that contribute to its self-described "electro lounge." Moreover, while the New Deal is from Toronto, Ontario, Blue Quarter is now based in Canmore, Alberta. (Note to the geographically challenged: Canada is a sprawling nation that spans three oceans, and the distance from Canmore to Toronto is roughly 2,000 miles and two time zones.)

Oh yes, plus the three members of Blue Quarter may not be of earthly origin. The band characterizes its composite identity as a manually operated spaceship. Drummer Jahanzaib "Bitou" Mirza serves as "alien negotiator," bassist Stephane Fortin is a "space mechanic," and Stickman Olivier is the "teletrance scientist." (Note to the semantically challenged: The group's cosmic reference may just be a metaphor.)

Mizra and Fortin formed Blue Quarter in early 2000, inviting Olivier to join and working from a Montreal base. The Chapman Stick has become a signature element, as Olivier's ten-string version of the instrument summons keyboard, guitar, and bass phrasings and can be visually arresting with its requisite two-handed technique. The versatility of the Stick allows Blue Quarter to move deftly from drum & double bass to elastic funk to jazz inflections. While these expressions can be undeveloped, at times they are dynamic, especially as the trio strives to refine and reconfigure the improvisational and compositional product of its unique instrumentation.

Blue Quarter (2002) ★ ★ ½

The band's varied "electro lounge" is evoked over these six studio tracks and an extended live cut, "SiLaLaSi" (it is a somewhat abbreviated debut, however, clocking in under 45 minutes). Blue Quarter does utilize the Stick to intriguing effect and the band offers complementary musicianship. Still, these genial permutations of techno jazz do not always carry a distinctive flair.

BLUES TRAVELER

www.bluestraveler.com
John Popper blows.
Thank you, and good night.

Actually, the truth is that increasingly he doesn't. While Blues Traveler certainly still delivers the signature tonalities from Popper's great harped vest, he has been moving away from the harmonica for some time, whether it be through his rich-toned guitar or just laying out. This is all the more true at present, now that the band has expanded to a quintet with Ben Wilson contributing both leads and fills on keys.

Blues Traveler's import cannot be understated, especially its role in the formation of the HORDE festival. As suggested during the introduction to Popper when he hosted the 2002 Jammy Awards, but for Blues Traveler it is possible that there would not be a Jammys, a Jambands.com, or a *Jambands* book. In March 1992, Popper called a summit of emerging improv-based groups to discuss the possibility of aligning for a summer tour that would bring them into larger venues and provide a national platform. Four months later, on July 9, at the Cumberland County Civic Center in Portland, ME, the first of the initial eight HORDE shows took place, presenting the Horizons Of Rock Developing Everywhere via the initial Fab Five: Traveler, Phish, Widespread Panic, Aquarium Rescue Unit, and the Spin Doctors (Béla Fleck & the Flecktones tagged in for Phish on the final few dates). HORDE expanded to a six-week tour in 1993 and over the next few years showcased worthy music—particularly to a younger audience unable to see such bands in the club setting—while helping define a scene that thrives today (and hey, if in 1998, Fastball, Paula Cole, and Marcy Playground didn't ring your bell, well, by year seven, the founders had earned a pass—plus they did the Lord's work

by keeping Col. Bruce Hampton on the bill with his Fiji Mariners).

The opening track on the band's 2001 disc, *Bridge*, its first release without founding bassist Bobby Sheehan, is entitled "Back in the Day." The prevailing image within this song, which addresses the passage of time, is music as a medium of transport. Indeed, a particular tune may carry a listener back to a moment in the past, evoking the sensory stimuli and even the thought processes associated with prior exposure to those notes. "Back in the Day" suggests that the same holds true for a vocalist, which can lend vitality to a performance or perhaps distract, depending on the singer's level of concentration. (Then again, he or she may be just trying to pinpoint the last known whereabouts of the car keys.) To this end, when Traveler pow-

Today's Traveler.

ers into "Slow Change," "Sweet-Talking Hippie," or "Gina," certain listeners occasionally enter that wormhole and re-emerge in the late '80s and early '90s when Blues Traveler seemed to own New York City. It is sometimes fashionable for longtime fans of a particular group to proclaim, "You should have seen them then," but in many instances this is little more than cultural capital, a means to boast about past attendance. However, in the case of Blues Traveler, without disparaging the current roster—which certainly has acquired a broader range and technique—the band was a beast to behold back in the day. Fronted by a wild-eyed, wide-bodied Popper, BT also featured guitarist Chan Kinchla with his gravity-defying tresses, Sheehan burning by his side, and Brendan Hill behind it all (while Popper is the man with the plan or at least the one who can hold his own with Howard Stern, you can't overlook Kinchla's contributions to much of the BT canon over the years, with Sheehan also participating as well as Hill, whose notable solo compositions include "Mountain Cry" and "Save His Soul").

Yeah, yeah, that's all well and good, but what about the Traveler of today? Well, before we get there one must consider a decade's worth of travails and triumphs worthy of a *Behind the Music* special (quite literally—BT was the subject of an episode that aired over Memorial Day Weekend in 2001). The band has a direct link to Bill Graham, who signed it to his management group at the behest of son David, with A&M Records releasing the eponymous debut in June 1990. Just over two years later, following the release of the group's second disc, Popper broke his hip in a motorcycle accident. Due to a slow healing process exacerbated by his weight, he performed while sitting in a wheelchair from December 1992 until February 1994. In 1995 the band's song "Run-Around" cracked the Top Ten on the *Billboard* pop singles chart (peaking at No. 8), which only begins to tell the story, as it remained in the Top 100 for nearly a year while garnering substantial airplay on other radio formats as well, including rock, adult contemporary, and modern rock (the song was freaking ubiquitous). Feeling a bit crispy by 1999, the band took most of the year off from the road following a brief January USO Tour of the Far East. In July, however, Popper required an emergency angioplasty to clear an artery to his heart that was blocked by 95 percent. One month later, Sheehan died at his New Orleans home due to complications from drug use (part of Sheehan's legacy remains his song "Mountains Win Again," which still elicits tears from certain listeners). By year's end, Chan's brother Ted (a member of Rhode Island-based alterna-funk band Dowdy Smack) appeared on bass. Keyboardist Wilson was added in early 2000, joining a newly slimmed Popper following gastric bypass surgery (the previous year's health issues had scared him straight).

"Back in the Day" references a realization that one might no longer belong—true in the sense that the band is now somewhat distanced from a scene it helped found. With the winnowing of the HORDE tour, the group is less involved in the summer festival circuit, and there has been no Bonnaroo for BT (at least not in the first two years). On the other hand, the band is certainly tapped into an aspect of the music industry that would benefit a number of younger groups in this book.

Traveler performs at radio showcases while still receiving airplay (albeit in mediated measure from 1995), appears regularly on the *Late Show with David Letterman,* contributes to film soundtracks (*Blues Brothers 2000, Ace Ventura: When Venture Calls,* and *Kingpin,* in which it appears as an Amish band), and is tapped for sundry music compilations (with *Ambercrombie & Fitch in Stereo* and the *Circuit City Sampler* slightly less glorious than *Carved in Stone,* a benefit disc to preserve Red Rocks).

The group's current music has a bit more grace and a bit less polish than in prior periods of its history. Most significantly, Kinchla still can riff while Popper continues to write verbose lyrics that often reward a scrutiny sometimes denied by the absorbing clusters of notes from his harmonica. "Back in the Day" retains an optimistic thought in suggesting, "If you're alive, you didn't finish the ride, no telling where it's gonna go." True too, as Popper blows and Traveler abides.

Live: What You and I Have Been Through (2002) ★★★

Both the song selection and the band's performance on this single disc taken from shows in late 2001 are sturdy yet not altogether spellbinding.

Bridge (2001) ★★★ ½

A well-founded opening salvo. Songs such as "Back in the Day" and "Pretty Angry" affirm Traveler's command.

Straight On Till Morning (1997) ★★★

While this release offers some ebullient moments, as a whole it meanders a bit too far from dulcet pop to more jagged rock realms. The results feel a bit too diffuse.

Live from the Fall (1996) ★★★★ ½

A testament to the vim and vitality of the original quartet.

Four (1994) ★★★★

Naturally. P.S. While "Run-Around" and "Hook" may have their detractors, they are affable tunes, and there are alternate shadings as well.

Save His Soul (1993) ★★★ ½

There is a contingent that deems this disc the most engrossing Traveler studio effort. But while *Save His Soul* presents a substantive batch of songs, many of which remain in rotation, some of the readings could be a bit more robust.

Travelers and Thieves (1991) ★★★ ½

A strong follow-up with a bit of a harder edge than the debut. Seek out the version with the bonus live disc *On Tour Forever,* which includes a 21-minute version of "Mountain Cry."

Blues Traveler (1990) ★★★★ ½

Raw and rambunctious, filled with enduring, endearing compositions.

Also:
Truth Be Told (2003)

Fan site:
www.bluestraveler.net

Discussion list:
www.theclerk.com/mailman/listinfo/blackcat

BLUESTRING

www.bluestring.com

There was a time when Bluestring referred to its sound as "saxofiddle," a novel description that likely was preferable to suggesting that its music often proved reminiscent of the Dave Matthews Band. However, personnel changes in 2002 (especially the departure of the fiddle player) led the group to reconfigure its approach. Placing more emphasis on percussion and acoustic guitar while carving room for saxophone player Brad Thomas to stretch out, Bluestring came into its own with a sound vigorous enough to intrigue Allman Brothers Band drummer Butch Trucks, who signed the group to his Flying Frog label.

The Athens, Georgia-based quintet retains a pop feel to its sound, stressing vocal harmony and winsome tonalities. The songs of principal songwriter and lead singer Clay Evans also often incorporate a wry humor (not surprising, since he once wrote parody songs for an Atlanta radio station). Meanwhile, bass player Chuck Thomas lends funk progressions that are complemented by drummer Jason Jones while percussionist Nick Prince lends zest. The group brought in a lead electric guitar player for its second release, *Pick Me Up*, along with a keyboardist, so it is quite possible that its tack will shift yet again. Still the band is likely to retain a lively sound that appeals to those who prefer melodic improvisation, as Bluestring typically is upbeat, engaging, and willing to meet the listener over the middle.

Pick Me Up (2003) ★ ★ ★ ½

Pick Me Up demonstrates that Bluestring's evolving sound continues to veer from its influences (although some Dave Matthews Band cadences remain on a few tracks). Clay Evans's vocals and Brad Thomas's sax carry the day, as the group digs in enthusiastically for some funk, straight-up rock, and even a bit of squonk.

Overthinking (2001) ★ ★ ½

At its best when Dave Matthews Band reference points disappear, here Bluestring yields funk, bluegrass, and some straight jazz undertones. Some solid evocative songwriting on tunes such as "Greatest Minds" and "Your Recovery," plus a taste of the group's live flair—for instance, the opening segue from "Professor Debreeze" into "Dinosaur."

BOCKMAN'S EUPHIO

www.euphio.net

This Missouri-based quintet offers a nod to a Kurt Vonnegut short story with its name. In the "Euphio Question" (originally published in *Collier's* magazine in 1951 and later collected in Vonnegut's *Welcome to the Monkey House*), the author describes the events that follow when a Dr. Bockman discovers a noise emanating from outer space that can deliver pure happiness. The band's name suggests that it, too, can serve as such a transmitter. (Of course if you really want to push it, the story actually also raises some questions about the artificial nature of the happiness, but hey, come on, get over it—Bockman's Euphio is still a cool name.)

As for the band's music (finally), the initial distinguishing factor is the dual keyboards. Andrew Weir, a former youth concert pianist, plays Fender Rhodes and synth. Joe Cosas counters with a Hammond organ, while also stepping in on trombone occasionally. The pair supplies a lattice of keyboard work, with Weir often initiating some sparkling, jazz-infused flourishes while Cosas counters with rich tones on the Hammond. Meanwhile, guitarist and vocalist Sean Canan, himself a former classical pianist, offers his own accents (he lends some solid phrasings, though his vocabulary still owes a debt to other notables such as Trey Anastasio).

Bockman's Euphio is a young, animated band still developing a sense of dynamics and working to focus its energy. Still, in spite of some touring limitations resulting from its members' student status (like Boston's Addison Groove Project), the group has built a solid Midwest following. Along the way it took top honors in 2001 at Cicero's Battle of the Jambands in Columbia, Missouri, winning studio time that would ultimately contribute to its 2002 debut, *Ladies and Gentlemen of the FCC...* The title of the release also hints at the band's humor, an apt trait for a Vonnegut-inspired collective.

Ladies and Gentlemen of the FCC...(2002)
★★½

Bockman's presents a number of songs that aspire to a live feel in the studio, with some arrangements that allow room for improv. The results are generally affable if not novel.

Discussion list:
http://groups.yahoo.com/group/Bockmans-Euphio/

THE BOMB SQUAD
www.bombsquadonline.com
Comparisons to old-school Deep Banana Blackout are inevitable. The Bomb Squad hails from a similar part of Connecticut, demonstrates a parallel affection for the progenitors of '70s funk, and, perhaps above all else, is fronted by DBB founding vocalist Jen Durkin. However, when compared with Durkin's former group during her tenure, the Bomb Squad's horns can be less strident and her vocals are a bit sultrier, at times pursuing more of a smooth-jazz feel.

Guitarist Ian McHugh took the lead in assembling the Squad. In the summer of 2000, just as his prior group EMCQ had started to gain momentum, vocalist Javier Colon left to join the Derek Trucks Band (and later departed to pursue a solo career). McHugh and the other EMCQ principals—including its brass section of Brad Mason, Mark Tragesser, and Mike Raskin—enlisted Durkin to fill in on a few dates, and she ultimately signed on, writing new music with the band.

The Bomb Squad started to come into its own during the late spring of 2002 when "Jenny Pipes" stepped up her commitment. She had been balancing her touring with Bernie Worrell and the Woo Warriors and her own project, Conscious Underground. Later that fall the Squad took a brief hiatus due to Durkin's pregnancy, though she performed into her eighth month—an entertaining, inspiring sight in its own right. While the band's lineup still does fluctuate, a gifted core remains (Mason, for instance, not only plays trumpet and flügelhorn, but is also a world-class performer on the EVI, a hybrid electric wind instrument in the synth/sax/trumpet realm). The Bomb Squad aspires to be a good-time party band with range, casting a variety of moods.

Sophista Funk (2002) ★★★

While much of the disc is driven by fast-paced, horn-infused funk (one can picture Durkin's patented whirls during the opening bars of "True Thang"), there is some fine counterbalance as well, with the slinkier "Hey Good Lookin'" and Latin-seasoned instrumental "Wherever You Are," "Keep on Movin'," and "Find Another Love" feel like lost mid-'70s soul classics.

BROTHERS PAST

www.brotherspast.com

Brothers Past is certainly staking out its own territory. The Pennsylvania-based quartet bucks the thematic trend propounded by many of the bands in this book with its acknowledgment that all might not be right in the world. This is not goth darkness—it's a bit subtler and more insidious, at times a compelling alignment of minor keys and paranoia. Still, Brothers Past does offer a palliative catharsis wrought from a gloom of minor keys and effects-laden collective improvisation.

The group's two releases demonstrate that the band certainly doesn't lack for ambition. On its debut, *Elements*, Brothers Past recorded a three-set performance and then reassembled it during post-production through some subtle tweaks and a fashioning of the title track from three disparate jams. On *A Wonderful Day,* the band structured its songs around the theme of insomnia. The disc relates the ruminations and frustrations of a wandering mind trying to stave off disturbing thoughts and find soporific ones. This cerebral approach may not make it to the stage (à la Lo Faber's *Henry House*) but it is quite possibly the first concept album devoted to this topic—with a Pink Floyd-ish, progressive, and, at times, pretentious feel to it (so hey, who knows?).

While Brothers Past merits praise for the conceit and execution of its studio endeavors (with varying degrees of success—see below), many still recognize the band predominantly for its live performances. In this context the group crafts true soundscapes, from nuanced ambient whispers to full-on techno declarations. The band's vocals are not its strong suit, and some find the group's extemporizations to yield plenty of tension without sufficient release, but Brothers Past does a fine job of slowly building on such themes until Tom McKee's keyboards and Tom Hamilton's guitar pedals quite literally effect change.

A Wonderful Day (2002) ★★★★

The band realizes the concept quite well, with a haunting if occasionally heavy-handed ode to insomnia. The songs are intentionally light on hooks and heavy on atmosphere, serving the band's intention. The results are mostly restrained and layered, though BP does tear loose on "Monsters Come Out at Night."

Elements (2001) ★★★

An inventive debut, yet a bit ponderous at times, overwhelmed by its own importance (for instance, the voice that opens the release with an ontological pronouncement). The vocals are ragged, but the walls of sound on the extended improvs are often forceful and intriguing.

BURT NEILSON BAND

www.burtneilson.com

For nearly a year, the prospects weren't promising for fans of the Burt Neilson Band. Following the final March date on its spring 2002 tour, the group invoked the "H word" (that's "Hiatus," for the uninitiated—which, in the wake of Phish's 26-month separation, has become de rigueur). Fans received a brief reprieve during the summer with a pair of shows, a stealth gig, and an announced performance at two festivals in Durham, Ontario's Frontiertown. However, the band members then moved on to other projects, and it seemed their BNB days were behind them. Then in late January 2003, the four musicians who had comprised the final incarnation of the group returned to the stage for a one-off date in Toronto that led to steady gigging in March.

For a number of years preceding the intermission, the Burt Neilson Band was one of the most well known Canadian jambands, in part because it helped to blaze a trail along with other groups that departed, such as Caution Jam, Milky Way, and One Step Beyond (which featured a pre-New Deal Jamie Shields). The BNB first came together in 1996 at Lakehead University in Thunder Bay, Ontario, through a series of informal local jam sessions that yielded the original seven-piece version of the group, which included two guitarists, a pair of drummers, and a trumpet player. As for "Burt Neilson," the group actually has no namesake; this appellation was instead selected as something of a goof (in alignment with a general comic tincture, which endures).

Jambands typically eke out a living on the road, and Canadian touring is especially difficult given the wide expanse of the country. This led to a winnowing of the roster, first with the departure of the trumpeter and the original kit player (replaced by drummer Gavin Maguire in 1998). In 2000, following the band's second album, *Orange Shag Carpet*, guitarist Daniel Denomme left the group. Culled from a March 2001 tour of Ontario, *Five Alive* became something of a misnomer the next year when percussionist Jeffrey Kornblum broke from the band. Throughout the group's tenure, however, principal songwriters and vocalists guitarist Mike Filipowitsch and keyboard player Jeff Heisholt, along with bassist Jeremy Little, have retained a focus on animated funk tunes with bright vocals and playful lyrics that often carry into piano jazz and guitar rock realms. The BNB does introduce the occasional bluegrass ditty and skank, though these elements often receive short shrift, as the band is most comfortable within the grooves.

Five Alive (2001) ★★★

This collection from the then-quintet's March 2001 tour offers a batch of older songs and some newer material. There are some invigorating moments, but a few of the jams feel similar in tone and temperament.

Orange Shag Carpet (2000) ★★★½

Spiked with horns, *Orange Shag Carpet* presents some spirited studio sessions. The brass complements sprightly keys and fluent vocals on the best of the jazz and funk forays.

Out of print:

Burt Neilson Band (1998)

C

CLUB D'ELF
www.clubdelf.com

In 1998 bassist Mike Rivard was given an opportunity to host a biweekly open session of players at Cambridge, Massachusetts, venue the Lizard Lounge. Rivard, a Berklee College of Music grad who remained in the area, had been much in demand over the proceeding decade performing with the Either/Orchestra, the Story, Morphine, Patti Larkin, and many others. As a result, those Thursday "workshops" at the subterranean venue soon became a magnet for available Boston area talent and other improv-inclined players passing through, including John Medeski, Reeves Gabrels, Dana Colley, Kenwood Dennard, Bob Moses, Duke Levine, Mister Rourke, and DJ Logic. Rivard's role soon became that of a composer and conductor for the shifting cast of musicians known as Club d'Elf.

The Lizard Lounge proved to be an apt home for the collective as there is no traditional stage or much delineation between artist and audience. Instead, the band members face one another in the center of the basement space locking eyes and instruments to create a music that Rivard has described as "Space Age Dixieland." Here the band members offer simultaneous expressions or lay out with Rivard as musical director—a role he has compared to pushing the faders on a console (although "Micro Vard," as he has become known, often has a light touch).

Club d'Elf also offers some of Rivard's composed pieces, which often have a Middle Eastern flavor to them. Still, much of any given evening is improvised with the core musicians contributing a cluster of rhythms: Morroccan Brahma Fribgane on oud (a Middle Eastern lute), Jerry Leake on tablas and percussion, Erik Kerr on drums, and Jere Fasion adding keyboards. Rivard himself sometimes plays sintir, a three-stringed bass lute. The sound varies depending on who joins the Club at a particular gig, as the additional instruments can include turntable, sax, trumpet, electric violin, and a range of vocalists and poets. While trance and dub permeate, sometimes the sound approaches John McLaughlin's classic Mahavishnu Orchestra with a contemporary spin.

As Above: Live at the Lizard Lounge (2000)
★★★★

Guest players on these performances recorded in late 1999 to early 2000 include Reeves Gabrels, Kenwood Dennard, DJ Logic, Dr. Didg & Mat, and Joe Maneri along with a dozen others. Many flavors are sampled here, from ambient avant jazz to world percussion to jungle to groove. There's often quite a bit happening simultaneously, less cacophony than blur, but the fact that Club d'Elf remains compelling throughout much of these two discs speaks volumes about the vitality of the project.

THE CODETALKERS
www.thecodetalkers.com

More often than not, when someone describes a particular project as a departure for an artist, it refers to music that careens away from convention. The opposite is true for Col. Bruce Hampton, relative to his current band, the Codetalkers. Indeed, contrary to most everything else in his career of 30-plus years, the Codetalkers produce songs that are melodic and even (gasp) catchy.

The Colonel is a legend. An inspiration. A longtime promulgator of "broken" music. His acolytes include fellow Aquarium Rescue Unit members Jimmy Herring, Jeff Sipe, and Oteil Burbridge as well as Derek Trucks, Mike Gordon, and many others. Frank Zappa was a longtime friend and champion of his efforts (when visiting radio stations, Zappa often compelled DJs to spin Hampton's releases). His vocals and guitar work are far from the traditional paragon, but he first held sway with intent and energy before anyone ascribed those traits to Neil Young. Plus, there's a healthy dose of performance artist running through his art.

Yet Hampton is not the principal voice in the Codetalkers. Instead, the quartet showcases the music of Bobby Lee Rodgers, who Hampton has described as "one of the best songwriters in the world." Rodgers's skills also extend to the guitar, mandolin, and banjo, and he is a former Berklee College of Music educator who has toured with McCoy Tyner, among many others.

The pair met in classic Hamptonian fashion with the Colonel guessing Rodgers's birth date and then inviting him pretty much sight-unheard to sit in with his band at a forthcoming gig (the relatively short-lived Planet Zambee). The relationship blossomed, and the pair eventually formed a new collective that predominantly presents Rodgers's music. Hampton will step up on vocals, though, particularly for some blues and soul classics as well as reworked versions of his older material. The core songs themselves have an accessibility that Hampton seemed to consciously avoid in his previous work. This is not to say, however, that there is no weirdness here—especially of the lyrical variety—it's just that there is an engaging melodic base to it all.

These compositions often become a platform for improvisation in the live setting. Hampton adds, "We're a jazz band masquerading as a rock band. We might do a solid hour of just improvisation at times, and then there might be none for an hour. It depends on the tune and the structure of the tune. They're different every day no matter what. We try to set different tempos and change the key a lot—just keep it fresh every day. But to me, I'd be satisfied with doin' one note and one chord. I'd never get bored. One note's all right with me, if everybody would be into it."

Indeed, while in some respects Hampton is less of a presence in the Codetalkers than in his previous groups, the Colonel's perspective informs the music as a whole. Rodgers confirms: "Bruce tries to destroy the band to see how strong it is. He's so off that if you're not on, it will stick out like a sore thumb. It makes you awake beyond belief."

The Codetalkers (2003) ★★★

Appealing melodies and skewed narratives predominate on the band's debut. The Codetalkers juxtapose funk and blues pockets with the less-conventional lyrical content of such songs as "Body in the Lake," "Did My Time," and "Saturn." Hampton steps up for vocals for two songs, a reading of Skip James's "I'm So Glad" and a compelling, persistent take on his own "Isles of Langerhan."

COMOTION

www.comotion.cc

String Cheese Incident's Michael Kang was the driving force behind this project, as he approached some of his favorite musicians for a collaborative recording venture. He tapped six players to join him in the studio: newgrass heroes Paul McCandless, Darol Anger, and Mike Marshall; the former Leftover Salmon rhythm section of Jeff Sipe and Tye North; and drummer Aaron Johnson. This roster carried an intergenerational element that Anger likened to the early days of the David Grisman Quintet, where "the younger guys were soaking up as much as they could from the older guys and the older guys were very much enjoying the blast of energy and enthusiasm of the younger guys." In January 2000 everyone's schedules aligned for one week, and the *Head West* sessions took place. Time constraints and geographic barriers limited the opportunities for collective composition, as most of the songs came to Comotion from the individual players.

The music that Comotion created during its week in the studio most likely sounds like nothing you would expect based solely on the personnel (or maybe not, if you recognize that these musicians enjoy confounding expectation). For the most part the band eschews bluegrass, drifting instead into the realm of progressive jazz, although there is also a strong Celtic element and hints of other genres, including reggae. Despite Michael Kang's role in assembling the group, it is McCandless's saxophones, oboes, and clarinets that often carry the sound, wrapped around Kang's mandolin or Anger's violin.

The band members cleared their swollen itineraries in September of 2000 for a nine-date tour to celebrate the release of *Head West*. At these shows the musicians exhibited a bit more of their bluegrass sides. The band also opened up a number of the songs with individual and collective improvisation. In addition, Comotion displayed an intensity and power beyond that of the album, which relies a bit more on texture and finesse.

Head West (2000) ★ ★ ★ ½

Interesting ideas abound, and the seven band members are both generous and responsive. The world's rhythms appear, from the reggae flavors of "Into Da Night" to the Hawaiian "Oh, Lei" to the extended "Celtus Mobius 2000" that closes out this release. At its worst, the music descends into lite jazz, yet just when things start to feel stale, someone reacts and redirects.

COOKOUT

www.cookout.net

There is often a pulsing insistence to the music of Cookout, which might lead one to assume that the band originates from a bustling urban environment. While Hattiesburg, Mississippi, may not seem to fit that bill, it does indeed serve as home to the quintet and its "jazz-fueled sounds for the modern ear." If you find this to be a curious dichotomy, it is fair to say Cookout embraces the anomalous as a means to "bring live musical risk before audiences with more finesse and balls than Evil Knievel in a tuxedo." Plus, frankly, music comes from within not from without, and at any rate, Hattiesburg (population 50,000) is the fourth largest city in the state. If you have any more questions on this topic take them to Afroman, who hails from Hattiesburg as well (more on him in a moment).

Sticking with regional stereotypes (what the hey), a group named Cookout that hails from Mississippi might be expected to deliver blues and soul sounds, however this band offers propulsive jazz seasoned with funk and a side of the abstruse. For a few years, Cookout's three lead instruments—Casey Robinson's guitar, Harry Crumpler's sax, and Ben Maddox's keys—swirled and swarmed, alternately comping and commanding. In January 2002 the addition of bass player Darrell Havard (joining drummer Brad Newton) brought another player to the fore. Havard (who had toured for some time with Afroman) introduced the Chapman Stick and its two-handed fingering technique that yields a percussive sound with sharp, staccato rhythms. The band performed more than 130 shows in 2002 with Havard and the Stick, as it continues to define its own sound while building on the traditions it relishes with urgency and aplomb.

Ear Fashion (2001) ★ ★ ★ ½

An assertive disc that often enfolds the listener with vivid organ runs, sax flurries, and incisive guitar. There's much more than groove here as the band also varies the pace with facility and confidence, building on flexible rhythms.

COUSIN FUNGUS

www.cousinfungus.com

Cousin Fungus originated in the mid-'90s as one of the very first, if not the first, Phish cover bands. It also holds the distinction of being one of the very first, if not the first, Phish cover band to perform with a member of Phish (come to think of it, the group may take honors here). On April 12, 1997, Jon Fishman joined the band on stage at Chuck's in Syracuse for a few songs, including "NICU" and "Slave to the Traffic Light." At that time Cousin Fungus was known alternately as St. Ash or Stash, depending on the vagaries of a given club's publicist.

After building a steady following in the Northeast while interpreting the music of Phish, the band members ultimately decided to focus on original material. In certain respects this was a bold move, as the group had developed some renown for its take on the Phish catalog. Ultimately, the band took the leap, changing its name to Cousin Fungus to mark this transition (alas, this new appellation did lack a certain subtlety, somewhat akin to Psychedelic Breakfast or any group founded after 2001 with the word "groove" in its moniker).

The band's path was complicated at the end of 2000, by the departure of keyboard player and primary vocalist Dennis Belline. For a few months CF toured as a trio, with guitarist Henry Stanziale singing lead and joined by his longtime bandmates and longer-time siblings, Chris on drums and Thomas on bass (which, incidentally, offered the group a prime opportunity to change its name to the Stanziale Brothers Band, but perhaps that's a bit of a mouthful). In June of 2001 the group added a second guitarist, Mike Sanchez, who began writing new music with the Stanziales, and Cousin Fungus released its second album a little more than a year later. As one can imagine, there is still a Phish presence in the band's music, although the group's current sound may more closely echo that of the Disco Biscuits. Sometimes the vocals can be a bit rough-hewn (as with the Biscuits), and the quartet is still working to develop some of its song ideas, but Cousin Fungus is striving towards defining its own space.

Share the Air (2002) ★★ ½
The band carves out more of an identity on this disc (against a backdrop colored by Phish and the Disco Biscuits) with some energetic readings of solid songs.

Thoughts of a Moth (1999) ★ ½
One can count off a number of Phish reference points on the band's debut, in which the group never fully elaborates on some of its more substantive ideas.

JASON CROSBY
www.jasoncrosby.com
Jason Crosby is the consummate utility player. A prodigy who began studying classical violin at age two and piano at four, he is also proficient at trumpet, French horn, viola, and guitar. Crosby traveled the world with the Long Island Youth Orchestra as a high school student, joined Solar Circus in 1993 at age 19, and currently juggles steady touring gigs with Susan Tedeschi, Shannon McNally, and Oteil & the Peacemakers. He also has taken to the road with Project Z, God Street Wine, and the Truth (a short-lived project featuring Oteil Burbridge and Leo Nocentelli).

As a result, when Crosby has the time and energy to work on his solo career, a number of world-class musicians are quite willing to chip in. His debut disc includes collaborations with Burbridge, Nocentelli, Derek Trucks, and Lo Faber (who produced the disc with Crosby). His most recent release offers appearances by Burbridge, Trucks, Tedeschi, McNally, and Jeff Sipe. In addition to dates with his own band, he has assembled a number of "Jason Crosby & Friends" shows with a number of the aforementioned players, plus Eric Krasno, Melvin Sparks, and Stanley Jordan.

Crosby's own music ranges from funk to rock to R&B to free jazz. He credits Oteil and Kofi Burbridge along with Sipe as his major influences, and such mentors certainly do encourage him to play "out." Crosby's approach is promising, but given his time commitment with other artists, his own endeavors are sometimes back-burnered or subsumed by their all-star feel, as his voice and that of his band are still emerging.

Four Chords and Seven Notes Ago (2003) ★★★ ½
Even more eclectic than his debut. Some of the songs with Shannon McNally's vocals have more of a traditional R&B feel, while the instrumentals can be more airy and aloof. The disparity can be jarring, but there are fine moments in each approach and top-notch players to carry it off.

Out of the Box (2000) ★★★ ½
A stellar cast is on board for Crosby's debut, co-produced by Lo Faber. Funk and jazz themes predominate, and if the songwriting isn't always singular the playing often is.

D

DARK STAR ORCHESTRA
www.darkstarorchestra.net/

A prank (of Ken Keseyian stature) took place on April 13, 2001, at San Francisco's Warfield Auditorium. The Dark Star Orchestra—which recreates specific Grateful Dead performances—was in the midst of presenting the Dead's April 13, 1980, show when Rob Eaton, who fills the Bob Weir role, stepped offstage midway through the band's first electric set (the DSO had opened with an acoustic set, as had the Dead on the date in question). Sliding into formation in his stead was none other than... Bob Weir, who played "Little Red Rooster," "Tennessee Jed," and "Let It Grow" before inviting Eaton back to join in for the set-closing "Wheel" and "Music Never Stopped." Weir's appearance with the group affirms the measure of support and respect this band has earned.

Dark Star Orchestra came together in 1997, when guitarist John Kadlecik and keyboardist Scott Larner decided to elevate the art and aim of a Dead cover band. DSO's mantra remains "Let DeadBase be your guide," as the group presents a range of shows from particular eras. However, the band doesn't just reproduce the set lists from a given date (a feat that would be satisfying enough for many Dead Heads), it also strives to do so with the same arrangements. Thus DSO has become something of a repertory company, as any given night may feature a lone drummer (for shows that took place during Mickey Hart's hiatus), a female vocalist (the Donna Godchaux era), or dual keys (the Bruce Hornsby/Vince Welnick period). In addition, the band's gear will change, as Eaton has a variety of amps that reflect those that Weir has employed, and the drummers reproduce the Rhythm Devils' stage plots (building "The Beast" for an appropriate '80s date).

The identity of the show that DSO interprets initially remains a secret except to the diehards in the room (or those who "cheat" by thumbing through their portable DeadBases). Then at the conclusion of the night, the group will announce the date and venue of the original. Following this—with a nod to tape traders—DSO often will encore with "filler," additional songs that may be from a different era.

The presence of tapers at Dark Star Orchestra gigs confounds some people who feel that any would-be listeners should seek out the originals. Still, the existence of a DSO trading community affirms the extent to which people get into the spirit of it all (plus the band does offer an interpretive art). A DSO show carries its own vibe and anticipation, with an element of Dead Head Jeopardy tossed in as well. Just remember, as the group itself will occasionally joke from the stage, "no wagering."

Thunder and Lightnin' (2003)

DAVE MATTHEWS BAND
www.dmband.com

Some of the musicians in this book have expended energy explaining why their groups are not quite "jambands." While these artists' assertions do not hold sway, when Dave Matthews makes such a declaration, he's persuasive. This takes nothing away from the Dave

Matthews Band, which is a model of grass roots success that has crafted a rich body of music, some of which will remain part of the popular music lexicon for some time to come. Plus, one has to appreciate the support the DMB has thrown behind a number of estimable groups profiled here, by offering opening slots on stadium and arena tours to artists such as Gov't Mule, Béla Fleck & the Flecktones, Medeski Martin and Wood, Robert Randolph & the Family Band, and Soulive.

When the Dave Matthews Band began gigging in 1991, its music had a pronounced element of improvisation. This is not surprising, given that most of the band members were seasoned jazz players (even teenage bass player Stefan Lessard had such predilections). However, the primary motivation behind this approach was a limited amount of material. Drummer Carter Beauford recalls, "I think that a lot of what we were doing in the early days was overkill. We didn't have a lot of tunes, and we had to stretch the daylights out of them to make it work. Now we're trying to focus on narrowing down and being precise in how we say it and when we say it." Guitarist Matthews adds, "We never wanted to be a jamband; that was never what we thought about. We just got together, worked up two songs and tried to get gigs. It was someone else who told us we were a jamband, and we said, 'Okay, whatever, we just play, and if people come that's a good thing.'"

The group also acquired the jamband tag through association. In 1994 Phish announced opening acts for only five of their shows, and in every instance it was the Dave Matthews Band (which resulted in a few onstage collaborations—the "You Enjoy Myself " on April 20, 1994, at the Virginia Hose Center in Lexington is a favorite of many). A year later the Grateful Dead invited the DMB to open a three-night stand at the Sam Boyd Silver Bowl in Las Vegas on May 19–21, 1995.

Still, the fact remains that the band, as it performs today, typically adheres to the arrangements. There certainly is room for solos, and Matthews affirms, "We want to have improvisation because we don't want to get bored, so we do make things up on the spot." In addition, certain guest performers,

Dave Matthews busts a string at HORDE, 1995.

in particular the Flecktones, tend to instigate some collective improv. Nonetheless, any given DMB show most often retains a reasonably tight focus on the songs themselves, as presented by the euphonious voices of the five band members. So while the Dave Matthews Band is listed here, frankly the group has been included only to explain why it shouldn't be included. The DMB is not a jamband but a pop-rock band, and a fine one at that.

Related article and shameless plug:

Relix, DMB cover story, October/November 2002 (It was while writing this piece that I first explored the topics discussed above. For more details, seek out a copy at your local library or order a back issue online at www.relix.com.)

Fan site:

www.nancies.org (This is one of many, but it is the most exhaustive, including set list archives, lyrics, and tablature.)

DAVID NELSON BAND

www.nelsonband.com

David Nelson has the lineage. He may not be a descendent of the FFV (then again, maybe he is—if one looks at the First Families of Virginia list compiled by President John Tyler's son Lyon, it does indeed include a Nelson). However, he can trace his musical roots back to the Bay Area coffeehouse scene of the early '60s, which in part spawned the San Francisco psychedelic music of a few years later.

To some degree, Nelson's career has been entwined with that of Jerry Garcia and the Grateful Dead. In 1962 and 1963, he joined Garcia on acoustic guitar as a member of the Hart Valley Drifters/Wildwood Boys (which included Robert Hunter on mandolin) and that band's successor, the Black Mountain Boys (alas, no Hunter). In 1969, John Dawson invited Nelson to lend guitar and vocals to the New Riders of the Purple Sage, who opened a number of Dead shows with Garcia on pedal steel and ultimately occupied Nelson well into the early '80s (in 1969 and 1970, Nelson contributed to the Dead's *Aoxomoxoa*, *American Beauty*, and *Workingman's Dead*). A few years later, after the "Nerps" stopped gigging, Nelson joined Jerry Garcia's acoustic band during its Broadway run at the Lunt-Fontanne Theater, documented on the *Almost Acoustic* album. Then he worked with a number of zydeco projects before the David Nelson Band came together in 1994, as an offshoot of the Gratefully Yours tour that included Tom Constanten, Matt Kelly (Kingfish), Merl Saunders, and other players who carried some association with the Dead.

The David Nelson Band quickly affirmed its vitality by introducing a spate of original material (including a number of collaborations between Nelson and Hunter). The DNB features Kingfish alums Barry Sless (electric guitar, pedal steel) and Mookie Siegel (keyboards, accordion), who, along with Nelson, joined Phil Lesh & Friends for gigs on July 2-3, 1999. (The lineup also included Steve Kimock and Bill Kreutzmann. Nearly five months later, on November 30, 1999, Lesh sat in with the DNB for its second set at a SEVA Benefit in San Francisco.) The band's rhythm section came to the group through prior associations: bassist Bill Laymon had performed with Nelson in the New Riders, and drummer Charlie Crane had worked with Sless in Cowboy Jazz.

The David Nelson Band remains rooted in the sounds that have engaged its members over the years. The quintet performs its own material predominantly, though it will also drop in an old-time traditional as well as the occasional Dead cover. Although Nelson has lost a smidge of his vocal range over the years, there is often an ease and warmth to his delivery that complements the compositions. While some listeners may deem the DNB's psychedelic country rock to be dated, many others welcome the genuine throwback throw down.

Visions Under the Moon (1999) ★★★

The country influences are a bit more prominent and the band a bit more restrained on this disc drawn from recordings at Portland, Oregon's Aladdin Theater that blend live performances and studio sessions.

Keeper of the Key (1997) ★★★ ½

Three Hunter/Nelson originals are among the highlights of this disc recorded at Baltimore, Maryland's 8x10 Club on May 6, 1995. The phrasings and tonalities are typically both comfortable and ebullient throughout this release.

Also:

Limited Edition (1995)

THE DEAD

www.dead.net

For some time, a glib one-liner has pro-claimed that this is the best Grateful Dead cover band on the planet. There's certainly an element of truth to this, especially when describing the latter-day incarnations of the Other Ones. However, after the group changed its name to the Dead in early 2003—emphasizing the continuity and stability of the current lineup—some felt this characterization seemed less apt (to be honest, though, it still may be the best Grateful Dead cover band on the planet).

When the Other Ones first emerged in June 1998 and headlined the Furthur Festival, the band's intent was to reinvestigate and revitalize the music of the Grateful Dead. Billy Kreutzmann opted not to participate, but Bob Weir, Phil Lesh, Mickey Hart, and Bruce Hornsby (graduating class of '92) did contribute. Two additional guitarists joined Weir: Steve Kimock (the logical choice to many) and Mark Karan (the dark horse candidate). Yet despite the guitar army, a number of Jerry Garcia's signature leads were interpreted through the propulsive saxophone of Dave Ellis (previously known best as a member of the Charlie Hunter Trio along with Jay Lane). John Molo, longtime Hornsby drummer and later one of Phil's Friends, sat behind the kit. While at times the sound was cluttered (as Weir noted, "With our approach sometimes it's real good and sometimes you need a traffic cop."), Dead Heads old and new praised the band's versatility and vigor.

The Other Ones 2.0 (or perhaps TOO.2, to invoke the popular acronym for the band), returned during the late summer/fall of 2000. The group had not performed the previous year, ostensibly due to Phil Lesh's liver transplant, but the bass player opted not to rejoin anyway and Alphonso Johnson (of Weather Report and Santana) appeared in his stead (and remained too low in the mix for some). However, Bill Kreutzmann was back in the game, to resume his 30-plus-year stint with drumming buddy Mickey Hart. The sax was gone, though, with Dave Ellis now focusing on his jazz career. Often it was Hornsby who spurred the band, bounding from his chair to connect with other players, typically Kimock ("We're the bookends of the stage," Hornsby stated in mid-tour, "but we probably look at each other more than anybody else. We're always playing off each other and there's a real close connection that we have."). The resulting shows were solid and robust if not always dynamic.

By the late fall, the Dead founders' private dissension about the group's business affairs became public, and ultimately resulted in a New Year's Eve showdown of sorts with the Other Ones performing at the Oakland Arena while Phil Lesh & Friends were across town at the Henry J. Kaiser Convention Center. Yet eventually the sides thawed, as publicly manifested by a performance from Crusader Rabbit on June 10, 2001, at Sweetwater in Mill Valley, California, with Bob Weir joining Phil Lesh & Friends for two sets (Warren Haynes sat out much of the night but performed on the encores). This paved the way for summer bills featuring Phil Lesh & Friends and RatDog, which in turn led to the appearance of the Crusader Rabbit Stealth Band at Lesh's New Year's Eve gig when three wizards atop a float during the parade revealed themselves to be Hart, Kreutzmann, and Weir. This ultimately

resulted in the formulation of another Other Ones, which debuted at the Grateful Dead Family Reunion at Alpine Valley Music Theater in East Troy, Wisconsin, on August 3–4, 2003.

The ensuing version of TOO eventually became the Dead, which is certainly fitting as its sound and spirit mirror the original. Jimmy Herring is the lone lead guitarist, melding some of Garcia's ideas with his own inventive flourishes. Lesh and Weir have each contributed a keyboard player, as Phil Lesh & Friends' Rob Barraco shares duties with RatDog's Jeff Chimonti. A few dates into the fall tour, Susan Tedeschi stepped in as well, sweetening the vocals (though in some instances it was clear she was picking things up on the fly and her contributions improved over the run). For its summer 2003 dates, the Dead announced that Joan Osborne would sing with the group. Indeed, at this point, the band is closest in intention and execution to its progenitor than any prior incarnation of the Other Ones. Some fans certainly revel in this fact while others hope this is only the starting point, and that the Dead will continue to introduce new music and take it further.

The Strange Remain (1999) ★ ★ ★ ½

This two-disc set drawn from the summer 1998 Furthur Festival captures the initial incarnation of the band with particularly assertive expressions from Dave Ellis on sax and Bruce Hornsby, who contributes confident vocals and keys. Meanwhile, the three guitar players mostly carve out room for each other on the fly. There is a vibrancy to the disc as the Dead challenges itself, reinterpreting its catalog and delving deeper into its jazz vocabulary, with results that are often absorbing.

Fan site:

www.otherones.net

DEEP BANANA BLACKOUT

www.deepbananablackout.com

The announcement on singer Jen Durkin's Web site in March 2003 proclaimed, "Never say never—disfunktional banana returns!" One can appreciate the rush of emotion that accompanied the news that Deep Banana Blackout's original lineup would reunite for a performance at the Gathering of the Vibes, an event that its members have been a part of since its inception. In more prosaic terms, Jen also explained, "I recently listened back to a live tape from a show in Burlington during our heyday in 1997, and it made me nostalgic about the music and the players. I'm excited to be back onstage with the band; it couldn't come at a better time. Taking the stage right before James Brown is a very old dream come true, and the VibeTribe is the perfect audience to share this pinnacle experience with."

This sentiment certainly rings true as the origins of DBB can be traced to Fairfield, Connecticut, cover band Tongue & Groove, which in the early '90s presented the music of Brown along with P-Funk, Aretha Franklin, Chaka Khan, and Sly & the Family Stone. When that group broke up, Durkin, along with bassist Benj LeFevre (Ben Carr), drummer Eric Kalb, and saxophone player Rob Somerville formed Back to Funk, along with Rob Volo on trombone, Jen's 15-year-old brother Johnny on percussion, and Fuzz (James Sangiovanni) on guitar and vocals (keyboardist Cyrus Madden would join a bit later). Fuzz helped guide the band towards an original repertoire by offering up a number of his own funk, rock, and Latin compositions and, according to Durkin, supplied the band's new name to her in a dream. The group started playing locally, and no less an artist than Maceo Parker created the signature Deep Banana Blackout chant. (John Scofield later appropriated the beats for his song "Blackout" on *Bump*.) Still, it was a performance at the second annual Gathering of the Vibes (a campground set on Friday night and a main stage set on Sunday) that catapulted the group.

Over the ensuing three years, the band's live show gained recognition for its loose vibe bolstered by tight rhythm and brass sections. In addition, fans were drawn to the galvanic vocals of "Jenny Pipes" (who had honed her chops at Berklee College of Music at the same time as Susan Tedeschi) as well as the curious fashion sense, scatological humor, and guitar riffs of Fuzz. ("What I've been trying to do is combine the best of everything: Have some cool funk grooves and some heavy rock riffs and some crazy solos that can be somewhat jazzy but take it to another level like Medeski Martin and Wood, who just go out and create chaos in their sound.")

While more than just a funk band, the genre remained at DBB's core, and the group often hailed its supporters as the Funk Mob. DBB became a national touring outfit within a year and maintained a strong connection to New Orleans, where it offered late-night sets and impromptu street processions, as well as New York, where DBB headlined successive New

Year's Eves at Wetlands Preserve in 1998 and 1999. In April 1999, Wetlands also hosted the group's "Boot Camp" residency (named after one of its songs), which included appearances by Clyde Stubblefield, Fred Wesley, Marshall Allen, Michael Ray, DJ Logic, and Peter Prince. At this time, however, the road began to take its toll on the group's lead singer (at a show at the Worcester Palladium on September 10, 1999, Durkin was unable to rise from the dressing room floor due to back pain) and she eventually opted to depart, performing her (presumably) last full show with the group in August 2000 at the Berkshire Mountain Music Festival. At this time Volo decide to move on as well, with his role handled by longtime Banana associate and Tongue & Groove alum, Bryan Smith.

Durkin's successor was Hope Clayburn, whose band, Baaba Seth, had recently dispersed. She distinguished herself with her presence on saxophone and flute as well as her determination not to emulate Durkin's vocals. Clayburn's tenure carried DBB further into smoky jazz realms, and some people preferred this era of subtler textures and collective instrumental prowess while others missed the all-out bombast of yore. Notable gigs in 2001 and 2002 included travels to Japan as well as opening a number of amphitheater shows on the Allman Brothers Band summer tour, with the horn section then performing a few songs with the ABB. However, road rigors, including the expense of supporting eight players, began to weigh heavily on the group, and when Kalb announced that he would leave at the end of 2002, the entire band decided to put things on indefinite hold.

But then the Vibes called once again, looking to hearken back to the original roster. Durkin, then performing with the Bomb Squad, had sat in with DBB for a few songs since her departure and was up for it. (There was even a bonus bit of Fleetwood Mac/White Stripes flair; the use of "disfunktion" on the singer's Web site likely referenced in part the fact that she would be returning to the stage with ex-husband Kalb as well as brother Johnny.) Volo, who had been performing with Fuzz's new project, the Gratuitous Sextet (along with Somerville and LeFevre), re-upped as well. None of the principals was entirely sure where this all might lead, but it is fair to assume that the Funk Mob will follow.

Release the Grease (2002) ★★★

The band is a bit restrained on the disc, which is not necessarily a bad thing as one of the hallmarks of the latter-era DBB is a strengthened sense of dynamics. Still, the title is something of a misnomer; while the musicians are in fine fettle, they do not deliver enough of those moments of all-out exuberance that one associates with the live DBB experience.

Feel the Peel (2001) ★★★ ½

Hope Clayburn and Bryan Smith are both in the mix for this studio effort, which in contrast to the previous two discs has smoother, more silken textures. This is not solely old school blaring funk but a rich, colorful mix of Latin, jazz, and soul. Still, on songs such as "Fire It Up," the band does just that.

Rowdy Duty (1998) ★★★ ½

This two-CD set is the signature release with Jen Durkin. She is in fine form throughout, and many of these songs remain DBB classics. The tones can feel a bit similar, and funk detractors may find it redundant at times, but it is a fine effort

Live in the Thousand Island (1997) ★★ ½

A solid initial salvo that defines Deep Banana's range and intent. Still, some of these studio readings of songs that can soar in the live setting feel a bit thin.

Related sites:

Fuzz—*www.fuzztunes.com*
Jen Durkin—*www.jendurkin.com*
Hope Clayburn—*www.hopeclayburn.com*

DEREK TRUCKS BAND

www.derektrucks.com

You wouldn't know it by looking at him, and you might not know it upon initially hearing him, but Derek Trucks is subversive. Some musicians have devoted themselves to contravening expectations, revitalizing many listeners in the process—performers such as Sun Ra, Cecil Taylor, and our own Col. Bruce Hampton, Ret. leap to mind. However, this recalcitrance is all the more resonant when it comes from a towheaded guitarist in his mid-twenties who carries an earnest if diffident stage demeanor. Trucks's music can be achingly beautiful and achingly broken, though as befits his perspective, his definition of experimentation is not altogether traditional: "I don't think pushing the envelope is going completely left or completely right. I think it's just a fire and intensity, more than people will-

ing to go out or play atonal or free." It is such an approach, facilitated by his artistry, that leads many to believe Trucks will contribute vital, consequential music to the canon for years to come.

And there's the rub. We're back in the realm of expectation again—something that Trucks has had to abide ever since he was first dubbed a prodigy. This is certainly understandable, as Trucks is a three-time winner of the National Spelling Bee and recently made inroads on the professional Scrabble circuit, taking top honors at a few events (for more on the splendor that is professional Scrabble, read Stefon Fatsis's *Word Freak*). No, no, wait a minute. Strike that. Trucks is actually a different variety of wunderkind altogether, one who opened ears with his slide guitar prowess at a time when the instrument nearly stood taller than he.

Derek is a nephew of Allman Brothers Band drummer Butch Trucks, so the ABB connection runs deep. Duane Allman long served as an inspiration to the young Trucks, who estimates that his copy of *Live at Fillmore East* had hundreds of bedtime spins during his early years. Trucks first sat in with the ABB at age 11 on July 11, 1990, for "One Way Out." Nine summers later he received a call from his uncle asking him to join the ABB on tour (Butch observes of Derek: "Duane invented this style of playing slide guitar, but Duane was just beginning to touch on what Derek is doing right now. Technically, Derek is much better than Duane Allman was, there is no doubt about it. Just listen to the records.").

But while Derek now belongs to his own group that delivers some of most powerful blues on the planet, and while early in his career he devoted much of his effort to this genre, it would be negligent to refer to the Derek Trucks Band as a blues band (heck, it might even be actionable). Through exposure to John Coltrane, Ali Akbar Kahn, Nusrat Fateh Ali Kahn, and Sun Ra, Trucks's music took on new hues and ambitions. (By the way, it is no accident that the third DTB release is named *Joyful Noise*, a phrase long associated with Sun Ra and also the title of Robert Mugge's 1980 documentary on the Arkestra.)

The extended Aquarium Rescue Unit family also played a role in Trucks's evolution, as bassist Todd Smallie—who has performed more than 1,600 shows with the DTB—came to join through his connection with ARU guitarist Jimmy Herring, having studied with him at the Atlanta Institute of Music. Smallie recalls, "In the transition we ran a lot of people out of the blues clubs. He used to say we'd Hampmotized them, gave them some Bruce Hampton music and just lost them."

Trucks's self-described world-soul, a hyphenate of global reach, would not be attainable without willing co-conspirators. In addition to Smallie, he is joined by drummer Yonrico Scott, another former Hampton associate. Scott performed in Broadway orchestra pits and on tours with Whitney Houston and Peebo Bryson before joining the DTB ("I went from playing Madison Square Garden to playing 50-seat clubs"). He serves in an avuncular role to Trucks (though unlike Butch, sans consanguinity) and his contributions became all the more vivid after a near-fatal heart attack just prior to a tour in October 2000. (Scott drove himself to the hospital in the throes of his attack.) On keyboards and flute, the most fecund songwriter in the band as of late is Kofi

Burbridge, elder brother of Oteil and himself an ARU veteran. In mid-2002 vocalist Mike Mattison from the duo Scrapomatic stepped in, drawing on the strengths of his two predecessors, Bill McKay (now with Leftover Salmon) and Javier Colon, to deliver stirring, soulful numbers while digging in on the Bobbie Blue Bland songs, as well.

The Derek Trucks Band can offer a majestic experience with emotional depth and stylistic breadth. Depending on the context, some audience members have felt a particular show to linger a bit on the mellower side (though again, this is often borne of ADD-based expectations). Others have found some of the Eastern-influenced songs and extended takes on such offerings as "Afro Blue" to be a bit far

Derek Trucks, focus and fire.

outside the frame. Trucks responds to such perceptions in observing: "There are enough people out there to entertain people and give them what they think they want to hear. I want to be a part of something that makes people question what they thought they wanted to hear."

Joyful Noise (2002) ★ ★ ★ ★ ½

A stellar representation of the DTB's world-soul. Guest vocalists Solomon Burke, Ruben Blades, Rahat Fateh Ali Kahn, Susan Tedeschi, and Javier Colon guide the band through a range of jazz, Latin, Middle Eastern, and blues tracks animated by the guitarist's own emotive counterpoints and ebullient support from his bandmates.

The Derek Trucks Band (1997) ★ ★ ★ ½

The recorded debut of the quartet (Trucks is joined by Smallie, Scott, and McKay) offers some tantalizing moments along with some less gripping ones. Trucks's ingenuity is made manifest through the band's interpretations of such songs as John Coltrane's "Naima" and "Mr. P.C." as well as Wayne Shorter's "Footprints." However, the original music often feels inchoate, as some of these riffs and changes could be developed further.

Also:

Soul Serenade (2003)

Out of print:

Out of the Madness (1998)

Discussion list:

www.lists.netspace.org/archives/derek.html

DEXTER GROVE
www.dextergrove.com

It can be unrelenting for Steve Drizos and Charley Orlando. As Dexter Grove, the two musicians currently average more than two hundred dates a year. However, since they typically perform on acoustic guitar and hand drums, they are sometimes a bit too portable. If they happen to be hanging out with friends or fans after completing a club date, the pair will often field entreaties to pick up their instruments and keep it going. "We used to do it all the time," Orlando laughs. "These days we're trying real hard to say no. Trying at least...."

The pair began performing together after Orlando's previous group, Doc Apple, broke up in 1993. It wasn't until 1995, though, that the two decided to go after their career full tilt. Positive feedback and road-friendly instrumentation instigated a series of continental crossings that continue to this day (Bob Dylan's "Never Ending Tour" has got nothing on DG).

Drizos and Orlando prefer to describe themselves as a two-piece band rather than a duo. The operative word, of course, is band, as Drizos often delivers basslines and melodies on congas, while Orlando's acoustic guitar carries effects that may approximate keyboards, bass, or alternate tones. As of late, on occasion Dexter Grove has also expanded into DG3 or DG4, touring with such players as moe.'s Jim Loughlin and guitarist Tim Herron. Some listeners have appreciated the augmented roster with its more robust sound, deeming the acoustic pair a bit limiting. Others prefer the tandem, drawn to its earthy, percussive timbres. In either context the band's self-classification as "acid folk" holds true.

Similarly in both settings, Drizos and Orlando are extolled for their interaction and anticipation, and in particular their gift for segues, even as they gain ground as songwriters (their originals can sometimes feel a bit repetitive and achromatic). At this point in the band's career, Dexter Grove can anticipate turnout from its faithful most anywhere in the nation, just as Drizos and Orlando can expect those requests for post-gig gigs.

Color Me Naked (2001) ★★ ½

Color is an appropriate word—following two tracks by themselves, Drizos and Orlando draw in other players including Kirk Juhas on keys, Tim Herron on electric guitar, and James Whiton on double bass. The results add hues, brightening some songs that otherwise feel plain.

Live Without a Crowd Vol. 1 (2001) ★★★

moe.'s Jim Loughlin and Al Schnier join the band on this set from the band's performance at the Aggie Theater in Fort Collins on November 14, 1999. DG presents some of its more captivating material, complemented by invigorating improv.

Live Without a Crowd Vol. 2 (2001) ★★ ½

It's the classic tandem on this disc from July 23, 2000, at the Canyon Recreation Hall in Yellowstone Park, Wyoming. Once more, some exhilarating musicianship and deft segues animate the effort.

Also:
True (1998)
Alive and Well at the Garden of Eden (1997)
420 (1995)

THE DISCO BISCUITS
www.discobiscuits.com

Some people just don't like the Disco Biscuits.

Such individuals likely will acknowledge the band's intensity and concede some degree of innovation, yet remain indifferent to the group's output. These folks may find the concept of an inverted or dyslexic song interpretation engaging intellectually, but when it comes to the Biscuits, they deem this a distinction without difference, finding little variance within a given performance let alone within a version of "Aquatic Ape."

And then there are the Bisco Kids. These mega-boosters cloak themselves in the group's music often to the exclusion and derision of all else. BKs marvel at the minutiae and savor the subtleties of the band's art with a fervor rarely matched by other fan communities. Jerry Garcia's famous quote regarding the fealty of Dead Heads comes to mind ("Not everybody likes licorice, but the people who like licorice really like licorice"), but in this case a more fitting comparison is one that promotes endorphin release, let's say a triple espresso with a yerba mate/ma Huang/bee pollen chaser.

One could not necessarily have forecast the extreme cuisine comparisons when four University of Pennsylvania students came together in 1995 (as "Zex Sea or the Capital Regime or the Party Tents, a new name for every other fraternity show."). The current quartet coalesced a number of months later, with keyboardist Aron Magner joining bass player Marc Brownstein, drummer Sam Altman, and guitarist Jon Gutwillig, and the band started to amplify its quantum of original music to supplement and eventually supplant its adept covers of complex improvisational rock. (Magner, who had gigged on the Philadelphia cocktail jazz circuit while still in high school, which led him to matriculate at Penn, recalls that there was some miscommunication prior to his first rehearsal. The band had expected a "40-year-old black jazz pianist named Aaron Magnum. When I walked into that first rehearsal, an 18-year-old kid with my baseball cap on backwards and my keyboard under my arm, they were all looking for Aaron Magnum.")

Magner needed some time to acclimate himself to the new idiom but eventually he took, as did the band, which rechristened itself the Disco Biscuits. (The name is a throwback, a chemical reference from an earlier era: In 1997, British journalist Sarah Champion edited a book entitled *Disco Biscuits* to celebrate the tenth anniversary of acid house music with contributions from Irvine Welsh, Jeff Noon, Alex Garland, Douglas Rushkoff, and others. She also compiled an accompanying double-CD set that included tracks from artists such as 808 State, Orbital, the Shamen, and the Orb. While one might not initially situate the Disco Biscuits in this realm, the band would certainly grow into the appellation.)

During the fall of 1997, Magner purchased a keyboard that would provide the catalyst for a sound that spawned two neologisms (and an abundance of acolytes). At the band's Halloween gig he debuted the Roland JP-8000, the keystone to a synth fortress that would soon surround him. He recalls, "I had the manual out during the show and I was figuring out how to use it. All of a sudden that keyboard player who previously was sitting in the background kind of playing air traffic controller, coloring different notes while Barber [Gutwillig] assumed most of the leads here and there, was putting out these sounds and rhythms that we hadn't been doing before. Sammy was saying, 'Wow all those crazy techno dance beats that I hear all the time from people's college rooms sound pretty cool over the weird sounds Magner's emitting.' Then Brownstein laid down this drum & bass bassline and we found ourselves in a different area." (An *Uncivilized Area*, as the band would dub this region on their next release.) Still, Magner was not altogether pleased with the initial results: "We sat in the key of *D* all night. I think eventually to switch it up we busted into 'Run like Hell' and then right back into *D*. Of course it was *D* with crazy sounds and cool drum beats and stuff like that."

Nonetheless, from this came trance fusion, the term often employed by the band to describe its ongoing efforts to morph (and Dusseldorf) genres. While the group's moniker may lead one to echo the Oracle and posit that perhaps the sound found the band before the band found the sound, Magner's machinery added a novel element that the group has not rendered a novelty, effectively integrating and aggrandizing his contributions. (Gutwillig's guitar work is a lofty balance of understated musings and sweeping anthemic gestures, complemented by Brownstein's grounded, head-whirling, tongue-displaced bass and Altman's solid, stolid drumming, with the vocals a bit less affirmative.) The totality of this experience has come to be described as "bisco" (this innovation also has yielded a phenomena that some refer to as bisco journalism, whereby particular writers have fallen over themselves and their text in order to craft new platitudes and descriptive phraseology in a similar way that Dan Bern's music seems to stimulate aspirations of cleverness).

The Disco Biscuits embody flux. These progenitors of trance fusion continue to fold in new beats, as any given show will draw on dub, drum & bass, rock, jungle, and sometimes jazz (with classical digressions as well). Similarly, the Biscuits reshape their music continually, with one dramatic manifestation being inverted versions of the songs— they flip around their compositions to perform the concluding passages before moving back into the beginning. The quartet also offers a dyslexic option, in which it cleaves an inverted variant and then returns to the passage formerly-known-as-the-outset much later in the night or at a subsequent gig (a related endeavor is the all-out refashioning of songs into different genres, which the band did throughout a show on May 28, 2003, including some heavy metal recasting as well as a rockabilly rave-up). This fluidity extended briefly to the group's roster, with Brownstein leaving the band for a seven-month span in 2000, when many referred to the group as the Triscuits. The tensions prior to Brownstein's departure, however, yielded one of the quartet's inspired notions: Unwilling to initiate an endeavor for its New

Jon "The Barber" Gutwillig and Sam "The Barbered" Altman of the Disco Biscuits.

Year's Eve 1999 show that would require extensive rehearsal, such as a rock opera, the band opted to improvise a score to the film *Akira*. This effort earned the Disco Biscuits a Jammy Award for "Jam of the Year." The group attempted this again during the fall of 2001, offering *Alice in Wonderland* on Halloween, followed on three nights by *It's the Great Pumpkin, Charlie Brown* and portions of *Koyaanisqatsi* and *Run Lola Run*. Despite these efforts, there is some perception of invariability to the group's sound that continues to polarize audiences. But as befits the music, swelling crowds suggest that there certainly is much movement.

Señor Boombox (2002) ★★★ ½

Rich in texture, *Señor Boombox* is a culmination of sorts, bursting the kernels of its antecedents. However, as a result, while the disc has "Floes," it doesn't always flow.

They Missed the Perfume (2001) ★★★★

The technological assimilation accelerates with Sam Altman programming all the drum parts. Some of the ideas pieced together via computer feel a bit too esoteric, but "Mindless Dribble" pulses at the heart of the disc and the band sinks in their hooks with "Home Again."

Uncivilized Area (1998) ★★★★

One of the most influential discs within these pages. With *Uncivilized Area*, the Biscuits go electronica. While the vocals remain raw and the improvisation is a bit more linear than what would follow, the results are kinetic.

Encephalous Crime (1996) ★★ ½

A bit rough and certainly rudimentary in the sense that these nine studio tracks display the constituent elements before the band put the trance into the fusion. The re-pressing of the disc jettisons an early live version of Zappa's "Pygmy Twylyte" in favor of a "Basis for a Day" from December 29, 1998, an exhilarating 22-minute anachronism.

Also:

TranceFusionRadio Broadcasts 01-03 (2003)

Fan sites:

www.discobiscuits.net
www.biscoradio.com

Discussion lists:

www.lists.netspace.org/archives/discussbiscuits.html
www.groups.yahoo.com/group/Digi-Biscuits/
www.groups.yahoo.com/group/biscodiscit/

DJ HARRY

www.djharry.net

"Hippie House" music is what DJ Harry (Antibus) calls it, and while he may not have fashioned a new genre (yet), he is onto something. To his credit Harry recognized the affinities between house music and the jamband realm. This is not an altogether new idea, as Harry himself has described his moment of epiphany when he encountered the Wicked Crew spinning in the lots after a Grateful Dead show at the Oakland Coliseum in December 1992. However he certainly took this to the next level with his own DJ gigs and then through the *String Cheese Remix Project*.

In 1994 Harry settled down in Telluride, Colorado, where he balanced recreation and avocation, on the slopes and later in the clubs, spinning house music and participating in the area's live music scene. One of the local groups playing après-ski parties was the Blue Cheese String Band, then a bluegrass outfit. As that band evolved into the String Cheese Incident, Harry continued to refine his own techniques. Then in July of 2000, he was given a DJ slot between sets at SCI's Horning's Hideout festival. Harry offered up his own take on the host band's music and as he began spinning "Texas," members of the group joined him onstage, performing the song live along with him. This sealed the musical relationship, and the band soon offered up the 24-track live recordings from its spring and summers tours, which Harry used to create the *Remix Project.*

While DJ Harry has helped to bring house music into a novel context (and exposed String Cheese and the jamband world to new circles as well), some wonder where he will take it from here. He has worked on Galactic and Phish remix projects, although he has not yet received the sanction from either band to release them. He continues to spin at post-String Cheese shows and also has collaborated with Dr. Didg. By its nature, house music is pulsing and repetitive, so while many find his efforts invigorating both in clubs and cars, others remained unmoved—your mileage may vary.

The String Cheese Remix Project (2001)
★★★½

DJ Harry scores in terms of idea and execution. The best of these mixes feels organic with a nexus to the original material, as on "Texas" and "MLT" (with guest saxophones from Karl Denson and Paul McCandless). The Remix Project falters only slightly on those few occasions where it sounds like standard house music with a bit of Cheese sprinkled on top.

DJ LOGIC
www.djlogic.com

DJ Logic is ubiquitous. Or so it often seems. From coast to coast, in contexts when one might not anticipate that a DJ could even fit, Logic (Jason Kibler) lends new textures to the mix. For example, few could have imagined a few years back that he would join Bob Weir and RatDog onstage for a single show, yet he's been on board for entire tours. DJ Logic also has recorded and performed with, among others, moe., Gov't Mule, the String Cheese Incident, Béla Fleck & the Flecktones, Vida Blue, and at the second annual Jammy Awards he appeared with Robert Randolph and the Del McCoury Band for "Swing Low, Sweet Chariot." (Del and the Boys had a gig across town that didn't allow time for a soundcheck, leaving the bluegrass legend somewhat unaware of what would transpire. So when Logic took a solo and started scratching from a recorded version of the song, this elicited a triple take from McCoury).

Logic has been working at his craft since he was a teenager, beginning as a solo DJ and then with the band Eye and I, which became part of Vernon Reid's Black Rock Coalition. Logic was just 18 in 1990 when Eye and I hit the road opening tours for the Psychedelic Furs, Ice-T, and Reid's Living Colour. The group disbanded a few years later, yet Logic continued to work with Reid. At one such gig, at CBGB's, Billy Martin was in the audience. Logic's gift for subtle improv intrigued the drummer, who invited Logic to open Medeski Martin and Wood's forthcoming *Shack-man* release shows at the Knitting Factory. This in turn led to collaboration onstage and later on MMW's *Combustication* disc, exposing Logic to new ears (including those of many fellow artists). The game was afoot.

The MMW connection brought DJ Logic into many new contexts, both with formal bands and looser settings as well (for instance, at the Berkfest All-Star jam in 1999 with Bob Moses, Oteil Burbridge, Fuzz, Nate Wilson, Karl Denson, Rob Somerville, and Dr. Didg, or at Wetlands on September 10, 2001, with Warren Haynes, Mike Gordon, and Stanley Jordan). His presence in such contexts occasionally elicits grumbles from fans who contend that he has a near-monopoly on turntable guest appearances. However, there is a reason for this: Logic thrives in such a framework—he embraces an improvisational aesthetic. For instance, he always supplements the 30 records he intends to use at any given gig with a miscellaneous section "in case we go somewhere we wouldn't expect." Musicians also appreciate his respect for their efforts, as he notes, "If it's not my band I'll just hang in the back and listen. I don't like to scratch up someone else's music. I'll just lend colors, pick my moment, and take them."

DJ Logic is often a bit more aggressive when touring with one of his own groups. Still, even Project Logic (which has included fellow Eye and I alum Melvin Gibbs on bass, when he is not out with the Rollins Band) is not a vehicle for his solos, but rather one that works from a collective improvisational dynamic. The band walks onstage and builds from an opening bassline or sample. Logic takes a similar approach with the Yohimbe Brothers, his latest project with Reid, which also features some heavy guitar work (Project Logic typically gigs without a guitarist). In most any context, one of Logic's hallmarks remains his affinity for jazz artists from the bebop era and beyond (he references Miles Davis on such compositions as "Miles Away" and "Kinda Bleu"). Indeed, in describing his penchant for improv, Logic observes, "I might reach into the miscellaneous records and take a Rahsaan Roland Kirk record with him free-styling on the flute and do a little beat-back spin thing and throw that up in there, with a drum & bass groove or something. I'm just trying to keep it creative while interacting with everyone else."

Yohimbe Brothers, Front End Lifter (2002) ★★★★

A dense, often chaotic collage. Logic does not scratch over the top, nor does the pair clear room for Reid to solo, as they opt for a layered approach. At times this leads to excess, particularly with their use of distortion. Still, this is often a dazzling if overwhelming mosaic of styles and sounds.

The Anamoly (2001) ★★★★

More eclectic than the debut, the individual tracks also are developed further as entities unto themselves. Numerous guest musicians contribute flavors ranging from Middle Eastern violin to jazz to jungle to straight-up funk. Yes, despite these disparate styles, there is a flow—an internal Logic to it all.

DJ Logic Presents Project Logic (1999) ★★★ ½
Logic and co-producers bassist Melvin Gibbs and Scott Harding assembled downtown

New York City neo-jazz all-stars (including the members of Medeski Martin and Wood and Sex Mob) for these sessions. There is a live, fluid feel to much of this release that balances textured experimentation with good-time groove.

DONNA THE BUFFALO
www.donnathebuffalo.com

Donna The Buffalo is on the cusp. Not on the cusp of national recognition, as the band, which first came together in 1987, recorded its last two studio discs on prestigious Sugar Hill Records, and has crossed the country multiple times to perform at such high-profile events as Bonnaroo and the Grateful Dead Family Reunion. Nor is Donna The Buffalo on the cusp of critical approbation, as the band's two Sugar Hill discs have received positive ink (and pixels). Moreover, the band is not on the cusp of festival success, as its GrassRoots Festival—which allocates profits to charitable endeavors—is now in its second decade, regularly drawing 10,000 people to an eclectic music bill in Trumansburg, New York (with a new event debuting in 2003 at the Shakori Hills Farm in Silk Hope, North Carolina). Instead, in some people's minds (including those of its band members), Donna The Buffalo is on the cusp of what is defined as a "jamband."

Without getting too reductive on the nature of a jamband, in listening to Donna The Buffalo one can identify the requisite

Donna The Buffalo at Bonnaroo 2002.

elements. First off, the band's music bounds from genre to genre, especially zydeco, reggae, rock, and old-time music (one apt, entertaining description is from Patrick Carr, who characterized DTB as "Ralph Stanley sitting in with Bob Marley's Reggae/Zydeco All-Stars"). As for the improvisational component, that is there as well, often with a Cajun zest and a hint of psychedelia. Some songs do remain succinct, however, while at other times the band may toss it around for brief solos akin to bluegrass.

Donna The Buffalo first came together as a group of friends with a shared passion for traditional acoustic music. Eventually they decided to play out, and took on the name Donna The Buffalo—a misheard variant of "Dawn of the Buffalo," which had been suggested through a Long Island accent (shades of God Street Wine). Over time, the group began to build on its sound, blending both electric and acoustic instrumentation with Tara Nevins adding many of the signature elements, from accordion to washboard to fiddle. Nevins is also one of DTB's two primary songwriters, and her compositions tend to have a country-folk flavor along with a reggae lilt, while Jeb Puryear's efforts gravitate towards zydeco. Donna The Buffalo's songs also often contain social messages (especially Puryear's contributions), and the band has made an effort to manifest such sentiments through events like the GrassRoots Festivals.

As for the cusp, in characterizing Donna's overall sound, guitarist Jim Miller (a former curator of entomology at New York's Museum of Natural History) doesn't eschew the jamband tag, but he emphasizes that—at its core—DTB's sound is "dance-oriented." Miller further suggests that Donna The Buffalo appeals to people "who might be sick of formulaic music or contrived music. I'm not giving us any credit there, we wouldn't know how to do that. We're simply friends and folks who just do this. I think that people like to see natural music being made and created on the spot."

Live from the American Ballroom (2001) ★★★

This double, live release is playful and often uplifting. Some of the jams can feel a bit repetitive, as they tend to mine similar zydeco-reggae grooves. Nonetheless, this is an inviting set.

Positive Friction (2000) ★★★ ½

Another pleasing studio effort from the group, with Tara Nevins distinguishing herself as a vocalist and songwriter. When taken as a whole, some of the songs do feel monochromatic, but there is an affable, breezy vibe to the disc.

Rocking in the Weary Land (1998) ★★★★

A strong balance of bright, varied songwriting that also conveys some social messages without being cloying or heavy-handed.

Also:

The Ones You Love (1996)
Donna The Buffalo (1993)

Fan sites:

www.gatheringherd.com
www.virtualmajic.com/theherd/

DR. DIDG

www.drdidg.com

It would not be inaccurate to call Graham Wiggins a mad scientist. In 1982 the Boston University physics major first encountered the didgeridoo at a small world music concert. This began an obsession with the Aboriginal instrument that led him to initiate a senior project on its acoustics and continue his research at Oxford University, where he completed his Ph.D. Wiggins's doctorate also ultimately yielded the tag Dr. Didg (this designation was solidified through a postdoc field trip to Australia, where he studied with the masters of the didgeridoo's circular breathing technique).

After Oxford, he began busking in the streets of London, where he met acoustic guitar player Martin Cradick. The pair formed Outback, a group that featured Wiggins on didg and Cradick on acoustic guitar and mandolin (two percussionists eventually joined as well). While Outback gained notoriety for its innovative instrumentation, recording two critically lauded albums, in the live setting the band rarely strayed from the arrangements of its songs.

It was not until 1993, during a late-night performance at the Glastonbury Festival shortly after Outback disbanded, that Wiggins began to improvise on the didgeridoo. He soon refined and expanded his looping techniques, which proved well suited to trance music and the English rave scene. By the end of the decade, he expanded his ambit and started gaining notoriety in the U.S., mostly through festival gigs at High Sierra, Berkfest, and String Cheese Incident's Horning's Hideout (where he jammed with the band and also with DJ Harry, initiating an enduring musical relationship—the pair have toured together, and Harry appears on Didg's *Dust Devils* release).

In the live setting, Dr. Didg typically performs with a drummer, bass player, and guitarist (Mark Revell was his foil and co-conspirator on guitar for many years). Lately the lineup has fluctuated a bit, and the group has not toured regularly. This has slightly hampered a sound that builds on the subtle ripples and fluctuations produced by a band that really locks in. Still, both in concert and on disc, Dr. Didg offers a novel approach to an ancient instrument, yielding hypnotic dance grooves.

Dust Devils (2002) ★★★½

Groove and layers abound. A number of standout tracks ripe for the dance floor; a bit less cohesive (though at times more intense) than *Seritonality*.

Seritonality (1998) ★★★★

This release presents the band live with the requisite remixes and samples. Captures the band's entrancing rhythms and vibe quite well.

Out of the Woods (1995) ★★½

Something of a transitional release from Outback to Wiggins's new incarnation, here there are some mellower moments and a jazzier flair as well. A fine effort, hampered at times by an inconsistent mood.

E

EKOOSTIK HOOKAH
www.ekoostik.com

Meet the Kings of Columbus. ekoostic hookah's Hookahville festivals are an Ohio institution, sometimes drawing upwards of 15,000 folks. More than a dozen fan sites are devoted to this group. Still, despite the depths of this fealty for a band that's been around since 1991, many people who know of ekoostik hookah have not necessarily heard its music. Not only that—its name may be misspelled more than any artist short of the Symbol formerly known as Prince (to be fair, though, this is not to due to any disrespect but rather the absence of a schwa on the keyboard—where is it, anyhow?).

So let's start with the name. When spelling ekoostik hookah, the h should be lowercase. As for the e, that is in actuality a schwa symbol, which in the International Phonetic Alphabet is represented by a lowercase backwards e. To remind you (your tenth grade English teacher probably covered this for about three minutes), a schwa is the indistinct vowel sound found in unaccented syllables (like the a in ago, or against, or...yes, acoustic). Fascinating, no? Okay, let's return to the band....

ekoostik hookah first assembled via an open mike night at a Columbus, Ohio, bar called the Southberg. Here current band members Dave Katz (keyboards, acoustic guitar, vocals), Cliff Starbuck (bass, vocals), and Steve Sweney (guitar)—all of whom were involved with other projects—hooked up along with original lead vocalist and rhythm guitar player John Mullins. The five musicians (including drummer Steve Frye, who left in 1993 and was replaced by current drummer/vocalist Eric Lanese) decided to commit to the new group, with Katz supplying the moniker that continues to confound. This band built momentum through 1996 until creative and personal differences with Mullins led to his dismissal, and the addition of current vocalist/rhythm guitar player Ed McGee (percussionist Johnny "Starcatt" Polansky would join a few years later).

In May 1994 the band hosted its first Hookahville, a low-key event for 1,000 fans on a piece of land owned by Katz and manager Jeff Spencer. In retrospect, an interesting aspect of this particular Hookahville is that it was opened by future hookah member McGee (then playing in a duet with Bill Creedon). The band put together another Hookahville a few months later for Labor Day weekend, moving to an amphitheater in nearby Bellvue and setting the pattern for two multiday camping events each year that continue today.

Artists who have appeared at recent Hookahvilles, and in some instances joined their hosts on stage, include RatDog, Béla Fleck & the Flecktones, Willie Nelson, the Dickey Betts Band, Little Feat, Medeski Martin and Wood, Leftover Salmon, and Galactic. Hookahville remains a precursor to both the summer and fall seasons, with the Memorial Day event typically the larger of the two, when Northern concertgoers are hankering for an outdoor festival.

While ekoostik hookah has built a national reputation through Hookahville, it continues to develop a concomitant fan base for its music. For some time the band's Buckeye support was something of an isolated phenomena, though as of late the momentum has picked up through two recent studio albums in relatively short order, the latter of which is the group's finest yet. The band's variegated sound is in many ways encapsulated by "Dragonfly," the opening track on the aptly-named *Ohio Grown*, as it moves from rock to a bluegrass feel with vocal harmonies and some counterpoint from guitarist Sweney. Sweney in particular has legions of boosters among Hookahheads, who deem him to be one of the most underrated players out there, citing his tone and facility with styles. (His analogue in some respects may very well be Max Creek's Scott Murawski—appropriate because there are some affinities between hookah and Creek, particularly a fervid regional fan base, though hookah is more active in terms of touring and recording).

Over the years, some have felt that the band's influences, especially the Grateful Dead, have been reflected too clearly in its music. However, ekoostik hookah has recently moved towards further distinguishing itself, and as the band continues touring internationally (including annual trips to Jamaica), it can expect the Hookah Family (a named adopted by some fans) to grow beyond its current sphere. ekoostik hookah just shouldn't expect anyone to spell its name correctly (without supplying the requisite word processing software).

Ohio Grown (2002) ★★★★
The best studio release by far. This one couples strong production with a winning batch of songs (as well as guest horns, violin, and chorus). Here the band makes use of the studio yet retains the spiritedness associated with its live shows.

Seahorse (2001) ★★½
There is a heavy psychedelic feel to this disc, a lack of clarity, which detracts from these compositions (some of which lack vigor as it is).

Sharp in the Flats (1999) ★★★
Recorded on April 18, 1998, at the Odeon in Cleveland, this double album is a solid representation of the band's live shows circa 1998.

Where the Fields Grow Green (1998) ★★★
This is the band's first disc with contributions from Ed McGee, and its first studio effort after a four-year gap. It offers pleasing takes of 11 songs (most of which remain in rotation to this day), at times with a pronounced Americana feel.

Also:
Double Live (1996)
Dubbabuddah (1994)
Under Full Sail (1991)

Related sites:
Official festival site—*www.hookahville.com*
Johnny "Starcatt" Polansky—
www.starrcatt.com

Fan sites:
Set lists and related archival materials—
www.dubba.com/ekoostikhookah.htm
www.hookahheads.com
www.hookahfamily.com
Fan-based organization devoted to aiding those in need that raises food and funds at hookah shows—*www.hookahfansforfood.org*

EMMA GIBBS BAND

www.emmagibbs.com

Let's start out by doing drummer Lauren Myers a favor: No, her name is not Emma. Instead, the band's namesake is former bassist Jeff Remberg's grandmother, who allowed the group to practice and provided snacks during its formative era. Also, since we're somewhere in the cognitive dissonance realm, it's worth noting that while the Emma Gibbs Band has some direct links to Widespread Panic (through producer John Keane and collaborating fiddler David Blackmon), the band's music is not that similar to Panic.

So how should one characterize the sounds of the Emma Gibbs Band? For a while, the Winston-Salem, North Carolina, group picked up on a reference in *Relix* magazine that described it as the future of alt-country. Such an encomium reflects the band's focus on its songs: folk mediations colored by mandolin, lap steel, dobro, and fiddle (and occasionally compared to the work of Son Volt), but also infused with driving electric guitar leads and draped with improv in the live setting. At present, though, the future of the band appears fluid, following the recent departure of lead guitarist Drew Cannon. The EGB has opted not to fill his slot (although it did replace Remburg with bassist Brent Buckner, and Myers has stepped in for drummer George Wallis). Multi-instrumentalist/vocalist Will Straughan has explained that losing the lead guitar "has opened us up," yielding "more space to sing and be creative." How the group will use that space and situate itself still remains to be seen. Songwriting will certainly remain a focus, but there are also potential new avenues for music, which has been consistently mellifluous and agreeable if not always innovative and striking. Still, Straughan and fellow frontman Richard Upchurch remain a resourceful tandem, and these developments bear heed.

Out to the Country (2001) ★★★

Produced by John Keane, with appearances by David Blackmon and Rev. Jeff Mosier, the title captures the mood of this disc, which also incorporates some gentler rock tones. Keane layers warm instrumentation throughout, and while the individual songs are not always memorable, they are often affable.

Also:

Seven Even (1999)
Emma Gibbs Band (1996)

ENTRAIN

www.entrain.com

To some degree, Entrain's music is difficult to define. The group has consistently offered energetic live performances, but at times it has deemphasized improvisational elements while at other times it has situated itself in the jamband firmament. Much of this dichotomy results from roster flux, as founder Tom Major and fellow Entrain stalwart Sam Holmstock have welcomed a passel of players into the group since its 1993 formation. (Hey, here's a thought: Since a grouping of geese is known as a gaggle, perhaps we should heretofore refer to a collection of players as a passel. Then again, maybe it's best not to be so doctrinaire about language given the varied reactions to the term "jamband.")

Still, throughout the first decade of the band's existence, Entrain's hallmark has remained a percussion-driven amalgam of blues, rock, calypso, and ska. Whether one characterizes it as a pop band, a jamband, or a rock band, Entrain is undeniably a dance band. Drummer Tom Major (who previously toured the globe with both Bo Diddley and Southside Johnny) formed the group in 1993 following a visit to West Africa that inspired him to assemble a beat-heavy outfit. The name is drawn from a phrase he encountered in Mickey Hart's book *Drumming at the Edge of Magic*, used in that context to describe a group of players locked in synchronously. As befit his goal, Major first tapped percussionists Holmstock and Rick Bausman from local (Martha's Vineyard, Massachusetts) bands the Ululators and Die Kunst der Drum. While Bausman would eventually depart when Entrain began a more vigorous touring schedule, Holmstock remained with Entrain on djembe, conga, and talking drum as well as trombones, keys, and washboard.

Soon after its formation, Entrain began a Martha's Vineyard residency at the Atlantic Connection in Oak Bluffs, yet word of mouth soon carried the band off-island. Still, the Vineyard remains central to the group, in part because summer visitors have spread the word to other regions but also because it has provided some unique opportunities, such as performing with President Bill Clinton on sax. However, the island base has also magnified some impediments to touring, and a number of players have rotated through the group. As for Entrain's sound, while there has been some variance with the personnel, Major's initial aim endures: to present winsome, propulsive music. The group's songs remain breezy, uplifting, and percussive. The extended instrumental breaks are not abstract or atonal—the band aspires neither to stun nor stupefy but rather to keep an energized audience in motion.

Rise Up: Live Volume 1 (2002) ★★★
There is a bright vibe throughout the group's first live release (with a second slated to follow). All seven credited musicians play percussion at some point on the disc during these 11 agreeable tunes that lend a pop feel to the world's beats.

All One (2000) ★ ★ ½
A friendly, Caribbean flavor permeates these tracks (a few of which were selected to appear in the film *Cutaway*). Former vocalists Brian Alex and Ned Nugent (no relation to Ted), share the duties on these songs, which can feel slight but also prove both airy and inviting.

Also:
No Matter What (1997)
Can You Get It (1996)
Entrain (1994)

FLIPOFF PIRATES
www.flipoffpirates.com
The Flipoff Pirates are often quick to emphasize their Ozark Mountain roots. They identify

the origin of their music as the realm where "hillbilly meets hippie." However, it's not easy to detect the relation of this geography to their sound, which is a hodgepodge of funk, reggae, jazz, and even some hip-hop stylings (the band covers Galactic, Bob Marley, the Red Hot Chili Peppers, and Cypress Hill, all of which can be heard in the group's compositions). On the other hand, if one were to take a gander at the hirsute quintet, one might get some sense of this locus.

The power of place likely impacted the pace by which the Flipoff Pirates developed their sound. While growing up in the Arkansas hills, the musicians rehearsed on a stage they built on land owned by the mother of bass player Jack Weeden. Here, working in relative isolation, the Pirates drew from the artists that inspired them while bringing their own perspective to bear, particularly through lyrics that convey a social consciousness. While the musicianship is solid (guitarist Matt Smith offers some searing runs), the songwriting still echoes the band's influences a bit too deeply (but Weeden's words do add flair). The Flipoff Pirates can be deemed progressive for their political inclinations rather than their musical ones, yet upon reflection the group does aptly describe its sound as "progressive, aggressive, modern Ozark Mountain funk junk."

Trillions of Voices Oneword (2002) ★ ★ ½

Jake Weeden provides the unifying element through his bass mettle and lyrics, which focus on the intersections between the personal and the political. The disc is often absorbing due to the Pirates' vigor, even if the band works through a range of musical ideas and doesn't always carry them too far from the sources.

FROGWINGS

www.frogwings.com

Here's a trivia question for you: Frogwings has performed with three principal vocalists—can you name them? Before we get to the answer, full credit belongs to Butch Trucks for putting the group together. When he assembled the first incarnation of Frogwings in 1997, one intention was to bring together the highest caliber of players with an affinity for improvisation, and when one looks at the band's lineup it is clear that Trucks was astute and some would say prescient in his selections. (Oh yes, the correct response to the quiz is that Edwin McCain initially sang with the band, then in 1999 John Popper stepped in, and the following year at the Jammy Awards, Susan Tedeschi supplied the vocals.)

The impetus behind Frogwings was Butch's desire to play some gigs with his nephew, Derek (this was before the younger Trucks assumed an official role with his uncle in the Allman Brothers Band). For a guitar foil, Butch tapped Jimmy Herring, one of Derek's mentors, then best known for his work with the Aquarium Rescue Unit (and now most recognized for his participation in Phil Lesh & Friends and the Other Ones). Butch selected Herring's ARU band mate Oteil Burbridge to play bass (and this would in time result in an invitation to join the Allman Brothers Band). Oteil's brother Kofi eventually joined on keyboards and flute (the elder Burbridge has now truly come into his own as a songwriter and performer with the Derek Trucks Band). Butch then filled out the sound with ABB percussionist Marc Quinones.

Audiences at Frogwings' limited run of live shows experienced a flurry, no, a blizzard of notes. During McCain's tenure the music had a southern blues and soul feel to it. When Popper stepped in (after McCain's label refused to let him participate), his presence added more of hard rock edge. He also worked up a number of songs with the band during a pre-tour rehearsal frenzy. It's hard to imagine when the players will be able to clear time for another blitz of performances. Still, one has to hold out hope for the return of the band that's short only on originals but long on chops, long on jams, long on just about everything.

Although the group's name shares an animal in kind with Trucks's Flying Frog Records, this does not bespeak any particular obsession with the amphibian. Instead, it references an aphorism that Trucks credits to the late Duane Allman. When Allman used to see people regretting some aspect of their lives, his response was, "Yeah, and if a frog had wings, he wouldn't bust his ass every time he jumped. Get over it." Through both band and label, Trucks's aim is to do just that.

Croakin' at Toad's (2000) ★★★★ ½
The band crackles on this release recorded at Toad's Place in New Haven, Connecticut (with the exception of the strident 16-minute "Eddie's Got a Boyfriend," which comes from the Wetlands Preserve). The dynamic between guitarists Herring and Trucks is worth the price of admission alone, but the rhythm section is propulsive, animating the sound with a number of creative fills and solos. Popper carries presence as well. While some of the songs with vocals can feel slight,

it is the charged, often boundless playing that elevates this release.

Related Web site:
www.flyingfrogrecords.com
(Butch's other Frog)

FUNKY METERS
www.funkymeters.com
Based solely on the ubiquity of "Cissy Strut," the legacy of the Meters is assured. Of course the band's catalog and musical importance go much deeper, but there is much to be said for the fact that when diverse musicians collaborate live on the spot, one of their common denominators is often "Cissy Strut." Just don't blame the song's originators for some of the lame, lifeless versions that have ensued.

In 1967 keyboardist Art Neville invited bass player George Porter, Jr., Porter's younger cousin drummer Zigaboo Modeliste, and guitar player Leo Nocentelli to join him in what would become New Orleans' analogue to Booker T. & the MG's. Then named the Meters (today's funky Meters incarnation wasn't formed until 1994), they soon gained notoriety for their variegated rhythms and tantalizing groove-directed improv that came to define instrumental funk.

Over the next decade, the Meters achieved an elevated stature both through original music and also by backing others. In the latter category, the quartet initially served as house band for Allen Toussaint's label and also appeared on such records as Dr. John's *Desitively Bonnaroo* and Robert Palmer's *Sneakin' Sally Through the Alley*. In 1975 the group performed a legendary gig aboard the Queen Mary at the behest of Paul and Linda

McCartney (released 17 years later as *Uptown Rulers: The Meters Live on the Queen Mary*). The Meters followed up on this by opening the Rolling Stones' American and European tours in 1975–76.

Although critically hailed, the group was not always commercially successful, and such pressures led it to disband in 1979 (with Art moving on to the most visible gig via performances with his siblings in the Neville Brothers). Nonetheless, the group retained its fervid enthusiasts, particularly in the music community, ranging from the Red Hot Chili Peppers (who re-recorded the band's "Africa" as "Hollywood" on *Freaky Styley*) to Galactic (who began as a Meters cover band). In 2001 the Meters, characterized by Porter as a prototypical jamband that stretched and segued in concert, received the Lifetime Achievement Award at the Jammy Awards.

A loose, unanticipated reunion at the 1989 New Orleans Jazz and Heritage Festival led to the next incarnation. Modeliste opted not to return, so Russell Batiste (later of Papa Grows Funk and Vida Blue) moved in behind the kit. In 1994 Nocentelli decided to leave the fold, and the group welcomed Brian Stoltz, who had recorded and performed in the Neville Brothers (also with Bob Dylan and Dr. John, among many others). The funky Meters then became an official entity.

Today the band still performs, albeit on an abbreviated schedule due to its members' conflicting responsibilities. (In early 2003, with Neville sidelined with health concerns, the remaining trio toured as PBS—Porter, Batiste, and Stoltz.) The funky Meters' live sets reference the group's past (sometimes directly in the form of a Meters medley) while introducing the players' more recent compositions, which carry the flavor of the classic Meters sound spiced up with their own zest.

In awarding the Lifetime Achievement Jammy to George Porter, Anthony DeCurtis described the Meters' music as "instantly recognizable" and "unfailingly fresh," noting that, "from the bottom to the top of their sound every aspect moves and sways in tricky rhythms." This description certainly applies to the current group, and in his brief acceptance speech, Porter affirmed the efforts of the band to remain vital, expressing appreciation for the award and adding, "Maybe in another 20 years I'll come back and get one for the funky Meters."

Fiyo at the Fillmore Vol. 1 (2003) ★★★★

The band originally released this live disc in 2001 and then reissued it in 2003 with a studio demo of "Too Funky" dropped onto the end (the take is solid but superfluous, given the version that opens the album). On *Fiyo*, the band manifests its vigor, dexterity, and craft in building on classic Meters sounds while introducing new songs, new angles, and new accents.

FURLEY
www.furley.net

In some respects, Furley's music is significant not only for what it is, but also for what it is not. The New York-based, six-piece band is an instrumental group with a horn section, yet it is not predominantly a funk/groove band. Instead it offers more layered compositions, at times with a fusion feel that invoke and embellish a world of sounds, from Latin to Brazilian to a Caribbean reggae lilt (with an

Irish bass player to boot). The band creates a self-described adventurous art that is complex and chromatic without being recondite. Yes, there is some funk too, although the band most mirrors a traditional funk collective through its eagerness to foster a convivial atmosphere.

Furley has been inhibited by its fluctuations in personnel. While bassist Colm Connell has been a steady presence since the group's initial incarnation began gigging regularly in early 2000 (with percussionist Vinny Commisso a stalwart as well), the current lineup was assembled more than two years later. One addition that carried a high comfort level was seven-string guitarist/synth player Joe Serrone (he grew up with Connell and the two have played together since they were teenagers). The other musicians—Nick Gianni on tenor sax and flute, Carl Obrig on a range of saxes, and drummer Ian Katz—have balanced the sound.

The roster change was accompanied by a name-attenuation from the original Vermin Furley (this was helpful from a public relations standpoint, as the earlier moniker had vague punk connotations). So for most intents and purposes, Furley is a new band and one that may distinguish itself, if it can stick together, build on its interplay, and continue to pursue its world fusion.

Dragon and Phoenix (2003) ★★★ ½

Furley exhibits a nice sense of dynamics on its debut, building moods with a montage of sound. While the band sometimes alters its bearings rather rapidly, most often this feels fluid and playful rather than arbitrary or forced.

G

GALACTIC

www.galacticfunk.com

You just might have them pegged all wrong. Then again, perhaps you'll distinguish yourself for mental acuity. The beauty is that either could be the case if you pronounce Galactic a funk band.

It all started with a thrash. When bassist Rob Mercurio and guitarist Jeff Raines were growing up in the Washington, DC, area, they were drawn to the straightedge punk sound of Minor Threat (Ian MacKaye, who founded both the group and Dischord Records, later formed Fugazi, a band known as much for its music as for its commitment never to charge more than $5.00 a show—a comparable pledge would likely lead to consecration in jamband circles).

Teenagers Mercurio and Raines began performing in a similar mode, though they remained open to other sounds. As the guitarist recalls, "Then I got *Maggot Brain*. It's a big day in anyone's life when they get *Maggot Brain*. I heard P-Funk and that was about it. We started our P-Funk cover band." The pair decided to attend college in New Orleans, with the academic merits of their institutions (Tulane and Loyola) incidental to what the music scene had to offer. Upon matriculating in 1990 they immersed themselves in that scene, while regularly playing with residents and their fellow students, including drummer Stanton Moore, who qualified in both categories and at the time was bashing with hard rock group Oxenthrust. (Mercurio remembers:

"He'd just be slamming on the drums. It's funny because now he uses so much finesse, and he's really into jazz, and getting more out of the instrument then just slamming it.") The bassist found himself in a session with Moore and then invited him to participate in one with Raines and keyboardist Rich Vogel, also a Loyola student, and so begot Galactic.

Well, not exactly. First came Galactic Prophylactic, an eight-piece, horn-imbued band (the name is a TV reference circa 1982— see if you can dredge up that one). The octet began performing at college parties and then gradually started gigging out before grocery chain Winn-Dixie filed a lawsuit and forced the band to dissolve. Huh? Well, okay, this is only partially true, as while the group did break up and Winn-Dixie did threaten legal action, there is not necessarily a correlation. What happened was that the group's lead vocalist, Chris Lane, had written a song entitled "Winn-Dixie Diva" and Galactic Prophylactic promoted a show with flyers that featured the supermarket logo, leading a less-than-amused corporate office to threaten a lawsuit unless the image was removed (the band made amends by removing all the posters). As for the breakup, this took place because the group's founders wanted to strip it down and see what they could do without the horns and the singer.

What followed for Mercurio, Moore, Raines, and Vogel was the Ivanhoes, a steady Monday-night gig performing only Meters covers as an exercise to get inside the music of the quartet that stands at the fore of funk. (The name Ivanhoes referenced the club where the Meters debuted in 1967, when Art Neville and the Neville Sounds winnowed themselves down on the venue's mandate from seven pieces to four: Neville on keys, Leo Nocentelli on guitar, George Porter, Jr. on bass, and Zigaboo Modeliste on drums. Oh yes, while we're on the subject of names, Galactic Prophylactic is drawn from a *Saturday Night Live* commercial parody featuring Eddie Murphy that aired during the premiere show of the 1982-1983 season.) The Ivanhoes performed at Benny's, a dive with vibe (the building would collapse a few years later), and it was here that the students tapped into the local music scene. At Benny's they met Theryl "Houseman" DeClouet, a singer with longstanding area ties (he was given his nickname by Ivan Neville and attended junior high with Cyril Neville) who was performing with Michael Ward and Reward, a group of rotating players including Mean Willie Green, Cornell Williams, and June Yamagishi. The Ivanhoes were quite taken with Houseman, and when the time came to record their debut they encouraged him to come in and write a few songs to add vocal tunes to their collection of instrumentals. From here they invited the singer to appear at a gig, and he soon became the band's "permanent special guest," taking the stage for a portion of every show. Some audience members are still confused by the elder musician's appearances, which at times can lend a disjointed element to the night. Over the years, though, the band has refined these transitions, making them much smoother (partly because its lineup crystallized with permanent sax player Ben Ellman, a former band mate of Moore's in the New Orleans Klezmer All-Stars).

With the roster in place, Galactic has developed its sound in part by working through a series of musical cycles, in a manner reminiscent of Phish. (And yes, this is a charged comparison, because over the years, Galactic, like many other emerging improv-proficient groups, has been likened to Phish in the broadest of contexts with the most tenuous of tethers—but hang on, this one is substantive). At various stages of Galactic's career (as with Phish) the group has emphasized a particular style and then ultimately moved on to another phase while incorporating elements of that mode into its tapestry. The band has built on its Meters infrastructure by delving into soul-jazz, drum & bass, country-blues, and hip-hop. Still, the initial core remains, as Raines notes, "That's defi-nitely the defining element of our band, the groove. A lot of people see us as a retro throwback band but I see us as a cutting edge kind of new groove band." This, in turn, is why listeners oblivious to the process may compare the band to its original Ivanhoe-spawned inspiration and miss the mark, yet others can hear the group working within the métier of the Triple Threat DJs and correctly aver Galactic's funk fidelity.

Vintage Reserve (2003) ★★★½

This compilation presents a cross section of Galactic's studio work (though it is not so burdensome for one to amass the totality, given that it spans only three discs). However,

Full-on Galactic as Houseman delivers.

it is the bonus material that ramps up this release, in particular two tracks from the Carnival Electricos show on March 1, 2003, with the Triple Threat DJs joining the group for "Doo Rag" as well as Big Chief Monk Boudreaux and the Golden Eagles along with the Lil' Rascals Brass Band on "Sew Sew Sew."

We Love 'Em Tonight: Live at Tipitina's (2001) ★★★½

This single live disc recorded in late November and early December 2000 does not fully deliver on the group's playful swagger. Still it does capture guitarist Jeff Raines moving through hill country-blues mode while the band as a whole lends a spry knack to many tunes including a cover of Black Sabbath's "Sweat Leaf."

Late for the Future (2000) ★★★★

Producer Nick Sansano maintains the clarity even as the band introduces a bit more fuzz and buzz. By far the most varied of the three studio discs, *Late for the Future* incorporates courser guitar riffs and brasher brass. Theryl DeClouet is well represented, with some of his richest contributions, though his presence on nearly half the cuts does eventually impede the flow.

Crazyhorse Mongoose (1998) ★★★★½

The band opens up its sound a bit on this fine second offering. The group makes better use of dynamics, finding delicate moments to complement its radiant grooves.

Coolin' Off (1996) ★★★★

The band's debut maintains a consistent, insistent funk feel with DeClouet lending soul to two tracks, most notably "Something's Wrong with This Picture."

Also:
Ruckus (2003)

Fan site:
www.galacticfans.com

Discussion list:
www.lists.netspace.org/archives/galactic.html

GARAGE À TROIS
www.garageatrois.com

Garage à Trois pretty much started out as the side project of a side project. In February 1998 Galactic drummer Stanton Moore invited a half dozen players to join him in New Orleans to record his solo debut, *All Kooked Out*. While these sessions mostly focused on the band's readings of funk- and jazz-flavored compositions (those of Moore, guitarist Brian Seeger, and some standards), the drummer remained in the studio after the group departed each day for some late-night improvisations with eight-string guitar innovator Charlie Hunter and purveyor of saxophonics Skerik (then best known for his role in Critters Buggin' and later to join Les Claypool's Frog Brigade). The resulting music sounded little like what would appear on *All Kooked Out*, delving more into electronic dance realms (with some odd, arresting effects as befits the players). The trio eventually decided to release these recordings as Garage à Trois, adopting the sobriquets of El Mangosta (Moore), El Balzac (Hunter), and El Guzano (Skerik).

The band's debut has a fervidly old-school approach. In keeping with the nature of the music—which was captured live without any overdubs—producer/engineer/Fog City Records founder Dan Prothero opted to release it exclusively on vinyl, as a four-song EP titled *Mysteryfunk*. The record's "handmade" quality is reinforced by its unique cover—each one is stamped individually using a letterpress. Almost equally unique, for a while the group's music was not available online, though a few brief snippets may now be sampled.

While Garage à Trois began as a one-off recording venture, the caliber of the musicianship as well as the ongoing amity of its players has led the band to perform publicly when itineraries permit. One notable early gig was a double bill that marked the premiere of another all-star collective, Oysterhead, at the Saenger Theater in New Orleans on May 4, 2000. Meanwhile, the group has expanded to a quartet (although the original moniker remains) with the addition of Skerik's Critters Buggin' band mate Mike Dillon on vibraphone and percussion. The band continues to reference the intentions of those initial sessions while introducing a steady (in)fusion of jazz and funk with some inventive, demented abstractions, strident intonations (and bonus color-coordinated outfits).

Emphasizer (2003) ★★★★

The band's approach is a bit more expansive than on its debut, in part due to gigging, which has bred familiarity and some working themes as well. This is a brash, galvanic collage of core compositions and improvisational experiments.

Mysteryfunk (1999) ★★★★

There's less than 25 minutes of sound on the band's initial EP of extemporizations. Still, this avant-dance record is often arresting and earns extra points for following through on its old-school aesthetic.

GARAJ MAHAL
www.garajmahal.net

In spring 2000, four players of varied experience yet comparable command and perspective met in San Francisco for a night of completely improvised performance. In addition to his own projects, guitarist Fareed Haque had previously lent his estimable chops to a range of prominent artists including Joe Henderson, Joe Zawinul, Ramsey Lewis, Cassandra Wilson, Dave Holland, and Sting. Shortly after leaving the Berklee College of Music, bass player Kai Eckhardt had performed in the John McLaughlin Trio with Trilok Gurtu and gone on to gig with Stanley Clarke, Steve Smith's Vital Information, and Billy Cobham's International Quartet. Guitarist Eric Levy was a former student of Haque (a professor of jazz and classical guitar studies at the University of Northern Illinois) with a similar precision and melodic flair. The three had come together through the invitation of former Steve Kimock collaborator Alan Hertz (KVHW), known for his dexterity behind a kit.

A responsive crowd and a corresponding assessment from the four musicians resulted in the formal creation of Garaj Mahal. Actually, the name itself came a bit later— JamBase founder Andy Gadiel offered his Web site as a forum to solicit potential monikers for the group. Hundreds of suggestions later, the band unanimously selected Garaj Mahal.

The appellation is actually quite fitting as it evokes the multiformity of the group's sound. The Mahal is the more contemplative side, with many of the songs incorporating complex time signatures and key changes. The Garaj reflects the blusier, funkier component that Haque often mentions in describing the group as a dance band. The guitarist's characterization may be true to some degree, though unlike the big bands of the '40s that he occasionally uses as a reference point, some of the music can be too angular and abstruse for such rhythmic response (particularly when the group passes around an idea and the players craft four variant solos). Such flourishes, however, also draw many repeat listeners to Garaj Mahal. Meanwhile, the diverse nature of the sound and the receptive ears of the group's audiences animate Haque, who lauds, "The opportunity to do almost anything that I would want to do, all in the same gig. I could play a classical thing, I could play sitar, I could play something bluesy or something really beautiful. That's all acceptable within this context, within this scene, and I think that's great."

Live Vol. 1 (2003) ★★★★

The first of three simultaneously released live discs, this is the most consistently compelling. Zakir Hussain appears on tabla for four of the six tracks, and at times the band follows him into Shakti terrain. While some of the compositions feel incidental, the players more than compensate with stunning phrasings and structures.

Live Vol. 2 (2003) ★★★

The funk is a bit more pronounced on this disc, along with some Zappa caroms. The focus mostly remains on Garaj Mahal's instrumental prowess, as the band's occasional singing can carry the listener and the group out of the zone.

Live Vol. 3 (2003) ★★★

The song that really jumps out is the 18-minute take on "Material Girl" that closes the disc. The transformation from the Madonna dance tune into gentle, graceful jazz musing is clever, but a little goes a long way. As with Vol. 2, some flat vocals provide a jarring juxtaposition to the otherwise elevated level of performance.

GIANT PEOPLE

www.giantpeople.net

The lone constant player throughout the recording and performing career of the Giant People is the band's founder, trumpeter Carlos Washington. Despite roster fluctuations, the group has rarely remained idle since its initial incarnation in 2000, playing more than 150 dates in 2002. The shift in personnel reflects Washington's evolving vision as he employs improvisation to brace an amalgam of jazz, funk, hip-hop, and sometimes even classical, creating a music that he refers to as new century soul.

Washington's journey to the Giant People (say, isn't that a Roald Dahl book?) carried him from the Marines on through Tiny Universe. Following high school he entered the Armed Forces School of Music and toured with the US Marine Corps Band, sometimes performing upwards of 500 shows a year (likely making the Giant People tour regimen feel breezy by comparison). After receiving his honorable discharge, he signed on with Karl Denson, joining the sax player's band for two years during which the pair often received encomiums for their interlaced horn lines. From here he decided to pursue his own vision, and he credits ska innovator Carlos Malcolm as a mentor when he assembled (and reassembled) the Giant People.

Washington, whose tone has been compared to Clifford Brown and Woody Shaw, also incorporates a range of effects to facilitate the band's many moods. Jesse Malloy joins him on tenor sax with a predilection for bop, and is fast-building a dynamic with Washington that the trumpeter once shared with Denson. Ignacio Arango, a Havana native, contributes some vibrant clusters on guitar. Prior to his emigration, Arango was a member of the Cuban Army Band (an analogue to Washington's Marine days) and later performed with famed Cuban trumpeter Arturo Sandoval. All in all, the Giant People's musicianship is impeccable, although they are still honing their songwriting skills and working to transform some memorable heads into rich, nuanced compositions. Sometimes the music can feel schizophrenic, especially on the band's studio release, which incorporates soul jazz, traditional R&B with vocals, and even an 11-minute "Tekno Jam." Still, there is noble intent and laudable delivery from a group described by its founder as "a soul burrito wrapped in a funky, fresh jazz tortilla."

Much Love (2002) ★★★ ½
The band's range is estimable, but the group occasionally stretches itself a bit thin on this studio debut.

Out of print:
Epic Soul Music: Live (2001)

GLOBAL FUNK COUNCIL
www.globalfunkcouncil.com

When Global Funk Council hit the road for 200 shows in 2002, Michael Smith held the keys (and the vibraphone as well). Smith, who wrote all of the material on the group's debut disc, *Keep on Pushin'*, assembled GFC in 2001. A veteran presence in multiple music worlds (he's backed Diane Schurr and released his own hip-hop/R&B disc), Smith surrounded himself with top-notch players who similarly wished to bridge the realms of jazz, funk, and rock with even a of bit of techno mixed in. The initial roster held some connections to the Greyboy Allstars (much) extended family. Smith had been a founding member of the Giant People along with former Karl Denson foil Carlos Washington before opting to pursue his own path. Percussionist Steve Haney toured and recorded with Greyboy, while drummer Eric Bolivar put in two years with Denson's Tiny Universe. However, given Smith's intention to push Global Funk Council on the road, Haney and Bolivar ultimately decided to move on.

The current Council is an eclectic collective. Guitarist Josh Suhrheinrich, a student and protégé of Fareed Haque, has also performed with trumpeter Arturo Sandoval and bassist Alonzo "Pookie" Johnson (Wes Montgomery, Freddie Hubbard) and previously led his own group, Soul Slipper. Bass player Jonathan Stoyanoff is a Berklee College of Music grad with a yen for complex compositions who certainly holds down the bottom, as evinced by his time on the road with guitarist Johnny A (Peter Wolf). The GFC lineup is still somewhat fluid with percussionists and horn players putting in limited stints. Given Smith's breadth of vision, a stable roster will lend focus and facilitate growth. Still, the group's animated, variegated grooves hold sway, and one has to assume that Smith will continue to integrate players of sympathetic spirit and talent. Plus, any new lineup will have an accelerated development, and if 2002 is any indication, there are plenty of Council meetings on the horizon.

Keep on Pushin' (2002) ★★ ½

This disc is a spirited amalgam of jazz and funk. On some of the tracks the grooves linger a bit too long, but before they become ruts a new idea typically swirls in and pushes the music along. There is a mix of vocal and instrumental tunes, the latter often conveying didactic yet beneficent messages such as "Take Your Reality Pills."

GNAPPY

www.gnappyfunk.com

Okay, so you're a quartet—bass, drums, guitar, and sax—creating music that yokes blues, jazz, funk, and acid rock. You'd like to reflect this musical conjunction with an evocative descriptive term other than the prosaic "jamband." Well, Texas's Gnappy leaps to the fore with panache by characterizing its sound as "acid blazz and junk" (a sportive handle that carries some resonance of *Village Voice* journalist Robert Christgau's "pazz and jop").

Gnappy first performed in the late '90s as a jump blues band based in Los Angeles (where guitarist Buck McKinney served as staff counsel in the business and legal affairs department of A&M Records). However, McKinney and

bass player Brad Bradburn eventually returned to Austin, where they recruited drummer Kevin Pearson and saxophone player Marcus Cardwell, a Berklee College of Music alum and veteran of Retarded Elf, a flashy, costumed funk collective. The quartet soon expanded its palette and grew apace with McKinney's entertainment law practice, the latter proving helpful when one of McKinney's clients, Lars Goransson—producer of such groups as Fastball and the Cardigans—agreed to work on the group's 2001 debut.

However, just as the disc hit, chaos ensued. First, Gnappy received an exorbitant web-hosting bill due to downloads resulting from its "featured artist" status on Napster. Then Bradburn and Pearson departed, as a slew of rhythm players floated in and out of the band, before the pair returned at year's end to resume the band's growth.

Gnappy admittedly owes a bit to such groups as Medeski Martin and Wood, Galactic, and Jacob Fred Jazz Odyssey. However, while the quartet's sound is most commonly situated in the realm of the two former bands, Gnappy does interject some characteristic ethereal abstractions that contribute the acid blazz (if not the junk).

Gnappy (2001) ★★★

While there is a familiar feel to much of the funk-flavored jazz and jazz-juiced funk on this disc, there is also aptitude and ebullience. Plus, the band lends its seal by introducing some open, meditative passages along with the odd bark or two.

Also:

Is This a Machine? (2003)

GOV'T MULE

www.mule.net

Matt Abts is a force. The drummer can power a band with the gonzo thunder of John Bonham as well as the clarity and dynamic of Billy Cobham. Not only that, he contributes some bonus visuals: When he's in motion, the colors on his well-inked arms meld together to form whirling, alluring hues.

Warren Haynes is a decent player himself. Maybe you've heard of him. He offers up a bit of guitar, does some singing, and writes the occasional song or ten. Perhaps you were there on June 29, 2002, at Deer Creek (aka the oh-so-cuttingly named Verizon Wireless Music Center) when Haynes tore it up for nearly six hours with three bands in his roles as mainstays of Phil Lesh & Friends, the Allman Brothers Band, and Gov't Mule. Let's face it: At times he's freaking Atlas with a slide, capable of hoisting a particular performance onto his black-shirted shoulders.

And then there's Maude. No come to think of it, Bea Arthur hasn't sat in with the Mule (yet) but consider this abridged tally of players who have: Jerry Cantrell, Jack Casady, Les Claypool, Bootsy Collins, Dirty Dozen Brass Band, Tinsley Ellis, John Entwistle, Flea, Béla Fleck, Marc Ford, G. Love, Roger Glover, Mike Gordon, Larry Graham, Peter Green, Kirk

Gov't Mule, Bonnaroo 2002, with Dave Schools digging in on bass.

Hammett, Jimmy Herring, James Hetfield, David Hidalgo, Paul Jackson Jr., Gordie Johnson, Kid Rock, Kevin Kinney, Sonny Landreth, Jonny Lang, T Lavitz, Chuck Leavell, Will Lee, Tony Levin, Dave Matthews, Larry McCray, Steve Miller, Zigaboo Modeliste, Jason Newsted, John Popper, Rocco Prestia, Vernon Reid, Chris Robinson, John Scofield, Son Seals, Kenny Wayne Shepherd, G. E. Smith, Chris Squire, Derek Trucks, Joe Louis Walker, Mike Watt, Bob Weir, Fred Wesley, Leslie West, Brad Whitford, Chris Whitley, Bruce Willis, and many additional artists who appear in this book.

Gov't Mule is the product of Allman Brothers Band tour bus talk. In the mid-'90s, Haynes and fellow ABB bassist Allen Woody were riding together between gigs, listening to Cream and lamenting the near extinction of the rock trio when Woody proclaimed, "You and me and the right drummer could pull it off." That drummer proved to be Abts, with whom Haynes had performed in the Dickey Betts Band in the mid-'80s. Abts had also worked with Mick Taylor and Ronnie Montrose (lest you've forgotten, the latter guitarist unleashed Sammy Hagar with the 1973 release *Montrose*. Ronnie sat in with Gov't Mule on January 31, 1998, which was also a notable appearance because the first concert Haynes attended, in 1972, was the Edgar Winters Group with Montrose on lead). Abts, Haynes, and Woody initially took the stage together for a loose post-Brothers jam at the Palomino in Los Angeles on May 12, 1994, and began some sporadic gigging in June. Three years later, no longer comfortably saddled with the "side-project" designation and eager to see where a full-time commit-

ment could carry the music, Haynes and Woody alighted the bus (and the ABB).

A superficial glance at the backgrounds of the three players left some listeners unprepared for Gov't Mule's tangible jazz component. Still, its members were exposed to the form from an early age, and this aesthetic became integral. Haynes notes, "One of my all-time favorite units is the Miles Davis Quintet with Wayne Shorter, Herbie Hancock, Ron Carter, and Tony Williams. When Gov't Mule is in that ethereal mode and we're playing off each other, we're trying to do in the context of a three-piece rock format what those guys were doing with a five-piece jazz format, which is to make the solos not just a statement by one individual but a statement by the entire ensemble." The guitarist similarly emphasizes the complementary nature of two styles that inform the band's sound, adding, "I think blues and jazz are the two true American art forms that have in common the fact that when they're played the right way the musicians can never do the same thing twice. Nobody locks themselves into any pattern of what they are going to play here or what they're gong to play there—it's all a flowing thing. Jazz is a much more complex scenario musically speaking, but they are both poured from the same stream."

The trio continued to amplify within these domains, at times through a maelstrom yet with precision and élan, until Allen Woody's death on August 26, 2000. (Woody's life and legacy were celebrated at the One for Woody show at Roseland Ballroom on September 21, 2000, with proceeds benefiting his daughter Savannah's educational fund.) For some time it appeared that Gov't Mule might remain inactive, but then in November Haynes and

Abts tentatively stepped forward for their acoustic Smile at Half-Mast Tour (the name references a poem written by Haynes that he read at Woody's funeral). From there the pair decided to enter the studio, musing about the various bassists, many of them Woody's idols, who would be perfect for particular songs. The two then decided to extend some offers, and after receiving affirmative responses, the *Deep End* sessions ensued, which ultimately featured more than two dozen bass heroes, including Jack Bruce, Bootsy Collins, John Entwistle, Flea, Tony Levin, and Chris Wood, with Bruce's participation especially significant, given Cream's initial trio inspiration.

The first of the *Deep End* discs appeared in October 2001, followed by *Volume 2* as well as *Rising Low,* a film directed by Mike Gordon that gyrates around these releases and their origins. (*Rising Low* garnered the Audience Choice Award for Best Documentary at the 2002 Newport Film Festival, even though the appearance of the enigmatic Joey Arkenstat on-screen and later onstage at Mule's December 31, 2002, show remains controversial.) To mark these efforts, Gov't Mule returned to the road with a rotating company of bass players: Andy Hess, Oteil Burbridge, George Porter, Jr., Greg Rzab, and Dave Schools. When asked if he would consider joining the band full-time, Schools replied, "Absolutely. If it could happen without jeopardizing what we're doing in Widespread Panic, which seems unlikely." (Incidentally, a good-natured debate churns as to which of these bands first introduced a cover of Tom Waits's "Goin' Out West," as both Haynes and Schools claim they first mentioned it to the other. The bassist laughs, "It's the only thing

Haynes and I disagree on, someone should go to the tapes." Well, we've done that and the score is in the Mule's favor: Panic debuted the song on January 20, 1996, while the trio first performed it a month earlier on December 14, 1995, although it is quite possible that each band came to it independently.)

Through the summer of 2003, bass players continued to move in and out of the lineup, and Gov't Mule remained a hybrid (a status shared by the band's equine namesake, which is the product of breeding a horse and a donkey). However, in September the group finally announced that Hess would join as permanent bassist, and many of the group's fans anticipated that his steady presence could further spark the trio (which often expanded to a quartet in the preceding months with keyboardist Danny Louis). A number of these boosters also hailed the stasis of Phil Lesh & Friends, which cleared Haynes's schedule for further songwriting and even (gasp) relaxation, as some felt he had worn himself a bit ragged by the end of 2002, even though the band remained a kicking ass. Still, these two developments loomed as propitious signs for the Mulehardy.

The Deep End, Vol.2 (2002) ★★★★½

While more disjointed than its predecessor, this is still a substantive effort. This disc expands the ambit of the Mule, including the prog-rock of "Sun Dance" (with Chris Squire), the Claypool-injected two-parter "Greasy Granny's Gopher Gravy," and the in-the-pocket take on Tower of Power's "What Is Hip?"

The Deep End, Vol. 1 (2001) ★★★★★

The strength of this disc is its cohesiveness

despite a stunning array of guest players. The bass battalion includes John Entwistle, Larry Graham, Roger Glover, Jack Bruce, Mike Watt, Mike Gordon, Stefan Lessard, and, on the final track, Allen Woody. The songwriting matches the musicianship of a roster that also includes John Scofield, Little Milton, and Page McConnell. A fitting one for Woody.

Life Before Insanity (2000) ★★★★

A bit heavier than *Dose*. This release is tight, taut, and tense.

Live…with a Little Help from Our Friends (1999) ★★★★★

Recorded on New Year's Eve 1998 at the Roxy Theater in Atlanta with many guest performers, this four-disc Collector's Edition is the way to go—a well-designed package with photos, notes, and sleek, efficient CD sleeves. As for the music, the 30-minute version of "Afro Blue" played as an encore that night with Jimmy Herring, Derek Trucks, Yonrico Scott, Bernie Worrell, and Randall Bramblett is worth the price of admission itself. Slightly skewed towards cover material (including "Spanish Moon," "Cortez the Killer," "Sad and Deep as You," "Third Stone from the Sun," and "War Pigs") due to the profusion of guests, Live offers some boisterous versions of the band's originals, including "Mule," "Thorazine Shuffle," and "Devil Likes It Slow."

Dose (1998) ★★★ ½

The first studio album after its members committed to the group full-time, here Gov't Mule plows through blues terrain with resolve. In addition, with "Thelonious Beck" the song title proves an apt referent for its music. Still, although the compositions are well founded, Dose's highlights include covers of the traditional "John the Revelator" and the Beatles' "She Said, She Said."

Also:

The Deepest End (2003)
Live at Roseland Ballroom (1996)
Gov't Mule (1995)

Fan sites:

www.mulebase.com
www.mulezone.com

Film site:

www.risinglow.net

Discussion list:

www.lists.netspace.org/archives/emule.html

GRAND THEFT BUS

www.grandtheftbus.com

The Canadian Maritimes are on the nation's far eastern coast, bounded by water (duh) and set apart from the inner provinces both in geographic and cultural terms. It is within this setting that a thriving jam music scene has emerged over the past few years, one chronicled by filmmaker Greg Hemmings in his documentaries *Revolve* (2001), which examines Nova Scotia's Evolve Music and Awareness Festival, and *A Head's Tale* (2002), which considers the broader context. Both films feature the music of New Brunswick's Grand Theft Bus.

The Fredericton brothers—bassist Graeme Walker and guitarist Tim—first assembled the group in December 2000 along with drummer Bob Deveau. They later recruited guitarist

Dennis Goodwin to add more accents to a sound that is often airy and ambient yet can also crunch into harder King Crimson terrain. One can also hear shades of the Slip, Steely Dan, and Tortoise in the band's music. Yet, buoyed by Walker's bright vocals and the group's gift for melody, Grand Theft Bus does strike distinctive chords, tottering only when it lingers on lighter funk. GTB also has merited acclaim for its segues, including some notable "seamless sets" with area group Jimmy Swift Band (JSB keyboard player Aaron Collier colors the GTB's debut recording). Charlie Hunter has also sat in with Grand Theft Bus, as the young band continues to make inroads beyond its home region.

Birth of Confusion (2002) ★ ★ ★ ½

The title is apt if only because Grand Theft Bus employs the studio framework to rearrange much of its material, creating some dichotomy between this effort and the band's live shows (a positive intent, no?). At times the music sounds like alterna-pop, at others there's an ambient jazzbo feel, all of which is buttressed by a keen emphasis on vocals. Some grooves recur over these 75 minutes of music, but there's still much to engage the listener.

Fan site:

http://thebusstop.cjh.net/

GREEN GENES

www.green-genes.net

Green Genes has helped develop and support the Lexington, Kentucky, improvisational music scene for more than a decade. The group began in 1993 as an acoustic trio, predominantly focusing on other artists' material (including bluegrass standards and selections from the Grateful Dead catalog). By the end of 1997, with the addition of a drummer and keyboard player, the group began electric performances with an increasing emphasis on its original music. As Green Genes built a local following, it started drawing in other notable acts for co-bills, turning its supporters on to such groups as Acoustic Syndicate, Yonder Mountain String Band, and Moonshine Still.

Kentucky is the bluegrass state, and Lexington is the heart of the bluegrass region, so it is not surprising that Green Genes draws on its indigenous music. (Quick discursive history lesson: In 1938 Bill Monroe broke from his brother Charlie and formed his own group, which he dubbed the Blue Grass Boys. He selected this moniker to reference his birthplace, home to a genus of grass [Poa] that contains bluish green culms. Monroe's band ultimately gained such acclaim for its defining characteristics—high, lonesome vocals, fiddle, mandolin, banjo, and upright bass—that the genre was named in his honor. But you knew all that, didn't you? Okay, except maybe for Poa. Anyhow, back to Green Genes....)

Green Genes founders guitarist Don Rogers and bassist Roddy Puckett continue to explore their roots with the New Kentucky String Ticklers (this quartet served as cultural ambassadors during a 2002 tour of Ecuador promoted by a US Embassy exchange program). Green Genes incorporates the bluegrass vocabulary but it also adds jazz and rock phrasings. The group's songs often juxtapose these idioms, although the band is still working towards originality in this realm. Nonetheless, after ten years of performing, Green Genes is playing to a wider scope, as evidenced by an invitation to the 2002 High Sierra Music Festival and additional touring outside of its old Kentucky home.

Green Genes (2001) ★★ ½

Brad Slutskin's keyboard runs often animate and elevate these nine studio tracks and two live cuts. Don Rogers is a solid foil on guitar for these songs that often build on jazz and bluegrass themes. While the vocals can feel incidental, and a few tracks drift towards more generic jam rock, this is a bright-hued debut.

GROOVATRON

www.groovatron.com

Indiana's Groovatron shares some common elements with Boston's Addison Groove Project. Like AGP, the group formed during the mid-'90s while its members were still in high school. There is also similar instrumentation, as both collectives incorporate brass. Plus, for the etymologically challenged among you, the two bands fashioned their monikers from the root word "groove."

Having pointed all this out, however, the two groups differ in their most significant component: music. While Addison currently works in a jazz/funk/electronica space, Groovatron often harks back to the involuted compositional style of Zappa and some of his modern jam progeny, most notably moe. and Phish. Indeed, while the band's name implies that the group is a mechanized implement of groove, the reality is that Groovatron will often depart such realms for a quirky instrumental break (or a decent joke). The band also places particular emphasis on its harmony

vocals, and all six musicians may contribute to a given passage. Humor is another animating factor as evinced by the group's lyrics, mien, and even the alternate band history on its Web site (alas, the CIA special teams force Acoustic Core just may be apocryphal). Groovatron imbues many of its songs with each of the aforementioned aspects, with an exuberance that will serve the group well as it continues to design it own sound and move further away from its influences and into its own spaces.

Yes, Have Some (2001) ★★

This is an amiable disc that captures Grooavatron's whimsy and verve, though much of the music remains steeped in the sounds of the band's pantheon (most obviously moe. and Phish). Still, the release manifests a vitality that bodes well for its future music (some of which has already emerged, as the disc was recorded a few years ago) via such songs as "Shaunza Night Sky" (with intentionally oblique harmony vocals reminiscent of Phish's "You Enjoy Myself") and "Satan Drinks Cheap Liquor."

Fan site:

http://markward.freeservers.com/groovaddicts.htm

GUEST

www.goguest.com

Hey, sometimes the '80s flat out ripped, right? Well, okay, not that often, actually, and the decade can use a bit of help. Thankfully, Guest is here to offer that up. A 20-minute version of Thomas Dolby's "She Blinded Me with Science"? Done. An invigorating take on the Fixx's "One Thing Leads to Another"? Look no further. Michael Jackson's "Thriller"? The Guest has got it covered.

Truth be told, the Athens, Ohio, quintet offers far more than that. For instance, before considering the group's original material, it's noteworthy that Guest also performs the music of the Band (the group presented a number of *Last Waltz* songs during its 2002 New Year's Eve show). Plus, Guest will drop in an interpretation of Pink Floyd's "Echoes" or the Disco Biscuits' "Humahumanukanukauapua'a" (always a treat to spell for audience members compiling set lists).

So while you can't judge a band by its covers, you can get some sense of its intentions. In the case of Guest, the group aspires to take its penchant for progressive rock and some current electronica ideas and balance them with the new wave's focus on the individual song—all animated by a skewed, often-absurdist humor. In theory this sounds like the irresistible force meeting the immovable object, and to be honest, there's definitely movement here. Still, it's an interesting amalgam, albeit one in progress. Meanwhile, keyboard player John Hruby and guitarists Drew Santer and J.R. Hecker sweeten the sound with their vocal harmonies. There's another consideration too, one that shares an '80s aesthetic, for as Hruby notes: "We still want to keep it danceable, though. We definitely want people to dance."

Entrance (2002) ★ ★ ★ ½

Guest's debut explores some varied landscapes without stretching itself too thin. It's an intriguing balance of poppier melodies and high harmonies with more complex orchestrations. John Hruby often becomes the locus with his prodigious vocabulary of keyboard sounds, while Count M'butu appears to lend percussive counterpoint on a few tracks.

HIWAY FREEKER
www.hiwayfreeker.com

Montreal's Hiway Freeker is quite literally three, three, three bands in one. Then again, maybe it's four. Frankly, who knows—there could be some other alter egos lying in wait. What can be ascertained is that on occasion the band members will cast aside their original music and perform under such guises as the Bob Dylan Project and Estrada. In the former context, Hiway Freeker transforms into a Dylan cover band. As Estrada, named after television's *CHiPs* actor, the group performs soul music and R&B songs originally recorded between 1977 and 1982. On any given night, Hiway Freeker may precede a set of original material with a cover performance, literally opening for itself. Here's hoping it receives two paychecks. (Fun fact: *CHiPs* went off the air in 1983, but because co-star Larry Wilcox left the series prior to the last season, many *CHiPs* diehards—quite possibly including the CHiFs (Canadian Hiway Freekers)—discount the last season altogether.)

As for the sound of Hiway Freeker proper, much of its music hangs on the rich, soulful vocals of Serena Southam. An actress with some theater credits to her name, Southam's captivating stage presence also contributes to Freeker's appeal. In at least one respect, however, the singer is overshadowed by her husband, guitarist/songwriter Paul Malin: He stands a strapping six-foot-seven-inches tall.

Visuals aside, the band's multiple identities reflect its versatility, as Hiway Freeker's music spans from psychedelic to blues to country, although Southam's voice may be best suited to her occasional role as sultry jazz chanteuse. While there is certainly virtue to this eclecticism and merit in its execution, at times it can carry the band from its most compelling asset, Southam's pipes. Still, this occasional drift may also be attributed to roster fluctuations, which may now finally be resolved, solidifying the lineup of Hiway Freeker and all its permutations thereof.

Shark (2002) ★★★ ½

Most of these songs are elevated by Serena Southam's majestic vocals, though the band does demonstrate its range on the animated, fiddle-fueled instrumental "Find the Hole (Part II)." Still, it is Southam's singing that carries even the slighter compositions in this diverse batch.

HOPE CLAYBURN'S 2ND BOOTY BATTALION

www.hopeclayburn.com

Can't restrain myself...must type it.... Over the past few years in numerous contexts, one refrain uttered to sax-deficient collectives has been...here it comes...you gotta have Hope (ahhh, that feels better).

Pun as it may be, it's true enough—groups ranging from Deep Banana Blackout to the Motet to the Tom Tom Club to the Allman Brothers Band have enlisted Clayburn on alto, baritone, and soprano saxophones as well as flute. Clayburn, who studied in the University of Virginia jazz program with John D'Earth, landed her first steady gig in the mid-'90s contributing to the world funk of Baaba Seth. When that group ended its run in 2000 after founder Dirk Lind pulled up stakes and relocated to Arizona with his wife and family, Clayburn found another opportunity that same summer following the departure of Jen Durkin from Deep Banana Blackout. While Clayburn's vocals do not offer the sheer, urgent power of Durkin, there is a richness to her intonations and her musicianship adds euphony (though truth be told, her vibrant, versatile sax can outshine her singing). When DBB suspended operations following its New Year's Eve 2002 show, Hope began to balance outside gigs such as Motet tours with a focus on her own band, the 2nd Booty Battalion (originally Hope Clayburn's Big Black Booty).

While Clayburn carries chops and charisma, as for her band itself, the 2nd Booty Battalion, it's really too early to tell. Although Hope is the driving force as primary songwriter and arranger, the group will likely flourish as a collaborative venture through steady gigging (and the bandleader is still drawn into other projects, as are the other members). Still, Clayburn has enlisted quite capable players, such as jazz guitarist George Turner, whose style often adds modern inflections to that of Wes Montgomery and Charlie Christian. Drummer Johnny Gilmore, a member of Corey Harris' 5 X 5, brings similar command. Indeed, it is quite possible that the group will blossom into an absorbing entity, as Clayburn is such an adept artist that one has to have...faith (you thought that was going somewhere else, didn't you?).

Hope Clayburn's 2nd Booty Battalion (2003)
★★★½

While fans of the latter-day DBB will likely appreciate the funk and Latin hues, there is more of a jazz chromaticism throughout this album, along with pronounced hip-hop shadings and a bit of the Delta. All in all, a tasteful effort abetted by plenty of guest players, though perhaps too diffuse at times, and one wishes Hope would step up to lend additional lead vocals.

HOT TUNA
www.hottuna.com

When you get right down to it, Hot Tuna is a blues band. This genre was the catalyst for founders Jorma Kaukonen and Jack Casady, and it continues to galvanize the two. When the United States Congress stepped in to decree 2003 the Year of the Blues, the legislature made a noble attempt to resuscitate a fading form, particularly the acoustic, porch variety that started it all. Yet Hot Tuna continues to vitalize this music nearly 50 years after its founders first paired.

Kaukonen and Casady met and initially performed on guitar together as teenagers in Washington, D.C., during the 1950s (in 2000 they were enshrined in the Washington Area Music Association Hall of Fame). The duo separated when the older Kaukonen left for college but reconnected in the mid-'60s when Jorma, who had relocated to northern California, invited Casady (who had since switched to bass) to join a group that would take on Kaukonen's nickname, Blind Thomas Jefferson Airplane (after seminal bluesman Blind Lemon Jefferson). While the Airplane gained popularity as an electric rock band, Kaukonen and Casady maintained an affinity for the music that had first moved them and began performing as a duo between sets at Airplane shows. RCA released Hot Tuna's live debut in 1970 (lore has it that the pair told an ashen label executive that they demanded to be called Hot Shit, but Kaukonen now deems this account apocryphal).

Three years and two discs later, with an expanded lineup (for instance, Papa John Creach played violin on occasion) and Kaukonen now on electric guitar as well, the pair disembarked from the Airplane (Casady doesn't enter the Jefferson Starship for another two decades—thankfully that band "Built This City" without him). Hot Tuna recorded and performed through much of the '70s, but by the end of the decade Kaukonen and Casady separated. The pair reunited briefly in 1983, then began picking again in earnest at the outset of the '90s. This time, Hot Tuna expanded to a trio with vocalist/guitarist Michael Falzarano, who introduced a number of his own songs into the repertoire. The three were later joined by Pete Sears on keys and Harvey Sorgen on drums, taking the group deeper into open, psychedelic blues realms, and Hot Tuna appeared at multiple Furthur Festivals. Throughout the decade the band became the definitive Relix Records act, as the label issued numerous new and archival releases.

While the quintet held appeal and certainly could work up some ferocious jams, many longed for the founding pair to return to their roots. As of late Casady and Kaukonen have obliged, gigging, albeit infrequently, as the Original Acoustic Hot Tuna (they will also occasionally collaborate informally at Kaukonen's Fur Peace Ranch Guitar Camp). The two remain vital artists. In 2002 Kaukonen earned a Grammy nomination with *Blue Country Heart,* a collection of songs from the Depression era with guest appearances by Sam Bush, Jerry Douglas, and Béla Fleck. The next year Casady issued his *Dream Factor* disc with Warren Haynes, Matt Abts (Casady appears on Gov't Mule's *Deep End Vol. 2*), Doyle Bramhall II, Ivan Neville, and Paul Barrere. Kaukonen plays on it as well, as the pair perpetuates a friendship while continuing to do the same for an art form.

And Furthurmore... (1999) ★★★

The quintet is featured on these 13 songs recorded during the 1998 Furthur Festival. Some Hot Tuna staples appear early on, followed by newer material, penned and sung by Michael Falzarano. Solid overall, although the former tracks never really cook and the latter do contain some blistering instrumental moments but are not altogether compelling.

Live in Japan (1998) ★★★

This disc presents a spontaneous acoustic set from Stove's in Yokohoma City on February 20, 1997, that purportedly took place because the stage was not big enough for the group's electric equipment. The sound quality wavers a bit, but the performances are sturdy, revisiting some of the material from the group's debut along with other standards and traditional tunes.

Burgers (1972) ★★★★

The first Hot Tuna album to feature predominantly originals. Stylistically, it draws from the first two releases with both acoustic and electric offerings.

First Pull Up, Then Pull Down (1971) ★★★½

Tuna goes electric on this one while adding Papa John Creach on violin and drummer Sammy Piazza. This release features two fine versions of Reverend Gary Davis songs, "Candy Man" and "Keep Your Lamp Trimmed and Burning."

Hot Tuna (1970) ★★★★½

Concise, powerful takes on the music that first riveted Kaukonen and Casady along with two Kaukonen originals carrying a sympathetic feel, "Mann's Fate" and "New Song (for the Morning)."

Also:

Splashdown Two (1997)
Classic Electric (1996)
Classic Acoustic (1996)
Live at Sweetwater Two (1993)
Live at Sweetwater (1992)
Pair a Dice Found (1990)
Historic Hot Tuna (1985)
Splashdown (1984)
Double Dose (1978)
Hoppkorv (1976)
America's Choice (1975)
Yellow Fever (1975)
The Phosphorescent Rat (1973)

CHARLIE HUNTER

www.charliehunter.com

Charlie Hunter has crossover appeal. No, not the sort that carries over to the pop music marketplace (which one might find mildly boggling given the fact that his 2001 *Songs from the Analog Playground* contained guest vocals from Norah Jones and Mos Def). No, instead, of the all the groups listed in this book, Hunter moves most readily from rock clubs to jazz chambers and back again. (John Scofield does the same, but not typically with the John Scofield Band listed within these pages.) Hey, not only that, but Hunter has opened for U2.

Indeed, one can fairly characterize Charlie Hunter as nonpareil. This designation begins with his instrument, an eight-string guitar designed to his own specifications by luthier Ralph Novak, which allows Hunter to deliver guitar leads and basslines simultaneously. Given the fact that he's been doing this for more than a decade, moving from the seven-string he initially commissioned, it is easy to look past one simple query: Why? (Control freak issues involving guitar and/or bass players?) Hunter's response is that he does not necessarily see himself as both a guitarist and bassist, but instead has attempted to replicate a sound he hears internally that draws on both elements but is also quite percussive and occasionally emulates an organ. (Still sounds like control freak issues, no? Well, maybe not.) The instrument reflects the idiosyncrasies of the artist who, over the course of eight albums and numerous tours following his 1993 eponymous debut disc, *Charlie Hunter Trio* (produced by Les Claypool), has serially fluctuated his roster of players. The results have

oscillated through straightahead jazz, funk, Afro-Cuban, and onward (Hunter delivers all of the above while interpreting an entire Bob Marley album on 1997's *Natty Dread*), but the sound often carries a groove that has hoisted Hunter beyond the habitat of the two-drink minimum.

Hunter's variegated career and reception extend beyond string selection and filling out a lineup card. He began active tutelage on guitar in the early '80s as a Berkeley, CA, teenager whose high school classmates included Joshua Redman and Dave Ellis (speaking of Ellis, this leads to a mystical, musical connection to Bob Weir: Three of Hunter's former band mates have gone on to work with RatDog, including Ellis, who is no longer with that group, Jay Lane, and Kenny Brooks, though Hunter himself has yet to make an appearance). After graduation Hunter moved to Europe, where he supported himself by busking for a few years (one of the skills he acquired during his tenure as a street performer is a gift for full-body percussion). He then returned to Berkeley and began teaching at Subway Guitars, where he became friendly with fellow instructor and future-Spearhead founder Michael Franti (incidentally, an oft-repeated aspect of Hunter lore is that he received his early fretwork lessons from Joe Satriani a few years before *Surfing with the Alien*, when Satriani was just the local guitar guy). Franti invited Hunter to join the Disposable Heroes of Hiphoprisy, his deeply political, equally innovative collective that opened dates for both Nirvana and U2 and recorded an album with Beat Generation writer William S. Burroughs before separating in 1993. Meanwhile, in addition to his own groups, Hunter has participated in two side projects: T.J. Kirk, his Grammy-nominated cover band (Will Bernard, Scott Amendola, and John Schott join him to perform the music of Thelonious Monk, James Brown, and Rahsaan Roland Kirk) and Garage à Trois (with Stanton Moore, Skerik, and Mike Dillon), a propounder of freaky, avant-funk.

When performing with his band, Hunter sits on the stage guiding the players through a multifold of modes and moods (the weight of his instrument and corresponding poor posture took its physical toll a few years back, leading him to a stool). Some club audiences have proven less engaged with the ensuing jazz abstractions, lamenting that the music is ill suited for all-out bodily expression. However, while it is rarely conducive to dancing, a steady beat often predominates to enliven many other listeners, including jazz-room head-bobbers. Indeed, as Hunter's instrument choice suggests, he is rather adept at placing the peanut butter in his chocolate (or is that the chocolate in his peanut butter), as he delivers his own fusion confection with conviction.

Charlie Hunter Quintet—Right Now Move (2003) ★★★★

Hunter refashions his group yet again with drummer Derek Phillips and an intriguing three-piece horn section: John Ellis (sax, clarinet), Curtis Fowlkes (trombone), and Gregoire Maret (harmonica). There is a looseness to this release, which carries both facility and felicity kindled by groove.

Songs from the Analog Playground (2001) ★★★

Mos Def, Norah Jones, Theryl de'Clouet, and Kurt Elling lend their cadences to two tracks apiece. As the title suggests, the success of this disc turns on the players' readings of the individual songs, both covers and originals, which certainly highlight the vocalists' affinities but as a whole prove a well-founded hodgepodge.

Charlie Hunter (2000) ★★★★

Hunter remains in motion, working with Leon Parker as on his 1999 disc (and adding two percussionists) but returning to horns with Peter Apfelbaum's tenor sax and Josh Roseman's trombone. A bit more funk than heretofore, as well as some bop and even a reggae lilt, set against a plaited rhythmic backdrop.

Charlie Hunter and Leon Parker—Duo (1999) ★★★½

The pair sound like a larger collective not only due to Hunter's eight-string but also Parker's penchant for playing any number of percussive implements. *Duo* mostly swings, from Afro-Cuban flavorings to cool, cool jazz.

Charlie Hunter and Pound for Pound—Return of the Candyman (1998) ★★★★

Following Calder Spanier's death, Hunter returns with a new rhythmic collective featuring Stefon Harris on vibes, John Santos on percussion, and Amendola back on drums. This is the disc that helped to pitch a tent with jamband audiences as it rarely loses its groove, though at times one wishes for a bit more of a dynamic with Harris.

Charlie Hunter Quartet—Natty Dread (1997)
★★★

Here the band rearranges the classic Marley album track by track in an instrumental jazz mode. One cannot deny the vitality of this band with Kenny Brooks and the late Calder Spanier on tenor and alto sax, and Scott Amendola behind the kit. The melodies remain if the reggae inflections do not, attesting to the might of the songs themselves. While "No Woman No Cry" receives a playful, inventive reading, for the most part this release holds merit for its achievement rather than the promise of repeated listening. A quintessential example of "your mileage may vary."

Also:

Ready...Set...Shango (1996)
Bing, Bing, Bing! (1995)
Charlie Hunter Trio (1993)

HYPNOTIC CLAMBAKE

www.hypnoticclambake.com

Hypnotic Clambake is something of a riddle. It may not enclose a mystery or serve as the marrow of an enigma, but feel free to think of it as a klezmer band wrapped in a bluegrass group inside a jazz combo. Oh yes, with plenty of Cajun seasoning and (you had to see this coming) a dollop of jam. Plus, not only does the group draw on a multiplicity of genres, but its bearings vary depending on who the members are at a given moment. As founder Maury Rosenberg relates, "If someone comes in and their forte is grunge fiddle, we incorporate it."

Rosenberg initiated the Clambake in 1990. At the time he was playing piano for the Boston Ballet, following stints in the Celtic rock band Border Patrol and the experimental outfit Psycho-Tec (with Dave Fiuczynski of the Screaming Headless Torsos). Although Rosenberg is fluid on all keyboards (musical ones, that is—his typing facility remains shrouded), his principal instrument is the accordion, and his efforts with Hypnotic Clambake draw on both zydeco and klezmer traditions. (If you're curious about the differences between these two, some of them are cultural—the former is a Creole music and the latter has Jewish origins—but there is also an instrumental variance, as in addition to accordion, zydeco emphasizes washboard while klezmer relies on clarinet.)

The players and their proficiencies have fluctuated over the preceding decade but the band typically has incorporated guitar, bass, and drums along with a bluegrass staple such as banjo or fiddle and often some brass as well. Beyond that, the inclinations of the members have dictated much of what follows, though Rosenberg composes most of the music—a mix of instrumental and vocal tunes that he vests with a wry, absurdist humor. The tenor of the improv has similarly shifted, and in some instances the band has eased back on this facet. Regardless, Hypnotic Clambake's approach has fostered a loyal fan base, acknowledged through the name of its O.U.R. Festival (Outrageous Universe Revival) that began in 1997 as well as the "pajama parties" the group has hosted for supporters in the know.

Varicose Brain (2001) ★★★

The songs on *Varicose Brain* exhibit characteristic deadpan humor, spry musicianship, and some spiffy studio edits. Overall, the disc offers solid performances and songwriting (though at this point, isn't "Ed McWoman" piling it on?).

Frozen Live Vol. 1 (1997) ★★★★

Hypnotic Clambake's first live release is a rousing and often ebullient collection of tunes from the 1996 version of the group (which includes future Jiggle/the Recipe bassist Chris Q). A deft melange of styles, from Rosenberg's originals through such covers as "Smokin' Joe Clark" and "Freedom Jazz Dance."

Also:

Kent the Zen Master (1995)
Gondola to Heaven (1994)
Square Dance Messiah (1991)

IRATOWNS

www.iratowns.com

Yes, Virginia, there is an Ira Towns. The Alabama minister is referenced in the group's name in a manner similar to New Hampshire resident Percy Hill (and with a bit more affection than, say, a gym teacher named Leonard Skinner). Childhood friends Brian Lewis, Sid Crigler, and Jack Hemby approached violinist Dan Campbell and drummer John Dent in early 1995 to assemble the group. The Iratowns soon earned recognition for their animated live sets that moved from '70s progressive rock to bluegrass and beyond, with a stomping cover of "Devil Went Down to Georgia" often closing out the night.

While all of the band members make solid contributions, it is Campbell's fiddle that often distinguishes the group. He becomes the lynchpin when the Iratowns work through traditional bluegrass, a Jean-Luc Ponty song, or an arrangement of "Welcome to the Jungle" fit for a barn dance. The group's original compositions reference all of these worlds, although they often have prog leanings with intricate, composed passages. This is also the area where the Iratowns most need to focus their efforts and continue to formulate engaging music with zest and complexity. The group lost a bit of momentum in 2000 when vocalist Hemby decided to leave the band, but a national search ultimately yielded Alabama native Steven Senn, and the pace accelerated once again.

A Series of Clicks and Whistles (1998) ★★ ½

Jack Hemby is still in the lineup for these nine originals and one traditional. The group's progressive bent resonates throughout this disc (which borders on the melodramatic at times without ever hitting it square). A number of passages prove energizing, though some of the songs lack individual bite.

Note: In addition to this studio disc, the group regularly releases live shows on its Web site.

J

JACOB FRED JAZZ ODYSSEY

www.jfjo.com

Without hearing a note from the Jacob Fred Jazz Odyssey, one can look at a set list and get a sense of the trio's élan. The group's catalog of original instrumentals includes such titles as "Thelonious Monk Is My Grandmother," "Daily Wheatgrass Burned a New Pathway," "Perfect Wife's Flannel PJs," "The Man Who Adjusted Tonalities," and "Muppet Babies Get Lost at the State Fair." These and the Spinal Tap reference in the band's name ("Jacob Fred" is whimsy as well) speak to the magnitude of their eccentricity and keen wit. A quick listen demonstrates that the band has the chops to match.

In 1994 University of Tulsa music student Brian Haas had already performed Beethoven's Piano Concerto no. 2 with the Oklahoma City Philharmonic (at age 17) and was looking ahead to the Van Cliburn Competition when he bucked the rigidity of his classical training and gravitated towards jazz. The result was a skronking septet named the Jacob Fred Jazz Odyssey, which quickly enveloped audiences with an absorbing, brazen cauldron of free jazz, funk, and even hip-hop beats. Soon after the band's 1999 national release, *Welcome Home,* some of the players began to ease back on their commitment to keeping the sounds fresh and on the road. So Haas and bass player Reed Mathis (who had joined the group

Skerik sitting in with the Jacob Fred Jazz Odyssey, Portland, Oregon, spring 2003.

straight out of high school) winnowed it down to a trio with a few players passing through the drum chair (including Brian's brother Richard) until former Ray's Music Exchange drummer Jason Smart took on the role in October 2001.

The current band carries an engaging swagger as a galvanic modern permutation of the jazz trio. While the Jacob Fred Jazz Odyssey has a number of compositions, in many instances the players prefer to improvise on a melody (or in search of one). Mathis employs a number of effects on his bass including a pitch-shifter, while Haas bounds from Rhodes to melodica to acoustic piano, with Smart often filling in the spaces with his own phraseology. One comparison is free jazz innovator Cecil Taylor—who has given his imprimatur to the group—but there are also more immediate funk grooves amidst the shifting time signatures. While the music can be abstruse, the band doesn't distance itself from the audience, as sometimes occurs in such contexts. Instead, the JFJO views their shows as a collective, participatory art. As Haas notes, "We step into the sweat lodge, detox, and bring the crowd with us."

All Is One: Live in New York City (2002) ★★★★

Recorded over two nights in March 2002 at New York's Knitting Factory, the first release from the current trio is a strident and often rousing mélange of melodies and abstractions.

Self Is Gone (2001) ★★★

JFJO's first release as a (mostly) three-piece band (various JFJO alumni guest on a couple of tracks). At times understated, at others incisive with many arresting flourishes, yet lacking some unity. A bit too staccato from track to track.

Welcome Home (1999) ★★★ ½

The national debut from the earlier version of the band (Haas and Mathis contribute only two songs, and a third is credited to the group as a whole). This is an interesting collective in its own right, with layers of percussion beneath players alternately contemplative and clustered in the fusion vein.

Also:
Telluride Is Acoustic (2003)

Out of Print:
Bloom (1998)

JAZZ MANDOLIN PROJECT
www.jazzmandolinproject.com

It's simple, elegant, and precise. No, not Jazz Mandolin Project the band, though a case could be made for two of the three (the trio's musical ideas are rarely all that simple). Instead, those adjectives refer to Jazz Mandolin Project the name. When Jamie Masefield first assembled players in 1993, he selected three words that effectively convey the essence of the group (and if that sounds like an easy task, consider the name of his side project, Grappa Boom).

Masefield grew up in a family of musicians (his grandfather played upright bass with Tommy Dorsey, Paul Whiteman, and others) and he started on the tenor banjo at age 11, taking lessons until he left for college. At the University of Vermont, he continued with the banjo, gigging in multiple area Dixieland bands. At the same time, he began woodshedding on the mandolin, which shares a similar tuning.

The musicians he emulated on this instrument were not traditional mandolin players, or even innovators such as David Grisman, but rather guitar players like Jim Hall, Bill Frisell, and Pat Metheny. (Masefield acknowledges Grisman as "the father of playing jazz with the mandolin," but places his work more in the swing context. The one mando player Masefield credits as a direct influence is the Aquarium Rescue Unit's Matt Mundy, and for a period the pair communicated regularly and played for one another over the phone.)

In 1993 Masefield initiated a series of monthly gigs at the Last Elm Café, a cooperative coffeehouse in Burlington. His intention was to work with a rotating roster of players to pursue a music that referenced his pantheon of guitarists yet also introduced classical influences and some worldbeat. This has remained his modus operandi over the past decade for what has been truly a Project, as none of the studio releases feature the same core players. The results are not typically conducive to dancing, which confounds some concertgoers but makes for a rich listening experience. (In the past, Jazz Mandolin Project has sought to emphasize the collaborative relationship between artist and audience through "The Collage," an improvisation that builds on ideas introduced by those in attendance. "The more abstract and the more ridiculous the better. They throw out the ideas, and we have a huddle where we pick out one of these ideas, and then we just start trying to play it.")

Throughout the group's history, as new players have entered the mix, they have allowed for new directions while introducing some of their own affinities. As of late, partic-

ularly through the effects-laden upright bass of Danton Boller, JMP has worked in some tonalities from the world of electronic music. During the spring of 2003, the Project expanded to a quartet at some shows with trumpeter Matt Shulman, a veteran of the downtown New York City jazz scene. JMP alumni include bass players Chris Dahlgren and Stacey Starkweather along with drummers Greg Gonzalez, Ari Hoenig, Gabe Jarrett, and Phish's Jon Fishman. (Phish band mate Trey Anastasio joined in the initial Last Elm sessions, and in 1994, Anastasio, Fishman, Starkweather, and Masefield did a run of shows as Bad Hat. Another Phish connection is Mike Gordon, one of Masefield's initial college collaborators, who is currently a member of the aforementioned Grappa Boom, and, to be clear, is the one who named that group.)

New York Yankees centerfielder/would-be jazz guitarist Bernie Williams remains an adjunct JMP member, having joined the band on stage at the 2002 Jammys. All in all, the group continues to fulfill the charge Masefield set out for himself in 1993, as he acknowledges, "The mandolin isn't a jazz instrument per se, so I'm trying to find a way to play the mandolin that sounds good and presents the sound that I hear in my head. I think that will be an ongoing process over my career."

Jungle Tango (2003) ★★★

The title track encapsulates the spirit of this disc, which does indeed draw from both modes. This is the richest, most diverse Jazz Mandolin Project release to date, with Masefield and drummer Ari Hoenig joined by bassist Danton Boller, percussionist Chris Lovejoy, and Gil Goldstein on piano and accordion.

After Dinner Jams (2001) ★★★ ½

As the name implies, this is a series of post-prandial improvisations. There is an affable looseness to these nine tracks that can feel impulsive but never quite reckless. The sound bridges *Xenoblast* and what is to come on *Jungle Tango*.

Xenoblast (2000) ★★★

Chris Dahlgren and Ari Hoenig are on board for the Project's Blue Note release. Here the band builds on some of the ideas from the previous disc, with some additional effects in the mix. A sturdy effort, although the compositions themselves lack some of the spark of their predecessors. (Trey Anastasio completists may want to pick it up for his contributions to "Hang Ten.")

Tour De Flux (1999) ★★★ ½

This time it's Chris Dahlgren and Jon Fishman in the bass and drum chairs for acoustic avant-jazz with mettle.

The Jazz Mandolin Project (1996) ★★★

A well-founded debut with Stacey Starkweather and Gabe Jarrett on bass and drums for this collection of light, bright compositions that carry both a classical and jazz feel (with some world music textures as well).

JEMIMAH PUDDLEDUCK

www.markkaran.com

Back in 1998, John Molo suggested Mark Karan for the initial Other Ones lineup, so it is fitting that the two have continued their musical association through Jemimah Puddleduck. Molo, who supplied Bruce Hornsby's backbeat for 20 years, joined Mickey Hart on drums during the first two Other Ones tours and went on to become an inaugural member of Phil Lesh & Friends. A few months after the Other Ones tour, Bob Weir tapped Karan to join him as lead player in RatDog. The next summer Karan assembled Jemimah Puddleduck on a lark for a show at the Ventura Theater, and the group gigged sporadically thereafter depending on open itineraries. When Lesh and Weir hit the road with the 2002 edition of the Other Ones, Karan and Molo were given an opportunity to spend a bit more time with JP.

The quartet intersperses blues standards (and should-be standards) with Karan originals. "A lot of it is more or less blues-based," he notes, "but rather than sticking to the 12-bar format, and when we get to the solos going around a couple of times in a blues progression and coming back to the song, it's more like we'll do the song, get to the solos, and then go to Mars for 15 or 20 minutes. It's an opportunity to play really good songs, it lets me sing, and it allows us to go to some unexpected places musically." Indeed, in this setting, Karan stretches his solos beyond what he typically does in RatDog. To this end, he is joined by JP charter member Bob Gross (Albert King, Delaney Bramlett) on bass, and recent addition, keyboardist John "J.T." Thomas, who performed with Molo for many years in the Range but whose multifaceted career began at age 20 with a stint in Captain Beefheart's Magic Band. Given its members' other projects, Jemimah Puddleduck will likely remain an intermittent endeavor but one that holds appeal for its players' many boosters.

Jemimah Puddleduck (2001) ★★★

Karan, Molo, and Gross are joined by Arlan Schnierbaum on keys for this collection of improv-fueled tracks culled from three shows that took place in July 1999, January 2000, and March 2000. Karan's three compositions are serviceable and the band has a fine taste in covers (including Johnny "Guitar" Watson's "You Can Stay but the Noise Must Go" and Gram Parsons's "She," which is interlaced with a bit of "Jack Straw").

JIGGLE

www.jigglethehandle.com

Okay, here's the *Reader's Digest* condensed version of Jiggle for the uninitiated. The group began as All You Can Eat in 1989, became Jiggle the Handle shortly thereafter, and jettisoned "the Handle" a decade later—not too long before its final performance at the Berkshire Mountain Music Festival in August 2001, followed by the band's first reunion show three months later. Jiggle has been gigging sporadically ever since. There you have it.

Okay, here's a bit more. The band is fronted by guitarist Gary Backstrom, the group's lone remaining link to the All You Can Eat days and one of the most underrated, fluid, melodic players in the Northeast (he's a particular badass on the acoustic). Backstrom originally was invited to step in and sing lead with All You Can Eat as a one-off performance for a battle of the bands. The group took top honors and then invited Backstrom to become a permanent member. The band changed its name soon afterwards, when the other lead guitarist left and Backstrom suggested Jiggle the Handle (a reference to the door handle of

his car that would spawn toilet jokes for about a decade until the group abbreviated the name to Jiggle).

A number of players rotated through until the roster solidified in 1998: drummer Greg Vasso, who came over from Max Creek a few years earlier wishing to gig more regularly; keyboardist Paul Wolstencroft from Planet Be, who had a pop-rock songwriting aesthetic and doubled as second lead vocalist; and dreadlocked, bass-playing golfer Chris Q, who stepped in following a stint with Hypnotic Clambake. A few years later the band added Michael Pujato, a percussionist born and raised in Chile who had since relocated to Nebraska.

Jiggle balances an affinity for deep improvisation with affection for its harmony-laced compositions, which often have a '70s FM vibe to them. The tone and texture of the group's jams are often compared to the Grateful Dead, though the group's predilection for Latin rhythms moved to the fore with the addition of Pujato. Following three releases and multiple national tours, the band members ultimately decided to ease off the road, with only Q maintaining a peripatetic lifestyle by joining the Recipe. However, Jiggle continues to regroup every few months with Backstrom, Vasso, and Wolstencroft at the core and drawing together Q and Pujato whenever possible. These gigs elicit particular enthusiasm from the Boston jamband scene, which Jiggle helped to ballast for much of the '90s.

Live at the Stone Coast (2000) ★★ ½

There are some solid moments on the disc, but it rarely captures the fire of the group. One does get a sense of the band's potential, though, on a crackling version of "Aliento de Vida" as well as a 16-minute take on "Fine Line."

In It Again (1999) ★★★

There is a bit of pop gloss on this release, which emphasizes the band's songwriting and its vocal harmonies. Nonetheless, a warmth predominates as the disc moves from calypso to reggae to Latin to straight-on blues-based rock.

Mrs. White's Party (1997) ★★

Mostly a studio effort with some live tracks. Backstrom and Vasso are the lone common players and the disc suffers from the lack of common voices. The playing is often laudable but the transitional group rarely carries it much beyond the sum of its influences.

THE JIMMY SWIFT BAND

www.thejimmyswiftband.com
"Alternative Music" no longer is alternative music. Now that a radio format has ossified around a particular style, it's fair to say that the descriptive term loses its cache. The true variant sounds appear to the left of the dial, on Mp3s and CD-Rs. Thus it is quite fitting that the Jimmy Swift Band took top honors as Alternative Group of the Year at Canada's 2002 East Coast Music Awards, since the band's improv-abetted electronic rock represents an alternative to the mainstream.

That bit of soapboxing is all well and good, but to be fair, some of the tracks on the band's first recorded effort, *Now They Will Know We Were Here*, do bear similarity to what one hears on "modern rock" radio. It is in the performance setting that the band pushes its songs, in a mode that some have compared to Pink Floyd (though JSB is certainly much peppier). While Craig Mercer is up front on vocals and guitar, much of the action is driven by Mike MacDougall, who is all over his seven-string bass. The Jimmy Swift Band's commitment to improvisation is evidenced by its seamless sets, which have taken place most commonly with Grand Theft Bus: one group will perform a brief set and then the other will join for a segue jam before taking over the stage (rinse, lather, repeat). The full band tag-in is a form long practiced by moe., which is why it makes sense that the JSB received an invitation to the 2003 moe.down.

Returning to awards, Mercer has garnered some interesting hardware. In 2001 he received second place in the Canadian National Songwriting Competition for "Drive By" (which appears on the group's debut). In 2002, Mercer took top honors from the Music Industry Association of Nova Scotia as Booking Agent of the Year, a job he has not relinquished even though he performs more than 150 gigs annually with the Jimmy Swift Band. (Your move, Chip Hooper....)

Now They Will Know We Were Here (2001) ★★★

Although the group tours as a quartet, there are nine players credited as band members on this disc, which offers some fine modern rock radio fodder. While this release is driven by crunching rock riffs, the Jimmy Swift Band does vary the pace, offering, for instance, some pulsing instrumentals.

Also:

Onward Through the Fog (2003)

JOHN SCOFIELD BAND

www.johnscofield.com

It's not as if any of this is new to him. Then
again it is. Listen to his contributions to Billy
Cobham's fusion configurations in the mid-
'70s with George Duke, Alphonso Johnson,
and the Brecker Bothers. Or put on one of his
soul-jazz discs from two decades later, such as
Hand Jive (1993) with Eddie Harris or *Groove
Elation* (1995). In both contexts one can detect
seeds, strains, and, come to think of it, stems,
of what would follow in jamband circles.

Then in 1998, John Scofield recorded *A Go
Go* with Medeski Martin and Wood and
toured in support of the disc with Medeski,
Wood, and Clyde Stubblefield (Billy Martin
was on his honeymoon). The John Scofield

Band is an outgrowth of that exposure and
experience—a quartet that builds on his
predilection "to do something hopping with a
jazz group playing funk" while introducing a
contemporary frame.

Scofield is one of the most celebrated and
influential jazz/rock guitarists of his generation. Fresh out of Berklee College of Music in
the early '70s, he recorded *Live at Carnegie
Hall* with Gerry Mulligan and Chet Baker.
From there he joined Cobham's band (a contrasting gig for sure), and in the following
years he went on to work with a number of
players, including Charles Mingus and Dave
Liebman before receiving a call in 1982 from
Miles Davis, who had recently returned to
performance following a six-year retirement.

An exuberant Sco hits it with the JSB.

"Actually he had his saxophonist Bill Evans [no relation to the jazz pianist of the same name] call and say 'Come to Cleveland' that same day," Scofield recalls. "And I said 'Okay I'll be there' to play with Miles. Then I stayed in his band for three years."

In the years to follow, Scofield often focused on his own projects, along the way collaborating with two guitarists of a similar stature: Bill Frisell and Pat Matheny. Then following *Quiet*, on which he played acoustic guitar, Scofield decided to make *A Go Go*. "I was a fan of MMW. I had heard their albums and I became convinced when I heard *Shack Man* that I should play with those guys because the style of music they played was so close to my own. Billy Martin's drumming has a certain kind of looseness and jazziness—it's a New Orleans thing. There has always been a kind of R&B that swung, and it turns out that a lot of it comes from these New Orleans drummers of 30 years ago. I've always tried to play with people who like playing funk type stuff, but they're hard to find."

In the years to follow, this quest has been easier for Scofield. (Speaking of New Orleans funk drummers, Scofield performed with one such player at the 2002 Jammys, Stanton Moore, as part of a quartet Scofield assembled that also included Skerik on sax and bassist Andy Hess, who became a member of Scofield's band.) His current drummer, Adam Deitch, a founding member of Lettuce and a fellow Berklee grad, makes the grade, as attested by his previous steady gig in the Average White Band. Avi Bortnick is a rhythm guitar player originally recommended by Charlie Hunter when Scofield toured in support of *Bump*, his follow-up to *A Go Go*.

("The thing about playing night after night in a two-guitar band is if they're both hot dogs like myself who want to blow solos all night, then it can get boring. In a band like the Allman Brothers there's singing so they break it up.")

Bortnick, whom Scofield poached from a career in architectural acoustics, plays another significant role in the band's current sound, as he is the one to trigger the samples. Scofield affirms, "I think in the general scheme of things to make jazz-rock work, jazz-rock-fusion, whatever you call this whole thing where we're a jazz group playing funk, to make that work it has to be something more than a string of solos over a vamp. I think a string of solos over a vamp gets boring. So for me the interesting things in jazz-rock have been the textural. Avi's rhythm guitar solos are a textural thing, and the samples are textural."

Some listeners who first encountered Scofield with *A Go Go* may be surprised or slightly put off by this direction, as textural is not a word commonly associated with funk. But it has long been Scofield's métier to refashion the familiar, and his current band takes him beyond the Groove Elation.

Up All Night (2003) ★★★★
The first disc attributed to the John Scofield Band, this one builds on the prior effort with command and vigor (and a sterling horn section as well).

Überjam (2002) ★★★ ½
Technically credited solely to John Scofield, this release presents three quarters of the current John Scofield Band (Jesse Murphy is

on bass) with appearances from John Medeski and Karl Denson. This is Scofield's most significant move towards incorporating sample beds and current electronic music, and while artistry and cool riffs predominate, the compositions themselves aren't as tantalizing as his preceding efforts.

Bump (2000) ★★★

A number of players rotate through this disc, including Chris Wood, Tony Scherr, and Kenny Wollesen from Sex Mob, Deep Banana Blackout's Eric Kalb, and Johnny Durkin, but it is Soul Coughing's Mark De Gli Antoni on keyboard and samples who galvanizes.

A Go Go (1998) ★★★★★

Scofield's collaboration with Medeski Martin and Wood opened doors, ears, minds, and (supply your own metaphor).

JUGGLING SUNS

www.jugglingsuns.com

So how about some more trivia? What do Juggling Suns have in common with Gov't Mule, Tom Tom Club, and the Breeders? If you said guitarist Mark Diomede, you'd be...wrong. (On the subject of Diomede's notable collaborations, however, he did once perform with Bruce Springsteen, and the group as a whole appeared with Julia Roberts in *Runaway Bride*. The musicians are in the film oh-so-briefly as a wedding band and as the Best Men, who perform at one of Roberts's suspended nuptials.) If your answer was Solar Circus, you'd also be wrong, but you'd be in the ballpark (albeit while batting .250). Indeed, the correct response is that each of the listed groups began as a side

project but went on to become the main focus of its principals.

Diomede co-founded Solar Circus in the mid-'80s as a Grateful Dead cover band, but over the ensuing decade the group began to focus almost exclusively on original music (releasing five discs with Relix Records along the way, plus jamming for an hour with Bruce Springsteen one night on the Jersey shore). By 1995 Solar Circus consciously limited itself to no more than one Dead song in any given show. Diomede, whose style certainly reflects an abiding respect for Jerry Garcia, began performing his tunes again in the fall of 1995 through a Monday residency at Cass' Café in Freehold, New Jersey (just a few months following Garcia's passing—a time when many longed to hear his music performed live). Diomede named the band Juggling Suns (the title track of Solar Circus' first release in 1989), presenting Dead songs and a few other covers as an alternative outlet for himself, Solar Circus bassist Kevin Kopac, original Circus drummer Brad Hall, and World Within keyboard player Gus Vigo.

The Cass' Café gigs soon developed a steady following and by 1997, with the break up of Solar Circus, Juggling Suns became a steady touring entity, introducing its own compositions and traveling throughout the East Coast and then to Japan. The group's lineup has shifted over the years, with Diomede and Vigo now joined by another Solar Circus alum, bass player Bruce Wigdor, as well as former Splintered Sunlight drummer Ivan Funk. Juggling Suns has never been doctrinaire about limiting its cover selections, so any given show may lean towards mostly original material or focus on that of the Dead (and others). The music of Garcia et al. certainly informs both Juggling Suns' songwriting and performance style, remaining at the core of its "cosmic dance music." This nucleus proves comforting and appealing to a community of fans drawn to such sounds, who maintain a steady orbit around the Suns.

Steppin' Off a Star (2002) ★★

The group's first studio album lacks much of the spark that animates its live shows. The readings often feel flat, as Mark Diomede's guitar is restrained, and many of the songs remain a bit too steeped in mellow psychedelia.

Living on the Edge of Change (1997) ★★★

The group's first release to focus on original material (1996's *Doorway to the Angels* mostly offers Grateful Dead covers), *Living on the Edge of Change* presents the band live as a quintet in 1997. While echoes of the Dead permeate (and will likely appeal to many Suns supporters), the music is at its most commanding when the band pushes itself into others realms, such as that of the Middle Eastern/funk instrumental "Tabla Rasa 97."

Out of Print:

Get Abducted (2000)
Doorway to the Angels (1996)

Fan site:

www.jugglingbones.com

JUICE

www.neworleansjuice.com

What's in a name? What is the power of place? These two questions become entwined when one considers the music of Juice. Or is it New Orleans Juice? Sometimes it's difficult to discern. On its debut disc the group is identified as New Orleans' Juice. On its second disc the apostrophe is dropped, and it is just New Orleans Juice, though the liner notes indicate that the songs were "arranged by Juice." The group's Web site is neworleansjuice.com, yet there the band most often refers to itself as Juice. So why should any of this matter beyond the all-important question of whether to file this entry under J or N? Well, in some respects it doesn't matter—other than the fact that this fluctuation parallels the inconstancy of the group's roster as well as the concomitant variations in its sound.

And what is "New Orleans" about Juice? These defining characteristics have changed over the course of the band's history. When bass player Dave Jordan founded the group in late 1995, Juice's then mostly instrumental songs emulated those of the Meters (with a dose of the Grateful Dead as well, yielding a sound the group described as "psychedeli-funk"). However, as musicians rotated through (only Jordan and harmonica player /co-vocalist Jamie Galloway appear on both of the band's releases), and Jordan's own tastes changed, Juice began to gravitate towards other New Orleans R&B icons, such as Lee Dorsey and Fats Domino (necessitating a bit less open-ended improv). One common thread may be Dr John, who has drawn from both worlds (and other orbiting spheres as well).

Particularly in the live setting, the band's music is animated by a fais do-do, celebratory spirit. Given the transitory nature of its roster, Juice is still defining its pursuits and the group's songwriting often remains beholden to its influences. While performing upwards of 150 times a year, though, Juice's shows continue to invoke the city nearly referenced in its name.

All Lit Up (2002) ★★½

Anders Osborne's production lends clarity to these 12 tracks in which the arrangements are a bit tighter than on the group's debut, placing more emphasis on the individual songs. The results are mixed. While the playing can be adroit—accented by Jason Seller's sax, Charlie Dennard's keys, and multiple guest percussionists—the songs themselves don't necessarily resonate.

Fortified (1999) ★★

This disc and incarnation of the band offer a bit more of the "psychedelifunk" that the group sometimes ascribes to its sound. The results make for a decent party album featuring a hodgepodge of styles building from funk, though the band's identity is sometimes subsumed by the festive vibe.

JUPITER COYOTE

www.jupitercoyote.com

JC is DIY. More than a dozen years into its career, performing upwards of 200 shows per annum, the band keeps things in-house, handling its own booking, management, and publicity. The group also manages its own label, though a few years ago it disbanded the aptly named Autonomous Records created in the early '90s to release and distribute its music along with that of such groups as Strangefolk, Blue Miracle, and Uncle Mingo. Jupiter Coyote did stray briefly, releasing 1998's *Here Be Dragons* with Roadrunner Records, but ultimately decided that the best path was to "Do It Yourself" (bringing this full circle for those of you still chawin' on that initial acronym).

Guitarists/vocalists Matthew Mayes and John Felty first met in elementary school. Their friendship remains at the core of Jupiter Coyote, from its origins as a cover band in the late '80s through its commitment to original music in 1990 and on to the present. For a while the pair supplied much of the musical dynamic in the group, with Mayes's guijo (an instrument crafted with a banjo neck and a Stratocaster guitar body) often juxtaposed with Felty's slide guitar (while Sanders Brightwell pushed the sound on bass). However, while Jupiter Coyote's music has long been described as Appalachian funk, it gained extra emphasis on the former term in 1998 with the addition of former Telluride Bluegrass fiddle champ Steve Trismen. The group employs sturdy musicianship that lends zest to songs often delivered by Mayes's deep, emotive vocals, which draw comparisons to contemporary John Bell.

The band has built a trusty cache of support nationwide through its near-perpetual touring, though to some degree it has fallen through the cracks. On a musical level, as evidenced by the two sides of its live release, a number of songs remain quite close to their arrangements while others allow the band to deliver on its propensity for improv (thus JC may be too "jammy" for one contingent but insufficiently so for another). In addition, on a practical note, the group has not played many of the larger recent festivals. To some degree, this is a product of Jupiter Coyote's independence, remaining outside the horse-trading of managers and booking agents. Still, these are matters of gradation, as the band has sold more than 150,000 albums and played to many times that number of audience members by remaining autonomous.

Waxing Moon (2001) ★★ ½

Waxing Moon offers a decent collection of tunes with comparable performance and production. However, one wishes for a bit more variation from Steve Trismen's fiddle, which at times yields Dave Matthews Band comparisons and carries a similarity to many of the tracks.

Jupiter Coyote Live (2000) ★★★

This double live set drawn from three October 1999 shows is well founded, balancing an emphasis on individual songs with some extended takes and fluid segues,.

Here Be Dragons (1998) ★★★ ½

A number of guests appear on this release, including Edwin McCain, Count M'butu, and Beth Wood. The emphasis here is on more mainstream, melodic fare, and to this end the group is rather successful.

Ghost Dance (1997) ★★★

This disc reflects the group's prior instrumentation, with guitar and guijo a bit more up front along with a tandem of percussionists. A sturdy sampling of mountain rock.

Also:
Lucky Day (1995)
Wade (1993)
Cemeteries and Junkyards (1991)

KARL DENSON'S TINY UNIVERSE
www.karldenson.com

KD has been that and done there. Strike that. Reverse it. No, on second thought reverse it once again. Karl Denson has indeed been all that, in recording with Lenny Kravitz, collaborating with Fred Wesley and Maceo Parker, co-founding the Greyboy Allstars, and engineering his own cosmology with the Tiny Universe. He's done it there too, traversing the globe in Kravitz's band, and with Wesley, the Allstars, and Karl Denson's Tiny Universe.

Denson grew up in Southern California in the '70s and '80s, immersed in jazz and funk. His social circles exposed him to James Brown, Sly Stone, and the Ohio Players, and while developing on the sax and flute, he sought out the records of Eddie Harris and Yusef Lateef along with most anything on the CTI and Prestige labels. (Producer Creed Taylor, himself a trumpet player, founded CTI in 1967, bringing on engineer Rudy Van Gelder and releasing music by Wes Montgomery, Freddie Hubbard, Stanley Turentine, George Benson, and Ron Carter, among many others. Prestige Records, founded in 1949 and another home to Van Gelder, issued records by Miles Davis, John Coltrane, Modern Jazz Quartet,

Thelonious Monk, and Sonny Rollins, and later by Jack McDuff, Rusty Bryant, Richard "Groove" Holmes, and Boogaloo "Joe" Jones.)

Denson (aka Diesel) developed a host of interests and performed in a variety of contexts, which is how he met Kravitz in 1988 while working on a session for Tony Lemans. (Lemans, a performer that some likened to Sly Stone, released his eponymous disc the next year on Prince's Paisley Park label. Unfortunately, Lemans died in an auto accident in 1992 at age 29.) The next year, Kravitz invited Denson to come in and blow a solo on "Let Love Rule," and the results inspired Kravitz to use Denson throughout the album and his next, as well as on tour until 1994, when he jettisoned the horn section. Meanwhile, Diesel released four discs of rela-

tively straightahead jazz between 1992 and 1995, all of which had comestible-themed titles (the third of these, *Chunky Pecan Pie*, also featured bassist Dave Holland and drummer Jack DeJohnette, whose work together over the years includes Miles Davis's *Bitches Brew*).

During this time period, Diesel also began to work with Fred Wesley, former trombone player and musical director of James Brown's band. (Maceo Parker produced some of these sessions. This was around one of the times that Wesley, Parker, and Pee Wee Ellis toured and recorded as the JB Horns, reclaiming some of their legacy. A number of Brown's band members have remained underappreciated over the years, including his classic drum tandem of Jabo Starks and Clyde

Karl Denson and Carlos Washington jam with Galactic.

Stubblefield, as much of the credit has been directed to the admittedly kick-ass James-errrr-by-contract-rider-Mr. Brown.)

While Denson was still gigging with Kravitz in addition to Wesley and his own band, a California DJ named Greyboy (Andreas Stevens) contacted him about recording a few tracks for Ubiquity Records' *Home Cookin'* compilation. Pleased with the sound, upon the release two years later of Greyboy's first full-length disc, *Freestylin'* (to which Denson also contributed), the pair decided to put together a band, inviting guitarist Elgin Park, bassist Chris Stillwell, keyboardist Robert Walter, and drummer Zak Najor (few names more closely resemble a typo than Zak Najor).

The Allstars went on to help popularize acid jazz in the United States, with Greyboy spinning tracks over the band's boogaloo. (Diesel has described boogaloo as "black hillbilly music" and also has said, "Boogaloo is about the late '50s. Dizzy Gillespie is one of the main architects. After bebop, Dizzy went back to his roots and started studying the Latin rhythms. He and Eddie Harris and Lee Morgan, who's one of my main boogaloo influences. It's when the beat straightened out.") By mid-1998 the band members were ready to move on to other projects, as Denson himself found the sound to be a bit too stagnant and retro.

Initially this new group toured under the Greyboy Allstar Sidecar Project umbrella, but within a few years of performing nearly 200 gigs per annum, the Tiny Universe eclipsed the Allstars in national recognition (though some fans still pine for Greyboy—now recognized as an all-star band given the players' subsequent efforts—and some of these supporters sated themselves through three

reunion shows in December 2002 and three more in August 2003). Karl Denson's Tiny Universe incorporates some of the styles and beats of Greyboy, but there is also a heavier R&B presence, a deeper funk, and hip-hop samples as well. Criticism has touched on the inconstancy of the lineup, which has hampered the band's growth to a degree. A number of players have rotated through the Universe, including Greyboy Allstars members Stillwell and Najor, as well as Carlos Washington (who departed to form Giant People), Mike Dillon (Critters Buggin', Garage à Trois), and Soulive's Alan Evans. Indeed, aside from the bandleader, none of the current members is original to the group, and Diesel has stated that one of the reasons he recorded 2001's *Dance Lesson #2* with an altogether different collection of players is he wasn't then content with the status of KDTU (a matter he soon rectified).

Meanwhile, some listeners are not fond of Denson's vocals, which appear on a number of the songs throughout an evening and on disc, not because his singing is inept (it is sound, if not stunning) but because they feel this aspect detracts from the band's instrumental prowess. The latter is further evinced lately with a roster that includes guitarist Brian Jordan, keyboardist David Veith (who holds the longest tenure in the group), bassist Ron Johnson, Chris Littlefield on trumpet, and the latest addition, drummer John Staten (this Giant People alum is not only a dynamo but was identified as the nicest person in the music community by Particle's Steve Molitz). As for KD's voice, it is evident that he is interested in offering far more than boogaloo (again, been that, done there), as the band's name itself references the broader orbit he aspires to maintain. A laudable goal, since, to paraphrase comic Steven Wright, it's a tiny universe, but you wouldn't want to paint it.

The Bridge (2002) ★★★½

There is tasteful playing throughout this release that offers many of the band's vocal tunes with guest turns from Fred Wesley, Michael Franti, Saul Williams, and Chris Wood. *The Bridge* yields some fine moments, many of the smoother variety, though some of the soul tunes never quite kindle.

Karl Denson's Tiny Universe (1999) ★★★

An earlier version of the band with only David Veith from the current lineup onboard. These six songs provide a bit more straightforward groove than the KDTU of the present (with a few sturdy vocal tunes as well).

As Karl Denson:

Dance Lesson #2 (2001) ★★★★½

Denson's Blue Note debut is the album that many were hoping to hear from him. These instrumentals sway between funk and jazz with an insistent attack from Denson and a mix of innovators that spans generations, including Melvin Sparks, Leon Spencer, Charlie Hunter, Chris Wood, DJ Logic, E.J. Rodriguez, and Ron Levy.

Also:

The D Stands for Diesel (1997)
Baby Food (1995)
Chunky Pecan Pie (1994)
Herbal Turkey Breast (1993)
Blackened Red Snapper (1992)

Fan site:

Karl Denson's Tiny Universe Set List Archives—*www.lukew.com/kdtu/index.html*

Discussion lists:

www.groups.yahoo.com/group/TinyUniverse/
www.lists.netspace.org/archives/kdtu.html

KOOKEN & HOOMEN

www.kookenhoomen.com

This San Francisco Bay Area collective brings art to its performance. Or perhaps that's performance to its art. ("Two great tastes that taste great together.") The band supplements its ethereal electronic musings with art installations by Robyn Hartzell, typically televisions with images painted on their screens plus a series of projections. Her contributions so enhance the music that the members of K&H often credit her as the "visual member of the band."

Nate Germick (Rhodes, synth, melodica) and Brian Mundy (guitar) met at Grinnell College in 1994, though the duo didn't come together until they each wound up on the West Coast a few years later. There they were joined by bass player Rob Gwin, who met Mundy through a friend in Chicago. The three decided to form a group that would draw on their enthusiasm for such performers as Aphex Twin, Tortoise, Herbie Hancock, and Frank Zappa. The band's sound is most recognizably reminiscent of the two former artists, though Kooken & Hoomen do delve into the complex scripting of Zappa, and their sound often mirrors a range of Hancock's periods.

Drummer Felipe Ceballos signed on in March 2000, and the band began to gig out. While rehearsing, the group met Hartzell, whose studio was next to their rehearsal space. She began to work at the shows and to design a full range of the band's graphic imagery (including the "bloopy things" that predominate). All told, Kooken & Hoomen create space music—not just because Hartzell often projects slides from low-budget sci-fi, but because there's plenty of room in the group's sound, which often can be minimalist, mellow, and diffuse.

Escuela (2001) ★★ ½

Escuela is self-assuredly mellow, which may distract a listener from digging in and hearing some of the nuances. While at times the band leans towards more generic, electronic-propelled beats with some butterfly jazz guitar licks, they do a solid job of sculpting their compositions, incorporating some subtler shifts and fills.

Also:

Gopal to Starwin (2002)

KUDZU KINGS

www.kudzukings.com

What the heck is progressive country anyhow? Isn't that an oxymoron? At any rate, it certainly elicits images of Jean-Luc Ponty screeching through "The Devil Goes Down to Georgia." Not that this has all that much to do with Kudzu Kings, as progressive country is just one descriptive term ascribed to the band's music—along with bluegrass, honky tonk, and good ol' improvisational rock.

As of late the Kings have gained some recognition for lending its guitarist, George McConnell, to Widespread Panic. While McConnell's departure in the summer of 2002

led the group to put some plans on hold, the band took after its vegetative namesake, a persistent weed that may briefly wither but rarely truly wanes. In fact, Kudzu Kings' original electric guitarist, Max Williams, had departed a number of years earlier, leading McConnell to switch over from an acoustic (and back to the instrument of his Beanland days, a group that also featured a pre-Panic JoJo Hermann). Over the years, a few guest players had also stepped into a Kings guitar slot, including Bucky Baxter (Bob Dylan, Ryan Adams) and Cody Dickinson of the North Mississippi Allstars.

Kudzu Kings draws on the surroundings of its Oxford, Mississippi, home—and not solely for its name. (Botany bonus: Originally from Japan, kudzu was brought to the US for the 1876 Philadelphia Exposition and later introduced into the Southeast to prevent erosion. Alas, it quickly ran rampant over horizontal and vertical surfaces, and the USDA declared kudzu to be a weed in 1972. It is estimated that more than 250,000 acres in Mississippi are covered by the creeping vine.) The cultural and physical environment provides a subject matter, especially in the initial songs penned by founders Tate Moore (guitar) and Dave Woolworth (bass)—loose ditties such as "Bar-B-Q Blues," "Panola County Line," and "Mississippi Mud." Inebriants similarly serve as reference points, not only in the music (the eccentric anthem "I Love Beer") but also in the band's stage demeanor, with its members offering the occasional spectacle of collectively ordering Jägermeister shots from the stage.

While Moore and Woolworth originally came together from the country & western perspective that remains at the band's core, the addition of other players including

Williams, McConnell, and keyboardist Robert Chaffe has carried the music into other corners as well. Here the musicians may exchange instruments or insults between songs, while offering spontaneous soliloquies (this aspect of improvisation is essential to the band's ethos, while the deep jam is not a component of every song). Like the vine, the group rarely strays from its geographic base, but its purpose and perspective likely hold wider appeal (plenty of people dig the alt-country thing, plenty dig the prog-country thing, and plenty more certainly dig beer).

Y2Kow (1999) ★★★½

A tinge more reverent than the debut, yet no less entertaining. Some of the ideas are cultivated a bit further with the introduction of additional accents.

Kudzu Kings (1997) ★★★

Mostly loose, animated songs in a country/Americana vein (with some liquid inspiration infused as well).

LAKE TROUT

www.laketrout.com

Some of the pleasure one can derive from digging in and engaging a group's music comes from tracking that band's artistic resolve. At times, the arc of a performer's career can take on an element of improvisation. The results may occasionally prove frustrating both for the artist and the audience, given the inevitable manifestation of expectation, but there often is a majestic quality to the curve. And hey, at least it keeps things lively—to wit, Lake Trout.

This Baltimore-based band has both entranced and alienated listeners along the way (the constituency of the former grouping certainly outpaces the latter). Lake Trout first came together as an instrumental quartet in 1994, with jazz and hip-hop leanings. A year and a half later, with the addition of guitar player Woody Ranere, the group also added some tender, melodious vocals and cracked poetry. By mid-1998 the sound gravitated towards electronica, and Lake Trout toured with DJ Who while folding elements of drum & bass into its improvisation. However, just as a swell of listeners came to associate the band with the burgeoning trance fusion realm, Lake Trout moved towards a modern rock sound in the Pixies/Toadies/Radiohead continuum (sax and flute player Matt Pierce has worked to carve out a role for himself).

Lake Trout retains fans that were first drawn to the band in each of its eras, and prior directives certainly resonate in the current sound. One steady element has been a captivating live show, resulting in invitations to share bills with a varied collection of artists including Blues Traveler, Oysterhead, the Dismemberment Plan, and Galactic. Lake Trout also performed at the 2001 Jammys with Marky Ramone and the Misfits' Jerry Only on "I Wanna Be Sedated" and "Blitzkrieg Bop." While the release of *Another One Lost* punctuated a de-emphasis on improvisation in the group's performances, given the band's history, steady listeners

Lake Trout, an ongoing (re)assessment.

anticipate an inability to anticipate where the music may lead and what may follow.

Another One Lost (2002) ★★★★½

Lake Trout melds alternative rock bombast with loops and ambient textures on this stark, sometimes brooding release that is empowered with the clarity of the production. A masterful modern rock album, though some people who are drawn to the sounds of *Alone at Last* may find themselves, well...lost.

Alone at Last (2000) ★★★★

Recorded live at Trax on December 9, 1999, this is the best of the discs to appear in the discontinued Phoenix Presents live series. DJ Who joins the group for some set pieces and segued improvisations. Drum & bass and electronica influences predominate, with the results both hypnotic and haunting.

Also:

Volume for the Rest of It (1998)
Lake Trout (1997)

Fan site:

www.binarycortex.org

LEFTOVER SALMON
www.leftoversalmon.com

Okay, play along for a moment. You can have one word to evoke the essence of Leftover

Salmon. What is it? Festivarians? Adequate, but that represents only a portion of the band's endeavors. LoSers? Actually, that's an abbreviation more than a descriptive term (and one that typically refers to its fans). Perhaps Mayor McCheeseniks? Actually, that's two words—keep trying, though.... Polyethnic Cajun Slamgrassians? Well, that's sort of cheating because it's the group's own tag, and at any rate, that's three words. BridgeBerters? Maybe, but that one would require a lengthy annotated footnote. Anahuacists? Ditto. A flat-out ripping cadre of musicians? A fine start, but by now you've abandoned any pretense of delivering a single word. Which, frankly, is just fine—the point being that it is not easy to encapsulate the Leftover Salmon experience in a succinct manner (just ask the band's prolix frontman, Vince Herman, often credited on "lead vocals and gibberish").

One might proclaim that Leftover Salmon is greater than the sum of its parts, but what the heck does that really mean anyhow? How does one apply it to music, ascribing values to individuals who then max out at some quantifiable point? In this best of situations, people's enthusiasms and affinities are boundless (okay, arguably within the realm of physical precepts and even then...). One of the joys of art is its dogged refusal to countenance any artificially imposed dictates. And this (made it, finally) is also the majesty of Leftover Salmon.

The group traces its origins to the Telluride Bluegrass Festival, though it never could be considered a bluegrass group. In 1989 banjo player Mark Vann traveled west from his Virginia home to the Fest and took top honors in the banjo competition. (Vann had spent nearly three years literally woodshedding in a cabin without electricity or phone—little to prevent him from devoting most of his time to the instrument.) One evening in the campgrounds, he was roused from his tent by a collection of pickers that included Herman as well as mandolin player Drew Emmitt. This encounter encouraged Vann to relocate to Colorado, where he eventually joined Emmitt in the Left Hand String Band, a group that incorporated traditional bluegrass instrumentation but did so with a less traditional repertoire (along with originals and traditionals, the group offered Allman Brothers Band and Little Feat covers). Meanwhile, Herman had started performing with the Salmon Heads, a band that placed emphasis on Calypso and Cajun music. Leftover Salmon came together in 1991 when some members of the String Band couldn't make it to a gig and invited a few Salmon Heads to fill in, including Herman. This hybrid entity found its name en route to the show, where the players talked through a synthesis of sounds that they would continue to deliver in the months to follow, once Leftover Salmon become a formal project (okay, formal is a poor word choice—let's replace it with the word "ongoing"), also drawing on country, ska, reggae, rock, jazz, and blues.

Leftover Salmon propounds a convivial atmosphere, and while its members take themselves none-too-seriously, they do approach their music with a reverence. Actually, that's not altogether accurate. While the players certainly possess an instrumental prowess, at times they are quite cavalier about how they employ it—offering, for instance, a version of "Hotel California" set to the tune of "Rocky Top," or, on the flipside, singing "Rocky Top" to the tune of "Smoke on the Water" (LoS also gained some early renown for its "Pasta on the Mountain"). Still, the band has long been hailed for its musicianship, particularly in the late '90s when the roster also featured Jeff Sipe (Aquarium Rescue Unit, Project Z) and Tye North with such celebrated guest performers as Del McCoury, David Grisman, Tony Trischka, and Sally Van Meter. These musicians have shared the stage not only with the band but also with a Mayor McCheese head liberated from a McDonald's playground a few years prior to Leftover's formation. (The head is now part of the band's lore, including repeated instances of its theft by other groups. For some historical accounts, visit www.leftoversalmon.com/mayor-kidnappings.html.)

Meanwhile, many feel that Herman has elevated the art of onstage blather to new heights (others would point in the opposite direction). This is all part of "Bridging the Bert," a phrase adapted from a fan's note delivered to the band that was misinterpreted due to poor penmanship (while it likely intended to proclaim that "State Bridge is the best," it seemed to read "State Bridge is the bert"). The origin of the phrase, however, is less important than what it has come to represent, albeit with a wink: a nexus of styles, sounds, perspectives, and, yes, mental states.

Due to its origins, Leftover Salmon retains a strong association and affection for the "Festivaaaaaall!" (to employ the exhortation often bellowed by Herman). Even though the band has gone on to headline at Telluride, its members continue to pick in the campgrounds—in 2001, Emmitt induced Sam Bush, Chris Thile, Peter Rowan, and Béla

Fleck to join such a jam. In addition, Herman has a penchant for "Anahuacing," a term that refers to musical ambush of unsuspecting campers, typically beginning with the singing of "Anahuac, anahuac, it used to be my home, but it's not anymore" (drawn from the Austin Lounge Lizards song "Anahuac," recorded on the ALL's debut, *Creatures from the Black Saloon*).

In 1999 the band sought to transplant the festival vibe and its penchant for collaboration onto *The Nashville Sessions*, which contains appearances by Earl Scruggs, Waylon Jennings, Lucinda Williams, Taj Mahal, John Bell, Fleck, McCoury, and many others. In certain respects, *The Nashville Sessions* anticipated the *O Brother, Where Art Thou?* phenomenon, and had it appeared a few years later, it might have been embraced by a much wider audience. In lieu of *O Brother*, however, the group later joined Cracker members David Lowery and Johnny Hickman to record *O Cracker, Where Art Thou?*, in which the musicians rearranged Cracker's material.

While Herman and Emmitt remain the lone founders of Leftover Salmon, they have infused their current band mates with the spirit that has long vitalized the group (though some potential audience members have been somewhat ambivalent about the new roster). After Sipe and North announced that their final shows would take place at the band's Planet Salmon Festival in September 2000, the band enlisted three like-tempered new players: keyboardist Bill McKay (formerly of the Derek Trucks Band), bassist Greg Gonzalez (who had toured with Matt Flinner Quartet and the Motet), and drummer Jose Martinez. A much more difficult and daunting loss was the death of Mark Vann due to skin cancer in March 2002. (Six months earlier, a community of players, including Fleck, Bill Payne, Paul Barrere, Peter Rowan, Pete Wernick, Todd Park Mohr, Bill Nershi, Michael Travis, Kyle Hollingsworth, and Jeff Austin, had joined LoS for a series of benefit performances to help pay for his medical care.) After touring with a variety of players including Jeff Mosier, Tony Furtado, and Matt Flinner, the band eventually welcomed Noam Pikelny on banjo, who counts Vann among his inspirations and icons. The band dedicated its next disc, *Live* (rhymes with give), to Vann, emphasizing the need to treat life as a daily celebration and to continue forging that nexus to Bert (and Ernie and Madison County and Folsom County and...).

Leftover Salmon and Cracker:

O Cracker, Where Art Thou? (2003) ★★★★
Aided and abetted by Cracker members David Lowery and Johnny Hickman, Leftover picks through the Cracker catalogue and rearranges many of the songs through Salmon's own playful vernacular (for instance, "Eurotrash Girl" as a country waltz and "Teen Angst" as a bluegrass breakdown).

Live (2002) ★★★★

Onstage antics are mostly absent from this live release drawn from performances during the first half of 2001. Instead, much of the focus is on Mark Vann's dexterous playing, which at times is part of a more textural, layered approach than an all-out perilous blur (but fear not, true believers, Vince Herman does kick up his heels a few times, as well).

The Nashville Sessions (1999) ★★★★½

Randy Scruggs produced this collaborative release, which introduces guest musicians on every track performing both original material and traditionals. As befits the locale, *The Nashville Sessions* is a bit heavier on the slamgrass side of the spectrum. Guests on this sparkling release include Randy and father Earl ("Five Alive"), as well as Del McCoury and his son Ronnie ("Midnight Blues"), Béla Fleck and Jeff Coffin ("Dance On Your Head"), Waylon Jennings and Sam Bush ("Are You Sure Hank Done It This Way"), and many more.

Euphoria (1997) ★★★½

The band's second studio disc is an agreeable representation of its stylistic hodgepodge. In some instances *Euphoria* does indeed achieve the state referenced by its title, though the performances feel slightly stifled at times.

Also:

Ask the Fish (1995)
Bridges to Bert (1993)

Fan site:

Set lists—*www.db.etree.org/losupstreamteam*
www.his.com/~vann/LoSstuff/losfans.htm

Discussion list:

www.lists.leftoversalmon.com/mailman/listinfo/festivalist

THE LES CLAYPOOL FROG BRIGADE

www.lesclaypool.com

Okay, trivia time. Can you name the one performer to appear at Bonnaroo, Ozzfest, Lollapalooza, the Jammy Awards, Woodstock, the Gathering of the Vibes, and the Reading Festival? Come to think of it, that's lame. Not the achievement, but the nature of the question, given the format in which it appears (indeed, if the answer weren't Les Claypool, what would be the point?). Okay, scrap that. How about this: Can you name the lone musician to record with Tom Waits, Kenny Wayne Shepherd, Gov't Mule, Jerry Cantrell, Vinyl, and the Les Claypool Frog Brigade? (Yeah, I tried to throw you with the build up to that last one but you probably answered Les Claypool anyway—no flies on you.)

Indeed, Claypool has had an eclectic, electric run since Primus first surfaced (and sucked) in the mid-'80s (actually, the sucking arguably came later). However, events took an odd turn (if you think that possible) after Claypool joined Trey Anastasio and Stewart Copeland as Oysterhead at the Saenger Theater for the Superfly SuperJam on May 4, 2000. With Primus on hiatus, the bass player began fielding offers to perform in other contexts, including the Mountain Aire Festival, the Gathering of the Vibes, and the Jammy Awards (where he collaborated with the Disco Biscuits, then the Triscuits, during their separation from Marc Brownstein). At Mountain Aire, the first of these gigs, he assembled a band that included Skerik on saxophonics (still a regular) along with Jack Irons, Tim Alexander, and Mirv. He named the group the Frog Brigade because Mountain Aire is also the site of the competition described by Mark Twain in his 1867 story "The Notorious Jumping Frog of Calaveras County." A month later, when Claypool performed at the Gathering of the Vibes, he enlisted RatDog members Jay Lane and Jeff Chimenti as members of Les Claypool's Rat Brigade. Ultimately, however, the Frog won out. (While we're on the topic of names, for a time the bass player called himself Colonel Claypool, though he eventually demoted himself in deference to the Colonel of Colonels, Mr. Bruce Hampton, and as of late has abandoned a military tag altogether.)

Initially the band performed material Claypool had written for Sausage and the Holy Mackerel (Lane had joined him in both projects) along with music from such prog bands as King Crimson and Pink Floyd. As for Floyd, while the Brigade initially presented "Shine On You Crazy Diamond," it soon began covering the *Animals* album in its entirety. ("I always wanted to play 'Pigs.' So we were sitting around deciding what we're going to do. Just coming off Primus, I wasn't in a big hurry to write tunes at that point. I had a bunch of tunes sitting around but I wanted to possibly use those with Oysterhead. So we were looking at various covers to interpret. I had always wanted to play 'Pigs,' it's one of my favorite songs ever but I never had the instrumentation. All of a sudden I had a keyboardist, and I've always told myself if I had a keyboardist I would play 'Pigs.' The next thing you know we're learning 'Pigs,' and I said let's learn the whole album; we'll do two sets and away we go.")

The Brigade builds on Claypool's signature aggressive, dynamic bass, and skewed, theatrical stage demeanor. Skerik is a fine foil in this context, as he offers a boisterous counterpoint through his sax effects. Dreadlocked guitarist Eenor thrashes in as well, while Jay Lane and Mike Dillon color and construct. Some can't get past Claypool's pinched, nasal vocals while others feel his voice serves the frenetic carnival rather well. In assessing his current endeavor, Claypool laughs, "I've done way more bass solos than I've ever done in my entire life. I'm doing all the things I was always told that nobody wanted to see. For years you sit down with your friends and you jam for hours on end. You drink beers and everybody trades licks. But it was never thought by anyone that I hung out with, that people might actually want to see that. That was something for the rehearsal space. It just blows my mind that there's this huge community of people that want to see players do that." Plus, unlike Primus shows, the audience typically doesn't hurl detritus at the stage.

Eenor (left) and Les Claypool of the Frog Brigade.

Purple Onion (2002) ★★★★

While *Purple Onion* is not likely to convert the uninitiated, others will revel in this release written, produced, and engineered by Claypool. The range of sounds makes for an auditory buffet (heavy on the prog-fried Primus and Psychedelic Sausage). While not every morsel ultimately proves enticing, you have to admire the spread.

Live Frogs Set 2 (2001) ★★★

Here the band offers its take on the Pink Floyd album *Animals*. It is certainly an impressive feat ("Dogs" is the keeper), though not necessarily a record that one will return to time and again (at least not while Floyd's version is still out there).

Live Frogs Set 1 (2001) ★★★★

This disc took honors at the 2001 Jammy Awards for Live Release of the Year. It opens with King Crimson's "Thela Hun Ginjeet" and closes with Pink Floyd's "Shine On You Crazy Diamond," with plenty of invigorating demented takes on Claypool's Sausage and Holy Mackerel material sandwiched between.

LETTUCE
www.lettucefunk.com

The initial *Lettuce Live* tape release indicated that the band's debut CD would arrive in January 1998. Four and a half years later, this promise was realized with *Outta Here*. Yet the band members had not been dawdling. In the interim, guitarist Eric Krasno founded

Soulive, and Sam Kininger joined him for a spell on alto sax. Drummer Adam Deitch took to the road with the Average White Band and later with John Scofield. Tenor saxophonist Ryan Zoidis toured and recorded as a member of Rustic Overtones. Adam Smirnoff played guitar with the Squad and ran a Brooklyn, New York, recording studio. Jeff Bhaksker played keys with Kudu. Bassist Erick Coomes began a career as a music producer. Yet through it all, these seven active, gifted players shared a fealty for the funk.

The band members' technical command should not be surprising given the fact that they met at the Berklee College of Music. Actually, to be precise, they met as high school students at the Berklee summer program, where Krasno and Zoidis walked the halls in search of like-minded players. Later, they all enrolled at Berklee, where their collective exuberance yielded the group's name ("Let us borrow your gear, let us set up and play in the corner, let us..."). Although they trailed off to pursue various projects, friendships endured, and the musicians came together when scheduling allowed for gigs and sessions, as reflected in the titles of such Lettuce compositions as "Reunion" and "Back in Effect."

Lettuce evokes the heyday of James Brown and P-Funk with some Headhunters swirled in for spice. Yet this is not a tribute band—the group offers original instrumental music that references its heroes and celebrates a sound, but does so with a modern musical lexicon. In the live setting the band also introduces some jazzier runs. Still, at the core is '70s funk. If you dig it, you'll dig it.

Outta Here (2002) ★★★ ½

Bounding out of the gate with Fred Wesley on the title track very much sets the tone. The enthusiasm holds sway, as John Scofield drops in as well, while Tonni Smith's vocals add soul to "Twisted." Lettuce lets loose on the live "Nyack" that closes the disc.

LITTLE FEAT

www.littlefeat.net

Just remember: Legends can still learn, too. During the summer of 2000, Phil Lesh invited Little Feat guitarist Paul Barrere and keyboard player Bill Payne to join him on the road for six weeks (Bob Dylan opened 31 shows, with Robben Ford and John Molo also Phil's Friends for this stretch). The results reverberated, as Payne explains, "Phil reintroduced to us the art of jamming, and also the art of leaving yourself open to play other people's music—the beauty and fun of it... We obviously have always done it in our way, but it really was a gift that Phil gave us. I can't stress it enough; it revitalized us."

Now, one should certainly exercise restraint before ascribing legend status to any group, but Little Feat does indeed merit the designation (even if "restraint" has not always been the band's byword. Indeed, Frank Zappa encouraged Feat founder Lowell George to leave the Mothers of Invention and form the new group not only in recognition of the guitarist's prowess but because Zappa, a freak with straight laces when it came to drug use, was uncomfortable with George's song "Willin'," which contained references to "weed, whites, and wine." Come to think of it, exercise was often neglected, as well, as George, a former devotee of the martial arts, weighed nearly 300 pounds at the time of his fatal heart attack). As a collective entity, the group that George assembled in 1969 with fellow Mother Roy Estrada on bass, Richie Hayward on drums, and Payne on keys remains a palpable presence and influence (some of the band's tunes have become rock standards, including "Dixie Chicken," which the Rock & Roll Hall of Fame selected as one of the "500 Songs that Shaped Rock & Roll." There is only one other group in this book that shares such recognition—feel free to ponder for a few moments).

As individual players, the current septet has contributed to numerous noteworthy sessions and tours, including those of Duane Allman, Gregg Allman, Joan Armatrading, Jackson Browne, Jimmy Buffet, Eric Clapton, Doobie Brothers, Bob Dylan, Buddy Guy, John Hiatt, Freddie King, Robert Palmer, Robert Plant, Bonnie Raitt, Bob Seger, Carly Simon, James Taylor, Tom Waits, and Warren Zevon. (Oh yes, as for the Allmans, their band is the other one from these pages that is represented in the Rock & Roll Hall of Fame's top 500 songs, for both "Whipping Post" and "Ramblin' Man." The Grateful Dead is on there too, with "Dark Star" and "Uncle John's Band." All in all, it's a solid list, but one might push for an additional Feat composition such as "Time Loves a Hero" to replace the Human League's "Don't You Want Me" or Duran Duran's "Hungry Like the Wolf," although such lists are designed for the kibbitz and quibble. Incidentally, one characteristic that the Grateful Dead and the ABB do not share with Little Feat is indoctrination into the Hall, though one has to believe that will be rectified.)

Four years into Little Feat's existence, the addition of three members who still remain with the group enabled the band to hit its stride (Payne certainly did, quite literally, along with many other piano techniques he introduced as Feat continued to move beyond its country roots-rock towards the syncopated sounds of New Orleans with a more pronounced jazz and funk feel). Guitarist Barrere freed George to focus on his slide playing, which he carried into terrain well beyond that of traditional Delta blues while introducing some rich tones and urgent sustain. Meanwhile, the rhythm section took on layers with Kenny Gradney replacing Estrada on bass and Sam Clayton joining on percussion. The first album with this roster, *Dixie Chicken,* buttressed the reputation not only of the band, but of its members. The group received critical approbation along with moderate mainstream support, while fellow musicians were among Little Feat's biggest advocates, often drawing in its members for studio work. By decade's end, the group's focus had dissipated a bit (an apt word to describe George, as his lifetime of indulgence ultimately bested him on the morning of June 29, 1979).

In the years following George's death, his bandmates mostly concerned themselves with other artists' studio schedules and tour itineraries until a few loose reunion sessions led to Little Feat's return in 1988, marked by *Let It Roll.* Barrere moved over to slide, and for a second guitarist the group nabbed Fred Tackett, who had known the band throughout its existence and had contributed a song ("Fool Yourself") to *Dixie Chicken.* For a vocalist the group considered two former collaborators, Bonnie Raitt and Robert Palmer, before inviting Craig Fuller (co-founder of the country-rock group Pure Prairie League, who shared a similar vocal range with George though his intonations often differed) and later Shaun Murphy, who began touring a few years afterwards when Fuller begged off the road. (Murphy, a veteran of the Seger and Clapton bands, appeared on each of Little Feat's studio records since *Let It Roll,* 17 years after she first charted a single with a pre-Jim Steinman Meatloaf as Stoney & Meatloaf).

Little Feat's live shows continue to introduce many of the songs penned by George along with older material and new compositions from the current roster, often embellished with precise yet playful soloing (and as befits its Zappanimated origins, things occasionally get a bit odd but never too spacey). The group has welcomed a resurgence of younger listeners through its association with Lesh and by building relationships with such groups as Leftover Salmon and String Cheese Incident. (SCI's Kyle Hollingsworth named Payne the nicest person in the music community in a *Bonnaroo Beacon* interview.) New ears also embraced Little Feat's cover of Phish's "Sample in a Jar," which emerged from a Mockingbird Foundation request for Feat to participate in a Phish tribute album. One suggestion for the record was Allan Toussaint's "On Your Way Down" from *Dixie Chicken,* later interpreted by Phish, though this raised some complexities. As the group joked, "So are we doing us doing them doing us?"

While Payne and his band mates graciously credit Lesh and others for revitalizing Little Feat, most of the impact flows in the other direction, as reinforced at the Lisner Auditorium on October 14, 2002, during a charity performance that included guest appearances by Sam Bush, Drew Emmitt, Béla Fleck, Warren Haynes, Vince Herman, Jimmy Herring, Sonny Landreth, and many others. The musicians presented much of the material from Little Feat's *Waiting for Columbus,* recorded at the Lisner nearly 25 years earlier, celebrating the band for its live efforts—a sentiment long shared by jamband enthusiasts.

Ripe Tomatoes Vol 1/ Raw Tomatoes Vol 1 (2002) ★★★★

Both of these two-CD sets are divided into the "Lowell Era," the "Craig Era," and "Little Feat Now." Despite the continuum, some will prefer individual discs from each period.

Live at the Ram's Head (2002) ★★★

Paul Barrere and Fred Tackett are on acoustic guitars for this performance from June 2001. This aspect adds some new hues to mostly familiar material.

Hotcakes and Outtakes (2000) ★★★★½

A four-CD box set with elaborate, amusing liners. The package offers essential cuts plus live tracks and "studio artifacts" dating back to the Lowell George era. A fine balance that should interest both newbies and stalwarts.

Chinese Work Songs (2000) ★★★½

This well-founded studio effort is marked by some unlikely cover choices, including Phish's "Sample in a Jar" and the Hooters' "Gimme a Stone."

Under the Radar (1998) ★★★

Vocalist Shaun Murphy plays a more active role in this collection that delivers tasteful playing even if many of the originals lack command.

Live from Neon Park (1996) ★★★

The version of "Dixie Chicken" feels boundless, though not all of the cuts on this two-CD set are equally dynamic.

Let It Roll (1988) ★★★★

Little Feat's return with Craig Fuller on vocals affirmed that the group was still capable of crafting bright, crackling compositions.

Waiting for Columbus (1978) ★★★★★

The band's only live album released during the George era remains a vital listen. The expanded version is the way to go, with two tracks cut from the original along with bonus material.

Dixie Chicken (1973) ★★★★★

The essential, influential Feat album as the group expands to a six-piece band.

Also:

Ain't Had Enough Fun (1995)
Shake Me Up (1991)
Representing the Mambo (1989)
Hoy Hoy (1981)
Down on the Farm (1979)
Time Loves a Hero (1977)
The Last Record Album (1975)
Feats Don't Fail Me Now (1974)
Sailin' Shoes (1972)
Little Feat (1971)

Fan site:
www.featbase.net

Discussion list:
www.littlefeat.net/_Comm/hoyhoy.html

LIVING DAYLIGHTS
www.livingdaylights.com

Living Daylights bassist Arne Livingston has the definitive response. When pressed to characterize the instrumental trio's sound, he'll explain that the group plays local music. The band first came together in Seattle but his comment does not exclusively target a geographic ambit. Livingston is instead describing the multiformity of players and performances that captivate him and drummer Dale Fanning and saxophone/flautist Jessica Lurie. The band absorbs these and delivers its own art through such frames without any consideration for a particular style, proceeding from an internal logic to craft music of a most personal, localized nature.

Well that's fine and dandy, but what the heck does the band sound like? In part, Living Daylights presents downtown New York jazz animated by African percussion and an array of bass effects that can prove buoyant or close-textured to suit funk passages or something a bit more avant. The lead voice typically belongs to Lurie's alto and tenor saxes, which are fluent in Zorn and Coleman yet offer varied accents and tonalities to keep the sound vibrant. Lurie's leads can be challenging, but she rarely jettisons melody altogether, and she can hit the sweet spots as well (which she continues to do in a variety of contexts—from her work with her own projects such as the Billy Tipton Memorial Saxophone Quartet and the Jessica Lurie Ensemble, to guest appearances, for instance, with the Dirty Dozen Brass Band at the 2002 Jammys. Her band mates similarly thrive in other settings: Livingston started playing with the Steve Kimock Band in February 2003, and Dale Fanning joins many of his wife Magdalen Hsu-Li's multimedia performances).

Before Living Daylights the band and *Living Daylights* the Bond film, there was living daylights the expression (as for the movie, frankly, the less said the better, though Timothy Dalton's dark and dour 007 is a fit contrast to the winking Roger Moore and a bit old school, in that his Bond is a smoker). "Daylights" is a centuries-old term referring to eyes, which is an apt phrase given the group's depth of vision. The members' spectrum of interests and inclinations also has rendered the collective a collaborative one, and over the years the entire band has joined others onstage, in particular the Slip. The two trios gigged infrequently as the Slipping Daylights (recordings circulate, and the groups also released a limited edition disc of its 61-minute improvisation from the High Sierra Music Festival on July 4, 1999).

As for the Living Daylights' own efforts, a dichotomy exists in that some listeners have found the group's sound overly experimental while others wish the band would push its music further beyond structure. Of course, many others are digging on the LD just as it is, rendering its three players local heroes to a boundless community.

Night of the Living Daylights (2003) ★★★★
The first live release from the band predominantly presents Lurie's material as well as Ornette Coleman's "Ramblin'" and Wayne Shorter's "Adam's Apple." The results carry more of an angular jazz swagger than *Electric Rosary*. Elizabeth Pupo-Walker from the Billy Tipton Memorial Saxophone Quartet adds percussion to four songs on this playful, incisive disc.

Electric Rosary (2000) ★★★★
Bill Frisell adds guitar to a number of the tracks on this crackling studio release produced by his longtime collaborator Lee Townsend. Each of the band members contributes songs to *Electric Rosary*, which offers clusters of funk and bop along with a number of Eastern European themes.

Also:
500 Pound Cat (1998)
Falling Down Laughing (1995)

LLAMA
www.houseofllama.com
If you were to make an assumption about Llama based solely on its name, you'd probably be mistaken. No, Llama is not a former Phish cover band that has started to introduce its own originals. Instead the name is a vestige of the group's original moniker, the Dahlia Llamas.

Similarly, if you were to draw conclusions based on the 11 songs that appear on the band's debut, *Close to the Silence,* you would likely make another error. Llama is not a modern pop-rock band, propped up by a creative recording engineer who offers up live shows that aim solely to reproduce radio fare with little interest in straying from the arrangements. Instead, as the hidden track on that disc suggests, while the band does have a gift for writing catchy melodies and hooks with a nod to both Toad The Wet Sprocket and the Dave Matthews Band, Llama also wants to stretch out, as well.

In some ways the band's story is akin to that of Lana Turner in the ice cream shop, but this one takes place in a pizza parlor. Ben Morton (vocals, acoustic guitar), Ben Brown (electric guitar), and Neil Mason (drums) were in their mid-teens when they began performing weekly gigs at Nashville's Guido's. Producers Kenny Greenberg and Matt Rollins came in one night, liked what they heard, and offered to produce a demo that the pair eventually brought to MCA Records. Label President Jay Boberg came down for a pizza-place gig and signed the band. Soon after recording *Close to the Silence*, the trio expanded to a quintet and hit the road in earnest. Llama has had some help along the way, not only from the label but also from supporters like fellow Nashville resident Bela Fleck, who makes a guest appearance on the band's debut. The group also garnered a slot at the first Bonnaroo Music Festival.

Llama continues to place emphasis on its songwriting and Morton's rich vocals. The quintet is still coming together as an improvisational outfit, moving beyond some simpler funk exercises into more textured realms. Regardless, this is a band with a melodic rock edge to it, one that holds particular appeal for those who appreciate such fare.

World from Here (2002) ★ ★ ½
A four-song EP that is sparer on the production side, offering a bit more of the acoustic/electric guitar dynamic. The disc closes out with "Serena," a funky nine-minute instrumental with some sweeping gestures as well.

Close to the Silence (2001) ★ ★ ½
This one sounds like a modern rock radio staple, which isn't to say that it's bad, just that it's comfortable (in a crunching, echoey kind of way). Ben Morgan's powerful vocals carry many of these songs in accord with the emotional charge of the lyrics.

LO FABER BAND
www.lofaber.com
Following God Street Wine's final three-night stand at Wetlands Preserve in December 1999, the band's co-founder/vocalist/principal songwriter Lo Faber seemed to vanish. He actually did disappear in many respects, moving from Manhattan to a converted barn in upstate New York to unwind (or perhaps he had to rewind—if you get it, you get it). There he built a studio and focused on production, working on a range of projects including Jason Crosby's debut and a double live CD from the concluding God Street Wine shows. However, he rarely played out and he didn't write much original material.

Two years later, a blizzard inspired him to write the first lines of the song "Magic Days," which in turn initiated a spurt of creativity that resulted in the "jam-rock opera" *Henry's House*. This double CD is a children's story that follows the adventures of a young boy and his friends who need to vanquish a trio of nefarious, magical foes (Bubsy Beals, Crafty Fox, and Volcano Boy). Over the course of four months, Faber wrote and recorded 22 songs, mostly in chronological order, working from two principles:

"When I got to the end of a song, I thought, 'What would sound cool musically here, and where does it lead me in the story?' For instance, I wrote 'When We Were Very Young' and I thought, 'The end of this tune is in *C* major, if I was playing live with a band I'd jam it in to *C* minor.' And that's what happens on the record. When I played with God Street we had a number of jams that really could go any number of places, and I tried to think in that mindset—if I had been jamming with the band and the whole album was a jam up to this point, where would I be trying to take it right now?"

While he recorded many of the rough tracks himself, Faber enlisted other musicians to help him complete *Henry's House,* most often three members of the Ominous Seapods (drummer Ted Marotta, bass player Tom Pirozzi, and guitarist Todd Pasternack), who would return home intermittently from tour to play on the latest tracks. The music itself builds on the God Street sound adding beat boxes, choral harmony, and a bit of electronica.

Faber had such an enjoyable time writing and recording *Henry's House* that it led him back to the road. He assembled as many of the core HH players as possible, including the three Pods and opera singer Angela Ford, making her debut in a rock setting. (Faber jokes, "When we were recording it was a little harder for her, she had to match my phrasing on all my vocals, and when you sing opera you're taught to sing a certain way and enunciate. Eventually I had to tell her that when she's singing my stuff, no more enunciation. Slur more.") The band worked up some God Street Wine staples in addition to the *Henry's House* material and began touring.

Meanwhile, Faber started exploring the idea of bringing *Henry's House* to the stage. Eventually he found an able accomplice in Kevin McGuire, a Broadway veteran and former lead in *Les Miserables* who also was Artistic Director of the Theater Company at Hubbard Hall in Cambridge, New York (relatively close to Faber's home). McGuire mounted a full production with the Lo Faber Band providing music and doubling to play some roles (Lo, appropriately, as Henry's father, Ford as the kindly Teacher Tess, and Pasternack as Bubsy Beals). The show opened to favorable reviews in August 2002, and Broadway prospects loom, even as Faber moves on to another extended song cycle (!) and tour.

Henry's House (2003) ★★★

The story has a few gaps (which were filled out in the musical), but the narrative still holds together through these 22 songs. All in all it's an energetic effort, sustained by the vocal readings. At times the album borders on excess, but hey—what do you expect from a jam-rock opera?

LOTUS

www.lotusvibes.com

The Lotus entry in our ongoing, oft-hyphenated, name-it-yourself sweepstakes (see the Ally, the Disco Biscuits, etc.) is "organic ambient trance-funk." And yes, once again, the band just about nails it. This quintet creates instrumental music in the livetronica vein that does indeed have an organic vibe—not only because the group uses percussion as well as a kit to color the music, but because its predilection for collective improv yields, in its finer moments, a sound unto itself.

The group formed at Indiana's Goshen College in 1999, though bass player Jesse Miller and his guitarist brother Luke have been playing together a bit longer. The Barr Brothers of the Slip are a reference point because of a common affinity for extemporization and to emphasize that Lotus is a young band whose stated influences include not only Herbie Hancock, Aphex Twin, and Babatunde Olatunji (an interesting triad in its own right), but also Sound Trip Sector 9, the New Deal, and, yes, the Slip. One characteristic the band shares with the New Deal is that much of its music is improvised in the live setting where the group typically builds on themes rather than songs. Unlike the New Deal, however, the Lotus sound is often dreamy and atmospheric rather than pulsing and insistent (and at times some find it too ethereal). The dynamic changed a bit in early 2003 when second guitarist Mike Rempel departed the group, yet this provided an opportunity for Lotus to enrich its palette by adding keyboards.

Vibes (2002) ★★★

The aptly named *Vibes* collects ten improvised pieces drawn from five live shows in the fall of 2001. Some of these soundscapes linger on a particular idea longer than they might, and the group is still defining its approach, but this is a fine first effort that gives one a feel for the band's big ears and nimble touch.

Also:
Germination (2003)

MADAHOOCHI
www.madahoochi.com

Sometimes all it takes is a locus, a means to gather, propel, and nurture a nascent music scene. In St. Louis, Missouri, three interlaced entities have served this purpose rather well: a venue—Cicero's (home of the Battle of the Jambands), a Web site—Moheads.com ("Serving the Midwest jamband revolution"), and a radio show—"Stumble in the Dark" (a two-time Jammy nominee hosted by James Mullins). This confluence has aided national acts, comfortable in the knowledge that they can route through the area and find a favorable environment. Of course, some beneficiaries have also been local bands, one of them being Madahoochi.

In order to receive such support, one needs to produce music that merits it. Madahoochi is well on the way. Originally formed in 1996, the group writes songs that aspire to vest colorful melodies with varied time signatures and complexities. There is certainly a pop side as well, accentuated by the warm vocal harmonies of Shawn Hartung and Scott Rockwood. Hartung's contributions also prove conspicuous, since the keyboard player is one of the rare female instrumentalists among her peers (and the lone female on keys in this book). While the band's singing often proves absorbing, Madahoochi continues to develop a signature instrumental sound, beyond solely a pastiche of many elements (groove-rock, roots, some jazz, a bit of funk). As of late the quartet is honing its approach and interplay through an extended residency at Cicero's. If this proves fruitful and Madahoochi's canorous songs carry it beyond the Midwest, the St. Louis jam-appreciation network will have served its goals and enjoyed some fine nights of music in the process.

Big Bang Medley (2002) ★★★

The disc offers a well-founded, euphonious collection of songs. Some hold only slight, fleeting appeal while others, such as the title track and "Shih-Tzu," certainly linger.

Also:

Movin' On (1999)

MARLOW

www.marlowmusic.net

Todd Pasternack has set a challenging course for himself. While he is best known for his guitar work with the Lo Faber Band and the latter-day Ominous Seapods, his Marlow project eschews explosive soloing to focus on the presentation of songs. Not only that, but much of the music he first recorded under the Marlow moniker carries a somber tone, chronicling a deteriorating relationship.

Pasternack expresses his appreciation for those listeners familiar with his roles in the Seapods and the Lo Faber Band, yet he acknowledges that, "There are times when I'm really conflicted with it. There are times when I'm like, 'Why the hell did I get into this scene when all I want to do is write solid songs and not have to worry about an audience saying when the hell are they going to jam already?' But I'm thankful to have support and I don't think I'm underestimating

jamband audiences. I think they get music like this." Pasternack is still developing as a songwriter, but some of his Marlow compositions certainly resonate, and a burgeoning fan base is responding to them.

Marlow has toured in a few incarnations. Initially, Pasternack took to the road with the members of the Lo Faber Band (including Faber himself) who had joined him in the studio to record his debut, *White Out*. He also has performed as a solo artist with Faber Band keyboardist Devin Greenwood on the No Repression Tour, and later with fellow Faber alum Angela Ford.

As for the band name itself, while Raymond Chandler's shamus comes to mind, Pasternack was inspired by another notable Marlow, the narrator of Joseph Conrad's *Heart of Darkness* (referencing that Marlow's famous journey in *White Out*). With his characteristic humor (which makes some of the *White Out* music additionally jarring) Pasternack adds, "I told my friends that I'm going to treat the name like Moby or Sting and they said, 'Dude, if you think we're going to start calling you Marlow, you're crazy.'"

White Out (2002) ★★★

Members of the Lo Faber Band back Pasternack quite ably for much of this release. At times it is a bit solemn and droning, but the best songs engage in an Aimee Mann pop-rock vein, including "The Goodbye Girl," the gentle "(Do You Wanna Fall) in Love," and "Under the Wire," which also hints at where Marlow might take some of this music in the live setting.

MAX CREEK

www.maxcreek.com

Max Creek endures. In 1972 the group was out there gigging steadily in the clubs, appealing to its stalwarts with a vivid, shuffling mix of original music and covers. In 1982 Max Creek was out there gigging steadily in the clubs, appealing to its stalwarts with a vivid, shuffling mix of original music and covers. In 1992 Max Creek was out there gigging steadily in the clubs, appealing to its stalwarts with a vivid, shuffling mix of original music and covers. In 2002...you guessed it: Max Creek was out there gigging steadily in the clubs, appealing to its stalwarts with a vivid, shuffling mix of original music and covers. The group has remained a steady presence—a New England fixture in particular—returning to many of the same venues over its 30-plus years of history (passing through multiple incarnations of Rhode Island's Living Room and Lupo's Heartbreak Hotel). While the band has put out a series of albums, it never has committed itself fully to national touring, instead very much embodying the ideal of music for music's sake.

While bass player John Rider is the lone founding member, the core has been in place for a few decades. Rider formed the group as a country trio when it came together in 1971. However, the band soon incorporated an electric blues side, tapping keyboard player Mark Mercier and 15-year-old guitarist Scott Murawski. While the two other founding members have long since moved on along with a few other players, percussionist Rob Fried signed on in 1979, joined in the mid-'90s by drummer Scott Allshouse.

For a long time, the band was closely associated with the Grateful Dead, as Creek first incorporated a number of the Dead's songs into its sets in the mid-'70s (marking it as one of the first groups to do so). Murawski recalls, "We weren't really a cover band, but that's what the bars were selling. So they'd bill us as a 'Tribute to the Grateful Dead.' We were like 'Stop, please.' But at least it was bringing the right clientele in, people who could appreciate what we were doing." At present, Dead compositions are fairly rare at any of the band's typically two-set shows of predominately original music. The most Grateful Dead one will likely hear is a traditional song associated with the group. Still, the band's psychedelic-tinged polyrhythmic roots music often does retain that Dead feel.

Max Creek has a vibrant fan base that often communicates daily via the message board on its Web site. The signature event for this community is the group's Camp Creek, which first took place in 1982 and has been held at the Indian Lookout Country Club in Mariaville, New York, since 1994 (in addition to multiple sets from the hosts, a number of groups perform, many of whom later sit in with Creek, such as Derek Trucks, Mike Gordon, Tom Tom Club, Jeff Pevar, and ekoostik hookah). Indeed, the supportive, family vibe that surrounds the group has resulted in numerous next-generation Creek Freeks. As Murawski notes, "The audiences have been basically 18- to 25-year-olds ever since I was 15. When I first started doing it, I was looking up at these older hippies saying, 'I'm out of my league.' Then I was the same age as everyone at the bars, and it just kind of stayed there for a while. Then slowly but surely

I started noticing that these kids were getting younger and younger. Now I'm playing to kids who could be my kids. It's kind of weird."

Spring Water (1998) ★★★

This release culls mostly newer originals from a two-night run at Hartford, Connecticut's Webster Theater. Some of this material has a familiar aspect to it, but the band's interplay and improv offers some sparkling moments.

Drink the Stars (1982) ★★★ ½

There is something of a dated feel to this double live CD that also features vocalist Amy Fazzano. Even so, there is a crackling, earthy energy to these songs, many of which remain Creek standards. *Drink the Stars* stands as a rousing document of a band completing its first decade of music.

Out of print:

Max Creek (1977)
Rainbow (1980)
Windows (1986)
XMCMC (1990)
Live at the Connecticut Expo Center New Years 1999-2000 (2000)

Related:

Scottness (2000) ★★ ½
Guitarist Scott Murawski interprets some Max Creek staples and newer originals in a more minimalist setting with drummer Scott Allshouse. At times the material outstrips the vocals, but this range of material that moves from demos to more polished offerings will certainly intrigue Creek boosters and interest others as well.

Selected fan sites:

Max Creek set list page—*www.max.creek.com*
Tony's Max Creek Page—
www.home.attbi.com/~heartbt/creek.html

MCCLOSKEY BROTHERS BAND
www.tmbb.net

The story behind the formation of the McCloskey Brothers Band puts a new spin on the phrase "mountain music." David and Todd McCloskey were riding a chairlift at Snowmass in their hometown of Aspen, Colorado, in the late '90s, discussing whether they should commit themselves fully to a band. As snow spiraled around the two, they decided to leave their decision to the elements, vowing to pursue a professional career if the weather cleared by the time they reached the summit. It did, indeed, turn out to be "sunny on top," which yielded a song and a record label of the same name along with the McCloskey Brothers Band.

While the band members are comfortable with grass both blue and new (David is a banjo instructor at the University of Colorado), their music travels a different trail. The brothers' banjo and mandolin are up front, yet these instruments are placed into a rock context, and the MBB most certainly does not offer high and lonesome vocals (there are decent harmonies, however). David and Todd, who located to Aspen in their youth, often write material that celebrates their surroundings in song and has a spiritual side to it as well. This earnest approach distinguishes the band a bit from their peers, even if the accompanying music is not always distinctive. Still, anchored by drummer Dan Menchey (Mucis) and bass player Steve Roseboom (Runaway Truck Ramp), the band is actively working on their sound, as David has started to play piano on a few tunes to vary the tones at some of their oft-lengthy gigs.

The McCloskey Brothers Band (2002) ★★★

The band uses the studio rather well to fill out these 15 concise tracks. While the banjo and mandolin are up front, the group also layers in complementary guitar and organ lines. The songs are melodious and well crafted, if sometimes commonplace. Extrinsic to the music but worthy of note is John Russell's gorgeous glossy photography of the Colorado landscape that accompanies the disc.

MEDESKI MARTIN AND WOOD

www.mmw.net

It was a long, hard road to Hookahville, but on Memorial Day Weekend in 2002, Medeski Martin and Wood finally made it. If you detect a wisp of sarcasm, it's no disrespect to Hookahville (or the Gathering of the Vibes or moe.down or Walther's Grass Roots Fest)—it's just that when John Medeski, Billy Martin, and Chris Wood came together for their initial gig in summer 1991 at New York City's Village Gate, the notion they would one day perform for thousands at an event like Hookahville was as remote as the notion they would one day be invited to record with Iggy Pop (which they were, for a few tracks on Iggy's 1999 release, *Avenue B*).

Medeski Martin and Wood are a jazz trio. They spent their formative years training and gigging in this context (actually, rather than formative years, let's call that era their pre-MMW days because, as with many vital bands

committed to improvisation, the group's sound is by no means static, and their formative years continue). Medeski began as a classical pianist in Florida, but an increased exposure and affinity for jazz as a teenager led him to enroll at Boston's New England Conservatory of Music to further his studies in both genres. Drummer Martin thrust himself into the New York jazz scene at age 18, both gigging and studying under other percussionists before his involvement with the Drummers Collective eventually led him to a European tour with Bob Moses. From there, Martin ventured into other projects, including a few years with Chuck Mangione's band (while Mangione and his flugelhorn are best known for 1978's "Feel So Good," now a lite FM staple, Mangione performed with Art Blakey's Jazz Messengers early in his career and retained an affection for bop while later moving towards Afro-Cuban rhythms, which is why he tapped Martin). Wood performed as a bassist in Colorado's all-state high school jazz orchestra before he, too, entered NEC (while growing up, Wood developed on his instrument apace with his guitarist brother Oliver, who has gone on to tour with Tinsley Ellis and is a founding member of King Johnson).

Indeed, it was a Byzantine path to Hookahville, and along the way not only would Medeski Martin and Wood come to be hailed by a nontraditional jazz audience, but would influence many younger musicians within the burgeoning jamband scene.

Some of the trio's initial exposure to these fresh ears took place via Phish. During the Vermont quartet's fall 1995 tour, Phish announced only one official opening act, MMW, for a performance at New Orleans'

State Palace Theater on October 17. In Phish's newsletter, the Doniac Schvice, Trey Anastasio introduced the sounds of Medeski Martin and Wood as "music that makes me want to drive too fast." Three nights prior to the New Orleans date, both bands gigged in Austin, with MMW emerging during the Phish show for "You Enjoy Myself" and Anastasio joining MMW for both of their late-night sets. (MMW subsequently sat in with Phish at the State Palace Theater gig.) As a result, a spate of new listeners—who otherwise might have guessed that "Medeski Martin and Wood" was an entity best consulted for personal injury litigation—sought out MMW's most recent disc and found themselves drawn by the insistent grooves of *Friday Afternoon in the Universe.*

(An aside to placate snippy folks who feel that Phish is given too much credit for broader developments within the current music scene: It is important to emphasize that MMW's music certainly stood on its own. Just as important, MMW acquired traction with this new crowd because they pursued a different mode of touring than many of their peers. Wood recalls that after he left the New England Conservatory, "I guess I assumed that what you do is learn jazz, then become a sideman to some famous jazz musician and move to New York. I just didn't know what else was out there. There were no role models. I'd seen lots of musicians go off and become sidemen so I understood that and where that led. But this style of rock 'n' roll touring in a van, sleeping on people's floors and eventually living in a RV together was just beyond what I thought of as a musician wannabe kid in high school. When we found ourselves in a RV, sleeping in RV parks and touring around

the US, it was just one big improvisation. There was no road map to follow; we were just making it up as we went along.")

Drummer Bob Moses and John Lurie's New York-based Lounge Lizards both played a role in Medeski Martin and Wood's inception and development. Moses was the conduit who pulled the three musicians together, as he first worked with Medeski and Wood while teaching at the Conservatory and then introduced the pair to Martin, a former student via the Drummers Collective. (Moses has led a fascinating life in music that began while growing up in New York City as the son of Richard Moses, press agent for such artists as Max Roach and Rahsaan Roland Kirk. Moses has collaborated with a number of players who passed through his childhood, including Kirk. He went on to work with Larry Coryell and Gary Burton among many others, and comprised one third of the trio on Pat Metheny's *Bright Size Life* along with Jaco Pastorius. Moses's more recent projects include his heralded post-bop releases *When Elephants Dream of Music* and *Time Stood Still*, as well as his Mozamba project, which places world music into a jazz frame. Moses also retained a long-standing relationship with Charles Mingus, joining him first as a 12-year-old in piano and drum duets. This experience later led Moses to pen a notable missive to the *Boston Phoenix* in July 2001 in response to an article on a local saxophone player presenting a Mingus tribute. In the course of this letter he excoriates younger players who fail to tap the source, referencing some within the jamband scene. The text appears at Billy Martin's Amulet Records Web site and is worth a read).

As for Medeski Martin and Wood's appellation, the trio has credited Martin's former bandmate in the Lounge Lizards, bassist Oren Blowdoen, with suggesting they use their last names. Blowdoen was a suitable source since MMW's sound owes a bit to New York City's edgy downtown jazz scene, and over the years the trio has continued to work with former Lizards Steven Bernstein (Sex Mob) and Marc Ribot while also backing Blowdoen on his 1998 release, *Luckiest Boy in the World.*

Against this backdrop, Medeski Martin and Wood have come to shape a sound that continues to galvanize listeners (including numerous developing musicians). One significant moment took place a few years after the group's inception when Medeski moved from piano to the Hammond organ (necessitated in part by MMW's mode of touring), which initiated a resurgence of vintage keyboards in jamband circles. Similarly, the band's work with DJ Logic on 1998's *Combustication* helped promote the use of turntables within this realm (while also initiating the ubiquity of Logic).

MMW have never solely presented simple, accessible grooves, but in the late '90s the band moved further into experimental planes—certainly to challenge themselves but also because, one senses, they wished to re-establish their jazz credibility. Still, any criticism levied at MMW's fan base from the music elite seems ill founded. As long as the band remains true to their vision, there's no shame in cultivating an audience beyond the rarified air of traditional jazz rooms (and F 'em if they can't take a joke). Moreover,

Medeski Martin and Wood, geared up in Chicago.

Medeski Martin and Wood have helped promote the work of other estimable artists along the way, such as John Scofield (they backed him on his *A Go Go* disc) and Bob Moses (in part through Martin's Amulet Records). Indeed, there's something to be said for advancing this campaign, especially when serving as deputized mayors of Hookahville.

Uninvisible (2002) ★★★★
While on the surface this disc is something of a return to the groove-oriented approach of MMW's earlier efforts, producer Scotty Hard folds in some abstract chatter from the Antibalas horns and DJ Olive's turntables, along with his own guitar and that of Danny Blume to advance the music.

The Dropper (2000) ★★★ ½
Guitarist Marc Ribot plays on a number of these tracks that often harken back to the group's downtown origins. Some snarling, sparkling moments, but generally the feel is a bit scattered on this avant mosaic, which also features Marshall Allen along with bonus percussion and strings.

Tonic (2000) ★★★ ½
The band's follow-up to the bustling *Combustication* is a live acoustic offering that jettisons the acid from the jazz. The band's swagger remains, though the trio is often in more traditional terrain building on bop. The rhythm section is particularly resourceful throughout these eight songs evenly divided between originals and covers (John Coltrane, Lee Morgan, Bud Powell, and Billy Roberts's "Hey Joe").

Combustication (1998) ★★★★★
DJ Logic joins in for this invigorating, influential effort that melds the band's experimental musings with a steady, pulsing core. Chris Wood in particular holds it down as the three other players embellish.

Farmer's Reserve (1997) ★★★
Also recorded at the Hawaiian shack that was home to its previous release, this is a spare, abstract, mostly acoustic improvisation that anticipates some of the ideas on *Tonic* rather than revisiting those of *Shack Man*.

Shack Man (1996) ★★★★
A bit less urgent than its predecessor, *Shack Man* is awash in playful, burbling funk.

Friday Afternoon in the Universe (1995) ★★★★ ½
Medeski's robust declarations on the Hammond organ, Wurlitzer, and clavinet as well as Billy Martin's limber retorts animate these zesty, capacious grooves.

Also:
It's a Jungle in Here (1993)
Notes from the Underground (1992)

Fan site:
Set lists—*www.mmwsetlists.com*

Discussion list:
www.lists.netspace.org/archives/mmw.html

MODEREKO

www.modereko.com

Modereko is an anachronism. No, not the band, just the name. The group's inception can be traced to the Bruce Hornsby tour bus of 1994. It was there that John Molo (drums), John D'Earth (trumpet), and Bobby Read (sax, clarinet, flute) would just sit together and jam, improvising to while away the miles between gigs. During these sessions, Molo expressed his resolve to create music from the bottom up, starting with drum grooves and then allowing it to flow from there without any predisposition to a particular style or genre. A few years later he achieved that end, working with guitarist Tim Kobza on the West Coast and then sending tracks to D'Earth and Read in Virginia to color them as they saw fit. The resulting project and de facto band became known as Modereko, a tag supplied by taking the first two letters of each musician's last name.

Following some initial live dates in spring 2001 that coincided with the album release, the group has toured infrequently and for limited stints due to the many commitments of its personnel, which has since evolved to include Molo, Read, and Kobza along with J.T. Thomas on keys (another longtime Hornsby collaborator, whose professional career can be traced back to his efforts with Captain Beefheart's Magic Band at age 20) and bassist Dan Conway. Of course, given the present lineup, quibblers may note that the name Modereko is no longer precise.

While the group's eponymous debut contains only 39 minutes of music, it swells with modes and images (incorporating funk, boogaloo, bebop, blues, Latin, and electronica with shifting segues between songs). This was by design, as Molo explains: "What we didn't want to do was make a jazz record or a jam record where we'd play a little bit of an instrumental then play a long solo and then come back. I just thought that had been done so many times."

When the band members' itineraries do align for gigs, both soloing and group improvisation play a significant role. (Molo, for instance, is comfortable with each, trailing back to his initial work with Hornsby in 1979 and on through his participation in the Other Ones and Phil Lesh & Friends.) One can sense a palpable esprit and mirth when the musicians step away from their other projects and stretch out with Modereko. The band has carried a bit less brass since D'Earth's departure, but Thomas has infused his personality into the project. To that end, perhaps Mocothreko or Mothcoreko would be more apt, but hey—remember what your grandmother always said: It's the music, not the moniker.

Modereko (2001) ★ ★ ★ ½

On these ten tracks the production feels precise yet a looseness of spirit prevails. The concise nature of these songs enables one to appreciate the nuances the band lends to an essence of funk braced by jazz and tethered by samples and other soundscapes to promote flow.

MODERN GROOVE SYNDICATE

www.moderngroovesyndicate.com

You know the groove, you dig the groove, these guys deliver the groove. No, strike that. Frankly, not everyone is down with the groove, and some people find it to be a bit played out (along with the word groove). If you count yourself among this contingency, slide on to the next entry. However, if you're willing to drop by the old school as long as there's a vitalizing new class, then MGS should get you moving.

Modern Groove Syndicate came together in 1998 as one project among many for its founding members who were entrenched within the Richmond, Virginia, music scene. The group also provided an opportunity for bassist Todd Herrington, drummer Joel DeNinzio, and guitarist Frank Jackson to get together and cut loose as they had been doing off and on since their high school days a decade earlier, when they gigged in local bands. The trio soon recruited keyboard player Daniel Clarke, then a music student at Virginia Commonwealth University who was performing with a number of groups, particularly jazz combos (Clarke later did a stint on the road with John Molo's Modereko). The addition of J.C. Kuhl, the tenor sax player from Agents of Good Roots, solidified the current lineup in early 2001 while providing a strident new voice and some additional visibility.

As of late the five Syndicate members have stepped up their collective commitment to the group, putting other projects to the side. The band's shows are marked by an upbeat, rousing engagement with jazz-funk, as each of the musicians steps to the fore and pushes the sound to new crescendos. While the group mostly performs original music, a vigorous nod remains to the sounds of the Headhunters, the Crusaders, and the Meters. As the five players compose and perform together with heightened regularity, it bears watching where the music will carry them (and one hopes this will include additional novel regions). At present, though, it moves the group with a zeal and exuberance that envelops and ingratiates.

Modern Groove Syndicate (2001) ★★ ½
These six songs were recorded in July 2001 soon after J.C. Kuhl came on board. The result is a bright-hued funk with jazz flourishes that speaks well for the band, even as it shouts out its influences.

Also:
Vessel (2003)

MOE.
www.moe.org
It is a curious thing indeed when formlessness becomes formula. To a degree, this happened with fusion as Miles Davis's *Bitches Brew* led us down a discursive path to Mahavishnu Orchestra and Weather Report, and then much, much further downward to Kenny G (who made an early name for himself in such climes, quite literally, by recording with the Jeff Lorber Fusion, which is likely more than you'll ever need to know about Kenny G[orelick]—beyond the fact that Pat Metheny excoriated him for "musical necrophilia" when he overdubbed himself onto Louis Armstrong's "It's a Wonderful World"). The jamband realm isn't G'ed out yet, but it does come with its rites and rubric, particularly as manifested by neophytes. The majesty of moe., by contrast, is that to a large degree the group charted its own hyphenated trajectory.

moe.'s journey to jamband (now there's a Discovery Channel special) is a product of a Buffalo, NY, music scene in the late '80s to early '90s that did not always delineate stark genre designations. Al Schnier, who joined the group in late 1991 as moe.'s third guitarist (though one soon departed, yielding a tandem with Chuck Garvey that animates the group to this day), recalls, "The people who came out to the shows were open to us playing with a honky tonk band or a punk band or a ska band. That informed our attitude that we could play, and all types of music, and maybe that could be our directive." The band's propensity for improv developed apace, initially mandated by a need to fill out lengthy sets of music because the area bars didn't close until 4:00 A.M. To keep itself engaged, moe. also came to vary the time signatures, creating music that can be deceptively complex. As drummer Vinnie Amico observes, "Some bands will do a roosty rock tune, and it will sound like a roosty rock tune. We'll do a rootsy rock tune and throw six bars of seven in there or a bar of seven and a bar of five, something weird like that." (You may know Vinnie from such prime numbers as 5, as upon joining moe. in 1996 the group quickly dubbed him "#5." This tag resulted from moe.'s inclination to burn through drum-

moe. in Las Vegas, February 2003.

mers, with five different players behind the kits on its first five releases. Within a few years, moe. ended the Spinal Tap era and Vinnie acquired a new stage name—his own—although he will still occasionally sign autographs as #5.)

There have been plenty of crappy name puns along the way (but to be fair, the lamest have not been of the band's own devising). The group took its name from the Bresler/Wynn song "Five Guys Named Moe" popularized by Louis Jordan, eventually winnowing it down to moe. in late 1990 when a roster change rendered the quint a quart. (Incidentally, future Derek Trucks Band drummer Yonrico Scott was in the national touring company of the musical *Five Guys Named Moe* featuring Jordan's music, which ran for 445 performances on Broadway beginning April 8, 1992.) As for wordplay involving the band's name (of which none will appear in this entry, as a moe.ratoriurm is in effect— uhhh, okay, starting now), the best known and most satisfying may be the moe.down, the group's festival that premiered over Labor Day Weekend 2000. It offers three days of moe. and pals, and given the band members' eclectic musical tastes, the lineup has included Ani DiFranco, Cracker, the Flaming Lips, and They Might Be Giants. (The moe.down has also been a family affair, with the musicians' young children occasionally scrambling onto the stage, plus a kids' tent with a bonus acoustic set by Schnier. Indeed, given the fact that moe. busted out the Wiggles' "Fruit Salad" in concert on June 7, 2003, one can't rule out a future appearance by Steve "Blues Clues" Burns, particularly since his *Songs for Dustmites* is a collaboration with the Lips'

Steven Drozd and Michael Ivins.) Then there's the moe.llennium celebration, the moe.'s Tavern show, the Heavy moe.tal gig, and, of course, the moe. or Les festival (the culmination of a summer run with Les Claypool's Frog Brigade), which led to numerous collaborative jams—a moe. bailiwick—as over the years the group has solicited the participation of many artists, including Bob Weir, Dickey Betts, Trey Anastasio, and Dave Matthews. John Popper joined the band for the sit-in-so-nice-he-did-it-twice appearances, playing at moe.'s request on April 19, 2002, and then returning the next night because he had enjoyed himself so mightily. Plus there's the often-imitated, never-duplicated tag-team segue in which musicians from another group take the stage and slowly supplant moe. for a song before the band's gradual return. Participants include the Ominous Seapods (June 20, 1998), Gov't Mule (May 2, 2002), and Umphrey's McGee (May 2, 2003). Finally, any name game must include a reference to the fan faithful, many of whom have brazenly dubbed themselves moe.rons.

Willingness to engage in such gleeful self-debasement is not only a testament to the band's proficiency at improvisation over a range of styles, but a reflection of the fact that the best of moe.'s songs have hooks (or legs, or leggy hooks—at any rate, they're catchy). Audiences have found that it can be all the more satisfying when the band returns from an improvised abstraction into a rousing, euphonious chorus. Indeed, the group's gift for composition piqued the interest of Sony 550 Records, and in 1996 moe. was among the first of its peers to sign with a major label. (This prospect is slightly less enticing nowadays, given the state of the recording industry and the fact that many groups can self-release discs, target their fans directly through the Internet, and receive much higher royalties. Then again, a major offers recoupable advance money for recording and tour support, better opportunity for airplay through leveraged relationships with radio stations, and—perhaps most significantly—the ability to convince one's parents that this whole band thing really is working out, and maybe the myriad job prospects afforded by that comparative literature degree can be deferred for a few years.)

The Sony experience, which bassist Rob Derhak jokingly describes as "our first deal with the Death Star," yielded two strong releases, *No Doy* and especially *Tin Cans and Car Tires*, even if the band had to suffer through the machinations of "the record company's shlonkey, whose job it is to steer you in whatever direction they want you to go without letting you know that's the case." moe. departed with humility checked and humor intact. (The musicians remain stage banter laureates—speaking of which, note to band: The untitled Chuck Garvey song that you refer to as "Assfinger," Chuck has [re]named "Bullet." No really, he has.)

In 2003 moe. released *Wormwood,* a logical extension and significant advance. A few years earlier the music had appeared to stall, perhaps a product of the Sony relationship and a play for radio, until the band moved past this by bringing back former drummer Jim Loughlin (#2) on percussion while re-examining its sound and embracing the jamband within. In part, the group began focusing on its segues, striving, as Schnier affirms, "to make them unique each time but also trying to make them as seamless as possible." As an outgrowth, moe. decided to record its summer 2002 shows in an attempt to transplant its live puissance into the studio by using the basic tracks, including segues, to construct a studio disc (this process also enabled the band to create a holiday album during sound checks on the road, entering the province of Kenny G—and hey, who would have imagined we'd return to Kenny, but again, there's the splendor of the segue). With *Wormwood's* live/studio amalgam, once again the group has pursued an intuitive yet novel and potentially influential course. This has become the moe. m.o., going back to the band's early days when, Schnier jokes, "We knew we wanted to create music that would cross all genres, we just never thought of it as a viable career option."

Wormwood (2003) ★★★★

An innovative hybrid that uses the studio to build on basic tracks from live performances. Instrumental segues keep it all fluid while retaining their own identities as well.

Season's Greetings from moe. (2002) ★★★

If you're going to buy a jamband holiday album, then this is the one for you. An affable collection that scampers back and forth across the bounds of reverence. At times one wishes the band would either be more faithful to these songs or bust them wide open. Finer moments include Rob Derhak's "Together at Christmas" (one of two original songs), which is rich in seasonal sentiment, and the version of "We're a Couple of Misfits," which is a bit less so. (Caveat: If you live or work somewhere that blasts holiday music exclusively from Thanksgiving through New Year's, then you NEED this disc.)

Warts and All, Vol. 2 (2002) ★★★★

moe.'s listserve helped to select this show from Tabernacle in Atlanta, GA, on February 23, 2002, as the second installment of its live release series. *Vol. 2* outstrips the original in overall achievement regarding song selection, exploratory improv, and all-out sizzle.

Warts and All, Vol. 1 (2001) ★★★ ½

Don't believe the hype (or at least the packaging)—this show actually took place on February 28, 2001 (not April 23, 2001), at the Scranton Cultural Center Ballroom. The inaugural installment of the band's live series has some gripping moments, though some of the newer material remains inchoate.

Dither (2001) ★★★ ½

Here the band distills its songs to their essences and then layers additional effects and instrumentation. Some spry and resourceful moments, but while the production expands, it doesn't always augment.

L (2000) ★★★★ ½

Winner of the 2000 Jammy Award for Live Album of the Year, this double live disc presents the band soon after Jim Loughlin's return on percussion (and beyond). Loughlin, along with Vinnie Amico, propels the band through a vigorous collection of fan favorites. Use caution if listening behind the wheel because you will exceed the speed limit.

Tin Cans and Car Tires (1998) ★★★★ ½

Along with *Wormwood*, the best overall studio manifestation of moe. Incorporating a string section, horns, talk box, and a chorus crafted around the F-word, this one has it all.

No Doy (1996) ★★★★

The brightest and poppiest of moe.'s discs. As a result, some listeners may enjoy this release the most, while others may find it lacks bite.

Headseed (1993) ★★★ ½

A major improvement from *Fatboy* in terms of clarity and composition. These relatively straightahead takes are vivid and assertive.

Fatboy (1992) ★★ ½

The band's initial studio experience (technically less a studio than the apartment of a friend with a multitrack recorder) originally appeared as a tape in 1992 before its re-release on CD seven years later. Despite remastering, it sounds a bit flat and the vocals slightly distant. Stalwarts will likely want to hear the early band's progressive funk on these eight tracks that include the retired "Long Island Girls Rule" and "The Battle of Benny Hill" coda along with initial passes at many others still in action, such as "Spine of a Dog" and "Sensory Deprivation Bank."

Out of print:

"Meat" (1996), 45-minute maxi-single
Loaf (1995)

Related discs:

Al & the Transamericans—*Analog* (2003)
Al.one (2001)

Related site:

www.alschnier.com

MOFRO

www.mofro.net

A band's description of its sound often proves edifying and entertaining, particularly if that group challenges prevailing trends. This holds true for Mofro's self-designated, alternating tags: "cheap ass funk straight off the front porch" and "Southern-fried soul straight off the front porch." The porch is evocative and essential, hinting at the acoustic blues that supplies one facet of the band's sound. However, as both phrases also suggest, there are other fundaments, as Mofro often slides from slinky funk to full-on soul rave-ups.

Although the group is from Florida and its music often references the state's social and physical environment, founders John J.J. Grey (vocals, guitar) and Daryl Hance (guitar, dobro) assembled the band in London. The pair had moved to England from Jacksonville in 1994 at the behest of a label that expressed interest in a demo. There they placed an ad for musicians in *Melody Maker* and began writing much of the material that would appear on the group's debut, *Blackwater*. The deal fell apart however, and Mofro returned to the United States and signed with Fog City Records. Then, in October 2001, shortly after the release of *Blackwater* and just as Mofro started to gig nationally and build momentum, a car accident with an uninsured driver sidelined the group. Eventually, following physical therapy, and with the assistance of musicians who played benefits to defray medical bills, the group returned to the road six months later, securing slots at the Bonnaroo Music Festival and the Gathering of the Vibes as well as tours with Vida Blue and Galactic.

Grey's lyrics often express exasperation with the increasing homogenization of daily life and correlate environmental desecration with the collapse of community. Grey explains, "I feel like there's something to be said about a culture that's going away and being replaced by pop culture which has no ties to any natural surroundings. It just floats in off the airwaves, it has no roots anywhere. The local culture that had time to develop in conjunction with the natural surroundings sort of gets destroyed, and everything's replaced by shopping malls and carefully manicured lawns that really isn't relevant to Florida's natural Florida." The band ballasts this perspective through music that is of the present yet also invokes the past. For those drawn to such instrumentation and attitude, this is a compelling combination.

Blackwater (2001) ★★★★

Mofro seasons J.J. Grey's southern howl with slide guitar and a dash of dobro while relishing the B-3. The 13 songs carry the listener from the front stoop to the juke joint and back via the swamplands. *Blackwater* trails off a bit at the end with some monotony but it is still an achievement.

MOOD FOOD

www.moodfood.net

If your sole Mood Food reference point is the knowledge that Grateful Dead keyboard player Vince Welnick has recorded and toured with the band, then you may misconstrue the group's intent. This San Francisco Bay Area-based group is not a Dead-inspired jam-rock collective. Instead, the group is drawn to darker fusion abstractions and the humor of Frank Zappa. Having said all that, it must be noted that over the past few years (particularly when on the road with Welnick), the band has dropped in some Dead covers, though they will bring their own affinities to bear—for instance, a run from "Help on the Way" into "Slipknot" into Herbie Hanock's "Sly."

Guitarist Tom Lattanand and bass player Andrew McIntyre relocated to San Francisco from St. Louis, Missouri, in 1998. The pair, who had gigged together during college, soon began creating music with Mitch Marcus, a multi-instrumentalist who typically performs on tenor sax, Fender Rhodes, and Hammond B-3. They then assembled a quintet with percussionist John Merrill and drummer Charlie Hall. However, it wasn't until a number of months later that the group effectively formulated its mood with the addition of Sylvain Carton, Marcus's longtime musical collaborator, who complements him on alto, baritone, and soprano sax (while also stepping in on guitar). A chance encounter with Welnick while the group was recording its debut disc in 2000 led to his contributions on two tracks and at some shows that followed the CD's release. Damon Hope, an alum of Merl Saunders's Rainforest Band, replaced Hall on drum kit in late 2001 and has added

vigor. The collective remains fluid in most every sense of the word, recently deciding to add vocal compositions, which often move the band away from raw, elemental jazz into more progressive terrain. This can render the sounds a bit schizophrenic, a description that is probably not unwelcome to a group that traces its origins to a moment when it "was jettisoned several years ago from a passing spacecraft."

Human Zoo (2002) ★★★ ½

An interesting amalgam of prog-rock, fusion, and groove that may or may not also be a concept album about an alien named Larry Palmetto. In contrast with the group's debut, most of these songs have vocals (and didactic lyrics), which sometimes do take the focus away from the band's strong suit, its musicianship.

Mood Food (2000) ★★ ½

The group's mostly instrumental debut fluctuates from the jazz-funk space into plain old space, with some interesting abstractions (if not always original ones).

MOON BOOT LOVER

www.moonbootlover.com

Peter Prince is a rock star. He may not play before 15,000 shrieking zealots every night or carry an entourage well into double digits (or even single digits, for that matter), but to see him strap on the Flying V and his moon boots, then bound on stage and let it rip only affirms that he is the quintessence of rock grandeur (or a super hero, but while Prince missed out on that profession he does capture the lifestyle through the artwork he's concocted for his group's discs, which emulates comic book covers).

For most of its career, Moon Boot Lover, the group Prince founded in upstate New York in 1990, has never altogether embraced the jamband aesthetic. Prince's characterization of the sound as "rocket soul" is apt, yet only hints at the blazing guitars and corresponding vocals. While the group incorporates elements of theatrics both in sound and style, it retains a strong sense of dynamics, so while MBL often surges with abandon it never quite goes over the top. Like many other groups that appear in this book, Moon Boot's musical amalgam (in this case rock/funk/soul) may have inhibited its mainstream reception because it eludes the pigeonhole. However, unlike these bands, MBL rarely pursues any extended improvisation. There are some blistering solos and nimble spontaneous segues but little all-out exploration.

Nonetheless, Prince and Moon Boot Lover remain entwined with the jamband scene. Soon after its formation the group competed in a battle of the bands in a cafeteria in Buffalo's State University of New York against the fellow fledgling musicians in moe. (The two groups would share a number of bills over subsequent years, including a brief Rock the Vote Tour in September 1996 where MBL's set segued into moe.'s with all the members onstage together.) As with most of the band's incarnations, the initial Moon Boot Lover lineup was a trio, with drum duties falling to Alan Evans. (Actually this was the initial lineup of the Groove, MBL's original moniker that was ditched during the groove-naming wave of 1990-1991, which, as it turned out, fell far short of what was to

come with the groove tsunami of 1998-2000. Say, there's a band name right there—Groove Tsunami). A few years later, Evans's brother Neal joined the group on keys for what would evolve into the Moon Boot Lover organ trio until the Evanses departed, eventually to comprise two-thirds of Soulive (Prince and the Evanses recorded one disc together as a three-piece, Catskill Martian Dogs, which remains unreleased despite occasional promises that it is in the queue).

Beginning in 2000, during stints between Moon Boot Lover tours (and lineups), Prince added vocals to the performances of other groups such as the Derek Trucks Band, Deep Banana Blackout, and Fat Mama. In June 2000 he hosted the Jammy Awards, performing with the Jammys Orchestra and offering up a solo song written for the occasion. Prince also shares a singular distinction with Dave Matthews in that he takes to the road with guitarist Tim Reynolds for acoustic shows, where he performs versions of his own music and select covers ("Oops!...I Did It Again" often proves the crowd pleaser).

Moon Boot Lover dates have been rare lately, however, since the inception of Peter Prince and the Trauma Unit, which features former Rockett Band guitarist Johnny Trauma, drummer Eric Kalb (Deep Banana Blackout), bassist Justin Wallace (ulu), and a number of keyboardists and horn players (Trauma describes the band as "the Rolling Stones fronted by Otis Redding"). In whatever context, though, Prince typically is a flurry of frenetic motion, proving that the timeworn footwear adage is right on point: You can take the boy out of the moon boots but you can't take the moon boots out of the boy.

Back on Earth (2001) ★★★★

The finest representation of the band so far, explosive and eccentric, yet, as the title implies, grounded. "Ali" would have been a stellar choice for the biopic.

Live Down Deep (1995) ★★★ ½

Recorded live in November 1994 at Bogie's in Albany, New York, *Live Down Deep* presents the Moon Boot Lover quartet with Peter Prince, the Evans Brothers, and bassist Jon Hawes. These offerings are often eruptive without proving excessive, as the group's performances captivate even if the individual songs do not always meet this goal.

Outer Space Action (1994) ★★★

A well-founded, modern soul record imbued by rocket power. Although some of these tracks fail to ingratiate, a number of others prove both spry and sly.

MOONSHINE STILL

www.moonshinestill.com

For Moonshine Still, it's all about the hum. You may want to reread that carefully—the hum. Keyboard player Trippe Wright (you may want to reread that carefully—Trippe) emphasizes that at the height of improvisation the band achieves an ecstatic state in which one's entire body is vibrating, and thus the hum. The group has aspired to this spasmodic condition since it first came together in the summer of 1996.

The Moonshine Still of the present may share only half the members who founded the group (bass player Ray Petren and vocalist/rhythm guitarist Scott Baston), but many elements abide. The band's sound remains buttressed by a collective pursuit for spontaneous musical connection. Drummer/mandolin player Will Robinson, who joined the band a few months after its inception, describes one aspect of this in a "Will Says" forum on the group's Web site as "one of those moments where you forget who you are and you feel connected to something that is greater than you. It is a feeling that, at least for me, is sometimes hard to find elsewhere in the world today. The music that we, and so many of our incredibly talented contemporaries play is a celebration, it is a communion, a group sharing in something greater than their personal selves, musicians and fans alike."

Additionally, the band retains an emphasis on vocal harmonies delivered by Baston, Petren, and Robinson. And then there's the group's name, a nod to history and hobby in the band's native Georgia while evoking images of "celestial light" and "the bootlegger spreading intoxicating joy." (A tangential NASCAR moment: In case you were unaware, moonshine stills also played a role in the origins of stock car racing, which evolved as a means to showcase the skills of renowned drivers who gained repute by crossing back-country roads carrying illegal liquor at high speeds to foil law enforcement officials. These ties were still manifested in 1967 at the Middle Georgia Speedway in Macon when federal agents found a moonshine still at the end of a 125-foot tunnel, beneath a 35-foot ladder, under a ticket booth.)

Moonshine Still's current lineup, which has performed together since 2000, presents an amalgam of blues, rock, jazz, and bluegrass that in the abstract does not diverge substantially from that of its fellow guitar-driven jam-band brethren. Even so, the buoyant leads of guitarist David Shore and keyboardist Wright do hold audience attention. Plus, the band brings a signature humor and vitality to its songwriting (representative tunes include "Nightcap at the Laundromat," "Coffee and Kind Buds" and "Carpet Cleaners"). While some administrative and creative fits and starts delayed its CD release, Moonshine Still is back on track and humming.

Moon Over Georgia (2003)

Discussion group:

www.groups.yahoo.com/group/moon-shinestill/

MOSES GUEST

www.mosesguest.com

Graham Guest has it all figured out. After completing an undergraduate degree and a master's degree in philosophy (Wesleyan University and Boston College, respectively) and entering a doctoral program at Tulane University, he returned to his home state of Texas to pursue a music career. However, as he assembled the first incarnation of Moses Guest in 1995, he returned to the classroom as a student at the University of Houston Law School, recognizing that it would be easier to develop his band while nestled in the snug cocoon of academe ("Thumbs up," says Dean Budnick, B.A., J.D., A.M., Ph.D.).

Moses Guest began as a trio named after Graham's great-great-great-great-great-grand-father. This origin of the group's name seems appropriate, as Moses Guest's music is steeped in American tradition with a rootsy folk-rock sound. The lyrics prove complementary, evocative, and often elegiac of bygone eras (there is a literary aspect, which one might anticipate from the macro-educated Guest, who has also written a semi-autobiographical novella titled *Love Letters from Waterville*). Guest's three band mates, in place since 1998, bring backgrounds in funk (keyboardist Rick Thompson), jazz (drummer James Edwards), and metal (bassist Jeremy Horton), which lend shades to Guest's alt-country compositions, especially in the live setting. Here the band also echoes the Grateful Dead, as Guest's guitar tone is reminiscent of Jerry Garcia, and the band often will dip into the Dead canon. Guest also cites Steely Dan as a major influence, which comes across less in concert than in the lusher sounds of the band's recent double CD, which incorporates a string section, sax, and dobro. The group's biggest challenge is to bring these songs to the stage and interpret them so they remain evocative of the past without sounding dated.

Moses Guest (2002) ★★★★

There's not much chaff on this double CD in which the quartet brings in a number of guest players to keep things vivid. The group uses the studio quite effectively to highlight its melodic roots-rock, by turns delicate and gruff but mostly robust.

Live Stages (2000) ★★★

A collection of originals propelled further outwards with a bit of blues boogie. Guest also sets the tone, quite literally, from the get go on "Into Jam," which is redolent of Garcia. Perhaps none-too-ironically, one of the songs that is the least Deadesque is the band's arrangement of "I Know You Rider."

American Trailer Home Blues (1999) ★★ ½

There are some solid moments throughout in this relatively straight-up Americana offering from the quartet.

THE MOTET

www.themotet.net

The Motet stands at the fore of the nascent "Electric Americubafrican Groove" movement that is building momentum in the United States. Well, okay, admittedly there is some hyperbole in that statement. While the Motet is not the only band out there empha-

Scott Messersmith of the Motet.

sizing Cuban and West African drum rhythms, Latin jazz beats, and a funk feel while introducing multilingual vocalizing into a deeply improvisational setting ("Hola and Akwaaba, Bembe Orisha!"), it does come close to singular status. As anyone who has experienced the full-on percussion tempest of the Motet can attest, there is indeed much movement, and the swelling numbers of persons who have witnessed such squalls can affirm its momentum.

Dave Watts devised the initial version of the band in Boulder, Colorado, during the fall of 1998, and for some time afterwards the group bore his name. Watts had settled in Boulder following the 1994 dissolution of Shockra, a Boston-based "psychedelic world funk" band. There he began playing with a number of area musicians, including Tony Furtado, and also reunited with fellow Berklee College of Music and Shockra alum Edwin Hurwitz in the jazz-folk quartet Skin. The Dave Watts Motet debuted about six months after Skin parted ways, with a loose roster of invited guests experimenting with the world's beats. Watts soon found a committed core of players including percussionist Scott Messersmith (who has since accompanied Watts to Cuba on a few occasions for cultural exchange and study), keyboardist Greg Raymond (who remains with the group), and vocalist/percussionist Jans Ingber (who left the Motet in fall 2002). When these musicians became significant, consistent contributors and the collective took on its own identity, Watts dropped his name from the band.

A Motet show can be an exhilarating experience, with six band members and special guests singing in varied tongues while juxtaposing genres and building a swell of polyrhythms on percussion instruments. To some degree, the fluidity of the band's music has been matched by the fluidity of its personnel. On the Motet's initial disc the group thanks nearly 20 former and adjunct members. This experience has rendered the group receptive to additional artists, and the Motet has toured with such players as Hope Clayburn and Cochemea "Cheme" Gastelum (and in a Jammy Award-nominated moment from the High Sierra Music Festival on July 1, 2000, the entire band crammed onstage with Deep Banana Blackout, the Slip, Living Daylights, Artis the Spooman, and Joe Craven).

While each new Motet member offers new avenues and options (recent additions include guitarist Mark Donovan and bass player Garrett Sayers), there can be transitional periods that carry some element of restraint (at times leading to a higher representation of straightahead funk, which is the least compelling of what the Motet has to offer). Still, the band thrives, with Watts touring the globe engaging new music and then "applying that towards what I've gained by studying at Berklee and the jazz concept of improvisation and a lot of the harmonic concepts that go along with a lot of the jazz traditions. Combining all of those worlds is really the goal." If we're to have a school of Electric Americubafrican Groove, then there's an apt mission statement.

Live (2002) ★★★★

The "W.O.W. Drums" segment that opens this release (drawn from March 2002 performances) is a fitting intro to this engrossing effort that affirms the band's affinity for the sounds of three continents, unified and animated by percussion.

Play (2000) ★★★

A tantalizing release that only loses momentum (briefly) during some of the more standard funk passages.

Breathe (1999) ★★★ ½

On this live collection from fall 1999, ten players lend contributions (including String Cheese Incident's Michael Travis, who appears on one track). The music visits some jazzier terrain but certainly scopes a wider geography, as well.

MOUNTAIN OF VENUS

www.mountainofvenus.com

Before we get to the music, here's a Mountain of Venus fun fact that says quite a bit about the demands of life on the road with a touring band. During the summer of 2002, the group decided to relocate from Boston, Massachusetts, to Fayetteville, Arkansas, as a direct result of its active gig schedule. The band members came to the realization that exorbitant Boston rents were even less justifiable while they were rarely in residence. Lafayette offered a moderate alternative along with a centralized base from which to initiate national touring. (Interesting, no? Well, at the very least, perhaps it will inspire you to head on out and support a touring act like Mountain of Venus when it routes through your town).

Here's a second MOV tidbit: The group recorded its debut release only two weeks after it formed in 1999. That decision to enter the studio in such short order certainly reflects the confidence of the players and the joy they derived from the music they had started to create. While the disc is uneven, one can certainly hear the dynamic that inspired the recording sessions, especially in the vocal harmonies of Tanya Shylock and Jody Cohen and the interlaced guitar rhythms offered by Cohen and lead player Mike Pascale. These elements continue to animate the band's sound.

Mountain of Venus has traversed the country gaining the support of audience members and musicians alike. Shylock, in particular, has been invited to the stage by a number of fellow artists, including the Big Wu, Perpetual Groove, and Max Creek. In addition, Steve Kimock was sufficiently taken with the band's music to invite MOV to open his 2002 New Year's Eve show, and the guitarist sat in with the band, as well. Mountain of Venus' sound is inviting and familiar, as one can often hear strains of the Allman Brothers Band and the Grateful Dead, particularly in its fluid jams. Still, there is a folkier, roots-rock side as well that often appears when the band changes pace with one of its more concise compositions. The quintet is still coming into its own as songwriters and as a collective, yet Mountain of Venus does distinguish itself with a solid balance of vocals and instrumentation.

Live Volume 1 (2001) ★★★

Shylock's vocals and her harmonies with Cohen energize this release. The band leaves ample room for improv, both within its song arrangements and in a segue from Little Feat's "Hate to Lose Your Loving" into the group's own "Over the Sky." At times a bit too familiar, but often well crafted and melodic.

Mountain of Venus (1999) ★★

Recorded two weeks after the group came together, *Mountain of Venus* does often feel like an opening statement. The first few of the seven songs are a bit plodding, but the pace picks up on the latter half of the disc. "Higher Ground" is a testament to the band's friendly vocals while "Song for the Children" creates an alluring mood.

Also:

Live at the Gothic Theater (2003)
Live at Cicero's (2003)

NERO

www.neroland.com

While Nero has been performing since 1997, many Americans first heard of the band through an online poll. As part of the Jambands.com 250 poll, readers were queried as to what music they were listening to at that very moment. Nero ultimately landed in the top seven, prompting many folks to check out the group's Web site. There they discovered that Nero is an active trio that played over 150 shows in 2002 (which is all the more impressive for a Canadian group, given the difficulties of touring over the wide expanse of that country).

When guitarist David Lauzon, drummer Jay McConnery, and bass player Shane Clark started rehearsing together, they had the opportunity to sample some of the equipment from Lauzon's father's Ottawa music store. This enabled them to experiment with a variety of tones and effects to build layered soundscapes that often seem to originate from more than three players. The result is Nero's self-described "jambient space fusion," a characterization that actually undersells the group. While there certainly are elements of electronic jazz, the band also offers solid funk riffs and, more significantly, some strident guitar work. It is in the juxtaposition of moods where the band is often at its most compelling. Original bass player Clark left after recording Nero's debut disc, *is it morning?*, but replacement Chris Buote effected a fluid transition.

While the group's efforts remain in flux by design, its biggest challenge is to deliver distinctive original compositions. Still, Nero's efforts have elicited positive response from both US and Canadian audiences, who have provided a vibrant web of support.

is it morning? (2001) ★ ★ ½

An oft-entrancing debut from the Canadian trio. At times ambient, at others a bit more aggressive. This disc is more successful in the latter area, especially when guitarist David Lauzon pushes beyond his reference points (Anasastio, et al.).

Also:

Soon (2003)

NEW DEAL

www.thenewdeal.ca

The New Deal is a happy little accident. Go back and listen to Franklin Delano Roosevelt's rhetoric during the 1932 Presidential campaign. Aside from the cool catchphrase, he offers little in the way of a concrete pro-gram—no specific legislation and only the most vague public policy pronouncements. Not only that, most of the programs crafted during his initial months in office (those opening 90 days that have since become significant for Democrat presidencies) were later invalidated by the Supreme Court, so his broader initiatives—the ones that would bear the legacy of the New Deal—evolved over time. Canadian musicians Dan Kurtz, Darren Shearer, and Jamie Shields likely were unfamiliar with the particulars of the Roosevelt administration when they decided to form the New Deal, but given the group's origins and current performance ethos, it is similarly serendipitous (though the Tennessee Valley Authority would quite literally pave the way for the Bonnaroo Music Festival).

The band emerged from drummer Shearer's weekly gig playing covers in a Toronto bar. Musicians rotated in and out at his behest, including bassist Kurtz and keyboardist Shields. At one point the three recognized that the audience paid them little heed and they began improvising in house-style music. Inspired by the results (even if no one in attendance shared this enthusiasm), the trio booked a gig at the Comfort Zone and pursued this same course to the polite applause of six listeners (conflicting recollections place the number in the eight to nine range). Again, the three were heartened by their efforts, if not necessarily the turnout, and decided to release a recording of the performance as a document of their sound and to seek out additional gigs. All they needed was a name, and they felt their intent to create live dance music of the sort that otherwise emanated from DJs turntables made "the New

Deal" apt. To underscore their music's origins, the group titled their 1999 debut, drawn from that initial show, *This Is Live*.

The New Deal's "live.progressive.breakbeat. house" did not have a natural constituency. Those in the dance club scene were accustomed to music from DJs and proved a bit snotty about live musicians stepping into the role (the band surmounted this to a degree early on when performing on bills with DJs by picking up in the same key—clubgoers often were absorbed by the sounds before they noticed the supplantation). Jamband audiences then gravitated to the New Deal, though observers doubted initially whether these listeners would countenance the sounds that reigned in clubland. Still, Shields held faith, given his experience wrought from his role in the funk/jazz outfit One Step Beyond (which had toured for a few years, developing an especially close relationship with Merl Saunders and often performing as his band). The New Deal's US debut at the 1999 Berkshire Mountain Music Festival affirmed Shields's sanguine expectation that their near-perpetual improvisation would enthrall. The trio gained traction within jamband circles as purveyors of a new form.

At present the band continues to respond to the challenge posed by their first show and maintains the vivid extemporization. Over the years the group has embellished some of the "hooks" discovered in the live setting (the band refers to songs as hooks to reflect their mutability). The trio will return to a number of hooks over the course of a performance, in part because audience members have staked out favorites, such as "Back to the Middle" from that opening gig at the Comfort Zone, which in the lexicon of hand signals that Shields often employs to guide his bandmates during improv has been represented by a lone index finger (given the title, though, he probably should be flipping them the bird).

Still, the New Deal longs to improvise, with the keyboardist typically supplying the chords and melodies while Kurtz delivers a corresponding run of notes with variations in feel and inflection, and Shearer aspires to mandroid status as a drum machine/human beatbox. This hybrid sound has captivated audiences in many circles, including Moby's Area One, the Coachella Festival, and on the road with Vida Blue as well as Herbie Hancock. In addition, the band inked a label deal with Jive Electro (they are no longer with Jive and, sadly, failed to share crudités with label siblings Britney and the *NSYNC boys when they had the chance). At present the three musicians are working towards varying their palettes and moods while remaining true to what first animated them during that crappy covers gig: facing the paradox of sustaining a New Deal (a pickle shared by the only four-term U.S. President in history).

NYC 5.30.02 + 6.01.02 (2002) ★★★★

This double live release offers an opportunity both to hear the New Deal build on some of their established themes while also plunging forward into all-out improv. The three players typically keep a repetitive art fresh through a tendency to discharge ideas before they stall the mostly insistent dialog (though at times the conversation does briefly drag).

Portland ME 12.17.99 + Guelph ON CAN 4.5.00 (2002) ★★★★

This repackaged reissue of the two EPs that

followed *This Is Live* documents the band's ensuing confidence, facility, and—particularly on the *Guelph* disc—velocity.

The New Deal (2001) ★★★½
The trio's first studio effort (though a number of the basic tracks were recorded live) affirms why the band calls these tracks "hooks." On occasion the results feel stultified, but often the group furbishes and then enriches.

This Is Live (1999) ★★★
A postcard from the dawn that is essential for New Deal fans and is still of interest to others. Some of these themes remain active though many here are protean, and at other times the trio does little more than retain the flow (which is still an admirable achievement).

Also:
Gone Gone Gone (2003)

Fan site:
Navidrome message board—
www.pub3.ezboard.com/bnewdealonline

Discussion list:
www.groups.yahoo.com/group/thenewdealhq/

NEW MONSOON
www.newmonsoon.com
This one gradually blew in from the East. Four of the seven members who comprise San Francisco's New Monsoon originally performed together in various incarnations at Penn State in the early '90s. In 1997 the first of these migrants, Bo Carper (acoustic guitar, banjo, dobro), began working with recent arrival Jeff Miller (electric guitar). Following the appearance of another former Penn State musician, Heath Carlisle (lead vocals), the trio began gigging with Carlisle behind the kit. Piano player Phil Ferlino debuted with the group three years later at the High Sierra Music Festival, after contributing to the band's first studio disc from the confines of an Allentown, PA, recording studio. By then he had become the seventh member of the group, as Carlisle had switched over to bass to accommodate drummer Marty Ylitalo, followed by Rajiv Parikh on tabla and percussion, and then Brian Carey on congas and timbales.

New Monsoon strikes a balance between the familiar and the singular, but has a penchant for combining instruments in a piquant manner. One is hard-pressed to name another group that in a single song may offer acoustic and electric guitars, didgeridoo, dobro, and ghatham (assuming one even can identify the ghatham, an Indian percussion instrument—T.H. Vinayakram introduced the ghatham, a mud pot with a narrow mouth, to many Western listeners through his mid-'70s efforts with John McLaughlin and Zakir Hussain in Shakti). Still, the sound is not altogether distinctive as the band communicates through psychedelic, jazz, Latin, reggae, and rock modes, and the group's songwriting occasionally founders when it adheres too closely to one of these approaches without pushing to define its own synthesis. The septet is among the vanguard of next-generation national touring bands, however, earning approbation for its novel polyrhythmic climate.

Downstream (2003) ★★★½
Although vivid vocal harmonies embellish some of the tracks on New Monsoon's second

disc, the instrumental songs tend to offer the brighter moments. In this context, the group most effectively delivers on its mingling of phrasings and fashions.

Also:
Hydrophonic (2001)

Discussion list:
www.groups.yahoo.com/group/newmonsoon/

NORTH MISSISSIPPI ALLSTARS
www.nmallstars.com

The Allstars are definitely on the friends-and-family plan. Brothers Cody and Luther Dickinson have been performing together for most of their lives, first gigging regularly as teenagers in the thrash trio DDT. (That name, of course, is a riff on the SST record label, original home to Black Flag and Husker Du. By the way, DDT also featured bass player Paul Taylor, who would move on to the band Big Ass Truck. And just for the heck of it, to show how convoluted and entwined this all is, Big Ass Truck guitarist Steve Selvidge is also well known to the Dickinsons, since their fathers used to perform together in Mudboy and the Neutrons).

North Mississippi Allstars bass player Chris Chew met Luther in the seventh grade and they played off and on informally thereafter, often with Cody—their first public performance was at their high school homecoming dance. Guitarist Duwayne Burnside joined in the fall of 2001—a few years into the group's career although he had known the Dickinson brothers for some time—at the suggestion of Othar Turner, a longtime Allstars supporter. (In 1996, the Allstars performed their first gig on a bill with Turner. In 1998, Luther would produce *Everybody Hollerin' Goat*, the debut release from the 90-year-old musician, a practitioner of the fife-and-drum tradition. Luther had first learned of Turner's musical proclivities many years back while watching an episode of *Mr. Rogers' Neighborhood* with his father in which Turner appeared with Jessie Mae Hemphill. "They played and my dad said, 'That's Othar Turner, he lives down the street'.")

And then there's the whole progeny thing. Duwayne is the son of R.L. Burnside, the Delta blues player who learned the guitar from his neighbor, Fred McDowell (and also performed on that initial Allstars bill). Cody's and Luther's father, Jim—a longtime collaborator with Ry Cooder and performer on the Rolling Stones' *Sticky Fingers*—did some work with Duane Allman and went on to produce numerous groups, including Big Star and the Replacements. (Luther appeared on the latter's *Pleased to Meet Me* album as a teenager. He recalls: "They wanted this one song, 'Shooting Dirty Pool,' to have comical, timely, heavy metal licks—some whammy bar and finger tapping. So Dad told them about me, and they invited me up there, it was pretty fun." DDT would later open for the 'Mats.)

The band's decision to incorporate a regional reference into its name is appropriate. Part of the North Mississippi Allstars fundament is the hill-country blues that McDowell taught to Burnside, who passed it along to the Dickinsons (along with other artists including another area citizen, guitarist Junior Kimbrough, whose juke joint the Dickinsons frequented). There is a simplicity and minimalism to this sound that allows Cody in particular to drop in a variety of contemporary drum beats (this also accounts for the success of *Come On In*, Burnside's 1998 album that incorporates looping and sampling techniques). There is also southern soul and boogie in the Allstars sound, and in Luther's use of the slide one can certainly hear the Allman Brothers Band. Another influence turned out to be future Widespread Panic guitarist George McConnell, who performed for many years in Beanland, a Mississippi group that also featured future Panic member JoJo Hermann on keys (the Dickinsons would later record and tour with Hermann).

North Mississippi Allstars' brash, rumbling sound drew critical praise and slots on tours with such national acts as Gov't Mule, Medeski Martin and Wood, and Galactic. (One interesting note is that during the early years, Chew often had scheduling conflicts caused by returning home for Sunday church or working as a truck driver, so other bass players sat in—including the Mule's Allen Woody and Chris Wood of MMW). While the band garnered acclaim from blues purists, they never were a hill-country retread, and over time they have continued to fold in other elements. One significant change has been the introduction of additional original material, having focused mostly on the music of McDowell and Burnside. In addition, while Luther originally handled much of the writing, recently Cody has been offering up compositions with more

Allstar guitarists Duwayne and Luther, sharing legacy and foresight.

of a pop flair. Meanwhile, Burnside's participation has freed up the group a bit—while he usually plays guitar he'll also spot Cody on drums so that the younger brother can do some picking or move to the washboard.

Like a number of the groups in this book, North Mississippi Allstars often feel they are misrepresented by a genre classification—though typically not as a jamband, but as a blues act (incidentally, the group's sets vary from night to night, with some succinct and fulminating, others more exploratory). Luther responds to the blues tag: "I think people have to put it into a category so they can put it away in their brain, but it doesn't matter to me. The category I'm most comfortable with is we're a rock 'n' roll band. I never claimed to be a blues band. Even with *Shake Hands with Shorty* we weren't doing traditional blues music. Over the past 20 years there have been people who liked to do old styles of blues to keep that alive, but that's not really what I'm into. Sometimes people ask me if we did a particular song to make the hardcore blues people happy and I say, 'Hell no, we do what we want to do.' That's our motto, we do what we want to do when we want to do it."

51 Phantom (2001) ★ ★ ★ ½

Produced by Jim Dickinson, this disc focuses on the group's own material. Many of these songs emerge from the hill-county blues and move towards the British blues-rock of the late '60s, though there is some gospel and punk mettle as well. While the band's influence predominates, *51 Phantom* offers a raucous ride.

Shake Hands with Shorty (2000) ★ ★ ★ ½

A cool disc that (re)introduces and interprets the music of Fred McDowell and R.L. Burnside, laying on some boogie and the occasional hip-hop beat for a jubilant offering that remains faithful to the spirit of the originals.

Also:

Polaris (2003)

NUCLEUS

www.nucleusmusic.com

Although three quarters of the musicians in Nucleus were raised in upstate New York, the band first came together in Arcata, California. It was there in the summer of 2000 that Pete Ciotti (drums), Piet Dalmolen (guitar), and Steve Webb (bass) of the recently dissolved jam-rock band All In The Family hooked up with saxophone player Matt Dickson. Dickson had previously guested with All In The Family on a co-bill with his soul-jazz group Velvet Jones, which also was winding down. The new quartet aspired to create music that built on its antecedents while incorporating new textures.

The band's sound has remained fluid. Initially, the four musicians melded their styles and also pushed into the realm of straightahead jazz. Then they introduced ambient/trance modes, with Dickson's sax lending an intriguing air. One common thread has been the band's yen to play free and leave song's arrangements behind. Nucleus, which relocated to the East Coast during the summer of 2002, retains its inventive spirit, even as—like many other young bands—it continues to shape its interplay and expression.

Live from the Center (2002) ★ ★ ½

Recorded at Quixote's True Blue on July 31, 2002, the six songs on this disc fill out 72 minutes. The vocals are a bit ragged, and at times some of the improvisation loses focus. Even so, there is solid interplay between sax and guitar throughout with some cool ideas from the rhythm section. The opener, "Pintos 'n Amber," introduces some of the band's many moods.

Nucleus (2001) ★ ★

This release reflects the inchoate Nucleus with more of a jazz feel. Solid musicianship, though at times the songwriting lacks originality and zest.

OLOSPO

www.olospo.com

The word "sassy" is rarely invoked these days to describe the efforts of a particular band, especially a quartet of men upwards of 25 years old. Yet fans of Olospo have directed this word at the Dallas group on a few occasions as a term of endearment (without any reference to the late, lamented *Sassy* magazine, which did indeed venture into music criticism with its "Cute Band Alert." No opinion ventured here as to whether Olospo would have qualified). Sassy, of course, is a synonym for saucy, and—Mike Myers's imagery aside—this does seem an apt description of a group that introduces itself to South by Southwest Festival attendees with the commentary: "Our songs gush FUN from every loud speaker, reflecting our influences, from XTC to Mr. Bungle to Steely Dan. Olospo is rare because we have depth. Our only objective at SXSW is to make jaws drop."

A bold assertion (jocose though it may be). Perhaps it is not all that unanticipated, however, given the group's connections to Walter Mitty (the fanciful title character in the James Thurber story and later the Danny Kaye film). In 1995, guitarist Chris Holt co-founded a band of that name and gigged regularly through the summer of 1999, gaining renown in Texas and beyond. When that group disbanded, Holt assembled a new collective with keyboardist Britt Morris, who now shares Holt's songwriting duties and was once a regular presence in the audience of Walter Mitty shows. Drummer Tom Bridwell had auditioned unsuccessfully for that group but later bonded with Holt over Zappa and PlayStation. (Olospo has formed an intra-band Madden Football League and reports on the results through its Web site, which incidentally is one of the more robust ones out there among emerging, independent artists. On a related game note, while not a PlayStation property, the "Super Mario Brothers Theme" is part of Olospo's live repertoire, though the quartet is not alone in this selection—it has long been an ulu staple.) Bassist Nick Ramirez is a fluid player who allows the group to move through the paces of the bands mentioned in Olospo's SXSW blurb, flavored with Phish and Zeppelin while also incorporating a funk and reggae feel.

Olospo remained somewhat bound to the southwest until December 2002 when

Ramirez received his college degree, clearing the group to pursue a national tour docket. As the quartet travels, it discovers a growing fan base familiar with its music via the Web and also through Olospo's participation in some of its home state's biggest events, such as the Austin City Limits Festival and South by Southwest. At the latter event, many felt that the band did indeed deliver on its pledge, as in the live setting Olospo typically is spirited, spry, and yes, sassy.

This Is the Pagoda (2002) ★★★ ½

A rare studio album from a young band—many of the tracks do indeed deliver the energy associated with Olospo's invigorating live shows. The 12 selections offer something of an amusement ride with crescendos, dips, and occasional flats, yet the swells certainly predominate.

Also:

Herbal Tea (2001)

OM TRIO

www.omtrio.com

As you may well guess, OM Trio attributes its name to John Coltrane and his support of the idea that "om" was the first sound in the universe and the origin point for all noises that followed. Some artists might deem this to be a daunting initial reference, but the musicians who comprise OM Trio are certainly self-assured. Such confidence is necessary for the many modes the band incorporates into its live shows, along with ever-vacillating time signatures and tempos.

As the band's appellation suggests, the sound is deeply rooted in jazz, and OM Trio did in fact record an album of mostly standards. Then again, the group's bass player identifies Bootsy Collins as his biggest influence and once held the bottom for East Coast jam-rockers Fatty Lumpkin. Comparisons to Medeski Martin and Wood are common, but mostly because the band is similarly configured as an organ trio—OM's sound is a bit more eclectic (and at times a bit less focused and cohesive). The group juxtaposes elements of funk, electronica, reggae, and even prog-rock, but then again, in 2001 the readers of the *San Francisco Bay Guardian* identified OM Trio as the area's "best jazz band" (no small feat), so all bets are off.

What is clear is that the band members first met in New Jersey and made it to San Francisco by way of Oregon. In June 1999 keyboardist Brian Felix, a student of Kenny Barron (Dizzy Gillespie, Freddie Hubbard, Ron Carter), traveled to Talent, Oregon, with Moscow-born drummer Ilya Stemkovsky and bassist Daniel Fusco. The three players began gigging as OM and released three jazz/avant-funk albums before Fusco left the group and the remaining two members relocated to San Francisco. There they soon added Lumpkin alum Pete Novembre (he had played with Felix in New Jersey funk band Velour) along with the word Trio (due to a name conflict with another group). The newly dubbed OM Trio quickly found sympathetic ears for its dexterous and often rumbling explorations in tonalities and harmonic structure with an impromptu Guns N' Roses cover tossed in as the moment dictates. The results can be too abstract for some audiences, yet as Felix notes, "We would much rather play to a roomful of ten people that are really listening and really being affected by us, than a room of 700 people where nobody is listening."

GlobalPositioningRecord (2003) ★★★ ½

There is a confidence and fluidity that suffuses this first studio disc from the current trio (with Netwerk: Electric's guitarist Jason Concepción on three tracks). This flow is all the more impressive because the music moves from avant-jazz akin to Medeski Martin and Wood to electronica to some edgier rock grooves. Be sure to hang out for the burbling Living Colour cover at the end.

OM Trio Live (2001) ★★★

These two discs draw from performances recorded on the West Coast between December 2000 and June 2001. While the individual songs rarely stand out, the playing certainly does, as the Trio is rife with improvisation ideas, at times perhaps a bit too much so—a sit-down with the 144 minutes of music on this release can be stupefying.

As OM (with Daniel Fusco on bass):

Meat Curtain (2000)
Jazz Trio (2000)
Clarified Butter (1999)

OMINOUS SEAPODS

www.ominousseapods.com

X-Men, Shmex-Men, cast aside that lowly group—the Ominous Seapods are the once and future mutants. Sure Wolverine's got some chops, but he has nothing on "The Old TP" (hang on). Well okay, the Marvel superheroes did come first. X-Men debuted at No. 1 in 1963, with giant-size X-Men premiering as the new team 12 years later, both preced-

ing the Seapods' initial gig in 1989. Still, what the X-Men have in longevity the Pods have in idiosyncrasy. And songcraft.

Of course, mutant is just one descriptive phrase within a broad lexicon fabricated by the band to define itself and its listeners. The group, founded by guitarist/songwriters Dana Monteith and Max Verna at the State University of New York, Plattsburgh, has characterized itself not as a jamband but rather as a gobi band, a reference to the nomads who travel from gig to gig (and frankly, but for a twist or two, the Web hub for this community could have been Gobigroups.com, with this book titled *Gobibands*).

In case you hadn't picked up on it yet, the Pods, especially the old-school Pods such as bassist Tom Pirozzi ("The Old TP"), were full of beans (sometimes quite literally—don't get the band members started on their stories of extended van trips and roadside fare). While the group placed an emphasis on its songwriting, it also interjected theatrics such as the donning of masks, the presentation of skits including a recurring scene between a green-thumbed musician and a state trooper ("Abraham Unleavenhead"), and belly bucking competitions. The individual songs often carried a similar perspective. For instance, in "Switchblade," Verna relates the story of how he brandished a concealed comb to intimate Knicks' announcer Marv Albert during an encounter in a Madison Square Garden rest room (no, not that kind of encounter). The Pods fans were correspondingly bent, often assuming personas that the group occasionally celebrated in song while showing a twisted, disproportionate love for the number 211 (February 11 is the date of a renowned show long before Ruben Studdard began representing the 205.

By the mid-'90s the band was within a crest of new groups, such as fellow Empire Staters moe., that were gaining national recognition. However, after signing with Jon and Marsha Zazula's Megaforce Records (actually its Hydrophonics Imprint), Verna elected to depart for a more sedentary lifestyle. The group then invited guitarist/vocalist Todd Pasternack ("The New TP") to join, with the transition occurring onstage on New Year's Eve 1998 when Pasternack appeared in a diaper during "Abraham Unleavenhead." Pasternack's arrival marked a transition away from some of the sketches (though not the comedy) as the band directed more of its energies to music. Following a few steady years on the road and another studio disc, the Seapods announced a hiatus, and in an odd, apt Podsian manner, the quintet's final show took place thousand of miles from home, in Baja, Mexico, during the summer of 2001.

The players moved on to other projects. Monteith began solo performances as Verna had once done. Pirozzi began playing with the Lo Faber Band, as did drummer Ted Marotta and Pasternack (the guitarist later formed Marlow). Keyboardist Brian Mangini put in a stint on the road with moe. and then joined RaisinHead (Pirozzi has recently come on board as well). Then in February 2003, a six-pack of Pods including all three guitar players returned for two performances that spanned the group's career and offered belly bucking aplenty. Looking back, one might contend that the introductory X-Men analogy was a bit too heroic, particularly since the Seapods opted to appear as the Legion of Doom, sworn enemies of the Super Friends, at one of its Halloween shows. One can also argue, though, that there is a certain amount of glory reserved for a band that takes care to ensure that both of its reunion shows included crowd-pleasing versions of its rousing anthem, "Bong Hits and Porn."

Superman Curse (2000) ★★★½

A solid, well-produced studio disc in which the band moves from country-inflected musings to straight-on rock raves-ups with a ballad for balance. The band's humor remains, although it is slightly subdued. Still, the quintet's songs feature a fine turn-of-phrase and some memorable melodies. Most of the material is recent, but the group does dig into its pocket for a version of "Bong Hits and Porn."

Matinee Idols (1998) ★★★½

This single live disc recorded over four nights presents some of the band's celebrated material from the Verna years, bookended by his songs "Blackberry Brandy" and "Leaving the Monopole." This release comes out charging, plateaus a bit, and then bounds to a close.

Also:
Jet Smooth Ride (1997)

Out of print:
Econobrain (1993)
Guide to Roadside Ecology (1995)
Matinee Idols: Late Show (1998)

Fan site:
Mutants of the Road Atlas—
www.dartmouth.edu/~jkm/MOThRA.htm

ONE-EYED JACK

www.one-eyed-jack.com

It's all too easy to romanticize the life of a touring musician. Music journalist turned filmmaker Cameron Crowe certainly stoked the embers with *Almost Famous*—his ode to those who bring their music on the road (and the journalists who report on it) can leave one feeling...stoked. Of course, if you were 15 years old and out there with Stillwater (or Led Zeppelin and the Allman Brothers Band), it is more than likely that three decades later you, too, would look back with wistfulness and wonder.

Which leads us to One-Eyed Jack (no, really). The group has been at it since the early '90s, bringing improvisational music to the live setting. No tour buses (or jets), but One-Eyed Jack has performed about 100 shows a year, which, when one factors in travel, rehearsal, and songwriting, translates into a near-daily dedication to the band—a commitment that one has to respect.

As for the music, there actually is some similarity to Stillwater (the fictional group from Crowe's film, lest you missed the reference above), since One-Eyed Jack often employs blues tones with a tinge of metal. Founded by guitarist Gary Gallagher as a "psychedelic garage band," OEJ has strengthened its sound over the years through an evolving roster of musicians. One significant arrival was Joe Boris, a vocalist and guitar player who joined in the late '90s and now writes much of the band's material. Most recently, percussionist Katie Schmidt has contributed vocals and percussion (Mickey Hart invited her to the stage for a jam he hosted at RhythmFest in 2002). They're not almost famous yet, but they are living the life, and there's something to be said for that.

Sunlight Blue Madness (2001) ★★½

Strong production lends clarity to these 12 songs while emphasizing their varied moods (from blasting guitar rock to power ballad). Although the music itself tends to build on standard themes and progressions, a number of the tracks prove quite vivid.

Also:

Live at the Lion's Den, NYC (1999)
Before Alone (1998)

ORDINARY WAY

www.theordinaryway.com

You can't fault Gordon Sterling's field vision. In 1996, as the sixteen-year-old prepared to play football for his Fairfax, VA, high school team, he suddenly felt a calling to assemble a band and deliver sounds equally celebratory and hortatory (Sterling's family is from Jamaica, and Bob Marley provided inspiration to this end). Sterling had little musical proficiency, but he spent the ensuing months devoted to the guitar while his friend Chris Stringfellow developed on the bass. The initial incarnation of the Ordinary Way appeared two years later.

At present the band is a septet with an avowed penchant to create music that is a synthesis of many forms, which guitarist Austin Mendenhall has described as "a sound more than a style." The doubling of vocals, percussion, and guitar along with robust keyboards yields rich, often radiant results. Some of the music is folk-pop akin to Rusted Root. At other times, it's an acid jazz variant with spoken word, dub beats, and electronic atmospherics. The Ordinary Way also delivers more straightahead, blues-driven rock. One particularly tantalizing element is Sterling's voice, a soulful instrument reminiscent of Roland Gift (Fine Young Cannibals). On occasion the lyrics can feel heavy-handed, and the music, while diverse, is not always distinctive. Nonetheless, the group is well on its way towards delivering on Sterling's initial vision and vibe.

Dojo (2003) ★★★ ½

An ambitious effort that moves from grounded expressions to more open-ended ethereal ones. The strongest tracks feature Gordon Sterling's mellifluous singing, though Sabienne Gustave's voice can be absorbing, as well. *Dojo* aspires to envelop the listener and achieves this aim in many instances.

Also:

Death and Taxes (2001)

Out of print:

Rising (1999)

OTEIL & THE PEACEMAKERS

www.oteilburbridge.com

All right, now is as fine a time as ever to test your knowledge of American film. Here we go: What musician in this book also appeared in a motion picture whose lead actor took home an Oscar for that particular movie? While you cogitate on that one, we'll take a moment to remind you that Oteil Burbridge, the bassist who is the founder, principal songwriter, and namesake of the band we will return to momentarily, spells his name

Oteil—that's "i before e except after t." Okay, okay, it's actually "except after c," but proper names don't count anyhow, though this all may explain why Oteil's name is commonly misspelled (less so over the years as his renown increases).

Okay, back to our game: And the answer is...Bruce Hampton, who appears in the film *Sling Blade*. Come on, Oteil would have been too darn easy, though as you may know he does appear as Lolo in the film *Being There*. (Peter Sellers received a Best Actor Oscar nomination for his role as Chance the gardener in that film, but he lost out to Dustin Hoffman for *Kramer vs. Kramer*. Billy Bob Thornton, however, took home a statue for *Sling Blade*, albeit not the Best Actor award, which went to Geoffrey Rush for *Shine*, but he did win the statue for Best Adapted Screenplay, which he wrote.) Burbridge also had a role in *Billy Jack Goes to Washington*, but he really made his mark in television, hosting a kids' show, *Stuff*, on Washington's WRC from 1978-1980 (and as for the Hampton film canon, Burbridge recommends the Colonel's appearance in *Getting It On*, a teen-romp from the early '80s).

Still, Oteil held a greater passion for music. He began on the drums and credits his years behind the kit to the rhythmic complexity manifested in his bass playing. Music was valued in the Burbridge home. For example, when Oteil was 15 his father issued a friendly challenge for him to learn Jaco Pastorius's parts on the apt "Teen Town" (from Weather Report's *Heavy Weather*) and Oteil complied, learning a phrase at a time. This turned him on to jazz (indeed, his father's intent was to supplement Oteil's funk vocabulary), as did the enthusiasm of his older brother, Kofi, who was still developing on flute and keyboards.

A number of years later, when Oteil ended up in Atlanta, one of his early groups, Knee Deep, included Kofi as well as drummer Jeff Sipe. In turn, Sipe (aka Apt Q-258) introduced Oteil to Hampton, who soon enlisted him for his weekly gig at the Little 5 Points Pub, which would eventually yield the Aquarium Rescue Unit. (The roster that would join the first few HORDE tours and initiate some stunning full-band segues into Widespread Panic: Hampton, Burbridge, Sipe, and Jimmy Herring, plus Matt Mundy on mandolin, remains the "definitive" ARU for many—if such a word can apply to an iconoclastic collection of players who aspired to spontaneity with most every aspect of their art.)

Following Hampton's departure from ARU in 1994 due to health considerations, the group invited Kofi to join along with vocalist Paul Henson, but by late 1995 the band eased up on its touring, and its players founded

Oteil Burbridge hitting the note on the 6-string bass.

other projects. Oteil did some brief touring with Frogwings and then in 1997 started to gig with the Allman Brothers Band (where he first began to play a four-string bass with a pick at the suggestion of ABB guitar tech Joe Dan Petty. At that time he also learned "Little Martha" on his six-string in an attempt to sway Dickey Betts's perception of the instrument). Meanwhile, with ARU in stasis, Burbridge had a cache of tunes and no outlet to play them, which led to the initial Oteil & the Peacemakers recording, *Love of a Lifetime* (1998).

A transformed version of the Peacemakers entered the studio a few years later to record the follow-up, released in 2003 on the Artists House label. (Artists House is a noble endeavor, founded by multi-Grammy-winning producer John Snyder, who worked with Ornette Coleman, Ron Carter, George Benson, Chet Baker, Etta James, and many, many others. He established the label as a nonprofit 501(c)(3) corporation to benefit its musicians, as the name implies.) One significant adjustment to the Peacemakers is that Paul Henson has come on board to sing—previously the music was all instrumental, other than Burbridge's scatting over his bass chords (most acknowledge his prowess here, though some feel that on occasion he goes to the well a bit too often). Another change took place within the bass player himself: Following a spiritual crisis exacerbated by the January 2000 plane crash that took the life of Joe Dan Petty, Burbridge emerged as a committed Christian. While mostly a shift in attitude and perspective, Burbridge also has incorporated some reference to this experience in his lyrics, as in the song "Thank You." Although

he does note, "It's such a heavy funk groove that people dance their asses off to it. It's cool, I can present my faith to people in a way that's not hitting them over the head." Indeed the music doesn't feel doctrinaire, particularly through the bright-hued, often brash contributions of keyboardist Jason Crosby, longtime guitarist Mark Kimbrell, and saxophonist Kebbi Williams. Oh yes, as for the name of the second disc, *The Family Secret*, this carries us back into the world of film. As Burbridge explains: "My other mission in life is to erase political correctness. I am committed to taking the power away from words that have been hurtful. The family secret is in the first five minutes of *Blazing Saddles*."

The Family Secret (2003) ★ ★ ★ ½

This is an impressive package with a DVD that offers video clips, interviews, sheet music, and even a bass lesson with Oteil. Paul Henson is on vocals, joined by newcomers Jason Crosby and drummer Chris Fryar. Burbridge writes most of the material with guitarist Mark Kimbrell and Fryar also contributing songs that delve into blues, funk, and jazz environments. The results are more varied than the Peacemakers' debut, and the group certainly kicks it a bit more (Kimbrell and saxophonist Kebbi Williams, in particular). Still, given the talent in the room, one might like a few additional chances to hear the band really cut loose.

Love of a Lifetime (2000) ★ ★ ★

Oteil & the Peacemakers' debut is a band album, not a bass album. He draws in some fine players including his brother Kofi (who also contributes a few compositions), Mark

Kimbrell, Kebbi Williams, and Regi Wooten. While the musicianship is tasteful, at times the songs themselves are a bit mired in softer, smooth jazz territory.

OYSTERHEAD

www.oysterhead.com

Give it up for the Superfly guys. In 1998, Superfly Productions debuted its SuperJam series, which has gathered a host of musicians who have not heretofore performed together. (Two such Jams include May 8, 2001—Carter Beauford, John Medeski, Me'Shell NdegeOcello, Joshua Redman, and Marc Ribot—and March 2, 2000—Henry Butler, Karl Denson, Stanton Moore, Leo Nocentelli, and Chris Wood.) Although these shows have taken place year-round, the

SuperJam has come to be associated with the Superfly During Jazz Fest Series (branding aplenty, no?) and for its May 4, 2000 event, the promoters had the instincts to hand the ball off to Mr. Les Claypool. The bassist turned to Trey Anastasio (the two had first performed together at the Laguna Seca Daze Festival on May 28, 1994, on a bill that included Phish and Sausage) and Stewart Copeland (the Police drummer, who has been devoting himself to film scores of late and produced "Dirty Drowning Man" on Primus' 1999 *Antipop* album). Rage Against the Machine's Tom Morello also was invited but demurred due to a scheduling conflict, yielding the gig to three forceful players and personalities (back to our spherical metaphor, Claypool observes, "When you're used to running with

Oysterhead's Little Faces, mid-tour 2001.

the ball all the time it's an interesting feeling to be tossing the ball back and forth and having everybody running together").

Claypool, Anastasio, and Copeland dubbed themselves Oysterhead, a name some view as a jesting reference to the perceived challenge of subsuming their collective egos. They rehearsed at Anastasio's Barn for a few days prior to the gig, working up some originals, with the initial riffs from these sessions incorporated into "Rubberneck Lions." In addition, the trio agreed on some covers that reflected their collective interests, including Led Zeppelin's "Immigrant Song" and Desmond Dekker's "The Israelites." The show itself at the Saenger Theater, which had sold out inside of ten minutes, proved by turns sloppy and spellbinding (and often a bit of both) as each of the three pushed the band in certain directions with the others not necessarily in synch (say now, there's a SuperJam: How about Justin Timberlake, Lance Bass, Sonny Rollins, Clyde Stubblefield, and Steve Kimock?).

While the musicians initially deemed the event a one-off, Copeland mixed some of the highlights from the two-and-a-half-hour show into 50 minutes and discovered that "I really could see that the gems were there, and if you clustered them all in one place, you've got a pretty sparkly thing." The results led the three to assume the Oysterhead mantle once again (a disquieting image, no?), regrouping at the Barn in April 2001 to record an album. A 20-show tour followed six months later in support of the studio effort.

The title of this disc, *The Grand Pecking Order,* is somewhat illusory, as there doesn't appear to be such a hierarchy within the band. Anastasio explains that "every aspect of that album was a three-way decision, from 'What mic are you going to put on the kick drum?' to lyrics." The music on the disc sounds like a synthesis of the three—despite the players' signature sounds, the results are sui generis. When performing this material live, the group expanded on these ideas, as Anastasio and Claypool's individual propensities surfaced a bit more, though Copeland's crackling contributions often kept the group grounded (or at least he tried). Other moments were given over to Anastasio's antlered Mattherhorn guitar and Claypool's headgear and goggles, along with the busting of chops (to supplement the showcasing of them).

One criticism arose over set lists, which, given the scant nature of the group's material, displayed limited variance (though in recognition of this, some simply yearned for additional covers). Anastasio recalls, "There was one night where I was on stage with Oysterhead after about two weeks being on tour and I really started to feel helpless in a certain way. From standing on stage with Phish for so many years I had this feeling that I wish I could inject some of that unpredictability and chaos into this formula. I was longing for it but I just couldn't do it. But after I walked offstage at that show I realized that was a ridiculous way to be thinking, and from that point on I said, 'Okay, we're doing what we're doing, enjoy it. It's not Phish, you know.'" Indeed, this also lies at the heart of some of the contemporaneous chiding, as the shows took place during a moment when fans were jonesing for a P-fix, whether Phish, Primus, or the Police. As the months passed (with all three bands performing again in 2003—imagine the payout on that trifecta), people have further come to appreciate the cabinet of curiosities that is Oysterhead. Those folks are fortunate, as Anastasio has emphasized that he views Oysterhead as "at least a two-off," granting him another opportunity to tee off on the Matterhorn (and Claypool to do the same).

The Grand Pecking Order (2001) ★★★★

The trio creates its own kinetic climate charged by a deep low end, melodic guitar riffs, and the vigorous snap of the drum kit. The tones are familiar, yet a listener is never altogether comfortable (in the best way possible—the music is not off-putting but in spots it can be droning).

P

PAPA GROWS FUNK
www.papagrowsfunk.com

While Papa Grows Funk certainly delivers on the promise of its appellation, this is only a starting point. The band retains a direct lineage to the legendary Meters and garnered Best Funk Band honors in *Offbeat* magazine's 2002 Best of the Beat Awards in its native New Orleans (a feat indeed). However, the group also builds on a lattice of swirling R&B inflections, sax-infused jazz, and some strident blues guitar.

The band's moniker also is a playful spin on the name of its founder, keyboard player John Gros. In early 2000, Gros, a veteran of George Porter, Jr.'s Running Pardners, was given an opportunity to assemble a band for a series of Monday night gigs in his home city. On drums he enlisted the agile, animated Russell Batiste, Jr. (the Funky Meters, Vida Blue), an iconoclast with a propensity to answer his cell phone in mid-jam. Guitarist June Yamagishi is a Japanese native with a blues background. He relocated to New Orleans in 1995, where he joined the Wild Magnolias and has performed and recorded with a number of his inspirations, including B.B. King, Shuggie Otis, Art Neville, and Dr. John. Sax player Jason Mingeldorff has contributed to a number of other area groups such as the New Orleans Nightcrawlers and Galactic. Finally, the bass player role has been shared by Peter V (Cyril Neville & the Uptown All-Stars, Mem Shannon) and Marc Pero (Smilin' Myron).

At the initial gig, the musicians worked from their common frame of reference, offering a generous measure of Meters material (no surprise there). Over the weeks and months that followed, the band evolved from a loose collection of friends and like-minded players into, well, a tight collection of friends and like-minded players. Gros began introducing his original songs (some of which feature his resonant vocals that have been compared to Dr. John's) and the entire band followed suit. Eventually the group's shows gained such acclaim that the players made a more formal commitment, touring both coasts. As the band continues to write new music that melds the musical leanings of its players, Papa Grows Funk may well gain further approbation, beyond the accepted artistry of its members and the band's live vigor.

Doin' It (2001) ★ ★ ★ ½

A robust debut. Some of the compositions remain in comfortable terrain, yet all are embellished by the group's crackling musicianship, especially Gros's vivid B-3, Yamagishi's bristling guitar, and Batiste's salvos on the kit.

Also:

Shakin' (2003)

PARTICLE

www.particlepeople.com

The year 2002 was one of Particle velocity. In June the band was one of only four to perform twice at the Bonnaroo Music Festival, including a late-night surprise set that carried well past sunrise. A few months later, the quartet backed Fred Schneider and Kate Pierson at the Jammy Awards for a romp through some B-52's classics that offered an invigorating, extended take on "Love Shack." Over the course of the year, the band traversed the country from its Los Angeles base to play a series of lengthy, animated shows while welcoming numerous guest musicians into the mix, such as Stefan Lessard, Page McConnell, John Medeski, Stanton Moore, John Popper, and Al Schnier, to name but a few. All of these helped garner the band a Best New Artist designation in *Relix* magazine's year-end issue.

So what is "space porn funk" anyhow? The description originally came from a fan, but the band often invokes it as an apt, elliptical, evocative tag for its instrumental music. Bass player Eric Gould has described the group's sound as "funk-improv-meets-ambient-electronic-groove." At a given moment other elements may predominate, as guitarist Charlie Hitchcock lends jazz chops (though at times one can detect a metal burnish to some of his runs). Steve Molitz, who is ensconced in a bank of keyboards, often serves as the "Launchpad," to reference one of the band's song titles (and Molitz's facial expressions alone are worth the price of admission).

A listen to one of the band's early shows (or its EP) demonstrates that Particle actively reinvests its tunes with new tones and textures (even to such staples as "Kneeknocker" and "Ed and Molly"). At times, one wishes that Hitchcock's guitar could be integrated a bit further into the collective improvisation beyond stepping up for a solo. It is important to recognize, however, that the band's sound is still evolving, and the current quartet has only been together since early 2001 (founding guitarist Dave Simmons, a lifelong diabetic, passed away in December 2000 just months after the band's formation). Nonetheless, Particle is a notable collective that fuses a party energy and vibe with some ethereal, cerebral passages. To this end, projectionist Scott Mackinnon has entered the fray, melding live video with computer-generated images to add visual stimulation and create a Particle accelerator.

Particle (2001) ★ ★ ½

This EP presents four signature Particle tunes. It opens with an early version of "Kneeknocker" that displays original guitarist Dave Simmons's restrained approach to coloring the sound. Charlie Hitchcock's more aggressive style marks the next three, which capture the band's oft-manic mélange,

Particle at Bonnaroo 2002

though there are many more broad strokes than the band currently brings to bear.

Fan site:
www.roadsabreeze.com

PEACH MELBA
www.peachmelba.com

Through an irregular yet not altogether unsatisfying chain of events, it may well be that Peach Melba's national name recognition is eclipsed by the name of its festival. The Athens, Ohio, quintet first came together in 1996 and recorded its debut disc, *From the Frozen Rosebud Emporium*, two years later, but with its initial Peach Tree Gathering on May 7-9, 1999, Peach Melba began a tradition with resonance. Over the subsequent years, each spring the band has welcomed a number of notable groups to one of the Midwest's first fests, including Schleigho, the Recipe, Guest, Ray's Music Exchange, and the John Mullins Band. Peach Melba obviously takes much pride in the event, and as the band continues to expand its tour ambit, it is quite likely that the relative notoriety will reverse.

Peach Melba performed in numerous incarnations before arriving at its current roster. Bass player Bill Nunley is the sole original member of the group, which began as a trio prior to adding 18-year-old guitarist

Morgan Washam in the initial months. Washam's current guitar foil, Brad Huffman, joined the group during its second year, along with drummer Brian Carey (percussionist Jim Embrescia, a friend of Huffman's, came on board a bit later). Throughout much of the '90s, Peach Melba also employed a female singer, most notably Kelly Pope (who appears on the band's debut disc), replaced later by Lea Birbilas. The latter's departure cleared the way for Nunley and Washam to handle all the vocals, and the initial results were decidedly mixed. While the pair has made strides, a stronger voice could further support the group's compositions, which are an amalgam of country, folk, and funk that the group sometimes refers to as funkabilly. Nonetheless, Peach Melba's fan base remains energized by the group's instrumental exertions, which enliven any Peach Tree Gathering.

No Preservatives (2001) ★★ ½

This disc captures the band in the fall of 2000, relatively soon after the current lineup solidified. It reflects both Peach Melba's strengths—good melodic ideas and complementary guitar swagger—along with one significant weak point: its vocals. There is also a tendency towards excess that can distract a listener from some interesting accents, but No Preservatives does still document two rousing nights in the group's hometown.

Also:

From the Frozen Rosebud Emporium (1999)

PERCY HILL
www.percyhill.com

It is always gratifying to be recognized by one's peers. Percy Hill experienced such a moment in 2000 when the Andover, NH, elementary and middle school teacher flew to California as a Disney American Teacher Award recipient. This was not the first such designation for Hill (founder of the Andover One-Wheelers Unicycle Team, which has performed at the Macy's Day Parade and the Fiesta Bowl), as he previously had been named Teacher of the Year by the American Association of Health, Physical Education, Recreation, and Dance, as well as Andover Citizen of the Year. Oh yes, he also has a musical namesake, and that group has experienced its own moments of recognition, including the 2000 Jammy Award it took home for *Colour in Bloom* as Studio Album of the Year.

Percy Hill began as a sextet at the University of New Hampshire in 1993. Here songwriter/ rhythm guitarist Tom Powley, lead guitarist Joe Farrell, and percussionist Zack Wilson pieced together the group, which also included Zack's younger brother Nate on keyboards (the initial bassist was Jeremy Hill, whose father, Percy, participated in the band christening process and eventually became its product). This lineup remained active for nearly five years, mostly performing in New England while releasing three albums of melodic, blues-based rock with soul that proved animated if not innovative.

Then in late 1997 Powley departed, followed by the rhythm section. This eventually led Farrell and Zack Wilson to refashion the band as a quartet with two veterans of the area music scene, drummer/vocalist Aaron Katz (Vitamin C) and bassist John Leccese (Groove Child, Kristin Mueller Trio). Katz's songwriting sparked the group, while the new pair also helped to situate the music more deeply in a jazzier pop realm that only heightened previous comparisons to Steely Dan (though Percy Hill remained in motion—for instance, in September 1999 it performed a gig as Geminatrix, focusing on instrumental electronic/dance music).

Nate Wilson was just 16 years old when Percy Hill formed, and while heralded from the get-go, over the past few years he has further emerged as a resourceful, responsive player. Wilson returned to school to complete his degree in music performance, which helped to keep the band off the road for much of two years. But when Percy Hill returned for three shows in September 2002, it did so with nine additional musicians, including a horn section arranged by Wilson. The group followed up with three more shows in April, again with brass, at times powered by vocalist Anastasia Rene. Still, it is difficult for an independent band to bring 13 players on the road, and the core quartet continues to work with other projects— Wilson and Lecesse with the Assembly of Dust, Katz with his own band, and Farrell in more low-key settings while also teaching music to schoolchildren in Maine. There is a certain frustration on the part of fans, who hope the band will continue to develop new music and offer it up in the live setting. Others see a majestic quality in the group's current approach, which is seemingly dictated solely by interest and inspiration (and while at this rate it looks like Leonard Skinner will

remain rock's most famous gym teacher, his name is misspelled, he's not much on a unicycle, and the Hill yet looms).

Percy Hill Live (2003) ★★★★
The Percy Hill big band interprets much of the material from *Colour in Bloom* along with some newer compositions. An occasional moment of clutter seems to inhibit the players, but these are still two vivid, lustrous discs.

Colour in Bloom (1999) ★★★★½
The 2000 Jammy winner for Studio Album of the Year contains top-notch production, which is all the more impressive from a self-release. *Colour in Bloom* offers melodic songs, some sophisticated arrangements, and energetic, affable performances.

Double Feature (1997) ★★★½
This live offering presents many of the best-known songs from Percy Hill's first incarnation. Some of the longer tracks do wane, but this two-CD set delivers a number of bright moments, particularly from Nate Wilson's keys.

Out of print:
Straight on Till Morning (1996)
Setting the Boat Adrift (1994)

PERPETUAL GROOVE
www.pgroove.com
To be honest, Perpetual Groove doesn't groove all the time. At least not in the sense that many people ascribe to that word, with bass and drums locking in a simple pattern to create a deep pocket, which guitar and

keys then reference and reinforce. The band is capable of that (check out "Bobblehead Funk" or its cover of "Thriller"), but there's more to its sound. At times there is a bit more tension, with complex progressions that willfully spill out of the pocket and circumnavigate the room before returning. At these moments on the groove continuum, the band is somewhere in the realm of the Disco Biscuits, a fitting comparison since the Biscuits' Jon Gutwillig and Marc Brownstein have performed with P Groove. Frankly, if one grants that the Biscuits have helped define a school of music called trance fusion, then the musicians in Perpetual Groove are upperclassmen (still developing and gaining speed).

P Groove guitarist Brock Butler and bass player Adam Perry met each other during their first year at the Savannah College of Art & Design. There they formed the initial incarnation of the group, which gigged for a couple of years until the two other players moved on. Butler and Perry continued to collaborate, and an open mic session yielded keyboardist Matt McDonald and drummer Albert Suttle, who officially joined in August 2001. McDonald often fashions the loops and textures that comprise a major aspect of the band's sound beneath Butler's guitar, but he is also a willing soloist. Suttle, who met the three other musicians while drumming 25 hours a week with the US Army, is the steady, rugged backbone that is essential to this music. Of course, just when an audience feels ready to anticipate the group's next move, the quartet will mix it up, adding a cover from Paul Simon or introducing a sax, banjo, or even an entire band to the stage (Moonshine

Still has jumped on board a few times). The group is still working outward from its influences, but it infuses them with its own concepts and constructs to cast a self-defined Perpetual Groove.

Sweet Oblivious Antidote (2003) ★★★

This is a solid studio debut for this quartet. There is a flow and cohesiveness that lends shape to the disc as a whole, though at times the individual tracks lack specific flavor. In some of its finer moments, however, the band envelops and echoes its melodic expressions.

PHIL LESH & FRIENDS
www.phillesh.net

The music played the maestro. According to Phil Lesh, this accounts for his decision to stop rotating players in and out of the Phil Lesh & Friends lineup and commit to a quintet. "In the first 30 minutes that the band played together we went to places that were new to me and very exciting," Lesh recalls. "We all looked at each other after those first 30 minutes and said, 'Whoa, what was that?' It stops you cold sometimes and you have say, 'This is impossible.' Although everybody in the band had played with me in other contexts with other musicians, this was the first time they all played with me together. I just didn't want to let that go because it was the closest to the shit, the real shit that it had been, and it just keeps getting closer. Of course, you never really get there, but that's the fun of it because it's infinite."

Although the roster coalesced in fall 2000, Phil Lesh & Friends debuted in April 1999, marking Lesh's triumphant return to the stage following his liver transplant surgery five months earlier due to complications from Hepatitis C. (This was not the first time Lesh had employed the "Phil Lesh & Friends" appellation—he had first done so in 1994 at a benefit for the Berkeley, CA, public school music programs, performing an acoustic set with Jerry Garcia, Bob Weir, and Vince Welnick. Oh yes, as for the legacy of the transplant, a grateful Lesh has delivered an "Organ Donor Rap" at every subsequent performance.) The initial Friends to join the bass player for a three-night stand at the Warfield in San Francisco included Page McConnell, Trey Anastasio, Steve Kimock, and John Molo. This group set the tone for much of

what has followed, in opening the run with a 39-minute version of "Viola Lee Blues."

From here Lesh began rotating players through the lineup, returning to many of the same songs with fresh ears, eyes, and appendages. The lone stalwart throughout this period was Molo, who first locked with Lesh during the initial Other Ones tour (Molo sat out a few shows in 1999, however, which leads to our trivia question: Name the two other drummers to perform with P&F. Answer in a moment, kids). Between May 1999 and September 2000, collaborators included Jorma Kaukonen, David Nelson, Paul Barrere, Billy Payne, Kyle Hollingsworth,

Phil Lesh & Friends at Red Rocks, July 2001.

Michael Kang, Al Schnier, Derek Trucks, Jeff Pevar, and Robben Ford (also drummers Prairie Prince and Billy Kreutzmann—our correct quiz response).

While unquestionably talented, the summer 2000 roster of Lesh, Molo, Ford, Barrere, and Payne never quite cohered or pushed the music to the fringe as many of its antecedents had done. Another criticism levied at this time was the prevalence of Lesh's vocals, particularly on Garcia songs rearranged to fit the bassist's register, which some felt sounded a bit off (one irony is that a few years after the "Let Phil Sing" chants prevailed during the GD era, an apt addendum might have been "But Not Quite as Much"). Lesh remedied this in the fall, putting together a P&F comprised of himself and four artists who had performed with him in previous incarnations and would become his steady band: Molo, Warren Haynes, Jimmy Herring (best known then for his work in Aquarium Rescue Unit and Jazz Is Dead but eventually to become guitarist in the Dead), and Rob Barraco (part of an intriguing journey that carried the keyboard player from covering much of the Grateful Dead's material in the Zen Tricksters to performing it with the Dead—when on stage with Lesh his facial expressions at times are the quintessence of beatific). Not only do all of these players share a predisposition for treks to the musical outposts, but Haynes has the pipes, and he increasingly took on additional vocal responsibilities. Moreover, to paraphrase Barry Manilow (an unlikely future Friend, but who knows?), Haynes writes the songs. Suddenly P&F, who had been relying on the Dead catalogue and select covers, began introducing

original material contributed by Lesh and his bandmates, often with lyrics by Robert Hunter. Meanwhile the group pursued what Lesh has referred to as psychedelic Dixieland music, whereby, "Whoever has the spotlight at the moment is the first among equals for now. Then someone else will take that position, or ideally what's created is a web of lines and relationships. That's the best way to perceive it. That's what Charlie Mingus said about his music. He said, 'Focus in front of the music and listen to the whole thing, don't try to pick out any one strand because you'll miss the totality.' That's how I ask the players to approach it."

After two years of steady gigging, by the summer of 2002 the future of the quintet (which some refer to as the Quintet or the PLQ) seemed in doubt. For one thing, Haynes was working it really hard, carrying a heavy tour load with Gov't Mule and the Allman Brothers Band (the ABB and P&F aligned their tour schedules for a few co-headlining shows in 2001 in 2002, and on two insane days in June 2002 Haynes pulled triple duty, performing with the Mule as well). Meanwhile, after Lesh reached a rapprochement with his former Grateful Dead band mates following a dispute over business affairs that had extended over a few years, the Other Ones reunited at Terrapin Station in East Troy, WI, and then set off on tour. Phil Lesh & Friends didn't perform for more than a year until an announcement that the five members would regroup for three shows at the Warfield in September 2003. Still, Lesh affirms, "Ever since my transplant my relationship to music has been tribal on the deepest level, and with this band it's almost automatic. I hate to say that because I don't want to jinx it. The alchemy is so strong that it's almost automatic the way our group mind can open up the pipeline for that eternal music that we're all trying to channel and funnel through ourselves so that it can exist in our plane." Good alchemists are hard to find these days, so one has to believe that P&F will endure in some form.

There and Back Again (2002) ★★★

Don Gehman (John Mellencamp, REM, Hootie & the Blowfish) produced this studio disc that strives to distill each tune to its essence (though given Robert Hunter's verbose wordplay, most tracks still fall in the five-to-six minute range). In this setting, some of the songs fare better than others, and Hunter's images and aphorisms remain vivid while Haynes's "Patchwork Quilt" is particularly affecting. All in all a robust release, particularly in conjunction with the bonus disc that offers four live tracks, including "St. Stephen" and "Dark Star" with guest Derek Trucks.

Out of print:

Love Will See You Through (1999)
Two live discs from an early incarnation of the band circa June 1999 with Steve Kimock, Jorma Kaukonen, Pete Sears, Prairie Prince, Zoe Ellis, and Caitlin Cornwell.

Fan site:

www.philzone.com—Jammy Award Winner, 2002

PHISH
www.phish.com

Don't hate them because they're beautiful. Come to think of it, don't hate them even if you're not quite sold on their pulchritude. (Before you rush to judgment on this one, though, check out the band all laced-up and frilly on the cover of *Rolling Stone*, an appearance the group acknowledged in quintessential fashion from the stage on February 14, 2003, by busting out the Dr. Hook classic. Shel Silverstein, who may be better known for his children's books than his music, even though Johnny Cash popularized his "Boy Named Sue," wrote "Cover of the *Rolling Stone*" for Dr. Hook in 1972—alas, two years before the initial issue of *Relix*, so there has been minimal musical crowing of that appearance.)

Actually, hatred is quite a hyperbolic sentiment, as most negative assessments extend no further than exasperation and envy, typically on the part of other bands' fans. Although on the topic of exaggerated reactions, Phish supporters maintain a fervent yet not altogether fawning relationship with the group. For example, at the close of Phish's July 30, 2003, show in Camden, NJ, immediately following a Burgettstown, PA, gig in which the quartet revisited several songs it had not played for some time (precipitated by a consultation of iPods loaded with a live repertoire spanning two decades), some audience members booed what they deemed to be a commonplace performance (within the Phish continuum, of course). Such a reaction is often wrought from a checklist mentality in which quality is defined solely by rarity. This happens with groups other than Phish, though at present it is most prevalent among a certain subset of Phish fans typically attending numerous dates on a given tour (but in this case, obviously not the preceding one). Extreme manifestations can suck the joy out of a particular concertgoer, and intervention is recommended, encouraging that person to ease up on the throttle a bit and take it one show at a time. After all, a set list of scarce songs does not equal an exceptional show...except when it does, as with July 29, 2003, in Burgettstown.

Another such example took place following the band's self-imposed hiatus, which began in October 2000, as some fans directed their ire at guitarist Trey Anastasio when he toured with a solo band, denouncing him as a tyrant, at least through snappy T-shirt slogans directing antipathy at a principal source of their once-and-future pleasure. ("The 'Trey is Wilson' shirts were nothing, you should have seen the notes people left on our tour bus," Anastasio chuckles.)

The cessation of public Phish performances, which extended from October 7, 2000, through December 31, 2002 (save three spontaneous songs at a wedding on December 1, 2001, 420 days following the band's last appearance, doood), certainly carried some impact, though the degree is still debated. The media often treated Phish's intermission as a jamband subsidy, speculating on which groups would benefit from the grant. (*The New York Times,* for instance, selected String Cheese Incident, to which SCI bassist Keith Mosely responded, "I think the band most likely to benefit from Phish taking a hiatus is Phish, really. They deserved to take a break, and after we've been together for however long, 15 years, I hope by God we get to take a year or two off as well.") In looking at ticket sales, a number of groups markedly increased their concert draws during Phish's two-year hiatus. One might argue, however, that any developing act would do the same over such a period, particularly given the increased interest in the jamband realm (which some would attribute to the Phish break, yielding a chicken/egg conundrum. Incidentally, one demonstrable effect was to vest "hiatus" with a new gravity—it became "the H-word" in certain circles, with one fan Web site relating a student's disruption of a vocabulary lesson by following up any mention of "hiatus" with the refrain "sucks").

Indeed, while it is likely that Phish's departure yielded little direct loyalty realignment from the group's fanbase ("Hmmm, Phish isn't playing so I guess it's the Cheese for me"), a case could well be made that the band's departure cleared the way for additional spending and energies to be directed at other groups, allowing fans to reconnect with live music at the club level and establishing a newfound immediacy that redounded to broad effect. (We'll see, though—that master's thesis is likely on the way or in the works.)

Still, with all due respect to artists such as the Grateful Dead, the Allman Brothers Band, and Jimi Hendrix (who certainly influenced Phish), no group has had a more reverberating impact on the jamband scene today. For instance, Phish's 1992 Elektra debut, *A Picture of Nectar,* has long served as the jamband primer (it has since been amended with pocket parts—the preceding law treatise pun is dedicated to the quartet's multitasking archivist/attorney, Mr. Kevin Shapiro). Here the band glides from genre to genre with fortitude, heralding an approach that does not necessarily privilege any of these modes, whether bluegrass, jazz, Latin, progressive, or straight-up, pounding arena rock. Numerous younger musicians and would-be musicians absorbed *A Picture of Nectar* as well as Phish's live shows, which then suffused their own measures and manners.

Phish is also an archetype in realizing the grass roots potential of the Internet. Many of these initiatives have emanated from the group's fans, some of whom began an e-mail discussion list in 1990 that became a Usenet newsgroup (rec.music.phish, the third such platform dedicated to one band, following groups created for the Beatles and the Grateful Dead), and then spawned the Phish.net Web site. A wave of additional sites followed, not only personal trading pages and those catering to the majesty of minutia (Ladies and Gentlemen, you are now free to peruse the Phististics of my friend and yours,

Trey Anastasio and Mike Gordon lift off, 8/14/93 (as heard on *Live Phish 07*).

the Timer, Zzyzx "David" Steinberg at Ihoz.com/PhishStats), but also a media archive (phisharchive.com), a women's organization (phunky.com), a fan story page (Pholktales.com), a paean to Phish lighting director Chris Kuroda (ck5.org), and a game site devoted to predicting set lists in a manner akin to a fantasy sports league (Phantasytour.com). The band in turn has moved its mail order ticketing to the Web and in 2003 created the *Live Phish* downloads series at Livephish.com, allowing fans to purchase soundboards that become available in the hours following each show.

Indeed, particularly due to these online efforts, Phish is certainly the most documented band of its contemporaries (and is accelerating towards such status within the broader annals of rock). In addition to the Web presence, this assertion factors in the organization's own self-cataloging and self-chronicling, fan distribution of the group's music in a multitude of media, and the proliferation of printed words—half a dozen books and counting, though the Rosetta Stone is *The Phish Companion* compiled by the Mockingbird Foundation, a nonprofit organization that directs funds to music education programs. (Incidentally, bassist Michael Elliott Gordon would now like to take a moment of your time to offer the following corrective to a reference he spotted in another book: "Mike's high school band, the Tombstone Blues Band, featured Kerri Keefe, a great blues guitarist from Hopkinton, MA. Kerri was Mike's early introduction to blues and early rock, and he showed Mike how to let that kind of music seep into one's soul." And now back to our entry...) Sometimes it

seems as if through these resources one can locate any gobbet of heretofore arcane Phish tidings and trivia, short of Mike Gordon's phone number (and come to think of it, that's out there as well, or least a voice mailbox that the bassist created in conjunction with his *Inside In* release).

Two overarching philosophies intertwine with Phish's improvisational ingenuity and oft-overlooked knack for melody to strengthen the fans' obsession. The first of these is a collective charge to bring a diligence and resolve to the music without taking oneself too seriously. Thus upon arriving at its current lineup in 1986, Phish engendered some accoutrements of doof, such as trampolines, vacuum cleaner solos, and drummer Jon Fishman's donut dress—but it did so against a vigorous backdrop of rehearsals in which the musicians viewed the band as a job (which one might well say it is, albeit with erratic hours and a general lack of urine testing), thereby punching in for daily sessions (one might also say that there's a particular postmodern profundity to the tramps and the vacuum cleaner, if not quite the dress).

Secondly, while much of the group's initial slew of songs featured complex structures and ricocheting time signatures, the lyrics could be nonsensical to the point of imperceptibility. Certainly this was the intent—a factor of the player's penchants and personalities—but it's also important to recognize that the band members and principal lyricist Tom Marshall were in their early to mid-twenties when composing many of these tunes (which, however, does not confer a free pass, since Gregg Allman wasn't yet 23 when he wrote, among others, "Whipping

Post," "Midnight Rider," and "It's Not My Cross to Bear").

Meanwhile, the band has also conveyed an inclusiveness that feels exclusive, welcoming everyone yet encouraging fans to dig in. Phish has facilitated this in a broad sense through mail order ticketing, and also—back in the day—by doggedly pushing to carve out an exception in its Elektra contract to allow audience taping at a time when the band held little leverage. Other specific examples (of many) include: sharing a series of musical clues with audience members (the secret language), allowing fans to participate in the selection of the quartet's first two musical Halloween costumes, tweaking concertgoers repeatedly with musical teases, engaging the audience in an ongoing game of chess during fall 1995 (both sides won a game), and creating festival weekends beginning with the Clifford Ball, in which Phish did not merely construct a stage but crafted an enveloping environment built around an elaborate art installation.

The group has also presented the occasional if-you-snooze-you-lose performances by offering late-night, unannounced sets at its fests or bookending big gigs with other momentous ones (as on June 26, 1994, in Charleston, WV, when the band performed the rare Gamehendge song cycle followed by a run-through of the band's *Hoist* release, or November 2, 1998, when it followed up the previous show's Halloween performance of the Velvet Underground's *Loaded* by interpreting Pink Floyd's *Dark Side of the Moon*, or the Great Gag in the Sky, which took place atop a control tower at 2:00 A.M. on the Sunday morning of the IT festival). Phish's second set from its 1999 Big Cypress New Year's Eve show encapsulates all of the aforementioned aspects, as the band rode to the stage atop a hotdog (the same one it used to fly over the crowd during the 1994 New Year's Eve gig at Boston Garden), revived a prostrate Father Time by feeding him prodigious amounts of Meatsticks—a reference to the band's song (and dance) of that name—before performing a set that exceeded seven and a half consecutive hours of music and included Anastasio's exhortation for the crowd to chant "Cheesecake" rather than applaud during a segment filmed for ABC's televised Millennium celebration program.

By mid-2000, however, some felt that the band had started to lose some of its direction and drive. Phish had consistently revitalized itself over the years by introducing new instruments or elements, and these observers couldn't foresee where the band would go. The answer, of course, was: away. The time off served its members well, with Gordon and keyboardist Page McConnell stepping up their songwriting while serving as bandleaders, a role often assumed by Anastasio for Phish. The quartet returned on New Year's Eve 2002 with minimal rehearsal of its older compositions yet a bounty of new material, delivering a run of shows abounding in energy if lacking in musical precision. Two tours later the vitality remained, complemented by a bit more meticulousness.

Back in the summer of 1992, when Phish opened a tour for Santana, some fans speculated on whether the quartet would ever be able to headline in such amphitheaters. One individual who entered the dialogue ended it with the question, "Well we like them, why shouldn't everyone else?" To a degree this has transpired, as Phish has become an estimable influence to a broad swath of its peers and many others peering up at the most celebrated of jambands. Hey, it's not Phish's fault. Then again, in the best way possible, it is.

Round Room (2002) ★★★ ½

This release feels somewhat akin to a rehearsal session (to the point where Trey Anastasio sounds as if he has a cold). While in some instances this looseness serves the songs (which are a bit more open-ended than those on the preceding few studio discs), some of these ideas warrant additional development.

Farmhouse (2000) ★★★★ ½

Farmhouse surpasses even *Billy Breathes* in terms of the band wringing the most from itself and its songs in the studio.

Hampton Comes Alive (1999) ★★★★

The final precursor to the *Live Phish* series, *Hampton Comes Alive* collects a two-night stand at Hampton Coliseum on November 20 and 21, 1998. Alas, there are no Frampton covers, but the band offers up plenty of others, including "Quinn the Eskimo," "Roses Are Free," "Gettin' Jiggy Wit It," "Tubthumping," and "Sabotage." All in all, two playful set lists and shows to match.

The Siket Disc (1999) ★★★

A series of raw improvisations drawn from the *Story of a Ghost* sessions, and named for engineer John Siket. The mostly formless, atmospheric improv is captivating upon first listen, in part because it provides a stark contrast with much of what one might expect from the band during this period. Still, these tracks do not altogether cohere and captivate with each additional spin.

Story of the Ghost (1998) ★★★ ½

The studio product of the band's funk era is at times surprisingly subdued (especially the vocals). Still, every sound feels precise and deliberate, beckoning the listener to don headphones.

Phish (The White Tape) (1998) ★★

Much of the music on these demos recorded between 1984 and 1986 had circulated among traders, though not with the clarity presented here. Frankly, the true excitement for many is in the track listings, which identify precisely who appears (and clear up at least one debate: "Ingest" and "NO2" are indeed different songs, the former written by Anastasio, the latter by Mike Gordon). This one is mostly for completists, or those who wish to monitor the band's development, with partial versions of "Divided Sky" and "Fluffs Travels" (and a version of "Alumni Blues").

Slip, Stitch and Pass (1997) ★★★★

Recorded in Hamburg, Germany, on March 1, 1997, this is the first official release with versions of "Mike's Song" and "Weekapuag" (alas, no "Hydrogen"). "Wolfman's Brother" is a highlight, and elsewhere one can find the band in a frisky mood, throwing down musical quotes (discover them for yourself).

Billy Breathes (1996) ★★★★ ½

Phish's first great studio album. A wonderful meld of composition and presentation that calls to mind the latter-day Beatles.

A Live One (1995) ★★★★★

A sparkling representation of Phish from this era. People go back and forth on the 31-minute "Tweezer," but it is often gripping as it unfolds. Other bright moments from these two discs include "Harry Hood," an audience-abetted "Wilson," and a definitive "Stash."

Hoist (1994) ★★★ ½

This may be the band's most straightforward pop release (of a sort). Still, many of these bright songs have an immediate appeal that doesn't necessarily linger.

Rift (1993) ★★★

The production is a bit leaden on this disc, weighing down some solid material that often sparkles in the live setting.

A Picture of Nectar (1992) ★★★ ½

An influential disc. However, in its to zeal to emphasize a multiplicity of moods, the band does not utilize the medium to pursue each of these tracks to its fullest.

Lawn Boy (1990) ★★ ½

Despite stereotypes levied at Phish, this is probably the only album in which the band appears somewhat ill at ease in bringing its live material into the studio. A number of these songs feel flat and unfinished.

Junta (1989) ★★★★ ½

Released in 1989 and then reissued by Elektra three years later with bonus live material from 1988, this is a relatively unvarnished studio recording from a callow band that is inventive and occasionally ebullient.

LIVE PHISH DOWNLOADS:

The band offers unedited soundboard recordings of its shows from December 31, 2002, onward at Livephish.com—*Live Phish 01* to *Live Phish 20*. Here are five recommendations from five years:

Live Phish 01 (2001) ★★★★

December 14, 1995, Broome County Arena, Binghamton, NY. A robust performance from one of the band's most popular periods.

Live Phish 07 (2002) ★★★★ ½

August 14, 1993, World Music Theatre, Tinley Park, IL. A second show from another strong era. A night of tantalizing improv embellished by quotes and digressions. The August 11 filler on disc three adds thunder.

Live Phish 15 (2002) ★★★★ ½

October 31, 1996, the Omni, Atlanta, GA. The band's take on *Remain in Light* is compelling and resourceful, serving to inform the sound throughout the era to follow.

Live Phish 16 (2002) ★★★★ ½

October 31, 1998, Thomas & Mack Center, Las Vegas, NV. This release not only presents a vivid interpretation of the Velvet Underground's *Loaded*, but also a crackling third set and an additional disc of highlights from the previous night.

Live Phish 18 (2003) ★★★

May 7, 1994, Bomb Factory, Dallas, TX. Skip right ahead to disc two to begin the band's first extended "Tweezer," broken up over 67 minutes with some rock radio staples to remain conversational in tone.

Also:

Mike Gordon—*Inside In* (2003) ★★★★

This is an odd yet affable soundtrack of sorts to Gordon's *Outside Out* film. Burbling, babbling passages predominate in spots, yet they never detract from the overall warmth of sound, if not always sentiment.

Mike Gordon and Leo Kottke—*Clone* (2002) ★★★★

A well-matched pairing of two iconoclasts features some compelling counterpoints to Kottke's fingerpicking.

Fan sites:

www.phish.net
www.phisharchive.com
www.mockingbirdfoundation.org/
www.ihoz.com/PhishStats.html
www.gadiel.com/phish
www.phunky.com
www.pholktales.com
www.ck5.org—perhaps the only fan site devoted to a lighting director

PORK TORNADO

www.porktornado.com

Pork Tornado is the oldest and most musically diverse of the Phish side projects that performed and recorded during the band's two-year hiatus. The five-piece group, co-founded by drummer Jon Fishman, is also the least

likely to initiate any improvisational flurries. However, Pork Tornado could vie for top honors in any hypothetical "Challenge of the Bar Bands."

The quintet began its career jukebox-style, at Burlington's Club Toast the night after Phish's 1997 Great Went. Five musicians from the Burlington, Vermont, area took the stage that evening and began calling out tunes to one another from a range of sources, mostly funk but also R&B with a bit of country & western tossed in as well. Fishman was joined by guitarist Dan Archer, keyboard player Phil Abair, bassist Aaron Hershey, and Joe Moore on saxes—all enthusiasts of various styles and standards, which they had at their fingertips (along with the ability to fake their way through, if need be).

As the group continued to gig, it started to introduce original songs with the stylistic multiformity of its cover selections. The band continued to build on the latter repertoire, as well—for instance, juxtaposing a Tornado tune, Moore's proclamation to "Kiss My Black Ass," with the "white trilogy," which moved from "White Room" to "Play That Funky Music (White Boy)" to "White Wedding." In the live setting Pork Tornado typically shares the proclivities of its audiences, keeping it loose-limbed and lively while staving off the last call.

Pork Tornado (2002) ★★★

An affable assortment of the band's originals, bounding from funk to blues to country-swing to honky tonk. The three wild cards are Archer's solo guitar piece "Fellini" as well as Fishman's attenuated "Organ" and colorful election chant, "All American."

PROJECT Z

The Z in Project Z stands for Zambi, which may be all you need to know for some sense of what's going on here. Oh yes, and the core trio is comprised of Aquarium Rescue Unit alumni Jimmy Herring and Jeff Sipe on guitar and drums, respectively, with longtime Bruce Hampton collaborator Ricky Keller on bass. Indeed, Project Z is built for speed and precision, with an underlying zeal to challenge the fundament of music through improvisation.

The band is a direct offshoot of the Apartment Project, a loose jam that Sipe (a.k.a. Apt. No. 258) hosted regularly at Atlanta's Little 5 Points Pub in the mid-to-late '90s. Whenever Herring happened to be in town, Sipe invited him to come down and join in. The Apartment Project, which then typically included Keller and percussionist Count M'butu, took the stage without a single song for extended sets of pure extempore musical conversation. More than a year later, someone handed Herring a tape of one of these performances. His enthusiastic response was echoed by Keller and Sipe, and Project Z was formed.

The resulting band perpetuates the musical ethos that is the essence of Zambi, Hampton's term for approaching music in the moment, without ego. Herring relates: "Our whole concept is to have Jeff kick off a groove, and then Ricky and I just start playing. We never want to lose sight of our original idea, and that is to totally improvise for real. Improvising to a lot of people means to go out there and play a bunch of stuff from your vocabulary. You go out there, you don't know what you're going to do, but you know you're going to be playing your stuff. But with us, we go out there and we don't have any preconceived notions of what

we're going to do. Sometimes we just detune the instruments to where there's no way you can fall back on what you know."

The results may not be everyone's cup of Z, but in the live setting it is often a stunning, sublime experience. Herring shares this reaction upon listening back to that first live show: "I heard stuff repeatedly throughout the night that I am just not physically capable of doing. If you lose yourself in the music, then it's not you doing it. That's what Project Z is for me."

Note: Ricky Keller died of a heart attack on June 22, 2003. An accomplished musician and skilled engineer with a kind soul, Keller also "embodied the spirit of the Z," as Herring relates. He will be missed.

Project Z (2001) ★★★★

There is a constant flow of music here, with some of the lengthier themes or songs linked by shorter interstitials, including three "Guitarguments" between Herring and guest Derek Trucks, along with appearances by Col. Bruce Hampton on Z phone. At times there could be a tad more shaping to this collection of studio improvisations, but Herring and Sipe are in fine fettle, with Keller a capable running buddy as the band moves from mood to mood, often with a fusion feel.

PSYCHEDELIC BREAKFAST

www.psychedelicbreakfast.com
Sometimes it's hard to get past a name. With so many entertainment options, folks will make occasional snap judgments based on rather superficial info. This being the case, there is no doubt that some individuals have looked right past upcoming Psychedelic Breakfast shows because, at first blush, the

band's appellation has the word "lame" written all over it. The name gets better upon further review, when one recognizes that it is a riff on the Pink Floyd song "Alan's Psychedelic Breakfast." If that doesn't help, folks should think back to the days when Phish was dismissed based on its moniker alone (with critics puffing out the "ph" with a dismissive tone). The Phish comparison is not inapposite, as on rare occasions PB will pull out a spot-on version of "You Enjoy Myself" (for instance, as a bonus fourth set on the "Jam Nation" radio show in January 2003).

Although Psychedelic Breakfast officially formed in 1998, guitarist Tim Palmieri, drummer Adrian Tramontano, and bass player Ron Spears first played together a few years earlier during their freshman year of high school. (In fact, Palmieri and Tramontano gave lessons to Spears following his suggestion that they create a band, and the bassist's development over the past few years has been a significant part of PB's efforts to shape its own sound.) A chance meeting with keyboard player Jordan Giangreco led to a jam session and, shortly thereafter, to the creation of the group. In addition to Phish and Floyd, the young musicians were also partial to Zappa and Zeppelin, and this amalgam of intensity and precision has become the band's hallmark, particularly through Palmieri's eruptive guitar swagger.

The Connecticut-based group playfully abandons restraint. For instance, in 2000, when the producers of Greenstock at Yasgur's Farm told the band it could exceed its one-hour allocated stint as it saw fit, the band obliged with a six-hour performance.

Similarly, the group typically comes blasting out of the gate, propelled by Palmieri's strident, quicksilver guitar leads and the complementary drumming of Tramontano, who has been described as a "spastic human metronome." At times this all-out assault can be numbing, as the band is still working on its dynamics (and its songwriting, which often needs focus), but many audiences prove spellbound by the results.

Bona Fide (2003) ★★★ ½
This September 2002 live disc, recorded at Pearl Street in Northampton, Massachusetts, is assertive and absorbing if a bit excessive. In addition to some reasonably well-developed originals, the band offers its take on "Hot 'Lanta" with guitarist Palmieri dueling it out with strident guest Seth Yacovone.

Deuce (2001) ★★ ½
The band's songwriting steps forward from its debut, with some more developed ideas and fewer collections of cool riffs. The lyrics still don't match the musicianship, which is often ebullient and tantalizing.

Psychedelic Breakfast (1999) ★ ½
Plenty of good ideas and solid playing, but not all that cohesive—with some goofy, distracting lyrics as well. This disc is the work of a gifted young band still trying to synthesize its influences.

R

THE RADIATORS
www.radiators.org

The preponderance of bands in this book should be so fortunate as to travel a path parallel to that of the Radiators. The quintet is one of the definitive New Orleans groups and a Jazz Fest staple (like the Cajun fare that also provides the fodder for some of keyboardist Ed Volker's compositions—remember kids, when you're having a crawfish boil, "Suck the Head"). The Rads are the product of a jam session that has resonated for more than a quarter century.

On January 28, 1978, Volker and two of his bandmates in the Rhapsodizers, guitarist Camile Baudoin and drummer Frank Bua, invited guitarist Dave Malone and bass player Reggie Scanlan for a garage session. Scanlan, who had recently worked with Malone in Roadapple, had also put in some gigs with Eddie Money ("He assured me that he was going to be big"—which turned out to be true largely due to the efforts of his manager, Bill Graham) and another quintessential Crescent City performer, Professor Longhair. Malone was a veteran of numerous groups, including a few with his brother Tommy and later John Magnie, who would go on to co-form the Subdudes (who then became the Dudes before returning as the Subdudes—and no, the Malones do not have another brother named Sam who enjoyed a brief career as a relief pitcher for the Red Sox before opening a Boston bar). Once in Volker's garage, the five musicians kept the music flowing for nearly five hours, after which they immediately committed to this new project if not its name, moving from Them Neighborhood Boys to the Weema Woppas, and finally the Radiators. (Fun fact: A few months after the group formed, on the other side of the earth a group with the same name began performing in Australia. These Radiators, with some personnel changes, are still presenting "classic pub rock" and sharing the news at www.theradiators.com, which is why the US Radiators are at www.radiators.org.)

Over the years, the group acquired a piscine association that has come to describe their music and spirited supporters. Phish Heads: Meet your predecessors and fellow travelers, the Fish Heads (this term evolved in part from Volker's description of the Radiators' music as "Funkier than a Fish Head"). Fans have maintained New Orleans-style Krewes in various regions of the country to celebrate the band and turn each show into an event when the Rads route through. The band has reciprocated by performing at such gigs as an annual private party during Jazz Fest (hosted by the SNAFU Krewe) as well as the invite-only Mardi Gras MOM's Ball (presented by the Krewe of "Mystick Orphans and Mysfits"). These same boosters maintain the band's set list archive, the BoulliaBase (natch), and have established a unique program at Radsfans.net—a Tip Jar for fans to kick in a bill or two to thank the band for a performance enjoyed via a live recording acquired through a trade (which, all in all, seems pretty fair, and what the heck, it's voluntary anyhow).

The Krewes particularly appreciate the festive spirit and fluctuating components of the Radiators' music. The latter trait extends not only to the band's improvisation but also to their song selection, as they draw on a cache of more than 1,000 cover tunes they have performed, as well as an excess of 300 originals. (That 300 figure reflects only the originals that make it to the stage. Volker is said to have written more than 2,000 songs, working up just a fraction of them for the Rads with fellow lead vocalist Malone. This "greatest hits" approach has yielded some engaging results, which Epic Records acknowledged in the late '80s by releasing three of the band's albums that received some steady radio rotation.) The resulting Cajun boogie is comprised of R&B, funk, blues, and psychedelic flavors, which some younger audiences find a bit old school since it most assuredly is—there's no trance fusion here. Meanwhile, one factor that may have curtailed some national recognition (if such characterization is apt for a band that has been hitting it for more than 25 years) is the lack of an essential live album that captures the full command and cadences of the group. A vault series seems in order, culled from the 3,000-plus dose of radiation the band has administered since 1978.

The Radiators (2001) ★★★ ½

A favorable return to the studio that presents the band's many hues. The songs are not always distinctive, but they are delivered adroitly with the Rads' inflections.

Live at American Music Hall (1998) ★★★

A collection of mostly newer material recorded at San Francisco's Great American Music Hall in September 1997. The intent is to vivify the compositions in this context, and the results are agreeable if not altogether rousing.

Bucket of Fish (1994) ★★★ ½

Two Minneapolis shows from June 1992 are represented on this live disc. The results do reflect some of the zest associated with the quintet's live show, but not the full scope of their material and mettle.

Total Evaporation (1990) ★★ ½

The title isn't so far off—this final Epic disc is the least successful of the three. The music is pleasant enough but rarely more.

Zigzagging through Ghostland (1989) ★★★ ½

A solid mix of older tunes such as "Red Dress" (originally recorded on the Radiators' debut), with some newer material. The songs may not quite have the spunk and the spark of the prior effort, but it is a solid studio representation.

Law of the Fish (1987) ★★★★

The band's major label debut feels like a greatest hits disc as it offers a number of the best-known songs associated with the group, including "Like Dreamers Do," "Love Is a Tangle," and "Suck the Head." Some of these could benefit from a bit more breathing room, but all in all, a fine effort.

Also:

New Dark Ages (1995)
SNAFU 10-31-91 (1992)
New Adventures (1983)
Heat Generation (1981)
Work Done on Premises (1980)

BouillaBase—set list archive—
www.ancientfurnace.net
www.radsfans.net

Discussion list (of one notable Krewe):

Krewe of Degenerate Music Junkies—
*www.groups.yahoo.com/group/KreweOfDegen
erate/*

RAILROAD EARTH

www.railroadearth.com

Railroad Earth first took motion during an informal "picking party" hosted by Andy Goessling. The multi-instrumentalist (guitar, banjo, flute, sax), best known as a founding member of the R&B/swing band the Blue Sparks from Hell, invited his longtime bandmate, fiddler Tim Carbone, and Todd Sheaffer, former guitarist and lead vocalist for From Good Homes. The three were so pleased with this initial session that they decided to continue the momentum, with Sheaffer writing some material and mandolin player John Skehan invited to join. In early 2001 the quartet tapped drummer Carey Harmon and upright bass player Dave Von Dollen to record an album as Railroad Earth, a name drawn from the Jack Kerouac prose poem "October in the Railroad Earth" (which opens *The Jack Kerouac Collection* CD box set, with Steve Allen tinkling away on piano).

The band's first official gig took place in May, and within months Railroad Earth had landed slots at the Telluride Bluegrass Festival, the Grey Fox Bluegrass Festival, and High Sierra (facilitated by the group's winsome compositions, solid musicianship, and

Sheaffer's notoriety through From Good Homes).

The group's friendly, bluegrass-flavored roots music holds appeal for From Good Homes stalwarts and even some listeners drawn to more traditional country (rendering it irrelevant to many that the point of origin for this down-home sound is New Jersey). Railroad Earth also has a burnished, poppier side while offering some Celtic nuances, jazzier passages, and an emphasis on vocal harmonies. At its shows, Railroad Earth balances tighter representations of its music with animated improv, as the group typically builds up steam and tosses it around bluegrass-style, building on the prevailing melodic ideas but never moving so far out as to lose sight of the song.

Bird in the House (2002) ★★★

The band adds some textures on its sophomore release but still retains its rippling, rollicking side. A bit more developed than the debut with an alt-country feel, this disc is defined by its engaging melodic songwriting accented by four-part vocal harmonies.

Black Bear Sessions (2001) ★★★

These sessions mark Railroad Earth as a popping, pleasing ensemble. While the sound is not necessarily inventive, there are some interesting turns, such as the group's takes on Tom Waits's "Cold Water" and From Good Homes' "Head."

Discussion list:

Earthboard—
www.groups.yahoo.com/group/earthboard/

RAISINHEAD

www.raisinhead.com

The prevailing trend among younger bands in the jamband orbit is to employ songs foremost as vehicles for flights of improvisation. Many of these artists fail to appreciate the full splendor of the music crafted by the Grateful Dead, in which the core compositions powered the engine. The six members of RaisinHead do aspire to deliver music in the latter mode, striving for an emotional engagement with the listener (and while the group's songs may not resonate as soundly as the work of Garcia/Hunter or Neil Young, they do forge a connection). The Grateful Dead is also an apt reference because while Rob Beaulieu founded RaisinHead in 2001, over the previous decade he and some of his bandmates performed in groups such as Slipknot and Box of Rain, which did interpret the music of the Dead (while other RaisinHead members, such as Ominous Seapod alums Tom Pirozzi and Brian Mangini, share these aims from a slightly varied perspective).

RaisinHead also merits citation as the only band in this book fronted by a former professional hockey player. After graduating from New York's Hamilton College, Beaulieu put in a European stint before returning to the US in the early '90s and turning his focus to music (alas, "The Ballad of Teemu Seleanne" remains unwritten). RaisinHead developed after Beaulieu invited Mangini to sit in for a few dates with his previous project. This resulted in an assist from the keyboard player's Pods cohort Ol' T.P., who then recommended drummer Scott Appicelli. Beaulieu also drew in his longtime associate Ted Grey

(Harvest) on guitar and vocals. As of late RaisinHead has toured with four lead singers through the addition of sax player Chris Scanlan. The vocalists' varied tones serve the music quite well, drawing some comparisons to the Band, given a similar approach to songwriting (and also a common eastern New York base). Still, RaisinHead is adept at improvisation, as along with his musical background, Beaulieu's years on the ice certainly have reinforced the value of changing on the fly (and you thought this was going to lead to a metaphor about goals).

Back to the Tracks (2002) ★★★

A sturdy first effort, moving from rootsier rock to ballad. The musicianship is adroit and the songs often inviting.

RAISINHILL

www.raisinhill.com

It's not always easy to dance to Raisinhill. That doesn't mean that people don't do so. But the band's music, which shifts tempos and moods (admittedly in a more languid manner than, say, Schleigho or the Jacob Fred Jazz Odyssey), often lends itself to the subtler physical expressions of head-bobbers. An increasing company of such individuals (along with some steady groovers) has frequented Raisinhill's shows ever since its three band members met and began performing at Bridgeport, Connecticut's Acoustic Café in 2001.

The trio's direction is not that surprising given that guitarist John Kasiewicz was a student of Ernie Stires at Goddard College where, like Trey Anastasio, he studied atonal composition. Kasiewicz shares another connection with the Phish guitarist: While at Goddard he met J. Willis Pratt and became a member of his band, We're Bionic, both recording and performing with Jon Fishman. We're Bionic also received a rare gig opening for Phish at the Pepsi Center on December 13, 1997.

Raisinhill sounds nothing like Phish, though. If anything, its improv parallels the instrumental flights of the Slip. While there certainly are aspects of Raisinhill's music that elicit jazz references (such as Brian Anderson's upright bass), the band also incorporates a funk feel, house beats, and even some edgier rock expressions. Kasiewicz's billowing guitar leads can vary inflections and flutter through changes with the efficiency of Bill Frisell. Meanwhile, drummer Jay Bond employs finesse and restraint to make his declarations count, while Anderson lurks beneath, occasionally angling upward with some darker tones. Raisinshill doesn't always stake out new territories, but the areas it does negotiate often captivate close listeners.

Raisinhill (2002) ★ ★ ★

The individual compositions may not resonate, but the disc as a whole creates an entrancing mood. Its 15 tracks balance more developed ideas with interstitial snippets that serve as apt segues.

RAQ

www.raqmusic.com

How best to introduce RAQ? There is a relatively famous photo (as these things go) taken during Phish's first visit to Colorado in August 1988. The picture captures Trey Anastasio and Mike Gordon carrying a keyboard across the street in Telluride with the Rocky Mountains looming in the background (if you're playing along at home, pull out your copy of *The Phish Book* and turn to page 43). Well, when RAQ made its Telluride debut nearly 14 years later, guitarist Chris Michetti and keyboardist Marc Scortino posed for a similar shot in that same location. The punch line is that there may be no band out there that sounds closer to Phish without actually covering the band's music. Yet the musicians in RAQ are sufficiently self-aware to acknowledge this and even initiate such a joke at their own expense.

While the quartet cites a number of influences ranging from Frank Zappa to the Greyboy Allstars, there is no escaping the fact that, particularly during RAQ's first year of existence, its sound often evoked the 1992–93 Phish era. Michetti is the source of much comparison, as his guitar tone, vocal intonations, and even his physical bearing can prove reminiscent of Anastasio (some even go so far as to charge that his glasses and choice of pants were copped from the Phish guitarist, to which he laughs that laser surgery and Chinos will put an end to it all). Come to think of it, the group is even based in Burlington, Vermont, if you want to indict them for esoteric matters.

It is important to recognize that RAQ is a young band. The group's initial lineup came together in the fall of 2001, and founding keyboard player Scortino stepped away from the rigors of touring a year later (yielding to Todd Stoops and offering an entertaining list of the Top 20 "Things I've Learned While Playing Keyboards in RAQ" on the band's Web site).

The fact that so many people readily compare the group's music to Phish's (during what many perceive as one of Phish's most enjoyable eras), speaks volumes about RAQ's artistry and energy. As the developing quartet continues to move away from that starting point, it could very well make for an interesting journey....

Shed Tech (2002) ★ ★ ½

A decent first effort, especially when you take into account it was recorded less than two months after the band's formation. If you're Phish-minded, jump to "Hot Wired" or "Guilty Pleasures." Otherwise, the opener, "Time Bomb," bounds along affably, while "Tunnel Vision," with its "sunshine sandwich for me" hook, reflects the group's impious side, as does the closer, "Welcome to the Donkey Show."

RATDOG

www.rat-dog.com

The backdrop can be a burden. No, not the tapestry that's hanging at the rear of the stage (though come to think of it, mandalas have heft when rolled up for load-out at 3:00 A.M.). Instead, the reference is to the weight of history, the associations and expectations that accompany artists, especially those who have enjoyed the long-standing support of a listening community.

The relevance to RatDog? Well, that stately, gray beard may distract you from the fact that founder Robert Hall Weir was but a baby-faced seventeen-year-old in May 1965 when the Warlocks settled into their initial residency at Magoo's Pizza Parlor in Menlo Park, CA (the group added Phil Lesh the following month, and by year's end had rechristened itself the Grateful Dead). For the near totality of his adult existence, Bob Weir has been BOB WEIR, and audience members come to RatDog shows in part to hear some of the chestnuts that Weir first roasted with the Dead more than three decades earlier. RatDog carries additional freight, as three shows into the band's initial tour Jerry Garcia passed away (RatDog took the stage on the evening of Garcia's death on August 9, 1995, for a cathartic, affirming performance in Hampton Beach, NH). So while the band is at its finest when delivering original material, which it does with puissance and aplomb, RatDog also offers a good measure of the Dead catalog, to the pleasure of many fans.

While RatDog interprets some of the Dead's songbook, Weir has not been content to stand pat, and the band's music and roster have remained dynamic. RatDog developed from the collaboration of Bob Weir and Rob Wasserman, who first performed together as a duo in the fall of 1988, shortly after meeting at a Willie Dixon gig. Given that starting point, it is fitting that the band initially gravitated towards the blues, and the roster included Weir's fellow Kingfisher Matt Kelly as well as the suave, stylish septuagenarian Johnnie Johnson on keys. (In 1953, Johnson—soon to be the Johnny B. of Goode fame—invited guitarist Chuck Berry to sit in with his Sir John Trio on New Year's Eve. Berry soon emerged as the frontman, and as he gained notoriety, the guitar player and the keyboardist would barnstorm, picking up additional players in the various cities they played. Johnson arranged some of the music, but the nature of his songwriting contributions remains a matter of debate—a 1999 multimillion-dollar lawsuit against Berry to collect royalties was dismissed because the statute of limitations had long expired. Regardless, in 2001 Johnson entered the Rock & Roll Hall of Fame on his own accord with an introduction from Keith Richards, who had gained an appreciation of Johnson while working on the 1987 concert film *Chuck Berry: Hail! Hail! Rock 'n' Roll*. Johnson performed nearly 70 shows with RatDog and he has continued in fill in on occasion, typically joining the group when it routes through his home state of Missouri. At the age of 77, he sat in for much of a show on March 22, 2002, including a performance of "Dark Star.")

RatDog's sound has transformed since the 1997 and 1998 departures of Johnson and Kelly, drifting closer to a jazz aesthetic (indeed, other than Weir, only one original RatDog member remains—chaw on that one, we'll be back for it momentarily). This transformation has been the product of such players as keyboardist Jeff Chimenti and Kenny Brooks on sax (who came on for fellow Charlie Hunter alum Dave Ellis in 2000). While Kelly played some guitar, the group did not add a steady, seasoned lead player until Mark Karan joined following his first stint with the Other Ones in 1998. Wassermann opted to move on in spring 2003 (although he continues to play some gigs with Weir), and keyboard player Rob

RatDog, the Grateful Dead Family Reunion, August 4, 2002.

Barraco sat in for a number of shows on bass, which prompted the Jambands.com headline, "Rob Barraco to Tour as RatDog Bassist (No, Really)," before Robin Sylvester took on the role, leaving drummer Jay Lane as the only other original member.

RatDog's readings of the Dead canon have accreted over time. It took Weir a few years before he introduced his signature tunes into the RatDog repertoire—"Sugar Magnolia" didn't debut until March 28, 1997, with "Playing in the Band" following three months later. To many minds, the more significant (and certainly unanticipated) additions came with the gradual appearances of Garcia standards such as "Bird Song" (which debuted on October 24, 1997), "Terrapin" (October 26, 1999), "Help>Slip>Franklin's" (October 16, 2000, Weir's 53rd birthday), and "Eyes of the World" (March 28, 2001). Not only has RatDog communicated these songs through a new voice, in many instances the band has transposed them significantly. Some of this is due to Brooks's efforts, as prior to joining the group, he notes, "Not only had I never seen a Dead show, but I had never listened to them. It was the kind of thing where I had no idea, and coming from this hardcore jazz background I really hadn't listened to rock, period. It was challenging for me to play because I didn't know what I was doing. The great thing is that Bob wasn't looking for cats who were in awe of him or blown away because they had been following the Dead on tour. He wanted cats who were out of the loop, which is why Jay and Jeff worked out so well." DJ Logic's extended runs with the group similarly demonstrate Weir's intent to keep the sound in motion.

As employed at the outset of this profile, the word "burden" typically implies the bearing of a load that has become wearisome and ponderous. But if one takes a step back, this characterization is imprecise and inapposite relative to the efforts of Bob Weir and RatDog. Weir views his preceding efforts with the Grateful Dead as a relief map to consult, for instance as the band searches for new destinations from the key of *D* when it launches into "Playing." Nuance is elemental as well, since Weir's vocals may take on a percussive role at a given show, if, as he says, "I'm having a particularly swell time with my consonants." Indeed, the band continues to push forward, as nearly a decade into its existence the old 'Dog aspires to teach new tricks.

Live at Roseland (2001) ★ ★ ★ ½

These paired discs draw on shows from Portland, OR, on April 25 and 26, 2001, to offer some agreeable interpretations of the Dead catalog. Particularly notable is the presence of Garcia material, including "Friend of the Devil," "Bird Song," and "Mission in the Rain." Still, as a whole, the release fails to deliver on the band's full resources, in particular some of its brasher, more angular playing as well as its canorous new material, of which only two examples are represented.

Evening Moods (2000) ★ ★ ★ ★

Aside from a tangy "Corrina," *Evening Moods* focuses on compositions debuted and developed by RatDog. The resulting collection may be Weir's strongest studio effort, with subtle accents providing equipoise to snarling leads.

Fan site:

www.ratdog.org

Sauce site:

www.weirsauces.com

RAY'S MUSIC EXCHANGE

www.raysmusicexchange.com

One of this band's achievements is delivering music that is both cerebral and heady (yes, there is dichotomy there). In the former regard, Ray's Music Exchange, which is comprised predominantly of players who studied at the Cincinnati College Conservatory of Music, produces a tantalizing contemporary take on jazz fusion. However, unlike some latter-day fusion efforts, which proved sterile and inaccessible, RME also draws in its listeners by incorporating worldbeat and funk. Not only that, but at its shows the group has also directly involved audience members by asking them to produce specific noises to enhance a collective jam and by soliciting themes for particular improvisations.

Guitarist Joe McLean founded Ray's Music Exchange in 1995, drawing in area musicians with a common vocabulary and vigor. Many were in school, however, and consequently more than a dozen players rotated through the lineup during the band's initial years, even as the group gained acclaim by winning the Cincinnati Entertainment Award in 1999 for Album of the Year and in 2000 for Best Jazz Group. While recording its first studio effort, *Turanga*, in 2001, the band winnowed down from a septet to a quartet (the players who moved on included drummer Jason Smart, who would join the Jacob Fred Jazz Odyssey, and keyboardist Paul Hogan, who

was writing a fair share of RME's material but entered graduate school at Columbia University's Computer Music Center where he began pursuing interactive performances).

The current quintet has retained its chops and a taste for experimentation, which draws approbation from fellow musicians, though at times the results can prove elusive to some audience members (in a manner akin to the defunct Fat Mama, winner of the New Groove Award at the 2000 Jammys). Moreover, because its members' interests are so expansive, Ray's is one of many projects for each of them. So while the band has toured nationally, making it to both coasts for the High Sierra and Berkshire Mountain Music festivals, by 2003 most of RME's shows were located in the Ohio area, leaving a core of listeners yearning for the group's playful give and take, hankering for the Exchange.

Turanga (2001) ★ ★ ★ ½

An inventive, at times abstract, studio debut. The band's horn-heavy fusion also samples world music from reggae to raga while incorporating some plangent slide as well.

Also:

ALIVEEXCHANGE (1999)

THE RECIPE

www.therecipe.com

Okay, let's dispense with the culinary pun right away and get to the matter at hand. While over the years the Recipe certainly has proven tantalizing, its ingredients have remained variable. So while many individuals have developed a taste for the group, this inconsistency has inhibited some listeners' cravings. (Note to figurative language philanthropists: All impressions aside, no metaphors were tortured in the creation of this paragraph.)

Founding guitarist/vocalist Joe Pritchard has long been the driving force behind the group. The Recipe emerged from an open mic night he hosted at Morgantown, West Virginia's Terrapin Station. Originally an acoustic duo dubbed Porch Party in the Can, the project became the Recipe in 1995, blending electric instrumentation along with the mighty vocal chords of Kristin Wolverton. The six-piece band soon found an audience beyond the Mountain State to share its enthusiasm for Appalachian folk, improvisational rock, and hillbilly funk (with some idiosyncratic lyrics—for instance, the guest appearance of *The X-Files'* Mulder and Scully on "Affected Specimen").

Wolverton remained with the group until spring 2001, recording three discs (the third of these, *Geode*, came out on the defunct Phoenix Rising label). During her tenure more than a dozen bass players passed through the group, including Rus Reppert, formerly of Barefeet & Company, who resurfaced a few years later on guitar. Although Reppert is no longer with the band, two other current members made triumphant returns after leaves of absence: original percussionist Tom Whelan and vocalist Julie Edlow, who joined after Wolverton's departure, yielded the stage to Cameron Lewis in spring 2002, and then reclaimed it later that summer. Given this pattern of Recipe reversion, some hold out hope that Hannah Ross (who left in spring 2002) may fiddle with the group once again (perhaps along with her banjo-playing brother, Amos, another alum). Nonetheless,

the group has been taking on new zest as of late with bassist Chris Q (Jiggle, Hypnotic Clambake) and Kris Kehr (Stone Poets) on mandolin, acoustic guitar, and harmonica.

In 1999 the Recipe hosted its first annual Family Cookout, a multiband festival in the hills of West Virginia. The event was inspired in part by multigenerational musical events that Prichard had attended with his family while younger: "I had been playing some electric guitar in rock bands at the time so I went there pretty reluctantly, but I was blown away. There were all these people in their eighties who couldn't even walk of their own volition but they just crushed on their mandolins. And they were out there because they just had it in their blood, they had to make music, and they enjoyed doing it together. There was this communal, community vibe to it." A similar spirit invigorates the group's fans, the Porch People—referenced by the band's second album title, a name that evokes a penchant for sociable assembly as a means to share the latest Recipe.

Night of the Porch People (1998) ★★★ ½
Although one wishes for a bit more clarity in the production, this doesn't mask the band's spark and spunk. The Recipe's psychedelic Americana/Appalachian roots rock is supported by solid instrumentation and spry, often arresting vocal harmonies.

Also:
All You Can Eat (2003)
Love Marble Hoe-Down (1995)

Out of print:
Geode (2000)

Porchparty—*www.porchparty.com*

Discussion list:

www.groups.yahoo.com/group/TheRecipe PorchParty/

REID GENAUER & THE ASSEMBLY OF DUST

www.reidgenauer.com

When Reid Genauer left Strangefolk in the fall of 2000, there were questions about whether he would return to the musician's life. He had opted to purse an M.B.A. at Cornell University, and some wondered if this experience would prove antithetical to his prior avocation. As it turned out, it only reinforced his yen for performance, and in the spring of 2001 he made some tentative steps back to the stage with solo acoustic shows. Over the course of the ensuing year, while still attending school, he continued to gig and then began to record, first by himself and eventually with a band.

Indeed, as Godfather Michael Corleone once proclaimed, "Just when I thought I was out, they pulled me back in." Or as Genauer relates, "I once rode up the chair lift with a priest. He was a young guy with sort of long hair, and I asked him why he chose to be a priest. It struck me as an unusual choice for a young, athletic guy. He replied, 'It chose me.' That's how I feel about music. My feelings have not significantly changed. I guess for a while there I lost sight of why I love it so much, in part because I was just tuckered out. But it's a wonderful release."

Genauer writes warm, engaging music that he delivers with passion. His lyrics examine and often celebrate the ramifications of quotidian dilemmas and impulses. While some criticize his songs' simplicities and platitudes, these are often their strengths because they are unabashedly inviting. Plus, such criticism fails to acknowledge Genauer's ability to turn a phrase or melody on its head.

The Assembly of Dust takes Genauer's core compositions and imbues them with its own stamp. Keyboardist Nate Wilson (Percy Hill) is flush with ideas and also adds inventive riffs to Genauer's songs from the Strangefolk catalog. Guitarist Adam Terrell often lends complementary ideas on guitar, supported by a spirited rhythm section—bassist John Leccese (also of Percy Hill), who contributes vocal harmonies, and Andy Herrick, an active presence behind the kit. As a singer, Genauer has the ineffable ability to draw listeners in, while as a bandleader one of his strengths a fine sense of dynamics, allowing him to intuit when he should step out of the way and let his bandmates carry the music before returning to cut loose with his robust vocals.

Assembly of Dust (2003) ★★★★

This disc offers concise yet animated arrangements of Genauer's material. The results are mostly engaging though at times slightly overproduced, with layers that detract from the strength of these songs, which is their immediacy and accessibility.

Related Web site:

www.stonechoirtablets.com
(Just who is Dr. Earnest Wonderbound III and what would he think of Joey Areknstat? Find out more about the social and cultural antecedent of the Assembly of Dust at this site.)

ROBERT RANDOLPH & THE FAMILY BAND

www.robertrandolph.net

Part of the joy offered by the live music experience is the act of discovery, whether of a song, a riff, or even a nuance. However, the first time that many concertgoers are exposed to Robert Randolph & the Family Band, they feel as if they've made the rarest of finds: a group that is equally dexterous and distinctive. It is this feeling that continues to galvanize listeners.

Part of this response originates from Randolph's pedal steel guitar. The instrument looks like a guitar neck on legs with foot pedals and knee levers that he manipulates to alter pitch while simultaneously picking strings with one hand and sliding a tone bar with the other. (The results certainly are reminiscent of a slide guitar, but the pedal steel offers some unique features, such as the ability to fly across octaves.) Randolph's particular instrument is also a variant, a custom-built 13-string that allows him to reach deeper chords.

Beyond this, Randolph is a captivating, charismatic performer. While seated for much of the show, his body remains expressive and as the mood hits he will kick out his chair and dance frantically, occasionally flinging his signature bowler hat into the crowd. Audience members who associate his zeal with religious fervor aren't far off the mark, as he comes from the "sacred steel" church tradition. Oh yes, the Family Band tears it up as well.

Robert Randolph grew up in a family of clergy at an Orange, New Jersey, House of God church where his mother served as minister and his father as deacon. This led him while in his mid-teens to the pedal steel, an instrument introduced into the House of God during the 1930s by Troman and Willie Eason as an alternative to costly pipe organs. (Henry Nelson was another significant early figure—for more on this development, check out the documentary *Sacred Steel.*) Randolph's gift for the instrument blossomed after studying in the late '90s with Ohio practitioner Ted Beard (who is invoked through one of the Family Band's signature songs, "Ted's Jam").

While Randolph learned about sacred steel players, he had little exposure to blues and rock musicians. So when a fellow parishioner introduced him to the sounds of Stevie Ray Vaughan, Randolph discovered a new source of inspiration (and he encountered Jimi Hendrix through Vaughan, hearing "Voodoo Chile" through his fingers). Not so long afterwards, when Randolph's sound was compared to the Allman Brothers Band, he revealed that he hadn't heard the group. However, he would do so soon enough—and even take the stage with the Brothers through a whirlwind series of events that began with a decision to record a demo. This led to a September 2000 date opening for the North Mississippi Allstars at the Bowery Ballroom, and the gigs followed from there (as did Randolph's involvement with the Word).

The group truly is a Family Band. Randolph's cousin Danyel Morgan is an active presence, both slapping and strumming on bass. Drummer Marcus Randolph is a multi-instrumentalist and an estimable steel guitarist in his own right (in the church setting, he has been known to switch places with cousin Robert). Keyboard player John Ginty (Santana, Lou Reed, Jewel), related in spirit if not consanguinity, provides a lucid counterpoint and complementary layers on his Hammond B-3.

The quartet's absorbing live shows soon led to a number of intriguing opening slots and invitations for Randolph to perform with the Dave Matthews Band, Widespread Panic, String Cheese Incident, moe., and many others. Randolph & the Family Band took home the 2002 Jammy Award for New Groove and performed at the show with the Blind Boys of Alabama, Derek Trucks, and John Mayer (the preceding year, Robert joined Del McCoury and DJ Logic for "Swing Low, Sweet Chariot"). The group also signed with Warner Bros. and began working on a studio release with Jim Scott, who has engineered recordings for such artists as Tom Petty, Sting, and the Red Hot Chili Peppers. As of late there has been sporadic criticism of the group's live shows, but comments relating to dynamics or static set lists often overlook the fact that this is

Robert Randolph, jubilant with bowler and pedal steel.

still a very young band. Indeed, Robert Randolph & the Family Band continues to engage listeners old and new—many of whom walk away with the flush of musical discovery, feeling sanctified.

Live at the Wetlands (2002) ★★★★

This disc showcases the band's métier, performing live for the faithful in this celebrated venue (includes a bonus intro from club owner Pete Shapiro). The six extended cuts highlight Randolph's spellbinding leads and the playful response from his band mates. Ebullient and invigorating, nearly to the point of exhausting.

Also:

Unclassified (2003)

ROBERT WALTER'S 20TH CONGRESS

www.20thcongress.com

Robert Walter's 20th Congress began as one of the Greyboy Allstar "sidecar projects" that began touring in 1998 when Greyboy started to ease up on its gigs. Two of the current projects, the 20th Congress and Karl Denson's Tiny Universe, have taken on such independent identities that they are no longer ancillary and may in fact outdistance the original group in terms of notoriety and appeal. So while the Greyboy members are close—in fact they reunited for a few celebrated shows in December 2002—Walter's group should remain an active, invigorating enterprise.

While the band's future seems secure, its roster remains in flux. Aside from Walter and his company of keyboards (Hammond organ, Wurlitzer, Fender Rhodes, piano), the only other senior member of Congress is fellow San Diego native Cochemea "Cheme" Gastelum, who plays flute and electric sax with a number of effects reminiscent of Eddie Harris (a musician perhaps best known for his composition "Freedom Jazz Dance"). Cheme performed with Walter for a few years during the early '90s in the punk and jazz collective Creedle, and when first assembling this band, Walter approached his old band mate and consulted with him to define a commonality of interests and intents. (Incidentally, Walter played drums with San Diego funksters Daddy Longlegs prior to his days in Creedle, and another member of that group was current Tiny Universe guitarist Brian Jordan.)

To some degree the results depend on the group's roster at a given moment, but the 20th Congress consistently builds on the boogaloo associated with the Greyboy Allstars, aided in part by Greyboy's bass player Chris Stillwell and guitarist Elgin Park, who pass through and step in on occasion. The group also delivers some straight-up funk, most recently abetted by guitarist Will Bernard.

There are also some jazz expressions in the music of Robert Walter's 20th Congress, often building from bop and facilitated as of late by drummer Joe Russo (Fat Mama). The band's original music often echoes classic modes while adding some new vocabulary, although the transient nature of the lineup has hampered its ability to develop a full lexicon (in part because Walter lends himself to many other projects). Still, Walter and Cheme remain compelling artists in most any context, and the band's namesake does remain committed to filling out the group

Robert Walter's 20th Congress at Shaw's Oysterfest.

with limber, resourceful players for any Congressional session.

Money Shot (2000) ★★★½

This release offers a nice balance of groove-driven tracks and more expansive expressions (which do sometimes wander). Walter performs on Hammond, Wurlitzer, Rhodes, and good ol' acoustic piano, varying the landscape quite effectively. Cheme's flourishes often guide the band out, while Stanton Moore's crackling ideas hold the focus.

Related (Robert Walter solo projects):

Robert Walter—*There Goes the Neighborhood* (2001) ★★★★

Walter composed most of the songs on this disc, which is a collaboration with some legendary jazz session players: original Head-hunters drummer Harvey Mason, guitarist Phil Upchurch, bass player Chuck Rainey, and Red Holloway (Jack McDuff) on tenor sax. The group is in fine form, offering deep pockets and percolating solos that serve the material quite well.

Robert Walter with Gary Bartz—*Spirit of '70* (1996) ★★★½

The Greyboy Allstars back Walter and former Miles Davis/McCoy Tyner collaborator Gary Bartz for these eight tracks. Bartz is understated and resonant throughout. His ideas don't always interlock with Walter and the band, but the results are often brash and playful.

Also:
Giving up the Ghost (2003)

RUSTED ROOT
www.rustedroot.com

When Rusted Root first gained listeners beyond its Pittsburgh, PA, base in the early '90s, one contingent described the group as "the finest Grateful Dead lot band in the land." While technically inaccurate, this characterization was not altogether inapposite. Like many of the musicians once alighting from VW buses on Dead summer tours, Rusted delivered a percussion-rich euphony through mostly acoustic instrumentation. Beyond the fundamental fact that the group never was a Dead lot band, the analogy is also ill chosen, as it neglects an essential element of the band's appeal: vivid, vivacious songs delivered through bright vocal harmonies. (If the lot premise were true, it would have been quite a moment when Rusted Root actually opened for the Dead at Three River Stadium in its home city on June 30, 1995.)

After his high school graduation, Michael Glabicki decided to form Rusted Root following a trip to South America, where he became enamored with primal polyrhythms. He recruited friend Liz Berlin, who drew in percussionist Jim Donovan, then a University of Pittsburgh music student, who in turn recruited Patrick Norman (initially a guitarist, Norman would later shift to bass). Vocalist Jenn Wertz, a photographer who met the band at a shoot, came next, as well as John Buynak, a multi-instrumentalist and visual artist whose graphic design work soon became entwined with perceptions of the band. Percussionist Jim Dispirito completed the roster in 1993. Audiences were soon enthralled by the group's vibrant, often celebratory performances in which each band member might seize a percussion instrument, and Mercury Records shared this enthusiasm in signing the group and releasing *When I Woke* in 1994.

During the years that followed, the band garnered platinum record sales while performing upwards of 150 shows a year, increasingly as an opening act on larger tours such as Page & Plant and Santana (the group's take on "Evil Ways" appears in the film *Home for the Holidays*, and since we're on the subject, other soundtrack appearances include "Virtual Reality" from *Twister* and "Send Me on My Way" from *Ice Age*). At times Rusted's appearances with these bigger artists became somewhat frustrating for the band's core audience, who longed for full performances in smaller venues, but these slots did offer exposure (for those keeping score at home, Rusted Root has performed more arena and amphitheater openers than any other group in this book, including runs with the Allman Brothers Band and Jewel). Meanwhile, in a slightly different context, Rusted also toured on the 1996 HORDE Tour and the 1998 Furthur Festival.

In 1999, citing some burnout and a desire for new exploration, the group announced a hiatus, and some fans wondered if it would return at all (Wertz had left in 1995, soon forming her band, Lovechild). Following tentative initial steps through a benefit performance at The Midwife Center in Pittsburgh during the summer of 2000, Rusted Root ultimately reformed with Wertz, recording a new studio disc, *Welcome to My Party,* a year later (minus Dispirito). The group's live show continues to offer an absorbing mosaic of sounds, though the set lists remain slightly static, and improvisation is now somewhat attenuated. Indeed, even though the band performed at the 2002 Jammys (offering three of its own songs in collaboration with Melvin Sparks, John Popper, and DJ Logic), the jamband designation seems to rankle Glabicki, who has stated, "If we are a jamband, we really suck at it." His self-assessment is slightly harsh and likely originates from a misperception of the term that excludes songcraft from its definition (and in fact, one group that embodies both facets of the duality that Glabicki identifies is . . . Rusted Root).

Welcome to My Party (2002) ★★★
Some of Rusted's traditional, familiar elements are de-emphasized in the production, which some longtime listeners may find jarring. While ultimately a sturdy effort, it lacks some exuberance.

Rusted Root (1998) ★★★
A bit more mature and less sprightly than the group's prior efforts. This eponymous effort takes a while to get popping, but it contains its engrossing moments, such as a version of "You Can't Always Get What You Want" with Hot Tuna.

Remember (1996) ★★★★
Jerry Harrison produced this album, the group's first after Wertz's departure. Along with its predecessor, this is one of the two discs that best capture the band's verve while also reflecting its melodious compositions.

When I Woke (1994) ★★★★
This disc is a favorite to many of the group's fans, as the animated opening move from "Drum Trip" to "Ecstasy" encapsulates much of what they enjoy about the band.

Rusted Root's Michael Glabicki.

Cruel Sun (1992) ★★★ ½

This release—the band's introduction to many listeners—is robust, spirited, and at times spiritual, though the group's songwriting would take on colors over time.

Related Web sites:

Liz Berlin—*www.lizberlin.com*
Jim Donovon—*www.jimdonovanmusic.com*
Jenn Wertz—*www.jennwertz.com*
Jim Dispirito—*www.jimdispirito.com*

Discussion list:

Rust Tribe—
www.lightlink.com/jesse/rr/howto.txt

S

SCHLEIGHO

www.schleigho.com

Math music. That is one phrase ascribed to the sounds of Schleigho, especially in its early years. This is not to suggest that researchers documented a rise in the standardized test scores of elementary schoolers exposed to Schleigho recordings (though that would be a glorious thing). Instead it is a reference to the often-dizzying array of nonconventional time signatures that the group introduces. This was particularly true of the few years following its 1993 formation, when this quartet of musicians' musicians elicited much approbation from fellow players. The plaudits persist although the sound has developed a bit, so while it remains complex the group also offers additional entry points for general listeners.

Although founding members Erik Egol (drums) and Jesse Gibbon (keys) first met and performed together as New York teenagers, Schleigho gelled at Boston's Berklee College of Music where Egol encountered Suke Cerulo (guitar, flute) and bassist Drew McCabe. This lineup toured and recorded through 1998, presenting seemingly boundless explorations into the jazz fusion terrain. Following McCabe's departure, the band added bassist Matt Rubano, who had performed with a number of artists, including Lauryn Hill. The sound then gravitated a bit more towards the funk side, remaining challenging but also steamrolling into grooves, often muscled by Gibbon on Hammond and Rhodes. (Meanwhile, Cerulo is one of the more tasteful and unheralded guitarists on the scene.) During the 1999 Jambands.com tour, Schleigho gained the attention of Allman Brothers Band drummer Butch Trucks, who signed the group to his Flying Frog Records label. Two years later, Rubano left the band, and Paco Mahone joined on six-string fretless and upright bass, delivering on both of his predecessors' affinities as the group's music now encompasses both modes.

Following a few years of playing upwards of 150 dates (including performances at the JVC Jazz Festival, the Gathering of the Vibes, and the High Sierra Music Festival), Schleigho took time off in 2002, and some wondered if the group would continue. During this period its members busied themselves with varied endeavors. For instance, Egol played with Lunch Money, a more mainstream pop-rock band, Gibbon toured with the Bomb Squad as well as Lucid, his own fusion group, while Cerulo did some solo gigs. These efforts lent a new vigor to Schleigho, though, and the band returned to deliver its defining amalgam of agitated passages juxtaposed with more contemplative ones. All of the group's songs are instrumentals, yet the results are certainly lyrical (which may not do much for your SAT verbal scores either).

Live at Ho-Down 2000 (2001) ★★★½

Four songs fill out the 70 minutes of music, and the ideas remain fresh throughout this disc. The 18-minute opening "Go Children Low" with Derek Trucks and Kofi Burbridge can be breathtaking, though it vies with a 26-minute version of "Matrices" for centerpiece honors.

Continent (2000) ★★★★

A cocksure and often inventive display of funk and fusion, this disc presents some bristling displays as well as some more spumous ones (the latter of which do occasionally drift too far into lite side).

Also:

In the Interest of Time (1998)
Farewell to the Sun (1997)

Out of print:

Schleigho (1995)

SETH YACOVONE BAND

www.sethyac.com

The original Seth Yacovone Band was quite different in intent, instrumentation, and execution from the one that tours today. In 1995, when Yacovone invited a handful of players to record his blues-based originals during studio time he had won in a guitar competition, he had no firm aim to create a touring band. However, this is what ensued, and while the collective performed exclusively in the state of Vermont at first, the group eventually altered its approach a bit and gigged across the nation and in Europe. This initial limited ambit and subsequent progression were driven in part by the fact that when the Seth Yacovone Blues Band (as it was then called) first came together, its namesake was only 16 years old.

Since his first public performance, Seth has amassed some estimable boosters in Italy and the US—perhaps most notably, Trey Anastasio. Phish's guitarist was one of the judges at the initial competition that brought Yacovone into the studio and has been a supporter ever since. When asked if he would consider adding another guitar player to his solo band, Anastasio pointed to Yacovone as the likely candidate if he were to do so. Anastasio has joined the Seth Yacovone Band onstage on a few occasions, and at the Worcester Centrum on November 29, 1998, Yacovone returned the favor at a Phish show, playing his own "All the Pain Through the Years" and dueling with Anastasio on "Layla."

Dropping the word blues from its moniker a few years ago signaled a move towards incorporating additional jazz and funk elements along with a newfound affinity for improvisation. Similarly, the personnel changed with the departure of a harmonica player and a second guitarist, yielding the current trio with drummer Tommy Coggio and bass player Steve Hadeka. Still, Yacovone's music is often steeped in the blues, just as Jimi Hendrix (one of Yacovone's inspirations) retained such a framework throughout his career. Yacovone's gruff vocals are well suited for the idiom as well (at times he sounds warmer, almost akin to John Fogerty, while in other instances he seems to be little more than shouting). There are also heavier, fuzzy tones to the band's sound that one associates with some of the classic British three-piece groups of the late '60s and '70s. Yacovone is still finding his way as a songwriter (his lyrics in particular have improved a bit), and the band is often at its best as a true improvisational outfit rather than solely supporting Yacovone's fiery displays. Even so, as the live shows attest, this lineup certainly brings a passion and power to the trio.

Standing on the Sound (2001) ★★★ ½

There's plenty to hear on this one, with the tracking divided into four sides as an ode to the (double) LPs that inspired the guitarist. This release does a fine job of distilling Yacovone's prior efforts while introducing newer concepts as well, with some funk and even a hint of prog-rock. A solid mix of shorter tunes and more expansive themes, this one comes closest to representing the current sound of the band.

Dannemora (2000) ★★★

This is the first release without the word blues in the band's name and the first from the current trio. The lyrics are an improvement from the earlier discs—Yacovone has a nice turn of phrase. While there are still some relatively standard blues originals, the band does push it on a few songs, especially "Mold I" and "Mold II," which build on two metaphors for the word quite successfully.

Yessir! (1998) ★★

A live disc that presents the band in a blues mode with the harp player still in the mix. Plenty of energy, and Yacovone takes some powerful leads as the group does stretch out a few songs, though mostly throwing it around for solos. It's Yacovone's songwriting here, not his stinging guitar leads, that feels callow.

Also:

In a Moment (2003)
Bobfred's Bathtub Minstrel (1997)

THE SHANTEE

www.shantee.com

Credit the Shantee for its use of dynamics. While many other bands with a propensity for improv like to come out slamming and don't deviate much from that level, this quintet is quite purposeful and effective in building moods. The band even delivers (gasp) ballads through the soaring vocals of Mike Perkins. This is not to say, however, that the group's intentions are always fully realized, as the Shantee is comprised of five relatively young musicians still working towards their avowed goal of crafting catchy melodic songs.

The band is currently based in Columbus, Ohio, not far from Denison University, where it first came together in 1995 (a slightly different, looser incarnation). The players have built relationships with the local heroes in ekoostik hookah, who have taken the stage with them on multiple occasions (and John "Starcatt" Polansky adds percussion throughout the Shantee's second release, *Hydration*). The two bands certainly share some supporters, though the younger group's sound is more vocally dramatic and poppier than hookah's, as the Shantee positions itself closer to the realm of roots rock.

Hydration (2001) ★ ★ ½

A bit more maturity in the songwriting and some solid production capture the band to good effect. Randy Browne's keyboards lend color throughout, and Mike Perkins's vocals elevate a number of the tunes.

Lands Unknown (1998) ★ ★

This release captures the young group full of energy and intent but still honing their craft. Even so, there are some nice moments here, including the title track, the jangly "Happy Song," and "Brotherman."

Also:

Four Now... (2003)

Fan site:

www.shanteeclan.com

SIGNAL PATH

www.signalpath.org

After learning that Signal Path's music had been described by an area radio station as "Missoula's hottest new electronica combo," one local wag responded, "Yay! That makes them the hottest out of, probably, one." Touché. And yet there is something rather majestic about being that one, eschewing any regional trends and pursuing music for music's sake.

In fact, such an aesthetic led Signal Path guitarist Ryan Burnett to form the group in 2001. He had been a principal member of the Montana organic funk-rock septet Abendego, which built a solid following over two years including a July 2000 gig at High Sierra.

However, Burnett's experience at that festival—with what he perceived as too many groups with similar intentions—led him to reconsider his efforts. Abendego folded in the fall of 2000, and Burnett began experimenting with guitar processors, samplers, and MIDI triggers. Eventually he found four musicians willing to traverse a similar path, including drummer Damon Metzner, who studied with Galactic's Stanton Moore; Ben Griffin, who performs on electronic percussion; New Orleans jazz guitarist Nathan Weidenhaft; and upright bassist Dion Stepanski. With this novel instrumentation, Signal Path began sampling its players' varied backgrounds while also leaning towards house and drum & bass sounds. The group's sound is still at the nascent stage, but there is a brash vitality to it that bodes well for what might follow. And if nothing else, Signal Path owns the electronica scene in Missoula.

Signal Path (2002) ★ ★ ★

These eight studio cuts position the band as a dexterous purveyor of livetronica. There is a unity here with the group's flexible rhythms and flourishes, even if the individual songs don't necessarily stand out on their own.

SKYDOG

www.skydogmusic.net

If you're at a Skydog show with your eyes closed, awash in the music, there are times when you'd swear you're listening to...Skydog Gypsy. Come to think of it, you are, sort of. Over the course of 2002, quartet Skydog Gypsy released its second disc, weathered the departure of a keyboard player, and re-emerged with an abridged moniker.

Skydog is a Georgia-based group, giving it a geographic nexus to its namesake, Duane Allman. The slide guitar innovator received his nickname via Wilson Pickett after a Muscle Shoals recording session in which Allman added some memorable licks to Pickett's version of "Hey Jude" (this was Eric Clapton's introduction to Allman, ultimately yielding the *Layla* sessions). Pickett actually dubbed the guitarist "Skyman" but since Allman's other nickname was "Dog," this transmuted into "Skydog."

Over the years, listeners have compared Skydog guitarist Dean Tovey less to Allman than to Trey Anastasio. Tovey himself credits a trio of J's as his pantheon—Herring, Page, and Hendrix. The band's music is pushed and accented by two Berklee-trained players, bassist Aaron Goldberg and drummer Allen Aucion. Former Ancient Harmony keyboardist Hal Month is the latest addition, and his vibrant contributions often buoy the band's "melodic funk fusion" within the firmament. Indeed, Skydog is proficient at the deep jam and continues to work at expressing some concise ideas in its songwriting while strengthening its vocal presentation. The addition of Month has animated the group, which now delves with élan into electronica spaces, even as it continues to deliver on those sounds favored by the original Skydog himself.

As Skydog Gypsy (out of print):
Should Have Brought Your... (2002)
Catalyst (1999)

THE SLIP
www.theslip.com

As befits its name, the Slip is elusive. Drop in for one song, live or on disc, and you may hear folky, melodic pop music. Stop by again and the trio may be off on an instrumental, improvisational bender with the drums at the fore or the bass taking the lead and the guitar in a percussive role. Either way, there is a grace, a spiritual component that suffuses the sound and, on occasion, the facial expressions of the band members (and while we're on visages, here's a pre-show diversion based on guitarist Brad Barr's mutable facial hair that some call the Barrb Q: before you and your friends see the band live, share an amicable wager on the state of Brad's chops—whether it will be full beard, stubble, newly shorn, clean with 'stache, etc.).

As for the band's apt appellation, this may be the quintessential instance of the muse choosing the artist. None of the current members was in the Slip when the band first came together at Tabor Academy circa 1990. By the time brothers Andrew and Brad Barr joined a few years later, the group had become something of an institution at the Massachusetts high school with numerous players rotating through the roster before moving on to college, including Sally Taylor, founder John Myers, and filmmaker Adam Mutterperl. The Barrs soon introduced original music into the repertoire and eventually welcomed bassist Marc Friedman as well.

Winnowed down to a three-piece, the resulting group remained intact while the members attended the Berklee College of Music for a few semesters beginning in 1995. (They soon found themselves within a fine

Berklee tradition: students who leave school due to success in the subject matter of their schooling. Friedman explains, "We wanted to pursue touring, making an album, and writing more tunes. Brad and Andrew ended up staying one more semester than I did. When I was there I was happy to be bombarded by the multitude of students and teachers, the infinite range of music that's out there as well as the different personalities and takes on music. Music is about communication and synching up with the right players and also about having the most open and free mind possible to put it in the right atmosphere where it can exist and be true. At Berklee I felt that I was lost in a sea of anxious bass players. I felt I had been there two semesters and I had a bunch to work on. So basically I just took it to my bedroom and started shedding like crazy while still keeping as many contacts as possible with the Berklee crowd.")

The Slip soon endeared itself to a New England audience, and the band's scope became national within a few years. In addition to its own music, the group maintained a commitment to a range of artistic forms, incorporating the work of poets, painters, and puppeteers into performances while also aiming to expose listeners to sounds they might not otherwise seek out (such as West African drummer Abdoul Doumbia or the free-form folk of Leslie Helpert). At times the Slip's music has been likened to jazz and it is certainly rooted in the genre, as the group credits such influences as Jaco Pastorius, Pat Metheny (whose *Bright Size Life* played a significant role in the Slip's decision to develop as a trio), and Bob Gullotti (who regularly performs with George Garzone and John Lockwood in anoth-

er fittingly named trio founded in 1972, the Fringe). However, the band members also grew up on classic rock (some of which Friedman references in his Kram Dangle project), while Andrew has studied with Doumbia in Mali. In addition, there is a Boho, earthy vibe that emanates and presents itself in the band's lyrics and spoken words, often focusing on purity and truth (the personal is certainly political within the Slip's "pleasant presence of the present tense"). The results can prove absorbing to musicians (Butch Trucks signed the Slip to his Flying Frog Records label, and Living Daylights performed with the trio a few times as the Slipping Daylights) and nonmusicians alike, which has carried the band into divergent settings, from the Newport Jazz Festival to Scullers Jazz Club, Japanese concert halls, and national rock venues. Through it all, the Slip's sets have reflected a relatively equal mix of instrumentals and vocals tunes—a ratio that further defies ready characterization and one that the prevailing forces in the balkanized mainstream music climate would decry as a branding error, a Slipup, which is exactly right.

Angels Come on Time (2002) ★★★★

The band's most cohesive album by far. The Slip creates a vivid environment for their pop, fusion, folk, and blues instrumentals and vocal songs. Some may find the results on the mellower side, but this disc is admirably unified, even in its eclecticism.

Live Is My Jumby (2002) ★★★

These five extended instrumental takes demonstrate the band's dexterity and acuity, as the players' fluidity embellishes each other's ideas even as they exchange roles. However, when taken out of context and lacking more melodic counterpoints, these abstractions often fail to galvanize.

Does (2000) ★★★ ½

A well-founded disc that focuses on the jazz instrumental side of the band, though some of its hues are washed out in the production.

From the Gecko (1997) ★★★★

There is a looseness and charm to the group's debut. Some of the passages are derivative (for instance, the echoes of Steely Dan in "Eube"). However, this release effectively taps into the animating spirit of the band, emanating a kinetic joy that is so essential to the Slip experience.

Also:

Live at Club Helsinki (2003)
Alivelectric (2003)

Fan sites:

SlipBase—*www.phrazz.com/slipbase/*
www.theslip.net

Discussion list:

www.lists.netspace.org/archives/theslip.html

SMOKESTACK

www.smokestack.org

One interesting consequence of Phish's long-standing eclectic approach (and that of other bands such as Leftover Salmon and String Cheese Incident) has been its impact on younger groups. Bands now have a freedom to create original music that moves from jazz to bluegrass to funk to calypso without con-cerns that audiences will deem this diversity confounding. Michigan's Smokestack is one such developing act that has embraced this aesthetic.

This is not to suggest that Smokestack sounds like Phish, because it doesn't (all that often). Instead, the Ann Arbor-based quartet, which came together in 1998, weaves keyboard-driven Latin and bluegrass strains through a jazz fundament (all of its members are students of this genre, and on occasion the group has performed a straight jazz set). To its credit, unlike some of its peers, Smokestack places a high value on song craft, and its improvisations often extend outward from a structured base with the occasional pop hook. The group similarly emphasizes its vocals, with keyboardist James Sibley and guitarist Chuck Newsome building the harmonies. One of the band's hallmarks remains its diverse musical palette, as suggested by the covers that it may drop in on any given night, from Thelonious Monk to the Police to String Cheese Incident to the Bangles (a lengthy take on "Walk Like an Egyptian"). Smokestack is a young band in the process of defining and refining its musical voice. It will be intriguing to see where this will lead and who will follow.

It's Coming Down (2001) ★★

Eclectic to a fault at times, as the move from bluegrass to funk to reggae to jazz on successive tracks shackles the band a bit, preventing Smokestack from digging in and developing a sound beyond this facility. The vocals are smooth, however, and there are some interesting textures on such songs as "Bodhi" and the Caribbean-flavored "Lag and a Foot."

SOULIVE

www.soulive.com

Field conditions were moist and mucky at the September 1998 High Sierra Music Festival (back during a two-year stretch when High Sierra took place during both Independence Day and Labor Day Weekends). But when Maceo Parker and his band walked on stage bedecked in their pressed white suits, they cast a mood and carried a strident authority that mesmerized many festival attendees including Alan Evans, the drummer in Karl Denson's new group (while leaving many others seeing trails). The lesson took. Six months

later, when Evans began performing with Soulive, which included brother Neal on keyboards and Eric Krasno on guitar, the new trio's garb proved just as swank (well okay, not quite, but they did don the suits). Parker resonated with Soulive in other ways as well. Over the years the band would perform both "Slow Maceo" and "Fast Maceo" while offering its own statistical variant on his "2% Jazz, 98% Funky Stuff."

With Japanese billboards, Dave Matthews collaborations, and a Rolling Stones opening gig a few years in the future, Soulive first connected during a jam session on March 2-3,

Eric Krasno and Neal Evans of Soulive.

1999. The Evans brothers had met Krasno more than a year earlier, when they were playing with Peter Prince in Moon Boot Lover, and the guitarist was getting his Lettuce project in motion. The three ran tape in the Evans's home studio, with Alan producing what would become the band's debut, *Get Down!* (punctuated by the opening track "So Live!"). Although they appreciated the results, Krasno remained committed to Lettuce while the Evanses lined up some gigs and sought to draw in a third player, taking suggestions from Krasno (Alan and Neal opted to find a guitarist, with Neal playing the basslines on his Hammond, which he continues to do to good effect, occasionally aided by a stuck key on the B-3). Then, with Adam Deitch's impending move from Lettuce to the Average White Band, Krasno decided to pull a Cheney (or, perhaps more accurately, the following year the future Vice President pulled a Kraz) and ended Soulive's search for a guitarist, stepping in himself to see where the music would take him (the answer, in short order, was across the US and then to Asia and Europe).

In 1992, Widespread Panic bassist Dave Schools and Blues Traveler guitarist Chan Kinchla jokingly created a word to describe the like-minded artists who banded together on the inaugural HORDE tour, landing on the arguably oxymoronic "neo-retro." There are few bands that better embody this term than Soulive. From the graphic design on its initial album cover (which Alan created to emulate the classic vinyl of the '50s and '60s), to its mode of dress and its sound, which often conjured up Grant Green or Jimmy Smith, Soulive cast an eye to the past. Nonetheless, a close

listen revealed not only the trio's deep affection for funk but the modern vocabulary of hip-hop with contemporary beats and phrasings, while the improvisations often shared this aesthetic in discerning and developing grooves (this is not to say the band didn't solo, with charges of excess occasionally levied at Kraz).

However one defines the Soulive sound, many listeners as well as players were soon drawn to it (the group won the Musicians' Award at the 2000 Jammys). Some early approbation came not only for the bandmembers' individual and collective chops but also for the artists they helped others to (re)discover, leading younger listeners to seek out Lou Donaldson, Green, Smith, and the progenitors of soul-jazz. Soulive helped locate and nurture a listener base, which assisted other emerging groups drawn to these sounds, through the aid of such early advocates as John Scofield (he appears on the band's *Turn It Out* release and joined the group at the 2000 Jammys) and Oteil Burbridge (who also guests on *Turn It Out*).

While the group often describes its sound as "soul funk" (typically in counterpoint to the jazz tag assigned through its fall 2000 contract with Blue Note), the three musicians have defined this term broadly while keeping their sound fluid. Thus in May 2001 Soulive announced the addition of Sam Kininger on saxophone as a full-time member and recorded *Next* as a quartet. A mixed response followed—some listeners felt the results lacked the intensity long associated with the group. Still, Soulive's modulations continued apace, and in spring 2002 it toured as the Twenty-First Century Soul Revue with DJs,

MCs, a full horn section, and backup singers. Six months later, the original trio returned for a tour (as did the sartorial splendor abandoned a year earlier). These shows were recorded for the *Soulive* live disc, and during the weeks leading up to its February 2003 release, the band presented a series of Wednesday shows in New York City. Each week was devoted to a different theme, ranging from jazz to hip-hop, funk, and R&B (guest players included Fred Wesley, Joshua Redman, Warren Haynes, Kenny Garrett, Ivan Neville, Me'Shell NdegéOcello, and J-Live). Dubbed the Stretch residency, it proved anything but that, as the group blithely manifested the many facets of its sound and proved well suited for the task.

Soulive (2003) ★★★★

A return to form (and frock). The trio approaches these songs with a control and composure (within its own freewheeling continuum) borne of three and a half years on the road.

Next (2002) ★★★

Sam Kininger is officially aboard for this effort, which carries more sophistication (as well as Dave Matthews, Black Thought, and Talib Kweli) than Soulive's earlier efforts, but at times the results (somewhat surprisingly) feel too soft.

Doin' Something (2001) ★★★ ½

The band's Blue Note debut features some well-founded, road-tested material. Stephanie McKay supplies the group's first lead vocals on "Romantic," and Fred Wesley animates a few of the tracks, though at times the trio is subdued.

Turn It Out (2000) ★★★★ ½

Soulive's first full-length disc remains a favorite of many. A mix of live tracks and studio recordings with appearances by John Scofield, Oteil Burbridge, and Sam Kininger, this release captures a kinetic band writing memorable heads, actively engaged with soul-jazz.

Get Down! (1999) ★★★ ½

An opportunity to hear the group in its initial days. While four of these five original songs on the EP were re-recorded for the band's first full-length disc, these initial takes recorded in the Evans's home studio carry more than a spark. When Velour re-released *Get Down!* in 2002, it added two live tracks from this era—covers of Lou Donaldsons's "Brother Soul" and Boogaloo Joe Jones's "Right On," which capture the spirit of these early months.

Fan site:

Soulive set list archives—
www.geocities.com/livesoulgroove/

Discussion list:

www.groups.yahoo.com/group/Soulive/

SOUND TRIBE SECTOR 9

www.sts9.com

"Let's try to move as one." This was the charge that Sound Tribe Sector 9 made to guitarist Fareed Haque before he performed with the band at the 2002 High Sierra Music Festival. Drummer Zach Velmer recalls, "Fareed rips. We all appreciate that but we do things a little differently. He understood and it really worked out." Some may question the nature of an invitation that seemingly carries a significant limitation, in denying Haque an opportunity to solo. Yet many others appreciate the course that may follow from placing the musician in an unforeseen, arguably boundless setting offered by the quintet's collective textured improvisation.

STS9's organica uses the latest audio technology to envelop the listener in a soundscape that draws heavily on live sequencing. It took some time to arrive here, since the band premiered as a trio in 1996 with Velmer, guitarist Hunter Brown (soon to be name-checked in the title of an early fan favorite, "H.B. Walks to School"), and bass player David Murphy. Then called Sector 9, the band took a significant step towards its current sound a year later when keyboardist David Phipps joined the three musicians at an Atlanta area benefit and remained a band member. (The group eventually learned of another Sector 9 so it added the additional two words to its name, evoking its community ethos.) Percussionist Jefree Lerner, a former student and drum tech for Jeff Sipe, joined a few years later and completed the current roster of players, though the group's lighting designer plays an integral role, and STS9 sometimes invites a range of visual artists to complement the music and create a viscid, multisensory environment.

And then there's the Mayan calendar (which fascinates Jam Nation co-host Jeff Waful to no end, along with the band's propensity to display an array of crystals on the stage). A significant aspect of Mayan cosmology is its division of the year into 13 months, each lasting 28 days to reflect the orbit of the moon. The name Sector 9 is a reference to the ninth baktun in the Mayan historical cycle. Each baktun in the cycle is comprised of 144,000 days. (But you knew this already, didn't you? Incidentally, this cycle is set to conclude in 2012, though the repercussions are unclear—some suggest that the modes of human thought will transform.)

Now, all this would fall into the "believe it if you need it, if you don't just pass it on" category, except for the fact that it has practical applications to the band's music. As Brown explains: "There's a tone that goes with every day. It corresponds with the frequency of the moon, the light of the moon that shines every day. That tone then relates to a note. If the frequency is say, 432, then that's true *A*. So then that day is an *A*. If we play a show that night we'll start off in the key of *A*, or maybe we'll play the whole first set in *A*, or maybe we'll end in *A* just to give respect." Indeed an earnest, spiritual element is tangible within the quintet's music, which its members have described as sacred.

Although STS9 eschews individual displays, the group floats into improvisational moments with élan. Some find the results too ethereal and repetitive, but many of these critics nonetheless acknowledge the band's ability to sculpt a euphonious collage (while recognizing the prowess of its players, in particular Velmer's vigor behind the kit). The reach of Sound Tribe Sector 9 is extensive. In addition to High Sierra and Bonnaroo, STS9 has played at Coachella, in each context to audiences appreciative of a group that challenges convention by producing music that is "free-form but structured." Just remember: This is an exhibition, not a competition—no soloing.

Seasons 01 (2002) ★★★★
This collection of live performances from the group's 2001 tour proves fluid and ambient.

While the individual tracks are not always gripping, when taken as a whole, the two CDs do resonate.

Offered Schematics Suggesting Peace (2000) ★★★½

This production was counterintuitive, as the band moved well into the contemporary electronic world yet recorded this release in an analog studio. Kofi Burbridge guests on a number of tracks that offer some absorbing moments but do not always cohere.

Interplanetary Escape Vehicle (1999) ★★★½

The studio debut from the group (then known as Sector 9) offers a glimpse of a band in development. While this is certainly a transitional step, and the band's funk and jazz roots remain discernible, there is a winsome appeal to such songs as "Moonsocket" and "H.B. Walks to School."

Also:

Live at Home (2003)

Out of print:

Sector 9 [Live] (2000)

Fan site:

www.soundtribe.org

SPEAKEASY

www.speakeasyband.com

Although its name references the prohibition era, Speakeasy's music is of the present. It was in the mid-'90s when three Springfield, Missouri, high school students formed the group, drawing heavily on the funk metal sounds of 311. When Shawn Eckels (guitar), Ryan Fannin (drums), and Tony Johnson (bass) moved on to college, however, they expanded their musical ambit to include progressive and improvisational elements. During this time, the group played out regularly and recorded two albums, facilitated by the area support of the MOjam Triad (that's MO as in Missouri—see the Madahoochi entry for details).

One phrase that has been ascribed to Speakeasy's sound on a few occasions is "dirty chops," which carries the unflattering image of band members' unwashed faces. Regardless, this does hint at another side of Speakeasy's music—a straightahead garage rock approach especially prominent during its early years. However, the addition of Marcus Chatman (who joined in March 2002 after his group Barefoot Revolution broke up) has shored up Speakeasy's vocal harmonies while adding an array of instruments for the group to layer into the sound (keys, trumpet, harmonica, cello, sousaphone, percussion). Chatman's contaminant-free playing has offered the band new avenues, though some raw hip-hop and urban funk does endure, as at any given moment the band can still get down and, well, dirty.

Cut of the Jib (2003) ★★★

The brash hip-hop opener commands attention but it is not altogether representative of what follows. Instead, many of the tracks offer sturdy soul ruminations, often against a backdrop of persistent funk and ska.

Also:

Baking Secrets (2001)
Frumunda (1999)

STEVE KIMOCK BAND

www.kimock.com

He may not necessarily have attained International Man of Mystery status, but Steve Kimock is enigmatic. Raised in Pennsylvania and transplanted to northern California in the mid-'70s, over the subsequent two decades he put in stints with numerous groups. Beginning with the Goodman Brothers, Kimock moved on to Keith and Donna Godchaux's Heart of Gold Band, Zero (which he co-founded with drummer Greg Anton in 1984 and soon included such San Francisco Bay Area luminaries as Bobby Vega, John Cipollina, and Martin Fierro), Kingfish, Little Women, and Merl Saunders. Jerome Garcia himself publicly acknowledged his own appreciation of the guitarist. (Kimock recalls, "It was awful sweet of him to say that. It was completely unexpected and unsolicited, and it was cool.")

Kimock acquired additional visibility in the summer of 1998 when he was named as a last-minute addition to the Other Ones line-up. When Phil Lesh returned to performing in April 1999 following his liver transplant surgery, Kimock began touring regularly with Phil Lesh & Friends (from P&F's initial run at the Warfield with John Molo, Trey Anastasio, and Page McConnell on through the fall of 1999, when Kimock departed for reasons extrinsic to the music). Nonetheless, other than on the West Coast where Kimock lived for many years (until recently returning to Pennsylvania), many people are familiar with the guitarist's name but remain unmindful of his music. (So perhaps it's not so surprising that his fan site is called FLOK.org for "Fellow Lovers of Kimock,"

which sounds like a support group—and come to think of it, it is.) Still, it is quite possible that Kimock's Q Scores will elevate and many more listeners will ride the K-Waves due to his present project.

Then again, perhaps they won't. Throughout much of his career, Kimock has made a point of pursuing whatever sounds may lure him with little concern for public expectation or mass appeal. (For instance, he doesn't read any evaluations of his music because "it just creates a kind of duality—this person thinks this about me, and I think this about myself. Pretty soon you're entirely in your brain, in your mind. I'm sure I've said this before, but if there's any place I'm trying to be with the music, it's in a flow state where there's none of that duality or anything that creates that kind of duality.")

His single-mindedness goes all the way back to his teenage years when he began an elaborate, extended rehearsal regimen that his high school principal eventually indulged on school grounds in order to prevent truancy. A similar commitment to his tone led him to delve into amp and speaker design (he relates some of the particulars in a *Relix* Tools of the Trade piece titled "Sound Hound"). In addition, to ensure that audiences can benefit from these efforts, and because he's not always willing to trust a given venue's speakers, he has often delivered performances through his own gear rather than a club's PA system.

The SKB evolved out of KVHW. The latter group's title is an acronym drawn from the first letters of the members' surnames: Kimock, his longtime Zero associate Bobby Vega, drummer Alan Hertz (now in Garaj Mahal), and former Frank Zappa vocalist

Ray White. This group first came together for a benefit performance in January 1998 and remained a unit for two years (though at the very end Ike Willis stepped in for White, lending another Zappa collaborator and W to the cause). The Steve Kimock Band picked things up soon afterwards with K and V often joined by either Pete Sears or Tom Coster on keys and a passel of drummers, including Prairie Prince, Jimmy Sanchez, and Hertz (the five tracks on the group's debut, *Live from the West Coast*, now out of print, feature Kimock, Vega, Sears, Coster, and Hertz).

The band took a significant step towards its current approach and incarnation with the addition of drummer Rodney Holmes in the fall of 2000. Holmes brought in a vivid performance style (he had worked with Carlos Santana and the Brecker Brothers, earning Grammys in both contexts) as well as his own compositions, some of which are steeped in electronica. Holmes also recommended guitarist Mitch Stein, his longtime collaborator in New York-based trio the Hermanators, and in March 2001 Stein joined the SKB, which remained a quartet and began to perform without a keyboardist. (Incidentally, Hermanator is the nickname of Austrian skier Hermann Maier, who experienced a 70mph "agony of defeat" spill at the Nagano Olympics yet picked himself up to win gold in the Super

Steve Kimock, a moment in the sun.

G and Giant Slalom.) Stein's contributions surprised some listeners, as he does not function solely as a rhythm player, but adds his own slashing leads and counterpoints. Vega left the bass chair to Richard Hammond and then to Alphonso Johnson, who remained with the band for more than a year. Living Daylights bassist Arne Livingston stepped in during the band's February 2003 tour and introduced his own penchant for complexity. Livingston, who has narcolepsy, has stated that he requires ongoing challenges to keep the synapses firing. He's on firm footing with the SKB because the time signatures are not standard and change drastically, though due to the grace of Kimock's songwriting there is a subtlety and flow, and the music doesn't hang on eccentricity.

While one might expect the Steve Kimock Band to serve predominantly as a showcase for its namesake, this is far from the case. Nor is the guitarist content with any past associations or Garcian imprimatur to dictate the sound. While recent experiments with samples confound some longtime listeners, many have come to accept and embrace the baffling of Kimock.

East Meets West (2002) ★★★★

These two discs collect performances from Yokohama, Japan (November 25, 2001) and San Francisco. Richard Hammond appears on the former set with Alphonso Johnson on the latter, recorded during the band's New Year's Eve run. However, the biggest variance comes not from the bass. but rather from the song selection, as the San Francisco side features two compositions by drummer Rodney Holmes, with "Sabertooth" incorpo-

rating samples that yield ambient improv. At times the music meanders, but with Kimock's fluid leads the results often prove sublime.

Live in Colorado (2002) ★★★★

These five tracks recorded in Colorado in February 2002 are representative of Alphonso Johnson's tenure with the band (minus the Holmes songs). This release offers a solid balance of uptempos and balladry, often within a few measures, as the band's sense of dynamics is laudable.

Out of print:
Live from the West Coast (2001)

Fan site:
FLOK—Fellow Lovers of Kimock—
www.flok.org
Kimocksphere—*www.kimocksphere.com*

Discussion list:
lists.netspace.org/archives/kimock.html

GORDON STONE
www.gordonstone.com
It was pedal steel guitar/banjo player Gordon Stone himself who once affirmed that some folks are born to be bandleaders and some have band leadership hoodwinked upon them. Okay, that's paraphrasing, but there is veracity to the sentiment. By the mid-'90s, Stone had served as Mike Gordon's banjo instructor and played on two Phish albums (*Picture of Nectar* and *Rift*), yet while performing with the bluegrass band Breakaway, he found himself restraining some of his impulses to push the music into jazz and improvisational spheres. However, after

some jam sessions with Jazz Mandolin Project's Jamie Masefield and bassist Stacey Starkweather, the two musicians encouraged him (or "tricked" him, as Stone has joked) into forming the Gordon Stone Trio (which would eventually morph into the Gordon Stone Band, often a three-piece).

Stone, who first moved to Burlington, VT, in the mid-'70s following a stint at the Berklee College of Music, has maintained eclectic aims and interests. In the years following his arrival, he worked with bluegrass projects and also in other contexts such as the Afrobeat of Zzebra (where he collaborated with future GSB member Russ Lawton) and the new wave group Decentz. Stone also retained an affinity for jazz and explored some of these ideas on his 1981 solo record, aptly titled *Scratchin' the Surface*. However, he never substantially addressed this music in the live setting until Masefield and Starkweather cajoled him to form the Trio.

While the original lineup was an intriguing one, vicissitudes soon carried Masefield and Starkweather on to other projects (including the Project) and Stone welcomed new players, some of whom later moved on, as well. The lineup with the longest tenure featured Lawton and bassist Rudy Dauth. However, in 1999 Trey Anastasio invited the drummer to tour with him and Tony Markellis in what would eventually become a ten-piece band (Lawton and Markellis co-wrote much of the material that later appeared on the *Farmhouse* album, and "First Tube" builds on a beat Lawton created for the Zzebra song "Shabadoo Day"). As of late, Dauth has pursued other endeavors, as well, with Stone drawing in other complementary players,

including Uncle Sammy's Brian O'Connell. The GSB's Phish associations cetainly summon fans, who prove mostly respectful, offering only the occasional cry for "Jibboo" ("Runaway Jim" is another request, though this one is more reasonable as the trio recorded it for its *Red Room* release). Meanwhile, Stone maintains connections with other bands, recording and performing with Strangefolk on multiple occasions and retaining membership in moe. guitarist Al Schnier's Al & the Transamericans (though as yet there has not been an outpouring of demand for the Gordon Stone Band's take on "Me & Pat & Bill & You").

Still, all in all, audiences remain engaged with the Gordon Stone Band's variable collective rhythms and its solo displays as well (Stone has been known to deliver a Thelonious Monk cover by himself on pedal steel). Although some listeners feel that the infrequent vocals introduced over the past few years don't lend much to the cause, the singing does add to the dynamics of the live show, suggesting that while Stone was once a reluctant bandleader he remains a proficient one.

Red Room (2001) ★ ★ ★ ½
Drummer Russ Lawton and bassist Rudy Dauth impart a lexicon of beats behind Stone's roistering banjo and plangent pedal steel. The band mostly situates itself in jazz environments, though a few poppier folk tracks also appear (and prove amiable if not altogether riveting).

As Gordon Stone Trio/Gordon Stone:
Even with the Odds (1998)
Touch and Go (1995)
Scratchin' the Surface (1981)

STRANGEFOLK

www.strangefolk.com

Okay, here's the rub. Right now, more than ten years into its history, Strangefolk's instrumental prowess and facility for improvisation are at an apex. The current quintet also has tighter vocal harmonies delivered with a heightened confidence and gusto. However, the band is still striving to rebuild its fan base following the departure of vocalist and co-founder Reid Genauer in September 2000.

The current Strangefolk is different from the band of yore. During Genauer's tenure, the quartet energized listeners with the sweeping hooks of his songs often reinforced by his emotive delivery (offering a fine contrast to those tunes sung by guitarist Jon Trafton and bass player Eric Glockler). At present, the choruses carry less of a rush, but the group builds more textures while varying tones through its three lead players.

Strange Folk (as it was originally known) first came together as an acoustic duo in 1991 featuring University of Vermont students Trafton and Genauer. After performing at coffeehouses and informal settings for a number of months, the pair drew in Glockler and drummer Luke Smith (both of whom were relatively new to their instruments, building a mutual vocabulary they have embellished over time). The guitarists continued on their original instruments, with Trafton's gear adding the Strange to the Folk.

"Reid and I started out playing acoustic guitars," Trafton recalls, "and that was fun, and it was kind of a novelty because I'd play it with all of these crazy effects—distortion pedals, wah pedals, and delays, and it seemed unique at the time. Then as we evolved into a band we kept that set-up." After more than 500 shows and two studio releases (plus a demo tape later released on disc), Trafton made a switch, because eventually, "I said to myself, 'I'm forcing this acoustic guitar to be an electric guitar, why don't I just make it easier on myself and play an electric guitar.' I did feel a little bit of pressure because that might have been our image, but I just decided to pick up the electric and go for it. I'm glad; I would never go back."

By the close of the '90s, Strangefolk had developed a national following within the burgeoning, vitalized jamband scene. During the summer of 1998, the group joined moe. and String Cheese Incident on the abbreviated Hoodoo Bash tour, which affirmed its standing. The band soon signed with Mammoth Records, and enlisted Nile Rodgers (Chic, David Bowie, Madonna, Mick Jagger) to produce its third studio effort. However, this disc remained in stasis due to corporate restructuring at the label, and Mammoth eventually dropped the band, which later released the aptly titled *A Great Long While*. Meanwhile, by the summer of 2000, Genauer found himself burnt out, especially with life on the road, and decided to enter Cornell Business School. His final performance as a Folk member was at the band's September 2000 Garden of Eden Festival (the group's annual event held in Vermont since 1996).

Following Eden, the three remaining musicians decided to keep it going. A few months later they held open auditions in New York for new players. Trafton recalls, "I was open to anything. The most far-flung instrument that came in was the didgeridoo. We just wanted to hear some talented people and see where we could take it. But while I was open to anything, I wouldn't accept just anything." Trafton and the band did accept guitarist Luke Patchen Montgomery, a singer/songwriter who had previously opened for Strangefolk with his similarly named Folkstone. The band also enriched its sound by adding keyboards, first by Scott Shdeed and later with current member Don Scott, who has stepped in as a soloist, joining Trafton and Montgomery in the latter musician's unanticipated role. "When Patchen first auditioned we could see he had some chops playing acoustic guitar, and then after he was in the band we realized he could play electric guitar, too. I think it's refreshing for Jon to have Patchen step in and take a solo every once in a while so that he doesn't always have to be the lead solo man." Bassist Glockler notes, "Now we have three competent solo players who trade off and switch it up. It's been fun. Sometimes Jon will say, 'I don't want to take a solo in this song, Don, you go for it.' A couple of other songs primarily Don solos on, and on some all three will take a lead and they'll pass the torch. A lot of times it's just the vibe on stage, and if one of them wants to take a solo he'll go for it." This approach animates Strangefolk's second decade of music.

Coast to Coast (2002) ★★★

This disc offers live music from the current quintet recorded during its fall 2001 and winter 2002 shows. These eight tracks demon-strate that the band is currently at its height as an improvisational collective (keyboardist Scott, in particular, shines). The 16-minute version of "In Deep," Montgomery's "Leave a Message," and Glockler's "Anchor" are all strong offerings. Some of the other tunes have a bit less zest, but all in all this is a step up from *Open Road* and a solid harbinger for the future.

Open Road (2001) ★★ ½

The first disc to feature the post-Genauer lineup (with Shdeed instead of current key-boardist Scott), this one feels a bit rushed. New member Montgomery makes a solid introduction with his four originals. Still, a few of the songs introduce appealing melody lines or riffs only to give way to more generic expressions.

A Great Long While (2000) ★★★ ½

Nile Rodgers produced this disc (originally slated for release on Mammoth Records until that label cut loose most of its acts). *A Great Long While* contains a good collection of songs (including the old-school favorite "Cabin John"), though some of the production is a bit too glossy, sacrificing intimacy and charm.

Weightless in Water (1998) ★★★★

The best of the band's Genauer-era releases, with all three songwriters making fine contri-butions. The disc opens with a move from Genauer's "Roads" to Trafton's "Whatever" to Glockler's "All the Same." There are fine takes on other Strangefolk standards as well, including "Valhalla," "Westerly," and "Oxbow."

Lore (1996) ★★★ ½

The band's first studio effort is a bit too loose around the edges, but the group more than makes up for it with some animated readings of such compositions as "Sometimes," "Lines and Circles," "Rather Go Fishin'," and "So Well."

Strangefolk (1994) ★★

A collection of early demos and two live tracks, this release is ideal for Folk diehards: it contains the only official recordings of "Reuben's Place" and "Rachel," plus studio takes and live versions of "Things that Fly" and "Like You Anyway."

Also:

Coast to Coast Vol. 2 (2003)

Selected fan sites:

Strangebase—*www.strangebase.com*
Home on the Strange—*www.frizhead.com*
Strangers Helping Strangers—
www.shstrangers.org/ (a charitable, fan-based organization that collects non-perishable food and donates it to organizations near the sites of Strangefolk shows—winner of the Community Service Jammys in 2000)

Discussion list:

Strangefolk fan2fan—*www.groups.yahoo.com /group/strangefolk-fan2fan/*

STRANGE PLEASURES

www.strangepleasures.com

Strange Pleasures has been instrumental in bringing improvisational sounds to Omaha. The group's music is only one part of the story, though. Strange Pleasures has worked to build a scene for like-minded area bands and fans, convincing other groups to route through the small Nebraska city between gigs in Chicago and Denver. While Strange Pleasures has weathered a number of personnel changes and continues to develop its own sound, the band members' good-natured proselytizing has garnered the group some national renown (and frankly, manager/sound engineer/lyricist Paul Pearson's role as a Jambands.com editor hasn't hurt either).

The quartet's lone original member is vocalist/rhythm guitarist Greg Beebe, who co-founded the group in 1995. Beebe, also the band's principal songwriter, credits Strange Pleasures' musical freedom with facilitating the roster changes (nearly 20 musicians have moved through SP). In addition, he indicates that this fluctuation has enabled him to clarify his own vision for the group. Still, on some levels this has inhibited the band's development, which relies a bit too heavily on the modes and moods of the Grateful Dead and Pink Floyd. As Beebe begins to work with a consistent core of players, these influences may very well recede into the mix, delivering further pleasures to Nebraska and beyond.

Waiting for Art (2002) ★ ½

Recorded relatively soon after the current incarnation crystallized, *Waiting for Art* shows that the band is still honing its own sound (the Dead and Floyd resonate throughout this release). To its credit, though, this studio effort has a live feel—especially on track four, "Van," and on through the "Van Again" reprise, eight songs later. Baywatch bashers (you know you're still out there) should be drawn to "Hasselhoff."

STRING CHEESE INCIDENT

www.stringcheeseincident.com

Don't forget it's not all hula hoops and fairy wings. Actually, let's pause and parse for a moment. While that introductory charge to the dismissive certainly carries validity, its very presence bespeaks a certain splendor. Think about it. What other band in modern memory warrants such a declaration?

The preponderance of winged concertgoers is attributable to the pomp and pageantry that has accompanied a number of String Cheese Incidents. The first of these, dubbed Dancing Around the Wheel of Time, took place on New Year's Eve 1999 with Peak Experience Productions spearheading a ritual component that yielded a dozen floats and a few hundred costumed dancers. The following August, String Cheese and Peak collaborated on the Full Moon Dream Dance spanning three days at Horning's Hideout, a woodlands site in North Plains, OR. In describing the event, John Dwork, the inimitable (understatement) co-founder, announced: "Besides being a great music festival, we are designing a wide variety of audience participatory activities based on the idea of 'mythic play.' We will use the four elements—air, fire, water, earth—as vehicles for identifying and exploring different aspects of the expressive arts. Participants will embody characters from the wide pantheon of Faerie lore as a way in which to more deeply experience this process. Air will represent the phools and thespians. Fire will represent the heroic arts such as fire dancing, juggling, hula hooping, tantra, etc. Water will represent the flowing arts, such as music. Earth will represent the building of art and those who support other artists. We will also

have a Royal Court of the Faerie King and Queen, which represents a fifth element of sorts—spirit. This group will set the event tone by performing interactive theater pieces throughout the weekend that will move us collectively through the different evolutions of the weekend's theme." Magic: the Gathering cards optional. Seriously, though, the collaborative aspect and visual impact of such events as the Academummy Awards, the Superhero's Ball, the Meeting of the Lost Worlds, and the Living Dream Experience mark an effort to transform the traditional concert environment (to achieve *Evolution*, the title of the DVD that presents the show on December 31, 1999). At worst, this spectacle has provided eye candy for the uninitiated, while at best it has offered an indelible, ineffable interactive experience.

While arguably String Cheese Incident is only indirectly responsible for the pixies, it has had a direct hand and hip in the hooping (and speaking of pixies—actually, make that Pixies—Killing Joke bassist Youth, producer of SCI's 2003 release *Untying the Not*, crossed paths with Black Francis, Kim Deal, and company over the years while working with the Verve, the Orb, Heather Nova, and many others. This connection affirms SCI's willingness to solicit new ears). The Cheese has supplied homemade hoops and instruction to audience members, particularly during a stretch in the mid-'90s, with some notable motion at the 1996 Telluride Bluegrass Festival. While the group has cut back on the lessons, it still promotes the practice by roping off hooper zones within venues when possible and stipulating that all manner of rings are welcome within the gates. (Technically speaking, a homemade hoop, often created with polyethylene piping and duct tape, is not a Hula Hoop®, which is a registered brand of Wham-O, Inc., the same folks who brought you the Frisbee® and the Superball®. BTW, for some healthy hooping be sure to check out SCI's Michael Kang as he simultaneously swirls and skis on the band's *Waiting for the Snow to Fall* DVD—and schedule a screening of the Coen Brothers' *Hudsucker Proxy*, the twisted tale of Norville Barnes, the Horatio Alger of hooping: "You know, for kids.")

String Cheese Incident is a product of that Rocky Mountain high, as all of its members relocated to Colorado, and the band's formation was a direct result of its founders' yen for the slopes. The nexus was Kang, a classically trained violinist and newly minted mandolin player who moved from Alaska to Crested Butte in the winter of 1992. ("All through college I hadn't really played the violin. Then when I picked up the mandolin it was strung the same way, so it was easy to pick up and play. So that was kind of the impetus—I could pick it up and play without worrying about intonation.") Kang began performing with guitarist Keith Moseley in a local bluegrass band called the Whiskey Crate Warriors, and soon afterwards, Bill Nershi, another recent arrival and guitar player, invited Kang to perform as a duo for some après-ski gigs. Nershi and Kang then asked Moseley to join, but granting that Nershi was the more proficient guitarist, Moseley moved to the bass. ("From the very beginning I was in way over my head. We were playing bluegrass and rock tunes, some jazz, some worldbeat stuff, and I was playing catch-up, trying to get up to speed on all that.") Michael Travis came in

next on hand drums, replacing mandolin player Bruce Hayes, who performed a few shows with the trio, and by December 1993, String Cheese Incident, originally the Blue String Cheese Band and then the String Cheese Conspiracy, was an entity (string cheese, the plasticized curd dairy treat, first appeared in southern California via the Armenian community in the 1950s).

Initially envisioned as a means to support steady ski runs, the band became fully committed to the enterprise by 1996, moving to Boulder and performing nearly 600 gigs over the ensuing three years. Stylistically, String Cheese at first characterized its sound as "funkalatino-afrojazzadelic bluegrass" with a defined emphasis on the fully named genre, but the band did not see itself as a bluegrass outfit. As Nershi explains, "We never worried that it's not right to have a percussion player in bluegrass music because we never tried to label our music as anything but going-out-and-having-fun music." (One word missing from the group's self-description is rock, and some listeners would prefer an elevation of the screaming guitar quotient, though Kang's electric mandolin often suffices.) The sound soon incorporated further jazz textures with the addition of keyboardist Kyle Hollingsworth, then of the band Durt, whom SCI courted and welcomed for a trial run before he agreed to join in mid-1996. At the same time, the Cheese began touring with its own sound equipment (a rarity for a band still gigging in relatively small clubs) as a means to ensure separation and clarity, which otherwise could be a challenge with Nershi on an acoustic. Hollingsworth recalls, "We bought a Mayer rig, which is one the

Grateful Dead used. We used that when we were playing 250-person rooms. We carried that in, set it up ourselves, and Kang would run the board from the front where he was playing, then run out and listen. We also had the best PA we could because the clubs we went into sometimes could make you sound really bad. It was scary sometimes, and it was all about making us sound clear."

Of all its contemporaries, String Cheese Incident most warrants comparisons to the Grateful Dead, not so much for its sound, but for its support. This latter term applies in two contexts: to crunchy tour nomads who share a common ethos, and to the team that works with the band. String Cheese is steadfastly do-it-yourself, from its SCI Fidelity record label to SCI Gear dry goods, Gouda Causes charitable wing, and SCI Ticketing, which in August 2003 made a commitment to take on the Empire when it filed a lawsuit against Ticketmaster (this likely will be a protracted struggle). The band's ties to the Dead are also now linear, as Bob Weir's longtime friend and lyricist, John Perry Barlow, has started contributing to the group's songwriting efforts, and Merry Prankster Carolyn Adams Garcia (aka Mountain Girl) is another visible, vocal

String Cheese Incident, Bonnaroo 2002.

booster. Still, any perpetuation of the Dead legacy is incidental to the band's own trails, which continue to originate from the mountains. Indeed, in *Waiting for the Snow to Fall* (the DVD documentation of the band members nurturing their inner ski bums during SCI's annual Winter Carnival tour of Colorado's resort areas, which in 2002 culminated with a Telluride slope-side set that allowed the quintet to downhill into the gig), Nershi relates, "A good night of music is just like getting some good turns down a really steep shoot. You get done and you go, 'Whew I'm still alive, that was great, that was really cool.'"

Outside Inside (2001) ★★★★
Producer Steve Berlin lends some pop punch to this bright collection of songs, which is the best translation of the band's anima into the studio.

Carnival 99 (1999) ★★★★
There is a flow to each of these two discs, drawn from performances in late 1998 and early 1999. The cover selections predominate, showcasing the band's multi-modes, from Jean-Luc Ponty ("Mouna Bowa") to the Neville Brothers ("Hey Pocky Way") to Wayne Shorter ("Footprints") to Jimmy Martin ("Hold Whatcha Got").

Round the Wheel (1998) ★★★ ½
Kyle Hollingsworth's first studio contribution carries the band into more pronounced Latin and jazz domains. While the playing is nimble and the songwriting sturdy, the results are not always as warm and vivid as one might expect.

A String Cheese Incident (1997) ★★★
A vivacious ten-minute take on Vassar Clements's "Lonesome Fiddle Blues" opens the band's initial live disc, drawn from early 1997. The band's original compositions offer animated passages, but few wholly standout.

Born on the Wrong Planet (1996) ★★★ ½
A number of guests join the then-quartet for this solid debut, framed more by bluegrass than at present. A sturdy sampling of the band's agility and approach circa 1996 with a complementary collection of songs, many of which remain staples, including "Black Clouds," "Texas," and "Jellyfish."

Also:
Untying the Not (2003)

On the Road: San Francisco, CA, December 28, 29, and 31, 2002 ★★★★ ½
Since the spring of 2002, String Cheese Incident has released its entire tour on individual discs as part of its *On the Road* series. One standout is the box set that collects the three shows from the 2002 New Year's Eve run, offering seven sets of music, including one backing Keller Williams. It is well packaged with a photo booklet presenting the band in full time-travel regalia, reflecting the night's theme.

Fan site:
www.friendsofcheese.com
SCI stats—*www.ihoz.com/scistats.html*

Discussion list:
www.lists.netspace.org/archives/sci.html

SWEET POTATO PROJECT

www.sweetpotatoproject.com

For now at least, the Big Wu becomes an immediate reference point when considering Sweet Potato Project. Like the Wu, which has about five years' seniority, Sweet Potato Project is based in the Minneapolis area and has built an audience through weekly gigs at the Cabooze (graduating from the Five Corners Saloon). The Big Wu has even taken an active interest in the Project, offering the band slots at its 2001 and 2002 Family Reunion festivals and an opening gig at its New Year's Eve 2001 show at the Roy Wilkins Auditorium. However, despite a shared affinity for improvisation, the two bands' musical pantheons vary. The Wu is deeply influenced by the Dead, and Sweet Potato Project is drawn more to Phish and Ween (with some Zappa tossed in for odd measure).

Aaron Gorton (guitar) and Tim Carrow (keys) typically lead Sweet Potato Project through a range of funk, jazz, electronic, and even reggae passages. Although the songs often contain some level of complexity, SPP also strives for the catchy melody. While the band's lyrics often evince a skewed sense of humor, they sometimes directly express a kinship with the audience. This dynamic should build as the band takes to the road for extended national touring and continues to develop its sound.

Dreamtime (2002) ★★

Energy and a friendly spirit permeate this release. In a few instances, the vocals are rough, and an over-reliance on the Phish lexicon proves confining. This release does hold charm, however, especially on the burbling funk of "Silly Saturation" and the palette of sounds that animates the ten-minute "Swamp Man."

SWIVEL HIPS SMITH

www.swivelhipssmith.com

The name Swivel Hips Smith accomplishes two goals in descending levels of importance (at least for our purposes). For starters, it is quite evocative, hinting at an oft-upbeat sound that aims to keep limbs in motion. At the same time, it serves as a tribute to a classic 1944 Disney cartoon featuring Goofy, riffing on the name of a character in "How to Play Football," which was nominated for an Oscar for Best Short Subject. (Alas, it lost to Tom and Jerry's "Mouse Trouble.")

The precursor to Swivel Hips Smith assembled at the 1998 summer Chautauqua Institute in southwestern New York. Initially performing as Bike Rent, the current founding core of drummer Luke Brown, bassist/ vocalist Chris Long, and guitarist/ vocalist Erik Swartz relocated to Colorado that fall, hoping to gig regularly. In this regard the group proved successful, remaining peripatetic for a few years making the rounds of Colorado, joined by Dan Rolls on sax and vocals and Shane Lieberman on guitar and vocals. The band's name transformed from Bike Rent to Latavon, before Swartz remembered the Disney cartoon and offered up the current moniker in 1999.

It wasn't until Swivel Hips Smith settled in Boulder in 2001 that it really began to expand beyond its self-described "funk-laden grooves." At present that means adding elements of ska, salsa, Middle Eastern phrasings, and even trance. The band's locus and tour history sometimes peg it as an archetypal eclectic Colorado collective (frankly, any state should be so lucky to have a reputation for nurturing artists with affinities for such a collage of styles). But Swivel Hips Smith continues striving to defy characterization— or at least traditional characterization— through its ongoing efforts to incorporate new tonalities while keeping those torsos swaying.

Homestyle Spread (2001) ★★

This disc is a snapshot of a young band ambling forward but not quite yet hitting its stride (it also presents an earlier version of the band without current saxophone/ keyboard player Seth Garland and a different sax/vocalist in his stead). Some of *Homestyle Spread* is perfectly affable, straight-up funk, but it's when the band incorporates other elements, from ska to Middle Eastern sounds, that things start to get interesting (though the bluegrass-flavored song at the end seems a bit perfunctory).

TALA

www.tala.ca

The tala is the rhythmic component of Indian music. It is a fixed cycle that contains a set number of beats. Its analogue is the raga, which relates to the melodic aspect of the music and contains a pattern of phrases. And no, knowledge of tala is not requisite to understanding the music of TALA, but neither is it altogether irrelevant since the group does incorporate some Indian modes. In addition, repetitive tala drumming does have some relation to electronic music, which is another facet of this Canadian band's sound. (Knowledge of the band's Canadian origin is not necessary to understand the music of TALA, but listeners may want to visit the group's Web site at tala.ca, not tala.com— the latter will take you to a site devoted to Texas Citizens Against Lawsuit Abuse, which truly has nothing to do with TALA, but in this brave new world of the hyperlink and the jam-band, segue is king, no?)

Steve Venkatarangam was attending university (that's college to our American friends) in Saint John, New Brunswick, in the mid-'90s when he began performing in a group called Fat Tala. When this act disbanded in 1999, Venkatarangam moved to Montreal along with fellow Fat Tala alum Jason Blanchard. There they ran into bassist Marc Lajoie, who had once played informally with Venkatarangam at college (that's university to our Canadian friends), and TALA soon ensued. Over time a number of players have passed through the group, with Venkatarangam the only extant original member of a quartet that now includes drummer Adrian Aitken, bassist Nick Grimwood, and guitarist Ryan Smith (the latter two joined following the recording of TALA's debut disc in spring 2002). The band's sound is layered with atmospheric electronic funk textures. TALA is well suited to this space, but some of its finer passages arise when it pushes into Indian and acid reggae vibes, at times colored with chimerical vocals. Many more such moments may loom if this roster can remain together and continue to explore the nuances at the edge of its sound while complementing its well-founded tala.

TALA (2002) ★★★

The band's debut is mellow, ethereal, and warm. The strongest tracks gain gravitas when TALA folds in the unforeseen, such as the wave of sitar or an odd vocal phrasing.

TEA LEAF GREEN

www.tealeafgreen.com

Tea Leaf Green embodies the excess-thumping adage, "When in doubt, go for the treble." No, not the pitch or the clef (though the band will freely make that move as well). This is treble as in numeric degree, i.e. triple, which is significant because the band's moniker incorporates no less than three separate marijuana nicknames of varied historical origin. Frankly, that—and the fact that the group hails quite proudly from the fine state of California—leads some to peg Tea Leaf Green at first blush as a psychedelic stoner band, which it is not (mostly). Rather than offering up an "Ode to Cannabis Cup Laureates Past," the band waxes rhapsodic about "Sea Monkeys," the "Hot Dog," and "Panspermic De-evolution" (Gee, come to think of it....)

TLG is among a swell of emerging groups from the San Francisco Bay Area helping to revivify the region's improvisational music scene. Along with such bands as New Monsoon, Ten Ton Chicken, ALO, and Mood Food, Tea Leaf Green, which formed in 1997, has carried a vigor and zest into area clubs.

By 2003 such appearances became less common while the group maintained a national touring presence with support for its balance of swirling crescendos, well-founded melodies, and loopy, whimsical lyrics (for instance, the words to "Sex in the '70s" typically elicit reaction: "Mama, tell me about the sex you had in the '70s.") Not only that, guitarist Josh Clark has the look (and certainly the shirts). With leads that occasionally invoke references to Trey Anastasio and two of the Phish guitarist's antecedents, Jimi Hendrix and Jeff Beck, Clark also exudes a rock star vibe that helps distinguish the group from some of its peers who lack a similar commanding figure.

However, while Clark lends both charisma and riffs, he is not the exclusive musical focal point. Keyboard player and lead vocalist Trevor Garrod often assumes that role with his spry expressions on Fender Rhodes, Hammond B-3, and synthesizer. Meanwhile, bassist Ben Chambers and drummer Scott Rager comprise a robust rhythm section. TLG also cultivates a Zappa ethos to accompany a pop-rock facet even as it flirts with funk and country modes. While some of the latter offerings can lack hues, the band continues to emend its approach, and Tea Leaf Green increasingly leaves its expanded audiences, yes, buzzing.

Midnight on the Reservoir (2001) ★★★

These ten studio tracks offer both melodic hooks and complementary technical flourishes, often furnished by Trevor Garrod's keys. Some of the songs fail to flare, but the best of them do carry heft and induce a hum.

Also:

The group offers recent show and archival performances through the "Tea By Mail" program on its Web site.

Out of print:

Tea Leaf Green (1999)

TEN MILE TIDE

www.tenmiletide.com

The bright, euphonious music of Ten Mile Tide builds on the efforts of its twin guitarists. This is no metaphor, as Jason and Justin Munning on electric and acoustic respectively are identical twins who share an alma mater and now a band. While at California's Stanford University the pair initiated some loose jams in the basement of Dinkelspiel Auditorium (fun to say, fun to type) with college roommates Marc Mazzoni (vocals, keys) and Steve Kessler (violin) along with their childhood friend Bryan Jayne (bass). While the group's first official gig didn't take place until post-graduation in November 2000, its collective history extends deeper.

Although Kessler's violin and some of Mazzoni's vocal cadences draw references to the Dave Matthews Band, a more apt comparison may be the current Strangefolk. Indeed, a number of individuals first learned of Ten Mile Tide after it opened a few dates for Folk in early 2003 and gained Jon Trafton's endorsement in the "Jon's Room" section of the Strangefolk Web site. Others first encountered the group (which didn't begin national touring until April 2002) through Cornerband.com and the Kazaa file-sharing platform, which Ten Mile Tide often credits

for its national recognition (and which also garnered it a brief CNN profile). The music itself is affable melodic rock with a tinge of Celtic influence, though the songs are not always as poppy as they might yet become— TMT is still working to bait its hooks. The band doesn't aim to be too complex or dissonant, opting instead for simpler, winsome grooves to engage a swelling fan base that crosses geography and gender.

Flow (2001) ★★½

There is a warmth to *Flow*, which features ten compositions on the pop-rock side of the spectrum. The best of these songs tend to be mellow and melodious, with keyboardist/vocalist Marc Mazzoni and violin player Steve Kessler often up front in the mix.

TEN TON CHICKEN

www.tentonchicken.com

Although the members of Ten Ton Chicken have progressive musical leanings, one cannot necessarily glean this from the band's sound. Much of this California quintet's mostly instrumental originals use keys and sax to deliver groove-heavy party funk. But then, just when you think you have it all figured out, guitarist Gary Morrell will burst forth with a solo that reflects his prog proclivities.

The band first came together in 1998, though it was not until the addition of saxophone player Jamison Smeltz and bassist Tom Fejes in December 2000 that Ten Ton Chicken really started to strut. Still, Morrell and drummer Rich DiBenedetto first played together in high school (and DiBenedetto later stepped in to join Morrell's band Now in the mid-'80s), and their familiarity certainly lends itself to the sound, particularly when the quintet strives for complexity. The group's name, taken from an apocryphal band in a friend's humor magazine, captures TTC's looseness and yen for the absurd, which also informs its sound (and occasionally springs forth between songs at a gig). While Ten Ton Chicken can deliver a forceful funk, the group is at its most inventive and compelling during those sophisticated arrangements and compositions that push the boundaries of groove.

Just Like In the Old Country (2002) ★ ★ ★

Just when things get too familiar on this mix of studio and live tracks, TTC veers left (for instance on "Loushka."). Jaimoon Smeltz's resounding sax arsenal helps to carry the sound into the corners and at times over the top. "Punchytime Jamboree" fulfills the promise of its title.

Also:

In Search Of . . . (2003)

TISHAMINGO

www.tishamingo.com

Tishamingo began its performance career as Revival, a name that is appropriate on a few levels. Guitarist Cameron Williams and drummer Richard Proctor began collaborating in the seventh grade and co-founded the Black Creek Band and Uptown Rudy before Williams left the Southeast for Colorado (and a new group, Jes Grew). However, when his informal post-gig acoustic jams with guitarist Jess Franklin (Jess Franklin and the Best Little Blues Band) resulted in the formation of yet another band, Williams enlisted his old friend Proctor (along with Best Little Blues Band bassist Stephen Spivey).

Revival is also an apt name because it references the song by the Allman Brothers Band, a group whose sound Tishamingo certainly echoes. On top of that, the band quite literally embodied the term during a month-long residency in August 2001 at a Tallahasse, Florida club. Each night, Revival presented one set of original material followed by a performance of an album in its entirety, ranging from *The Allman Brothers Band* to *Led Zeppelin*, *Black Sabbath*, Derek and the Dominoes' *Layla*, and Jimi Hendrix's *Axis: Bold as Love*.

Now known as Tishamingo, the group's live shows are mostly devoted to a burgeoning catalog of original material. Most of the songs build from blues progressions, though the band continues to broaden its scope (as well as its instrumentation, often performing with a keyboard player—Jason Fuller, in many instances). Tishamingo's interlaced guitars typically galvanize, with some Delta slide and the occasional acoustic interlude lending zest. The vocals are roughened and robust, in the realm of Warren Haynes or John Bell. The band's snarling sound captured the attention of John Keane (Widespread Panic, Brute, Cowboy Junkies), who agreed to produce Tishamingo's self-titled debut in 2002—a favorable introduction to the band. Keane's measure of respect continues, as he makes the occasional guest appearance when the group routes through Athens, Georgia.

Tishamingo (2002) ★ ★ ★ ½

John Keane produced the band's debut and even drops in a bit of pedal steel and banjo. This disc offers a number of solid blues-based cuts (with some Allman Brothers Band feel to them), including "Whiskey State of Mind" and the more expansive "Tradition" and "Pete's Lament," while changing the pace on the more stately "Way Back Home."

TONY FURTADO & THE AMERICAN GYPSIES

www.tonyfurtado.com

The fact that Tony Furtado actively eschews any particular genre association or label makes him the ideal subject for these pages (Tony, welcome to a club sufficiently kaleidoscopic and chaotic for even Groucho Marx to avow membership). However, Furtado's renunciation carries additional weight as many listeners have come to associate him with bluegrass picking. Indeed, the fact that his current group is not a bluegrass project remains one of three common misconceptions about Furtado. (The second is his age. Some people assume Furtado is in his mid-fifties, but they are likely confusing him with progressive bluegrass legend Tony Trischka, though Trischka himself seemingly complicated the game of identity swap. When asked, "If Béla Fleck is the next Tony Trischka, who is the next Béla Fleck?" Trischka's response was: "Tony Furtado." As for misconception number three—nope, no relation to Nelly.)

In 1987, while still a California teenager, on something of a lark Furtado made the pilgrimage to the Walnut Valley Festival in Winfield, KS, where he took top honors at the National Bluegrass Banjo Championship. Victors are not permitted to defend their titles in successive years, but Furtado reclaimed his in 1991. (Other notable Winfield winners include Alison Krauss [1984, fiddle], Chris Thile [1993, mandolin], Mark O'Connor [multiple flat-pick guitar and fiddle victories, including a Twofer in 1977], and Jamie Janover [2002, hammered dulcimer]. In the wake of the festival acclaim, Furtado embarked on a bit of a traditional path by touring with fiddle player Laurie Lewis and her band for a few years. From there he began working on his own projects that did delve into more progressive realms. However, in the mid-'90s, inspired by the work of Ry Cooder, he spent an intensive few years working up his skills as an acoustic slide player, and he now performs on both instruments. (Indeed, in a Jambands.com review of the 2003 Old Settlers' Music Festival in Austin, Chris Gardner wrote of Trischka's claim to the "I'm So Good on Two Different Instruments that It's Really Not Fair to the Rest of You Chumps" trophy.)

Over the years, Furtado has toured with a number of players who have supported him while simultaneously pushing the music into deeper fields. His current collective, the American Gypsies, is comprised of musicians who match his interests from Celtic to bluegrass to jazz to blues. The Gypsies includes bassist Myron Dove (Santana, Steve Winwood, Al Jarreau), drummer Aaron Johnson (Darol Anger-Mike Marshall Band, Comotion), and guitarist Gawain Mathews (a trained jazz player, he also performs with Matt Flinner, who incidentally took the honors in the Winfield mandolin competition in 1991). The group's versatility also renders it particularly welcoming of guests, many of whom have joined the band for songs, shows, and even tours, including Anger, Paul McCandless, and Jessica Lurie. A typical gig offers Furtado solo segments in addition to the full-band performance, delivering tight arrangements that reinforce his virtuoso status along with passages that move beyond (in such a setting, the group most often exchanges some inspired solos rather than pushing it too far into exploratory realms). Sometimes Furtado is characterized as a member of the new American Roots movement, but he is not so geographically constrained, and such a description similarly denies his group's full florescence.

American Gypsy (2002) ★★★★

This disc balances solo tracks, guest players, and permutations of the current band. Divided between traditionals and Furtado originals (with Mike Nesmith's "Some of Shelly's Blues" interjected, as well), blues, funk, Celtic, and bluegrass are only the initial reference points for what follows. There is exuberance in much of the playing, while Furtado offers up a number of ballads that carry emotional resonance without being overly solemn.

Also:

Live Gypsy (2003)

Earlier projects:

Tony Furtado Band (2002)
Tony Furtado & Dirk Powell (1999)
Roll My Blues Away (1997)
Full Circle (1994)
Within Reach (1992)
Swamped (1989)

TOPAZ

www.topazmusic.com

Cellist Erik Friedlander is the driving force behind TOPAZ, a New York City quartet that incorporates sax, bass, and percussion.

Friedlander, son of the famed photographer Lee, has toured with Joe Lovano and John Zorn, recorded with Laurie Anderson and Dar Williams, and sat in with Hole during the taping of its MTV *Unplugged* performance. Friedlander founded TOPAZ in 1996, and the group has released two discs, its eponymous debut (1999) and *Skin* (2000). Actually, come to think of it, while it is a cool band, TOPAZ has nothing to do with the subject of the present entry (a collaboration could prove intriguing, however, and it is feasible, given a shared geographic base).

The Topaz in question is another NYC group proficient at improv, but this one is named after its founder, Topaz McGarrigle. The tenor sax-blowing transplanted Texan (thus the ubiquitous cowboy hat) formed the first version of the group in 1998, emerging out of a weekly jam session at Tribeca's Bell Café. Prior to this, McGarrigle had founded the Future Freedom Ensemble, an acid jazz collective that also included trombone, upright bass, tablas, and a live DJ. (The Ensemble captured the attention of young director Kris Isacsson, who commissioned the group to score his film *Man About Town*. It would win Best Short Film at the Sundance Festival, and Isacsson would go on to direct Julia Stiles and Freddie Prinze, Jr., in *Down to You*.)

From the outset, the emphasis of Topaz (the man and the band) has been to blend musical sophistication with rhythmic inducement (to keep the good people up and dancing). The sax player has emphasized that his version of early '70s future funk is "just jazz over dance beats, which is what jazz was originally." To this end, Topaz has achieved notoriety in somewhat saturated groove circles, with national tours and festival performances at events such as Gathering of the Vibes and Bonnaroo 2003. For some time, the group included bassist Jason Kriveloff, drummer Christian Ulrich, Ethan White on Wurlitzer, and Squantch on trombone and didgeridoo—all of whom balanced other musical endeavors, as well. At present the only remaining original player other than the namesake is guitarist Mark "Tewar" Tewarson (who may also pick up a sitar and viola when so inclined). The pair is joined by former Project Logic drummer Steph Roberson, Borahm Lee on keys, and Stu Brooks on bass. This roster has lent its own accents, carrying the group a bit more into dub and trance territories even as the bandleader maintains a mission of movement.

The Zone (2001) ★ ★ ★ ½

A fine collective effort. The resourceful production builds on the band members' interplay to yield an insistent, insidious collage of solos and collective crescendos (though some may find the group's occasional vocalizing of the choruses a bit off-putting).

Listen! (2000) ★ ★ ★

The opening cover of Donald Byrd's "The Emperor" (from the trumpeter's Ethiopian Knights) is a fine introduction to Topaz's take on jazz/funk. However, more than a dozen players contribute to this disc, and on occasion the focus wanes. The improvisation is generally lithe, although it can feel a bit lite, criticism that also applies to the songwriting.

Out of print:

The Shrine (1999)

Discussion list:

www.groups.yahoo.com/group/topaz/

TRICHROMES

www.trichromes.com

Following the passing of Jerry Garcia in 1995, Grateful Dead drummer Bill Kreutzmann left the San Francisco Bay Area for Hawaii, where he occupied himself with scuba diving, digital art, and his organic farm (Grateful Greens). After a few years on Kauai, he put in a brief stint with island-based trio Backbone but never committed to hitting the road again with any vigor. However, in 2001 an extended San Francisco sojourn resulted in the formation of the Trichromes.

The roster includes a number of players long associated with the San Francisco music scene. Vocalist Sy Klopps is the alter ego of Herbie Herbert, original Journey manager who also worked with Santana in the late '60s through the early '70s. When the Trichromes first performed in October 2001, Neal Schon assumed the lead guitar mantle and recorded on the group's initial EP before ultimately returning to the road with another incarnation of Journey. Guitarist Ralph Woodson (the Sy Klopps Blues Band) has since added his fiery guitar to the mix (Woodson first received area acclaim in 1982 when his band Togetherness won a Battle of the Bands at the Berkeley Community Theater, having closed out the set with a 12-string acoustic version of Hendrix's "Hear My Train a Comin'"). Bassist Mike Dipirro is a versatile player who appears on upright with his hybrid bluegrass trio, Free Peoples, and on electric with the Trichromes. In addition, after the current lineup crystallized, Kreutzmann took some rehearsal tapes to longtime Grateful

Dead lyricist Robert Hunter, who lent his words to eight songs (in a few instances Pete Sears later came in to help write music, as well).

The summer of 2002 saw the Trichromes touring in support of their eponymous debut recording. The group opened a number of amphitheater dates for Phil Lesh & Friends and also performed at the Grateful Dead Family Reunion. The band holds particular appeal for fans of the old school, psychedelic blues-rock of the late '60s and '70s, as there are fewer bands currently creating that sound. Dead Heads also credit the group for carrying Kreutzmann back into active musician mode, which facilitated his reunion with Mickey Hart, Phil Lesh, and Bob Weir in the Other Ones.

Trichromes (2002) ★★★

Many will find pleasure in the opportunity to hear Robert Hunter's imagery set to music over eight songs (even if these tunes often lack the melodies and grace of Hunter's earlier work with the Dead). A worthy debut, though at times the band sounds a bit too restrained (guitarist Ralph Woodson does have his moments of flight, but one wishes there were a few more).

ULU
www.ulu.net

Open your eyes: The world is awash in musical ulus. There is Britain's ULU venue, located at the University of London Union (which some have compared to New York's Irving Plaza with a bonus abutting swimming pool). There is director Ulu Grosbard, who directed the 1995 Oscar-nominated *Georgia*, featuring Mare Winningham and Jennifer Jason Leigh as sisters with contrasting singing careers as a folkie and a punker. There is the Hawaiian ulu tree that is often hollowed out to make drums (and surfboards). And then there's ulu the band, which has been interweaving crackling, popping funk and jazz instrumentals since 1997 (alas, not as long as the distinctly nonmusical ulu knife, which has been around for five millennia longer—a fact that may explain why a Web site devoted to the cutting implement is at ulu.com while the quartet's online home is ulu.net).

ulu began in the early '90s as a series of conversations between Syracuse University students Scott Chasolen and David Hoffman. The keyboard player and drummer discussed playing together in some context, but it all remained quite theoretical until the pair graduated and came to recognize that music provided a beatific corrective to the post-baccalaureate malaise. The pair eventually welcomed bassist Justin Wallace and performed as a trio for a short while before a *Village Voice* ad drew in guitarist Luca Benedetti and his friend and fellow former Berklee College of Music student Aaron Gardner, who played sax and flute. This version of ulu toured as a quintet for a few years, releasing two albums before Benedetti left the group in November 1999, preferring to remain in New York City and pursue projects there rather than tour (his final performance with the group is captured on *Live at Wetlands Preserve 11.19.99*).

Over the next three and a half years the remaining four players toured as an organ-driven quartet, typically layering a jazz dialect over a vast funk bottom. The standard musical comparison made by the media during this era, which will be steadfastly avoided here, was to Medeski Martin and Wood (oops, damn). While both groups create genre-bridging instrumental music, this comparison certainly overlooks Gardner's presence on sax and flute. Moreover, MMW's sound is more angular, experimental, and at times academic, often eschewing the pocket altogether, while ulu's pocket can be so deep as to swallow an appendage (plus MMW is not likely to bust out the "Cantina Theme" from *Star Wars* or the music to *Super Mario Brothers*).

While ulu thrived following the departure of Benedetti, the same could not be said when Hoffman and Wallace left the group in the spring of 2002. Chasolen and Gardner kept it going, drawing in a few new players for what some fans referred to as "newlu." These additional musicians were competent, but the group lacked the requisite chemistry to electrify. However, by fall 2002, two new players facilitated such a surge: drummer Josh Dion (an animated musician who bookends the stage with Chasolen—the pair are sometimes likened to two flailing Muppets) and bassist Brian Killeen (a native of tract-housing landmark Levittown, NY, whose residents have also included Eddie Money and Zippy the Pinhead cartoonist Bill Griffith). Lately ulu has introduced some strident cadences while also doing more with keyboard samples and sequencing, even as it references the funk and jazz progenitors, keeping the sound from pushing too far towards the cutting edge (which is fine, as the ulu knife already dominates that space).

What's the Deal (2002) ★ ★ ★ ½

This live recording affirms the vitality of the original quartet (to hear the quint in fine fettle seek out a copy of the *Live at Wetlands* release). These seven original compositions carry the band from snappier funk to melodic jazz to more atmospheric electronic expressions, all of which are elevated by playful, assertive improv.

Also:

Nerve (2003)

Out of print:

Live at Wetlands Preserve 11.19.99 (2000)
ulu (1998)

UMPHREY'S MCGEE

www.umphreys.com

This is a story of Umphreaks and geeks. Let's stick with the former, as one can make a strong case that this coalition devoted to the music of Umphrey's McGee boasts one of the finest tags in fandom. There are only a few other communities with equally apt appellatives. You have to give moe.rons and LoSers high marks for comparable designations that also merit bonus points for sportive self-denigration. Still, all of these folks have nothing on Dead Heads, a term with an etymology one can trace back to the mid-nineteenth century that often referenced those who would loiter in taverns solely for warmth. One cannot make such a charge of Umphreaks, who have certainly held their own, for instance burning more than 500 discs of live shows and distributing them throughout

Colorado in anticipation of the band's debut appearance (a campaign that proved quite successful, as the group blew out the rooms during its April 2001 run).

And as for the geeks? Well, the band did form at Notre Dame, where keyboardist Joel Cummings's senior thesis was titled "Schubertian Sonata Form and Anachronistic Modulatory Technique" (not quite "The Man who Stepped into Yesterday"). But fear not—there will be no aspersions cast upon the fine men and women of Notre Dame (especially not large ones like Jerome Bettis, Nick Buoniconti, and Mark Bavaro, nor jaunty ones such as Regis Philbin). Besides, the members of Umphrey's McGee are closer to geeks in the old

school sense of carnival performers drawing together an audience hankering for curiosities (such as fluidly dropping Mozart passages into a jam, followed by a Mötley Crüe quote, and then some reggae measures before things really start to get weird—just follow the riffs of Jake Cinninger, aka Sideshow Jake). At any rate, the geek label likely won't faze a band that titled its studio debut *Local Band Does O.K.* and gigged originally as Fat Tony before founding guitarist Brendan Bayliss suggested they brand themselves with the current moniker, a variant on a cousin's name.

Umphrey's McGee is often described as a next-generation progeny of the jamband scene (the winning line belongs to Benjy Eisen

Umphrey's McGee, Bonnaroo 2002.

and his *Relix* profile on the group, in which he writes, "In the admissions office of the Jamband County Club, Umphrey's McGee's application is letter-perfect"). Indeed, while UM has emphasized original material since its first gig, the group's initial choice of covers soon reflected affection for the sounds of Phish ("Mike's Song," "Antelope"), Medeski Martin and Wood ("Bubblehouse"), and moe. ("Rebubula"). To this end, one of the gratifying UM moments at the 2002 Bonnaroo Musical Festival (beyond its own performance) took place during moe.'s set when guitarist Al Schnier handed his guitar to Bayliss, who delivered the composed section of the song that had been an Umphrey's staple a few years earlier. (moe.'s respect for the younger group became manifest on May 2, 2003, during moe.'s gig at the Orpheum Theater in New Orleans. Umphrey's was the recipient of moe.'s patent-pending, full-band handoff: UM emerged during "The Faker" and remained onstage for "Glory" while moe.'s players exited gradually and later returned as the Umphrey's guys retreated slowly and moe. launched into "Kids.")

Still, while the band began with common jamband reference points, its tastes were certainly much broader as well (see Cummings's thesis—no, really, see it) along with some harder rock, jazz, and pop. Not only that, but as the group expanded beyond a quartet, the equation changed. First there was the addition of Andy Farag on percussion in 1998, then four years later drummer Kris Myers stepped in when Mike Mirro left to pursue a medical degree, and, most notably, Cinninger joined in late 2000 (the guitarist, whose tastes run to Blue Oyster Cult and T. Rex, carries technical skills with a head for the shred and had previously shared UM bills with his group, Ali Baba's Tahini).

Umphrey's McGee is also commonly defined by the careening trajectories of its music. The group has codified this with what it refers to as "Jimmy Stewart," a portion of the evening in which it plots to move from particular keys or tempos while remaining interlocked (by the way, the name is not a nod to the involuted film roles selected by the actor but rather a reference to the "Jimmy Stewart Room" where the band first attempted this performance approach, at the wedding reception of fans Jeremy Welsh and Laura Bossardt on September 8, 2001). While some criticism is directed at the group for the celerity with which it moves from idea to idea, many others hail this same facility. Bayliss has jokingly attributed this characteristic to the band's collective attention deficit disorder, though others might point to paradigm shifts within the culture that have necessitated an altered span of focus. Nonetheless, the group's supporters rarely get too reductive about it—they're just happy that the band members are Ritalin-free so they can keep their Umphreak flags flying.

Local Band Does O.K. (2002) ★★★★

This is the band's studio debut, following three live recordings (released initially in part to help secure gigs). Flexible rhythms and ricochets prevail on this album, which often feels like progressive rock without the swollen heads. The vocals are affable, but it is the instrumentals that ingratiate, particularly the precise guitar leads that can display a metallic tinge before the band kicks into electro-fusion or a Latin snap.

Out of print:

One Fat Sucka (2001)
Songs for Older Women (1999)
Greatest Hits Volume III (1998)

Fan sites:

www.umphreaks.com
www.umphiles.com

UNCLE SAMMY

www.unclesammy.com

Over the years Uncle Sammy has been the poster child for all things jamband. The group typifies both the best and the worst of the realm. In the former category, the quartet undeniably possesses chops (all four musicians trained at the Berklee College of Music), and the players are comfortable and confident when charging into improvised spaces. However, like some of the group's peers, Uncle Sammy has sometimes given vocals short shrift. Moreover, the band has been eclectic, perhaps to a fault, drawing from funk, Latin, jazz, rock, and reggae, which has somewhat inhibited the opportunity to develop a style of its own. Nonetheless, the quartet has maintained an East Coast presence, building on regular gigs at the Wetlands Preserve (US recorded its *Naturally Preserved* album at the club) and steady festival appearances (including multiple years at the Berkshire Mountain Music Festival).

Uncle Sammy formed during the summer of 1997 with its initial shows at Cape Cod's Beachcomber. Within two years, the group had worked up a number of funk and jazz originals while earning plaudits for its instrumental flourishes (especially for its players' potent solos—initially the band did not emphasize its collective improvisation; this developed over time along with its singing). Bass player Brian O'Connell often steps forward to display his command of the Chapman Stick (he received a Bassist of the Year designation in 2001 from *Revolving Door*, the western New York music guide). Drummer Tom Arey keeps pace with a light touch yet also the ability to lay it on (there are plenty of Arey-heads out there). Guitarist Max Delaney, whose leads initially revealed affection for Trey Anastasio, has come to incorporate a lattice of jazz and Latin cadences. Beau Sasser proves resourceful on keys, while his vocals remain the group's strongest (his register is similar to Donald Fagan's, which has allowed the group to drop in the occasional Steely Dan tune).

Uncle Sammy played more than 100 shows in 2001 and neared that figure the next year, but in 2003 its members found themselves pulled in other directions. Arey put in an extended stint with the Global Funk Council. His bandmates also worked on other projects, such as O'Connell's string of dates with Gordon Stone. Still, the arrival of an impending Uncle Sammy studio release, produced by Mike Keneally (Frank Zappa, Steve Vai), could very well motivate the band to pick up the pace and possibly even outdistance its earlier efforts.

In the Barn (2002) ★★★

A strong performance from a spontaneous barn set (hence the title) during a rain delay at the 2001 Gathering of the Vibes. While the sound quality of this audience recording does inhibit some enjoyment of the two discs, there are quite a few fine moments that effectively capture the essence of the band's live show, including signature covers

("Windjammer" and "Teen Town"), Uncle Sammy originals ("Feeling Optymystical," "Recycle Now," and a version of "Ladybug" with Addison Groove Project's Ben Groppe on tenor sax), and an amalgam of the two (Steely Dan's "Peg" sandwiched within Uncle Sammy's "East St. Louis").

Out of print:
Naturally Preserved (2000)
Live at Broadway Joe's (1999)

Discussion list:
www.groups.yahoo.com/group/unclesammy/

VIDA BLUE
www.vidablue.net

Former Major League Baseball pitcher Vida Blue was born in the state of Louisiana, so it is appropriate that the genesis of his musical namesake occurred in the same locale. In September 2001, Page McConnell, Oteil Burbridge, and Russell Batiste first came together in a New Orleans studio for six days of recording. Phish keyboard player McConnell had been relatively quiet during the first year of Phish's hiatus, but then, as he recalls, "Over a short time span I happened to see the Allman Brothers Band and the Funky Meters. A little light bulb went off and I thought this might be a nice little trio."

McConnell's expectations were not immediately realized. The trio came together and improvised under Page's direction, seeking to discover an organic sound and feel. It took time for the three to coalesce, perhaps in part because this was the first time they had played together (somewhat surprisingly, Burbridge and Batiste had not even previously met). McConnell recalls, "The first couple days we didn't get much material down, and I was wondering if this was going to be as good as it might be. But then we sat down on day three and played what would become the song 'CJ3.' It had a techno electronica feel to the intro, and from there it took off. That was kind of the first time that we felt we really came together."

This approach likely held appeal for these players partly because it was a departure for each of them. Burbridge typically negotiates the intersection of jazz and blues with his group the Peacemakers as well as with the Allman Brothers Band. Batiste's genre focus can be gleaned from the names of his principal projects, the Funky Meters and Papa Grows Funk. Meanwhile, McConnell eschewed the grand piano, his standard instrument with Phish, for a synthesizer, organ, and electric piano in this new context. In addition, McConnell, who rarely wrote any music with Phish, had the newfound responsibility of crafting lyrics (these ranged from the gentle epigrams of "Electra Glide" to "Who's Laughing Now," a cautionary tale about overindulgence that references John Belushi, Chris Farley, and Jackie Gleason).

The band put together three runs of dates in the months following their initial sessions (with Mike Gordon and Trey Anastasio joining them at New York's Roseland Ballroom on New Year's Eve 2001 during the "Light Up or

Leave Me Alone" encore). In general, audiences enjoyed the trio's two-hour live sets, though some found the sound to be too mellow and ethereal, at times akin to a modern take on Miles Davis's electric jazz of the early '70s. Still, most everyone grew energized when Vida Blue threw a curveball with such covers as the Steve Miller Band's "Fly Like an Eagle," Led Zeppelin's "No Quarter," and John Lennon's "Instant Karma."

Vida Blue (2002) ★★★★

Given the lineup, it's somewhat surprising that the music is often atmospheric rather than bounding and playful. McConnell's comfortable vocals are well suited for the easygoing "Most Events Aren't Planned" and "Electra Glide." The band fulfills its promise on "CJ3," a 12-minute instrumental in which McConnell and Burbridge play through a number of themes, with Batiste adroitly interposing himself.

Also:

The Illustrated Band (2003)

VINYL

www.vinylgroove.com

While Vinyl certainly anticipated the musical curve, one gets the sense that its eight bandmembers don't care all that much about their prescience. The group came together in 1995 as a loose association of friends who practiced in the garages of Mill Valley, California. The music they were drawn to was decidedly old school (hence the band's name), a mix of funk grooves, Latin percussion, and dub reggae. Within a few years of Vinyl's inception, a number of younger bands

had also latched upon a groove-laden sound. Yet Vinyl seems undaunted, as the group keeps it going, still creating the music that sparked its formation (the band tours nationally but often gigs around its northern California base).

Vinyl's instrumentation permits the freedom to slide from genre to genre with players laying out or coloring a particular song. Percussionist brothers Antonio and Sean Onorato join drummer Alexis Razon to offer up complex rhythms and to lock in and power a groove. Similarly, the horn section of Danny Cao (trumpet) and Doug Thomas (saxophone, flute) may offer burnished sounds reminiscent of Tower of Power or cadences more suitable for reggae. Meanwhile, bass player Geoff Vaughan, guitarist Billy Frates, and keyboardist Jonathan Korty also serve varied contexts. The group's robust collage has earned it numerous festival gigs, including the Newport Jazz Festival, Berkshire Mountain Music Festival, and the High Sierra Music Festival. Supporters include Phil Lesh, who joined Vinyl for a set of music in 2000, and Les Claypool, who played on the group's third disc, *Flea Market*.

While the group's general intent hasn't changed materially since its early days as a professional outfit, the results are certainly much tighter. Over time, Vinyl has eased up a bit on individual soloing, opting to keep the show dynamic lively by shifting modes. Typically this happens from song to song. as the band doesn't get too postmodern or ostentatious about it by tearing through multiple styles within the course of a given tune, retaining fealty to individual genres as befits its vinyl roots.

Flea Market (2001) ★★★★

This release moves away a bit from the bounding funk of its earlier efforts to present the band's experimental side as well as more of a worldbeat flavor (which is not to say it's devoid of groove). Along with 14 originals, the lone cover tune is an intriguing reggae arrangement of George Gershwin's "Summertime."

Live at Sweetwater (1998) ★★★½

The storied venue in the group's home locale of Mill Valley, California, serves as backdrop to a spirited performance of some agreeable songs. The percussion section shines throughout, as does keyboardist Korty, all supported by Vaughan's steady bass.

Vinyl (1997) ★★★

A rousing, grooving introduction to the band's many resources. Some of the individual compositions lack individuality, but the execution is bright.

WIDESPREAD PANIC

www.widespreadpanic.com

Maybe it's a northern bias.

As Widespread Panic approaches its third decade of existence, the group doesn't seem to get its due. The band has performed on three continents, appeared on both Letterman and Leno, and packed arenas and amphitheaters over multiple evenings, yet it is not feted with the attendant enthusiasm commensurate with such accomplishments. Then again, maybe the perception of a short shrift is itself biased, in that it fails to account for tremendous southern support of a group that drew over 100,000 boosters to its 1998 CD release party in Athens, GA, swelled the fairgrounds beyond comfort at the 2001 New Orleans Jazz and Heritage Festival, and anchored the initial Bonnaroo, closing out two nights from the main stage. It turns out there is every need for Panic, thank you very much.

This is all familiar to the group, though, as people have long misconstrued the nature of the band and its sound. Widespread Panic was bereft of guitar jangle when it came together in mid-'80s Athens, despite contrary expectations when it toured outside the area. Bassist Dave Schools recalls, "People would see 'From Athens, Georgia, Widespread Panic,' and they were showing up in white linen shirts and black vests wanting to hear R.E.M.-type music." The band also found itself imbued with a Grateful Dead signet, especially since it had introduced a few Dead covers in the pre-"Touch of Grey" era, at a time when scant other groups in the South were interpreting this music. (These tunes represented only a small portion of the Panic cover canon, let alone the totality of its catalog, as from the outset the group emphasized its originals. Still, by 1989 the band cut bait on these songs because they had become something of a millstone and were now prevalent on other groups' set lists. Spreadheads particularly lamented the departure of "Cream Puff War," which the Dead had stopped performing in 1967, and their plaints were heeded when Panic closed out its 1995 Halloween show with the tune. It is the band's tradition to introduce new and rare covers on that holiday, along with its own obscurities like "Coconut," which it played almost exclusively on October 31 between 1992 and 1997. That song is now back in rotation, as is "Cream Puff War." Incidentally, "Bird Song" and "China Cat Sunflower" currently are the Dead compositions that fans would most like Panic to revisit, though the band may be best suited to bring back "New Speedway Boogie.")

Another classification that didn't sit right with the members of Widespread Panic is jamband, a term that the group predates and for a time actively recoiled against, although it now acquiesces, to a degree. (Schools offers, "Yeah we're from Athens but we don't sound like R.E.M. and yes we're a southern rock band but we don't sound like Molly Hatchet. I guess we're a jamband but we don't sound like the Grateful Dead. All these labels lead someone to think that you're going to sound like something else, and that's not fair.")

Still, while there have been misperceptions regarding Widespread Panic's music, the band has been able to redress them through its efforts on the road and in the studio. Particularly in its early years, Panic's sound was quite dense and viscid—syrupy in texture, but by no means mawkish in message. If not quite an acquired taste, it certainly was

Widespread Panic—Mikey and JB on dual guitars and perches.

one that didn't reveal its full flavors on initial ingestion. Cognizant of this, the band came to average more than 150 shows per year in the early '90s, veering from the southern circuit to reach New England in 1989 and the California coast a year later, sustaining a sprawl and spreading the Spread (say that ten times fast). Along the way the group continually assessed and advanced, adding percussionist Sunny Ortiz in 1989 and touring with Dixie Dregs keyboardist T Lavitz in 1991, inviting John "JoJo" Hermann (Beanland) to take on that role a year later. The band's self-scrutiny also led it to begin working with set lists in 1994 as a means to ensure a full rotation of songs (this process is documented in *The World Will Swallow You,* one of a few films devoted to the group, such as *Panic in the Streets,* which captures the massive 1998 CD release party in downtown Athens, as well as 1992's *Live at the Georgia Theater*, directed by Billy Bob Thornton, who would later create a video for "Aunt Avis"). As for the song selection, on the day of each gig the band is presented with a master list, and then, Schools explains, "The ones in black we played last night, there's not a chance we're going to play those again. Then the songs in red were two nights ago and the ones in green were three nights ago—if we feel like it we could play one of those. Then everything else on the list is fair game."

Meanwhile, the band was not plagued by an inability to translate its music to another medium. Panic recorded a steady succession of studio albums featuring substantive compositions founded on blues-rock, and the group rarely foundered as it folded in other idioms. By the mid-'90s, vocalist John Bell's emotive growl began to peal from the FM dial. Increasingly, Spreadnecks, Spreadheads, and Spreadweb habitués pursued and promoted Panic (the online denizens comprised one of the earliest and most strident virtual music communities).

Producer John Keane (R.E.M., Indigo Girls, the Cowboy Junkies) is one of many individuals with whom the group has maintained a longstanding, collaborative relationship. Keane first met Panic in 1986 and has worked on every disc since the band's 1988 debut, *Space Wrangler,* with brief time off for good behavior during albums two and three (Keane is also a musician who has played with the group on many occasions, most often on pedal steel, as well as an author, penning *A Musician's Guide to Pro Tools*). The band members have also maintained relationships with other artists whose work they've respected, making a point of covering material written by Bloodkin's Danny Hutchens and Eric Carter ("Makes Sense to Me," "Can't Get High," "Henry Parsons Died"), Jerry Joseph ("Climb to Safety" plus more than a dozen other Joseph originals, with J.J. as guest vocalist), and Vic Chesnutt ("Aunt Avis"—we'll return to Vic momentarily, but here's a trivia question: Name the first Panic studio album that did not include one cover song). As for Chesnutt, the band's veneration has led it to back him for two studio efforts, *Nine High a Pallet* and *Co-Balt,* collectively attributed to Brute. (Chesnutt, who has been confined to a wheelchair since a car accident as a teenager, has many other enthusiasts, including Michael Stipe, who produced his first two albums, and artists who recorded his music on the *Sweet Relief II* compilation, such as Smashing Pumpkins, R.E.M., Madonna, and Garbage.) Another significant figure has been Col. Bruce Hampton Ret., as Bell has emphasized that from the moment the Aquarium Rescue Unit opened for the band, taking eggbeaters to instruments for portions of that set, Panic has never been the same (Bell provides the introduction on ARU's self-titled debut disc, and it was Panic who foisted the group onto the initial HORDE tour, resulting in some of the more electric moments of the shows during the full band segues between the two groups).

Two of Widespread Panic's colleagues and companions came on to help the group through the exceptionally difficult summer of 2002, following guitarist Michael Houser's diagnosis of terminal pancreatic cancer. Guitarist George McConnell (a former Beanland bandmate of Hermann's who first appeared onstage with Panic in 1993) and saxophone player Randall Bramlett came out to support and enrich the sound (Keane did the same during a brief April tour).

Houser, the band's namesake (one day he amended his customary tag, "Panic," to dub himself "Widespread Panic"), had first met fellow Georgia student Bell in 1982, and they began performing as a duo before adding Dave Schools in 1985, followed by a crop of drummers until they recruited Houser's high school friend Todd Nance a year later for the first incarnation of the band (Kelly Jo Davis lent vocals to some early gigs but never committed to the road—she eventually married another band associate, guitarist Tinsley Ellis). Houser most often produced his lingering leads while seated onstage in a chair, with his billowing hair usually obscuring his face from the audience. (For a brief period in the late '80s he stood, but back problems returned him to his rear, where he felt most comfortable, without any posing or posturing. Sometimes Houser joked about a browbeating he received as a 15-year-old for a lack of stage presence from friends who joined him in basement jam sessions.) Houser remained onstage with the band until early July when his illness prevented him from continuing, though he did continue to produce music and completed his solo album, *Door Harp*, before passing away on August 10, 2002.

Houser's wish was for the band to go on. So following the summer tour, the five members entered the studio, eventually inviting McConnell to join them for a recording that broke from tradition, in that the group created the songs during these sessions (and to answer that trivia question: *Ball* is the first studio release comprised solely of band-written material). Out of respect for Houser, Widespread Panic then returned to the road in April 2003 (McConnell—who certainly found himself in a difficult position—received some censure from fans who felt he didn't always mesh with the band's sound and hampered its ability to communicate effectively and collectively, but he also received some upgrades along the way). However, by late summer the group announced that it would follow through on longstanding plans for an extended sabbatical at year's end. Fans soon consumed themselves with traveling plans, striving to gorge themselves with Panic, little concerned with whether others deemed the group underrated, overrated, or even aerated. Spreadheads also awaited possible archival releases from the band while upping their quantities of recordings from the group's 2,000-plus gigs, seeking out the digital medium and, if need be, the analog, high bias alternative.

Ball (2003) ★★★★

Stately if not altogether somber, the band broke with tradition by building these songs in the studio. The results are the most multifarious of its recording career, pushing more directly into Latin jazz and funk. Keep it spinning following "Traveling Man," the final song Mike Houser brought to the group.

Live in the Classic City (2002) ★★★★½

This three-disc set presents the April 1, 2000, show at the Classic Center in Athens, followed by snippets from the preceding two nights. Guests abound on this vivid representation of the band from this era (some Spreadheads may decry the lack of rarities in the song selection, but others will deem such criticism immaterial).

Don't Tell the Band (2001) ★★★½

The arrangements are a bit less condensed than on prior efforts. This both serves and detracts from songs that are comfortable yet not always commanding (the band's bright take on fIREHOSE's "Sometimes" is certainly worth a listen). The bonus disc comes with four tracks that would later appear on *Classic City*.

Another Joyous Occasion (2000) ★★★

This live release fails to capture the full spark and sizzle that emerged from the collaboration with the Dirty Dozen Brass Band during Panic's summer and fall 1999 shows.

Till the Medicine Takes (1999) ★★★★½

The sextet's deft reading of Jerry Joseph's "Climb to Safety" is one highlight of a lustrous release that draws in a number of guests, including Dottie Peoples, Colin Butler, and the Dirty Dozen Brass Band to lend punch (in addition, Todd Nance is sturdy in his vocal debut on "You'll Be Fine").

Light Fuse, Get Away (1998) ★★★★★

The first live release from Panic presents two discs of material from the 1997 tours. An essential offering for the aggressive, animated improv, but just as significantly for the felicitous compositions that provide the pulse.

Bombs and Butterflies (1997) ★★★

The musicianship remains tasty and tasteful, though some of the compositions fall somewhere between a rut and a groove.

Ain't Life Grand (1994) ★★★½

The first of the band's discs to gain national airplay (for both "Airplane" and "Can't Get High") is a solid studio effort, yet it lacks some of its predecessors' resonance.

Everyday (1993) ★★★★

JoJo Hermann joins the band for its third release that remains on many fans' short list of studio favorites. There is some similarity of tone throughout, as the band inhabits its own clime like the live shows from the era.

Widespread Panic (1991) ★★★★

T Lavitz appears on keys, and Sunny Ortiz is on percussion for this eponymous disc often referred to as "Mom's Kitchen." This one holds up quite well, with Bell-owing vocals rumbling through a thick sound that complements some gripping compositions by Panic, Van Morrison ("Send Your Mind"), and Danny Hutchens ("Makes Sense to Me").

Space Wrangler (1988) ★★★★ ½
On "Driving Song" the band invokes "an honest tune with a lingering lead," setting the tone for much to follow. This lucid debut offers a number of songs that remain essential Panic, including "Chilly Water," "Porch Song," and the title offering. Capricorn re-released *Space Wrangler* in 1991 with three tracks from subsequent sessions, including an engrossing pairing of Robert Johnson's "Me and the Devil Blues" and the Talking Heads' "Heaven."

Also:
As Brute with Vic Chesnutt:
Co-Balt (2002)
Nine High a Pallet (1996)

Related:
John Hermann—*Defector* (2003) and *Smiling Assassin* (2001)
Michael Houser—*Door Harp* (2002)
Barbara Cue—*Ditch Lilly* (2002), Todd Nance project
Slang—*The Bellwether Project* (2001), Dave Schools project
John Hermann and Barbara Cue—*Louisiana Truckstop* (1999), Todd Nance project

Fan sites:
Set lists and stats—
www.everydaycompanion.com
Panic Fans for Food (winner of Jammy Awards' 2002 Mimi Fishman Memorial Award for Community Service)—
www.panicfansforfood.org/
www.spreadnet.org

Discussion list:
www.lists.netspace.org/archives/spreadnet.html

WILL BERNARD & MOTHERBUG
www.willbernard.com
Will Bernard is a consummate San Francisco Bay Area guitarist, a musician's musician who has contributed to a number of notable endeavors. However, despite the enthusiasm of his peers, Bernard has maintained a low profile and a limited geographic ambit (most often gigging locally). If he can devote himself to a particular project such as Motherbug for an extended period of time, it is likely that he will garner wider renown.

Prior to earning his composition degree from the University of California, Berkeley, Bernard attended Berkeley High School where he joined its Jazz Ensemble, which boasts such distinguished alumni as Peter Apfelbaum, Dave Ellis, Charlie Hunter, David Murray, Lenny Pickett, and Joshua Redman. Bernard went on to collaborate with Hunter in T.J. Kirk, a quartet that celebrated the pantheon of players referenced by its moniker: Thelonious Monk, James Brown, and Rahsaan Roland Kirk (the group's second release, *If Four Was One*, received a Grammy nomination in the best Contemporary Jazz category in 1997). The musicians invoked by the name T.J. Kirk hint at the range of influences and affinities that Bernard brings to bear on guitar. Bernard has also worked extensively with Apfelbaum in the

Hieroglyphics Ensemble and beyond, and recently toured with Robert Walter's 20th Congress and Living Daylights.

While Bernard founded a handful of groups in the late '90s, his band Motherbug stirred particular interest. Bernard's compositions carried this quartet away from the jazzier leanings of T.J. Kirk into an even funkier context, with keyboardist Michael Bluestein serving as a foil on Hammond B-3 and Fender Rhodes. The two received vigorous support from a rhythm section comprised of bassist Keith McArthur and drummer Jan Jackson (both of whom previously had joined Bernard in the band Pothole). However, conflicting gig commitments have limited Motherbug's ability to perform. Indeed, Bernard has gone on to tour the East Coast with an alternate incarnation that he has dubbed Otherbug, featuring Justin Wallace (ulu), Joe Russo (Fat Mama), and Marco Benevento (Jazz Farmers). One hopes that in the near future Bernard will have an opportunity to focus on his music with steady collaborators to showcase his fluidity and fancy as a guitarist and composer.

Motherbug (2000) ★ ★ ★ ½

This release moves from lounge to funk to groove-jazz (with some spoken word dropped in as well), yet there is a cohesive quality to it all. Bernard is often the principal voice, yet he wisely allows Michael Bluestein to swell forth on such tunes as "100 Cha Chas" and "Baldy Wonderland."

KELLER WILLIAMS

www.kellerwilliams.net

Keller Williams is singular. Audiences unfamiliar with his live shows may not know that Williams performs unaccompanied by other musicians, as the stage is gear-laden with nearly a dozen guitars, a bass, a mini-drum kit, a theremin, and a passel of enigmatic electronic devices (a Jambands.com 2002 April Fool's headline announced: "Keller Williams to Break Up"). However, this characterization as singular also works in the other sense of the word, since the total K-Dub musical experience—encompassing his songwriting, performance style, cover selection, and instrumentation—certainly is striking (an apt participle, as Williams often muses about that hypothetical glorious day when his musical success will permit him the luxury of building a bowling alley in his basement. One may well interpret this as wry commentary on the nature of commercial success and excess from a man who sings about his aspiration to be a "One-Hit Wonder." Then again, maybe Keller just wants to bowl in the buff).

In the early '90s Williams began gigging steadily as a member of a Virginia-based quartet and took an indirect path to his solo career. At the time he was playing with the All Natural Band, primarily on the acoustic ("I did play a little bit of electric, too, but only rhythm"). His fellow bandmates wanted to pool the money from their gigs towards making a record. Complications arose, however, when Williams wanted to dip into the gig money because, unlike the other players, he didn't have another job to support himself. Ultimately he opted for solo performances as his additional form of employment, and when the All Natural Band split up, he stuck with his day job (which calls to mind "Day Job," the Garcia-Hunter song that became the source of much vituperation when it debuted on August 28, 1982, ultimately leading the band to cut bait. Was the song itself too didactic? Did the fact that it mentioned work render it verboten? Or was the music itself too innocuous? One wonders if the contemporary fan base of another group would be similarly agitated by a tune that counsels one to retain one's daytime gig "until your night job pays." Williams—who has performed a few dozen songs from the Dead catalog over the years but not "Day Job"—did his share of tour, working menial jobs and then hitting the road with his lone responsibility "to get inside before the lights went out").

Keller's performance style is often compared to Michel Hedges's self-described "violent acoustic" efforts, though Williams's voice is more supple and carries a broader range (this comparison is somewhat irrelevant, since Williams typically plays a ten-string guitar rather than a 12-string, having removed a pair at one point early in his career to ease the tension on the bridge of an older instrument and then enjoying the resonant results). Like Hedges, Williams most commonly goes it alone onstage, though his show offers a bit more than the sound of a man and his guitar. His efforts take on additional layers through a looping device called the JamMan (which he first encountered while opening for Victor Wooten. Incidentally, Bob Sellon, who credits himself as the system programmer for the JamMan—a modest way of saying he invented the darn thing—has identified Les Paul as the first to develop a looping system, though the initial versions required an artist to sync to the loop time and not vice versa).

Williams clearly is no Luddite, but he emphasizes that his tracks are not preprogrammed, and he also introduces additional auditory accompaniment, at times using the body of his guitar to percussive effect and at others employing the mouth flugel (one is tempted to call him a master of mouth flugel—the means by which he emulates horn sounds sans brass, though to be accurate one must identify him as its lone practitioner, at least under that designation). In concert Williams does not offer an abundance of spiraling guitar leads, but he has ingratiated himself to jamband audiences through his acrobatics. He works without a set list in heavily segued performances, and deep into a particular song one can watch him divining a path as he diddles, daddles, and doodles (occasionally he noodles). Some have also suggested that Williams's status as a lone performer infuses his art. Having assigned but a single word to each of his album titles, he notes, "The very first album was called *Freek*, and it just went from there. I don't have any kind of philosophical answer. I kind of wish I had started to form a sentence, but that idea came later before I put in all those nouns and verbs. It's just short and simple. I think one word says it all in some cases. I think it will probably remain that way, too. I like saying a lot with one word; you try to put your imagination behind it."

While typically he is onstage by himself, Williams's report card nonetheless indicates that he plays well with others. Prior to his *Home* release in 2003, each of his studio efforts drew in other musicians, including 1999's *Breathe*, which he recorded with String Cheese Incident. Williams first encountered the Cheese in 1995 soon after he relocated to

Colorado. Going from fan to tour opener and collaborator, the Keller Williams Incident performed dates at the inaugural Bonnaroo as well as SCI's 2002 New Year's Eve show (in which, due to the evening's time travel theme, Williams appeared in a stylish white suit circa 1977, and the group donned disco finery for some Bee Gees covers as well as KW originals). One team that Williams has not yet joined is the Keller Williams Realty team, though the national franchise of agents is homesteading at KellerWilliams.com ("my mom keeps encouraging me to play a company picnic"). Indeed, for the latest on the man who would be band, Kellerwilliams.net is the place where you can keep in the loop.

Home (2003) ★★★★
The first studio solo album from Williams finds him playing all of the supporting instruments. There is warmth to the resulting disc, which is a bit gentler and more contemplative than its predecessors, though it retains the songwriter's wry humor.

Dance (2003) ★★★
Williams remixes a number of the tracks from *Laugh*. On the best of these he teases the connections to the progenitors yet folds in something new (as with "Tweeker" or "Barber"). When he strays at times, the results feel a bit too much like generic electronica.

Laugh (2002) ★★★★½
Here the guitarist records in a trio with Tye North and Dave Watts. All in all, this is his most successful studio disc in terms of composition and performance. Playful moments predominate.

Loop (2001) ★★★★
A sparkling representation of Williams's live show at a time just after his initial explorations with the JamMan.

Breathe (1999) ★★★½
String Cheese Incident backs Williams on this release, and Cheese fans will likely enjoy hearing the group in this setting. While the hues remain bright, this combination doesn't serve all the songs, some of which lack piquancy.

Also:
Spun (1998)
Buzz (1996)
Freek (1994)

Fan site:
www.k-dub.org

Discussion list:
www.lists.netspace.org/archives/keller.html

THE WORD
www.whatistheword.com
This project's inception came from John Medeski (Medeski Martin and Wood) and Luther Dickinson (North Mississippi Allstars) discovering that they both had been avidly spinning the recently released *Sacred Steel* compilation. This disc presents steel guitar gospel music, which has long been essential to the House of God church based in Florida. Medeski and Dickinson made loose plans to record an instrumental gospel record and they eventually blocked out a few days in October 2000. In the interim, North Mississippi Allstars bass player Chris Chew discovered a follow-up recording, *Sacred Steel Live*,

which included one track by a young pedal steel guitar player named Robert Randolph (whose church in Orange, New Jersey, shared the musical tradition of the Southern Pentecostal ministry). Quite serendipitously (or perhaps something more), Randolph had just started to perform New York City gigs with the Family Band, and one of these shows just prior to the recording sessions was an opener for the Allstars at the Bowery Ballroom. Medeski attended the performance, taking it all in alongside the Allstars, and at the end of the night the four musicians asked Randolph to join them in the studio. Thus came the Word.

Randolph's perspective and his pedal steel served the band well during these sessions. As a form of tribute, the band opted to record a few songs from the original *Sacred Steel* release and opened with two written by Glenn Lee, who had recently died of cancer at age 32. The band also arranged some traditional spirituals as a nod to the hill country sounds of the Dickinson Brothers, "Blood on That Rock" and "Keep Your Lamp Trimmed and Burning." They also worked up a version of Albert Brumley's "I'll Fly Away," which would be popularized in vocal form a few months later through Gillian Welch and Alison Krauss's soaring efforts on *O Brother, Where Art Thou?* Dickinson and Medeski added two originals inspired by the sounds that had first moved them.

The Word first toured on the East Coast in the summer of 2001 and the following January out West. The band was a powerful presence from the get-go, though the consensus was that the quintet really coalesced over time. A few critics suggested that with

Randolph's steel joined by Luther Dickinson on slide a little went a long way, but most seemed positively overwhelmed. Indeed, the Word represents one of those instances where deep promise is served through such a temporal assembly of players.

The Word (2001) ★ ★ ★ ★ ½

Robert Randolph's presence lends quite a bit to the project. The group's take on "Joyful Sounds" sets the tone, and "I'll Fly Away" is sublime. The two compositions by Medeski and Dickinson seem slightly misplaced, but all in all this is a powerful release and an important one that gives further exposure to the sacred steel tradition.

X2

www.x2jamband.com

Keyboardist Johnny Neel and drummer Matt Abts first met in the late '80s when they joined the Dickey Betts Band. The two band members worked on Betts's *Pattern Disruptive* disc and played a number of live shows before the Allman Brothers Band reformed in 1989, whereupon Betts drew Neel (and DBB bandmate guitarist Warren Haynes) into the fold. Neel toured and recorded with the Brothers for a few years before leaving to work with his own group, Johnny Neel and the Last Word.

In 1994, Haynes reunited with Abts to form Gov't Mule, and over the years the Mule tapped Neel to lend his keys on multiple occasions. Neel and Abts resumed playing together again on a more regular basis in 1999 in Blue Floyd, which offered up rearranged takes on the Pink Floyd catalog. When that band ceased touring in 2002, the pair decided to record and perform together as X2, the Experimental Duo.

The pair's approach is decidedly old school, as Neel doesn't employ sampling or sequencing but rather fills out the sound by jumping back and forth from keyboard bass to organ, synthesizer, and clavinet. In concert and throughout the band's debut disc, Abts kicks out a bed and Neel plays over it and reacts, leading Abts, in turn, to respond. At times it can feel a bit like a clinic (for better and worse) and even somewhat anachronistic given the instrumentation, but the pair's enthusiasm is palpable. At many shows the two will follow up an experimental opening set with a second set of blues, rock, and soul covers, often drawing on notable musical friends who live in the area to elevate the energy even further.

X2 (2002) ★★½

Abts and Neel develop ideas on the fly over these nine mostly improvised pieces. The pair builds playful melodies over some robust grooves, though at times the results do feel like exercises.

Y

YAMAGATA
www.yamagatamusic.com

For a while in the late '90s, Yamagata played an essential role in the Memphis improvisational music scene. The group hosted a biweekly jam at the Taphouse with a number of local players at a time when few other area venues wanted to support such music. In some respects, Yamagata's initial groove-laden sound had some relation to the celebratory spirit of the jam. This is reflected in Yamagata's debut release, *Eveland*, which also contains multiple guest appearances from the Taphouse jam alumni. Eventually, on the appeal of that record, the group moved on, touring regionally and then nationally. As it did so, Yamagata changed some of its personnel as well as its approach, moving away from a groove orientation (with an admittedly heavier edge) to a more progressive rock sound.

Connect, Yamagata's second record, reflects the group's current sound with the present quartet. One dramatic change has been the band's decision to perform an increased number of vocal tunes (nine of the 12 on *Connect*, versus one, with Kelly Hurt guesting, on *Eveland*). Guitarist Joe Austin has started singing lead, and his high register along with the nature of some of the group's material has elicited comparisons to Rush (although, frankly, he's not quite in Geddy Lee's range). Still, this is only one facet of the band's sound as, unlike the Canadian trio, Yamagata has four members, with Jeff Waldon performing on sax. His contributions very much carry the band at its best into a realm of its own, offering elements of prog complexity and some harder edges along with a jazzier side. It's an ambitious sound that the band is still defining and finding its way into, particularly as the group continues to write new vocal material. Fans of the earlier incarnation of the group may need to adjust expectations, but there are a number of familiar aspects, including the band's intensity.

Connect (2002) ★★

This disc captures Yamagata's current direction, mostly with vocals and a prog-rock bent. A number of the songs have a similar feel, and they can drone on a bit (as can the vocals), but there are quite a few compelling riffs and progressions.

Eveland (1999) ★★½

An earlier Yamagata in terms of players and purpose. The band carries a groove with a guest horn section and keyboards. Although few of the songs prove distinctive, there is a heavier tinge, which at times does vest a number of the tracks with vitality.

YONDER MOUNTAIN STRING BAND

www.yondermountain.com
Truth be told, fortuity has played a role in the Yonder Mountain path. There is no other acoustic outfit with a corresponding degree of support and enthusiasm from jamband listeners, and this is partially happenstance. Yonder Mountain String Band has benefited from something of an *O Brother, Where Art Thou?* bump along with sustained appearances on festival bills. These performances have high-lighted juxtapositions with preceding acts yet have also shared a predilection for improv and a broad musical taste that resonated with listeners. But you make your own luck, which Yonder has done through sturdy musicianship and songcraft, generating appeal while deftly segueing from its high lonesome originals to a transposed take on Michael Jackson's "Don't Stop Till You Get Enough" or a lilting version of Jerry Garcia/Robert Hunter's "They Love Each Other."

In many respects, Yonder Mountain String Band is the embodiment of contemporary jamgrass. The group is comprised of upright bass, banjo, mandolin, and guitar, yet offers far more than bluegrass breakdowns, straying into spacier spheres. Traditionalists who quibble with YMSB's designation as a bluegrass band—not necessarily because of its open-ended approach but more for its instrumentation (the band is fiddle-free)—still show respect for the group. Yonder garnered an invitation to perform at the Grand Ole Opry as well as multiple slots at the Telluride Bluegrass Festival (and to be clear, the band isn't bearing the bluegrass badge—YMSB saved such a traditional tune as "Rocky Top" for its pseudonym, the Cosmic Bowling League, when opening for itself on New Year's Eve 2002 at the Paramount in Denver). The jamgrass handle also applies when tracking the bandmembers' musical development, as bassist Ben Kaufmann first encountered bluegrass though Phish's efforts in this realm while guitarist Adam Aijala made the journey via the Dead and Old & In The Way.

Yonder Mountain String Band formed in late 1988 in Nederland, CO, where one of its early advocates was Leftover Salmon's Vince

Herman (when the quartet debuted at High Sierra in 1999, the festival program promised quality entertainment from the band, per Vince). However, Herman is not the lone booster. Over the past few years, collaborators have included Tim O'Brien, Sally Van Meter, Jerry Douglas, Darol Anger, and Mike Marshall (O'Brien and Van Meter produced the group's first two studio discs). All four YMSB members sing and write music, though mandolin player Jeff Austin is the most prolific and the closest to a frontman the group has (banjo player Dave Johnson completes the lineup). Long a staple of the festival circuit, the band decided in 2002 to draw on that experience with its inaugural String Summit at Horning's Hideout in North Plains, OR, which has come to offer six sets of Yonder and in its opening year presented a slate of performers that included newgrass paragons Hot Rize and the David Grisman Quintet. Yonder Mountain String Band's music typically remains high energy, in part because its listeners sometimes lack the patience for down-tempo selections (similarly, the band's inclination to encore into a single mic can prove challenging depending on the room and the audience). The quartet is a true collective, outdistancing its individual members' proficiencies while carrying a spirit and verve that often leads new listeners to experience the group in much the way that Austin described its 2001 New Groove Jammy: "It was an unexpected chocolate cream in the middle of the box."

Mountain Tracks Vol. 2 (2002) ★★★★
Recorded during the fall of 2001, this live offering delivers a radiant balance of original music and covers, including a reggae-infused take on John Hartford's "Two Hits and the Joint Turned Brown" and a logical extension of the Rolling Stones' "No Expectations." Be sure to hang out for the hidden, single-mic transposition of Pink Floyd's "Goodbye Blue Sky."

Town by Town (2001) ★★★
Tim O'Brien produced *Town By Town*, which often delves thematically into the bluegrass idiom with generally pleasing results.

Mountain Tracks Vol. 1 (2001) ★★★ ½
While the disc concludes with an absorbing 18-minute passage bookended by J.J. Cale's "If You're Ever in Oklahoma," it's the band's own material that stands out on this live release, in particular Jeff Austin's "Keep on Growing" (with a bonus Toshian scat).

Elevation (1999) ★★★
A well-founded, affable debut, with solid songwriting contributions from all four band members and guest musicianship from the likes of Darol Anger, Mike Marshall, and producer Sally Van Meter.

Also:
Yonder Mountain String Band & Benny Galloway—*Old Hands* (2003)

Discussion group:
www.groups.yahoo.com/group/yonder/

Z

ZEN TRICKSTERS

www.zentricksters.com

The Zen Tricksters' latest CD is titled *Shaking Off the Weirdness,* and one can imagine that the weirdness in question refers to the band members' associations with Phil Lesh.

While the band has written and recorded original material, for many years it was best known for an ability to deliver inspired versions of Grateful Dead material. Guitarist Jeff Mattson and keyboardist Rob Barraco had been the core of the Zen Tricksters line-up since Barraco joined in 1989. Ten years later, Lesh, who was still rotating players in and out of his band, happened upon a copy of the group's *A Love Surreal* disc. Impressed with the band's aptitude for translating live jams into the studio setting (and apparently unaware of the Tricksters' association with the Dead canon), Lesh invited Mattson and Barraco to join him for a rehearsal session and then for a Phil Lesh & Friends run at San Francisco's Warfield on October 7-9, 1999. A month later he tapped Barraco for a P&F tour, which led to a regular gig, resulting in Barraco's departure from the Tricksters (Barraco's story took a further turn when he became a member of the Other Ones in August 2002).

While this was an extraordinary course of events, change has become commonplace for Mattson, who began with the Volunteers—an earlier incarnation of the Zen Tricksters—in 1979 (Barraco joined after the name was changed to the Tricksters). This group, which featured the vocals of Jennifer Markard, garnered notoriety as the leading East Coast-based Dead cover band at a time when there were many groups vying for such honors. When Markard left the band, however (occasionally she will still take the stage on guest vocals), Mattson became the only Tricksters player with a direct lineage to the Volunteers.

During Mattson's tenure, the group has often performed more than 200 dates a year, holds the all-time record for most performances at New York's Wetlands Preserve, and has the distinction of performing at every Gathering of the Vibes from 1996 (when it was Deadhead Heaven) through 2002. So it's not surprising that Mattson and mainstay bassist Klyph Black decided to keep the Tricksters on the road as a trio (with Tom Circosta), even shaking things up by embarking on an acoustic tour in 2002.

Particularly since the release of its 1996 debut disc, *The Holy Fool,* the band has tried to strike a balance between its own material and the Dead's (though they also play other covers, including songs by the Band and Dylan). Depending on the personnel and place of performance, the Zen Tricksters have weighted their set lists more heavily on either original songs or those of the Dead. Regardless, Mattson's tone and a number of his lead ideas remain reminiscent of Garcia, which holds appeal for many individuals who had minimal opportunities to experience this sound in the live context. At present, however, and especially as a trio, the band tends to reference the sound of the Dead rather than recreate it.

Shaking Off the Weirdness (2002) ★★★

This acoustic disc is a nice change of pace for the Tricksters, demonstrating Mattson's feel while Black picks up a few instruments, including a dobro. Barraco returns for four songs, and Jason Crosby and Buddy Cage also pitch in. The release has some bluegrass leanings and, once again, a pretty high comfort level.

A Love Surreal (1999) ★★★

Despite the title nod to Coltrane, this one owes more to the saxophonist's ethos than his output. Most of these songs have a familiar feel, though as Phil Lesh has suggested, the band does capture a live feel on tracks such as "Goin' Down Slow."

The Holy Fool (1996) ★★ ½

Although the band walks through a number of styles and moods on this disc, the variety still tends to reflect that of the Dead. Still, there is some good songwriting and corresponding performance (with a hint of studio sheen).

ZYRAH'S ORANGE

www.zyrahsorange.com

In the liner notes to its second release, *Body*, Zyrah's Orange acknowledges its sources of inspiration, which include Beck, Emmylou Harris, Daniel Lanois, the Keith Jarrett Trio, Percy Hill, and the Grateful Dead. Shades of all these artists appear in ZO's sound. One can drop in *Body* for a shuffled spin and, depending on which track is summoned, a listener might peg the trio as a funk combo, a modern rock group, or boho jazzsters. Indeed, ever since the group's formation in the mid-'90s, Zyrah's Orange has remained on the eclectic side of an eclectic genre.

The group has the potential to push the bounds of jambandom. However, there has been some resistance, especially from listeners in the scene who have found a portion of ZO's songs situated too closely in the alternative rock/pop realm (then again, the band's "8 Words" rated in the Top 30 on the Jambands.com 1999 year-end radio charts). A roster shake-up in 2002 has modified Zyrah's approach, with founder vocalist/guitarist and principal songwriter Elliot Page and drummer Dan Gullotti now joined by bassist Aaron Kravitz and expanding to a four-piece with keyboardist Ben Kuris. As a result, Zyrah's Orange has moved confidently into the electronic rock realm, accompanied by some darker tones. This has broadened the Boston-area group's listener base, although it has de-emphasized some of the quirks that contributed to the band's "Mass. Groove appeal."

Body (2000) ★★★ ½

The album doesn't necessarily flow, but there is a unity in multiformity, whether serving up an alterna-pop song or a jazz/funk workout.

Also:

Mind (1999)

JAM BAND, JAM-BAND, OR JAMBAND?
How We Got There and Why It Matters (Somewhat)

In many respects, the impetus for this book (and certainly this essay) arose from a question posed by a musician after his band had performed on our "Jam Nation" radio show. "Jambands.com?," he asked, "What did you have to do to get that URL?" The glib answer, of course, is, "Register it," which I did not offer at the time, instead explaining that when we created the Web site back in 1998 there was minimal recognition of the term "jam band" (a LexisNexis search will bear this out). However, over the intervening years, due partly to efforts made at the site, Relix magazine, and elsewhere, the term's usage has blossomed (you may prefer another verb—perhaps one with fungal connotations, or maybe something viral will do).

Every once in a while I receive an e-mail from a student or a journalist or a student journalist asking if I am responsible for the term jam band. The tone is generally amiable and not too prosecutorial, and for a few years my stock response was that I had popularized it (to my mind, jam band has been floating around in the parlance of an obsessed few for quite a while, particularly through the incipient online bulletin boards and newsgroups, and among the tapers I remember out there in the early '90s—certainly by the initial HORDE tour in 1992). But the nature of these inquiries started to change as their frequency increased. They came to focus on etymology and definition as well as the proper spelling of the term, since the mainstream media gradually picked up on it but offered variants ranging from jam band to jam-band to jamband (in most instances preceded by the words "so-called").

The truth is, I stumbled over the spelling question for many months because I am no prescriptive grammarian. And from the outset I never aimed to name a genre or validate that process (and as for whether we are indeed describing a genre, I now answer affirmatively, but hang on...). There is no question that when we started we used two words—jam band—although I always found that combination to be a bit prosaic. Frankly, back in 1998 when I first completed a book on the music of these groups (the work that in turn named the Web site), I toyed with a series of innocuous titles that would avoid any type of catchall phrase (I was eventually dissuaded by a few people, including my wife, who brought an interesting perspective to bear as her tastes run far afield). If I had recognized that the term would carry some traction, I might have opted for something with a bit more jazz to it, like the Seapods' Gobi, Dave Schools's and Chan Kinchla's neo-retro, or perhaps an altogether different tag.

Since I've now invoked the word jazz, let's take a side step and turn to the nature of music definitions for a moment. What does it mean to be a jazz band? A rock group? Alternative? Is there anything inherent in any of these terms that conjures a particular style or form? Or are we left with Supreme Court Justice Potter Stewart's tried-and-true pornography pronouncement: "I know it when I see it." Not only that, but how does one define these forms? Bluegrass can be identified through its instrumentation. You can start to define blues by its time signatures, but once you supplement that by introducing its historical backdrop, I argue that you concede relativism and the import of context.

This leads us to "jamband." Once I recognized that people were actually using this tag as a descriptive term for the music rather than the name of a Web site covering new artists and nuances, I made the move towards jamband. This has been our term of choice for a few years now. I think it carries a bit more grace than jam band. And I like the fact that it is a neologism. We're not just trying to say, "Hey look at these bands, they jam, they are jam bands." There's more to it. I feel that jamband suggests a flow, a fluidity that marks the music the term tries to encapsulate. And at any rate, I suggest that it is at least an empty vessel, a form that finds function through context.

For me the defining component of a jamband is its musical variegation. Part of this certainly references the dynamic nature of the bands' performances, which incorporate ample measures of improvisation. But there is an additional aspect that is extrinsic to the live setting (which is why, for instance, we retain a Studio Album of the Year award at the Jammys—to my mind, a jamband is not exclusively marked by its live efforts). This other component is a penchant for bending and blending established genres. Phish isn't a bluegrass band, a jazz band, a blues band, or a funk band, although at a given moment it may deliver any of these styles. Instead, Phish is a group that melds and intermingles these forms into its particular flow of music. It is a jamband.

Some artists are uncomfortable with the term. I can appreciate that. No one wants to reduce his or her art to a one-word description. That process seems limiting. On the other hand, sometimes the nature of language requires us to convey a broad idea with a word or two. Regardless, the beauty of socialized exchange allows us to expand and expound, to find the gradations, the humor, the majesty, of it all.

So I contend that there is indeed a swell of bands out there that do not fit into any traditional categories. Furthermore, these groups are not built for the increasingly balkanized world of commercial music where, for instance, when recording an album one needs to set the kick-drum microphone just so in order to even raise the possibility of airplay on the radio format of choice. These artists' live shows vary so significantly from night to night that increasingly they are offering immediate downloads and performance discs to their fans. The jam prefix doesn't mandate a disregard for songcraft. In fact, the best of these artists deliver commanding compositions that draw on a palette of varied sounds, which in turn are further embellished and animated in concert. The results have inspired the creation of a fan community drawn to this true alternative.

The term jamband may not be sexy or ironic, but it does feel apt. I also argue that the word offers clarity and distinction, because in part it manifests the endeavor it seeks to characterize. Plus, above all else, it is only a starting point, because by using formal language to represent harmonious sound we are applying concrete to the formless and infinite. This certainly holds true in jamband circles, where any such struggles serve only to bolster that commonly held precept: "Remember, dude, it's all about the music...."

The Genesis of Jambands.com

As for the origins of Jambands.com, I will leave that to the site's co-founder, Andy Gadiel, who has long since moved on to focus his energies at JamBase.com. Both Internet hubs evolved out of e-mail exchanges and later phone conversations between Andy and myself (he lived in Michigan at the time, and I lived in Massachusetts). Jambands.com is truly a product of the Internet age, as while I knew of Andy through his Phish Web page, and we had attended many of the same shows over the years, I never met him face-to-face until many months after we started rolling....

As with most things in life, the concept for Jambands.com evolved naturally over time. It was back in the spring of 1998 when I was living in Lansing, MI, near my alma mater, Michigan State University, and working as an assistant on a doomed summer music festival tour. Part of this festival's scheme was to develop a magazine showcasing the types of bands playing the event, as well as heavily promoting the festival itself.

While in the process of doing research, I heard that Dean Budnick was writing a book about the emerging scene of bands, not coincidentally the same bands being scouted to play the festival and to be featured in our magazine. I had known Dean's name as most people in Phish circles did—as the guy who wrote the first book on the band (The Phishing Manual) back in 1996—so I dropped him a line and we started talking.

Dean filled me in on what he was doing, and we exchanged thoughts about this whole emerging scene of music, his book ideas, and our common interests in music. Dean's calling his book Jambands seemed logical at the time. I don't remember exactly what was being considered back then, but that term was being thrown around a lot, and the whole concept was kind of evolving in that direction. Here was a bunch of bands playing in their towns or around their areas that were all connected by a common consciousness surrounding the music. Inspired by the Grateful Dead, kept current by Phish, and progressing all the time by new and innovative bands, the music clearly had a link that would not only unite the bands themselves but also a very large community surrounding them.

To promote the forthcoming Jambands, Dean wanted to register Jambands.com so people could read about the book, check out excerpts, and even order it online. At some point right after our initial phone conversation, I thought about the idea behind Jambands.com as something more than a book promo. I had been running with a recent theory that the actual address of a Web page should reflect what you would expect to see if you went there. Applying that to this idea, if someone typed "Jambands.com" into their Web browser, they should also get jamband news, reviews, essays, tour dates, links, and information about the entire emerging scene.

I wrote Dean an e-mail immediately, and he loved the idea. From there, the concept was born. Dean organized the writers, and I got the technical side worked out. For a few months we worked on fleshing out the idea so we could launch something to be proud of, and at the end of September 1998 we unveiled the first issue. Every month, Dean delivered the stories from enthusiastic writers all over the country, and I would tackle the Web element by organizing and formatting all the info into the site.

Synchronically, during that time my tastes in music had evolved to include bands even beyond the highly addictive Phish. I had even developed a section of my Phish page called "Phriends of the Federation," which offered links to the official Web sites of other bands that I liked at the time. If people liked a band listed and also liked another band, they would e-mail me about it. If the band fit, I'd add it to the list. Before long, the list swelled. It became clear this specific musical taste and community was a nationwide phenomenon encompassing hundreds of artists and hundreds of thousands of music fans.

It was around the same time I started talking with Dean that I was staring at this list of links to official band Web sites and thinking to myself, "What if instead of sending people to these individual pages to learn about the band and where they are playing, we brought their show information to one central site for people to go to?..." It was upon this concept that the Tours Calendar (now developed into JamBase.com) was born. Creating a centralized database of tour dates and information for thousands of bands around the world evolved along with the magazine Web site of Jambands.com, and together they grew to help inspire and promote a burgeoning music scene.

Built largely upon the motivation and enthusiasm of the fans, both Jambands.com and JamBase.com have remained created by the fans, for the fans. Much of the content is contributed on a daily basis by site visitors, and both sites are reflective of the community at large. Although run separately today, both sites contain a community feel, remaining true to the integrity of the music being promoted and dedicated to supporting quality artists, while bringing together a vibrant and positive community of music lovers.

—Andy Gadiel

AN AWARD, A SHOW, BUT NOT NECESSARILY AN AWARD SHOW:
Anatomy of a Jammy

It is a night that embodies improvisation on most every level. What else can you say of a show that pushes into its seventh hour with a climactic final jam featuring Trey Anastasio, Warren Haynes, Bob Weir, John Popper, and others poised to tear it up, only to have the spotlight wrested from them to a second stage held by a relatively unknown Jamaican toaster and a fairy-winged flautist who had scampered backstage a few minutes earlier? Welcome to the Jammys, everybody, where just about anything can happen (a night where, as show co-founder Pete Shapiro laughs, "You know at least one person on the back of the T-shirt isn't going to be there...along with a half dozen not on there who will...").

Ever since we first formulated the idea in late 1999, the Jammy Awards show has thrived through a confluence of brain-numbing prep (the phone calls and faxes begin eight months in advance) and serendipity. In the latter category, for instance, Frogwings' performance at the 2000 Jammys was possible only because we realized about three weeks out that the Allman Brothers Band had a day off while routing through our general vicinity. This allowed Butch Trucks to pinch a tour bus, roust his nephew Derek, Susan Tedeschi, Jimmy Herring, Mark Quinones, and the crew, and get them to the show. In another instance of Trucksian fortuity, Butch was feted in a black-tie affair by the Alzheimer's Association at New York's Waldorf-Astoria Hotel the evening after the third Jammys, which enabled Warren Haynes to draw in the ABB the night before for a surprise appearance in the Gov't Mule slot. Pete has described this as "the convergence, the Perfect Storm of events that allows the show to go down as it does."

Of course, we've had our share of misses, too. Maybe we were naïve, but we were giddy nonetheless at the possibility that Paul McCartney would join us in 2002 when his tour carried him right through New York on an off night (there's always next year). In 2001 Me'Shell NdegéOcello left cell phone messages just prior to showtime indicating that she wouldn't be able to attend, yet unbeknownst to us she showed up anyhow (but didn't perform). That same year we lost Talib Kweli earlier in the day due to creative differences regarding his performance with Soulive, but we pulled in Black Thought from the Roots for a version of "Billie Jean."

Still, we've only lost one person during the course of the show itself: Al Franken, our putative presenter of the lifetime achievement award to the Grateful Dead in 2002. (Although through no fault of his own, Col. Bruce Hampton almost did not make it onto the stage a year earlier when some miscommunication led the Steve Kimock Band to perform without him—thankfully, Derek Trucks invited him out for a powerful "Lovelight" with Robert Randolph and Yonder Mountain String Band's Jeff Austin joining in). As for Franken, he stormed out five minutes before he was set to present the award to Bob Weir in honor of the Dead as the show had run too long for his taste—which is understandable, because we were an hour behind schedule—but he did flee the building halfway through "Soulshine," the final song from Gov't Mule, just moments before he was set to appear, which I tried to communicate to his back as I chased him onto 53rd Street where he went in search of his limo. It's sort of sad—he was wearing his "Grateful Dad" shirt and everything.

As you might imagine, Al has a slightly different recollection of the evening, and when I asked him to respond he offered this take: "The organizers of the Jammys had originally asked me to host the event, but I couldn't because of other commitments. I did agree to present the lifetime achievement award to the Dead (humbly—I am an enormous Deadhead), but I had told the organizers that I would have to get out by a certain time—I believe midnight—because I had to get up at 4:30 the next morning to catch a plane. I was assured that I would be out by then, and was asked to come around 10:30 or so. (I am not certain of these times, because this is months ago.) I arrived at 10:30 and happily listened to music and went backstage and got to meet Leo Kottke, a hero of mine. I told the organizers I really had to be out by midnight, and they assured me that I would. As it became clear that the show was running over—which shows do—I told them I'd try to hang in till 12:30 or so, but I really had to leave then. At about 12:30, it became clear that it was going to run longer, so I said I'd hang till 1:00, but that was it. More assurance, etc., and I could tell that these guys didn't have control of the show (it's the Jammys, for godsakes), but that, of course, was the problem. It just kept going on. Finally, at 1:00, the group onstage started a new number, and there seemed to be no end in sight. So I expressed my regrets and left. I didn't storm out, and there was no limo. I'm sorry that they took it the wrong way. I hope especially that Bob [Weir], whom I didn't get to see that night, knows that I worship the ground he and Phil and Mickey and Bill walk on. I just had to get some sleep."

As the person beseeching Al's backside, I stand by my characterization and respectfully suggest that his time perception is slightly exaggerated. As for the limo, whether or not he eventually found it, I know it was out there because we were the ones who provided it for him. I would also counter that we did indeed have the show in firm control (okay, until the RatDog changeover, but Al likely was in bed by then), however, we freely let it go at times—for instance during the Gov't Mule set, enabling Trey Anastasio and John Scofield to join in on "Sco-Mule." Still, all in all, our will is not ill, and thankfully we had the prescience, or one might say dumb luck (Al?) to have Senator Patrick Leahy deliver his remarks via videotape, which suited the event quite well.

With any luck, there's something to be said for persistence, as well. By the time you read this, the fourth installment of the Jammys either has taken place or is on the horizon. By now I will have made my annual entreaty to Christopher Guest, Michael McKean, and Harry Shearer to appear as Spinal Tap and/or the Folksmen, as I have done since year one (actually, I added the Folksmen request in year three, after I saw them open for Tap at Carnegie Hall, a number of months before their film *A Mighty Wind* opened). With any luck they will be hosting this year, but as with Sir Paul, if not, then hopefully one day (I'll knock on that door again and again, just like I do with Sonny Rollins and John McLaughlin).

Don't look for Dee Snider, though (not that you were, necessarily). We had an entertaining idea for him back in 2001 at a time when he was hosting a morning radio show in Hartford, CT, on WMRQ, the same originating station of our "Jam Nation" program. Dee informed us, most respectfully, that he was not fond of our ilk (and I genuinely don't begrudge him this because he acknowledged that while others like this music, he just doesn't get it). Ween also passed that same year, but not before yanking Pete through a series of quasi-requests involving Dickey Betts and David Lee Roth that didn't go anywhere (but that was prior to their Bonnaroo appearance, so who knows…). As for others who were unable to host, the topic summons the trauma induced by that agent who passed and then browbeat me for the incorrect usage of a vocabulary word ("ascribe," if memory serves)…which led me to explain in oh-such-a-polite manner via e-mail that I actually hold a Masters in English and a Ph.D. from an accredited university, followed by a concise discourse on the meaning of the word in question. (I freely acknowledge that this was probably my weakest Jammys moment—and if he's reading this, I do apologize. But hey, he came at me first. I did nothing but defend myself. I'm a freaking writer, and that was an unprovoked slap at my toolbox. I wouldn't dare tell him how many moist towelettes he should push for in a contract rider. No, no, just kidding—I really do regret my lack of courtesy and restraint. It still bugs me. I should have let it go.)

Incidentally, the fact that we even approached Dee and Dean (Ween) reflects a transformation that took place from year one to year two (again, as I mentioned at the outset, the show has been an improvisation). I'll return to the awards shortly, but as for the performances, much of our intent in the first year was to represent the broad lineage of the players within the jamband realm. Thus we had our participants perform the songs of artists who had inspired them. Deep Banana Blackout offered up Santana and Frank Zappa, the Slip delivered Bob Dylan, Soulive and John Scofield interpreted P-Funk (briefly, before moving into Scofield's own "Hottentot," which seemed fair because Sco was obviously an influence on the trio). One slightly modified tribute came via the New Deal, as we asked them to present their take on a Bill Monroe song (they stuck with it for a few bars before diving into their progressive breakbeat).

By year two, Pete's idea was to modify this approach and instead imbue the show with an element of improv through collaborations of players who had not previously performed together (and in some instances had not even met prior to soundcheck). The inspiration for this notion came in part from the kinetic moments that took place through such combinations during our first year, especially Les Claypool's pairing with the Disco Biscuits, who at the time were on the outs with Marc Brownstein and "needed" a fill-in bass player.

So, beginning in the spring of 2001, Pete and I began pacing around our pads spitballing combinations over the phone (something he was quite adept at, given his IMAX film *All Access*). We came bounding out of the box at that year's Jammys with the Del McCoury Band joined by Robert Randolph & the Family Band and DJ Logic for "Swing Low, Sweet Chariot." Del's triple take when Logic began scratching a version of the song made the night for me, which still had five hours to go. Other people were particularly digging on Tom Tom Club with Michael Franti, the Biscuits with John Popper and Stanley Jordan, and Les Claypool's Frog Brigade with Junior Brown and Paul Shaffer. (Shaffer was actually slated to play with the Biscuits, but slid over to the Frog Brigade set when it turned out we were running late— fancy that. That year we also made it onto the JumboTron at Yankee Stadium through the performance of centerfielder Bernie Williams and the Jazz Mandolin Project. (JMP's Jamie Masefield maintains high standards, and my recollection is that he was somewhat leery heading into the day of the show, but any concerns were allayed during an extended dressing room rehearsal that afternoon. The musicians were disturbed only by Marky Ramone and Jerry Only of the Misfits [there to perform with Lake Trout], who arrived and began banging on doors demanding a Bernie sighting. All in all, Bernie was a mellow, affable presence whose only issue was a need to relocate when someone sparked up.)

We continued this collaboration theme into the third year with pairings that included the B-52's and Particle as well as moe. and Blue Öyster Cult. (The latter was unquestionably favored by the crew, many of whom came to the lip of the stage and banged it pretty hard during "Don't Fear the Reaper.") We also took this idea to one of its extensions when we promised Scofield that we would bring in whomever he chose so long as he assembled a new configuration of players, which is how Stanton Moore and Skerik flew in from the West Coast to join Sco and Andy Hess.

But let's not forget that while the Jammys is a satisfying evening of music, it is also an awards show. (No, really, it is—even though when Paul Shaffer arrived in 2001 he turned to me and busted, "Where are the awards? This isn't an awards show, you're putting me on...." I think he would have been a bit more impressed with the Jammy Awards 2.0, in which the J sweeps into a Fender guitar neck, as opposed to my original idea that served us the first two years: ten-inch-wide Paul Revere trophy bowls. Hey, speaking of bowls, that reminds me: Suffice it to say that our 2001 host Jim Breuer's heavy-lidded stoner thing is not an act. The man lives the dream.)

We have always emphasized the conviviality of the night—our initial tagline was "a celebration of the scene"—but from the moment I brought Pete my concept of the Jammys to develop and embellish, my hope was to acknowledge exemplary artists and individuals within the jamband scene (folks may deem the music "all good," but frankly, some of it is even better). To determine the award nominees, we decided to strike a balance between the views of fans and insiders. One concern here, as you can imagine, was whether the awards should be a pure popularity contest, in which case those performers with the largest constituencies would have an advantage (then again, perhaps if most people in the community support something, it should be so honored). Now what we do first is query a panel to limit the field to worthy candidates, so that any winner is, indeed, worthy, and will represent us all rather well. Typically, a month before we present the final nominations for fan voting, I e-mail a few hundred writers, managers, musicians, and other scenesters asking for their input, after which I tally up the replies (my lone mook was in 2001, when I was so taken with the cross section of Live Performance of the Year nominations that we ended up with 16. The next year I held strong at half a dozen).

I've been real pleased with our ability to recognize deserving endeavors through the awards and shine some light their way. The example that leaps to mind is Percy Hill, winner of Studio Album of the Year in 2000 for *Colour in Bloom*. The band put that album together basically on a shoestring budget, yet it is an indie disc that sounds major. I also thought it was cool that Les

Claypool's Frog Brigade pulled a relative upset the next year in taking Live Album honors for *Live Frogs Set I*, the release that marked Les' entree into our world. moe.'s win in 2002 for its late night set at Bonnaroo (the band's second Jammy, following the Live Album award for *L* in 2000) acknowledged a significant summer festival along with a lengthy guest-laden performance that is underrepresented on the Bonnaroo DVD.

The acceptance speeches have also yielded some entertaining moments. In 2002, after winning Tour of the Year, Trey Anastasio, Jennifer Hartswick, and Cyro Baptista sang their thank you's amidst the Phish hiatus to the tune of *West Side Story*'s "Gee, Officer Krupke," including the lines, "...We've tested all your patience, yet you've been tried or true/You're sick of Pork Tornado, you're sick of Vida Blue/If I would just stop talking, you would get your wish/Stop this shit and give us back our Phish..." Two years earlier, when the Disco Biscuits won the award for Jam of the Year honoring their December 31, 1999, set in which they improvised a score to the film *Akira*, guitarist Jon Gutwillig made a point of immediately crediting bassist Marc Brownstein for his efforts—suggesting to some that Brownie would be back, and he did indeed rejoin the group three weeks later. The next year, after Jeff Waful received the Radio Show award, he heard the hometown crowd cheering for Bernie Williams, who had stepped onto the other stage preparing for his performance with JMP. Waful, a tortured Red Sox fan like myself (remember when Williams "nearly" signed with Boston after the 1999 season?), leaned forward and charged "Go Red Sox!" to the boos of many. (Incidentally, Waful has the dubious distinction of winning Jammys in two categories that were discontinued the following year: Jambands.com Writer and Radio Show. Frankly, he almost didn't win for Radio Show because I had disqualified "Jam Nation" from the nominations due to my involvement. But Waful insisted I was unfairly prejudicing him so I relented—and caught a bit of flack for it—although, FWIW, "Jam Nation" did win the voting fair and square, which was assiduously monitored by *Relix* Associate Publisher Kathy Stoddard.)

The Lifetime Achievement award has become another essential element that helps to define the night. The first year this proved somewhat loose, as B.B. King accepted via videotape, and Pete had to hustle 30 blocks uptown with a cameraman to present the award and a commemorative pair of Jammys jammies before hauling ass back to Irving Plaza, rewinding the tape, and handing it to the projectionist sight unseen, hoping for the best (and it was indeed a fine moment). The second year the award went to George Porter, Jr., who accepted on behalf of the Meters (with an introduction by Anthony DeCurtis, who has been with us as a presenter all three years—quite gratifying) and all was well, except that we had to cut short our final Meters jam due to curfew. (One of my enduring memories of Jammys 2001 is Pete on the side of the stage during the Biscuits slot, the final one prior to the closing jam, frantically swirling his finger around to indicate that they should wrap things up while Gutwillig and Popper repeated the gesture back at him and shrugged their shoulders, feigning unfamiliarity with this signal.) In 2002 I thought Lifetime winner Bob Weir delivered a wonderful speech that stressed the lineage of the jam back to Louis Armstrong and other antecedents. Franken had fled, but the videotaped intro by Senator Patrick Leahy was fitting, as were Jammys host Popper's remarks (the Blues Traveler frontman really brought the best of all worlds to the hosting gig—he has an intimate knowledge of this music, yet he's deft of speech, fleet of foot, and freaking funny. Plus, Popper's a trouper. Who else could host a seven-hour show with intermediate guest performances, wander off, saunter back, and just turn it on? He also agreed to wear some really dorky pajamas in something of a pre-show suggestion/challenge that led a staffer to dash off and score a pair. Oh yes, as for hosts in addition to Popper and Breuer, Peter Prince did an admirable job our first year. He even wrote a song for the occasion. I just wish we had given him a bit more to do...).

Once the show starts and we're in motion, things have proceeded relatively smoothly (if protractedly) over the years. On the evening of the Jammys our biggest headache typically has been the guest list. The issue is that there are limits to how many people we can squeeze into the venue, and, despite our best efforts, we often have not received the names of the performers' comps until shortly before the show. (We strive to be accommodating, since no one is compensated for their participation—although we do cover travel, etc., so that in theory no performer has to dip into pockets substantially for the event.) This is the one factor that has held up the night each of the three years. In fact, the Jammys is the only show I've attended where the VIP line outside is longer than the one for those who have purchased advance tickets. This is where Pete and *Relix* Publisher Steve Bernstein now take it upon themselves to ease the flow by walking the VIPs they recognize into the venue. "One of my Jammys highlights," Pete recalls, "was the first year, being outside all stressed out wondering when we were going to get started, and then walking in and seeing we were underway. The Jammys Orchestra was up there with Scofield and Merl Saunders, and everyone was grooving out." (That first year we put Fuzz of Deep Banana Blackout in charge of our house band, the Jammys Orchestra, which also included some of his DBB bandmates, Marc Friedman from the Slip, Sco, Merl, and many others. The next year we went with the Derek Trucks Band, who backed up a few Jim Breuer bits along the way, followed in 2002 by the Tom Tom Club joined by the Dirty Dozen Brass Band horns.)

While the Jammys began through a conversation I initiated with Pete, and we continue to squawk about the show months in advance (with the input of Steve, Kathy, Jon Schwartz, and Team *Relix*), the Jammys would not have achieved any measure of its current success without the production team, in particular Jeff Webster. It's one thing to say, hey, wouldn't it be cool if we put all these collaborations onto two stages and then bring it to a close with a jam that takes place across both of them? but it's another thing to make that a reality. The Jammys thrives because people like Webster take it deep, architecting the stage plots and changeovers. "We don't have the budget of a festival or a big TV awards show," Pete observes. "We should have a budget many times what we do relative to what we pull off. And all that goes to the crew. They put their heads down and do it the way it needs to be done."

Webster was preceded by moe.'s Chris Burrows, who handled the production side in the first year along with Ken "Skip" Richman but was on tour during Jammys 2001, which left Webster to figure out how to use both stages in a reasonably cost-effective yet top-shelf manner. (Hey, not only that, but his crew gave me fashion tips when I lost my tuxedo pants while walking the dozen blocks to Roseland from my hotel in 2002—my penguin garb has been another steady element—and advised me to go with my shorts, tux shirt, and coat. All was well, to my mind at least, until Bob Weir came over to make his acceptance speech and looked me up and down with a semi-withering glance as if to say, "You, my friend, look like a schmuck.")

And there you have it: the Jammys. In 2002 it was the kind of event that moe. guitarist Al Schnier didn't want to leave, even though he had a gig at B.B. King's (as he'll note, however, the moe. slot was billed as a post-Jammys performance, so no matter how late the show ran he would still be on time, which gave him an opportunity to participate in what *The New York Times* would label the Jam of the Titans). Jammys 2002 was the kind of event that offered its share of moments to Mystic Bowie and Flute Girl during that final jam before the colossal figures on the other stage asserted themselves and eventually led us into a "Gloria" that raised the hackles on my neck when everyone in the room seemingly pumped their fists in unison with the chorus.

The Jammys. It's a night of music and awards and music and rewards and music. It's a true celebration of the scene. See you there this year (and if anyone found a pair of tux pants on 8th Avenue on October 2, 2002, please float them my way...).

Jammy Award Winners

2002

Lifetime Achievement: the Grateful Dead (presented by essay contest winner Bill Stites)
Live Performance: moe., Bonnaroo Music Festival, June 23, 2002
Tour: Trey Anastasio, summer 2002
Live Album: Widespread Panic, *Live in the Classic City*
Studio Album: Trey Anastasio, *Trey Anastasio*
Archival Album: Phish, *Live Phish 11*, November 17, 1997, McNichols Sports Arena, Denver, CO
Song: Gov't Mule, "Soulshine"
New Groove: Robert Randolph & the Family Band
Fan Web Site: Philzone.com
Mimi Fishman Memorial Award (community service): Joshua Stack, Panic Fans for Food
Grahamy Jammy (industry award for support of the scene): Annabel Lukins

2001

Lifetime Achievement: The Meters
Jam: Phil Lesh & Friends with Mike Gordon, December 31, 2000
Live Album: Les Claypool's Frog Brigade, *Live Frogs, Set I*
Studio Album: Phish, *Farmhouse*
Release: Grateful Dead, *Ladies and Gentlemen...The Grateful Dead*
New Groove: Yonder Mountain String Band
Fan Web Site: Etree.org
Mimi Fishman Memorial Award (community service): Mockingbird Foundation
Topper/Zahn Award (industry award for support of the scene): Howie Schnee
Radio Show: "Jam Nation," radio 104, Hartford, CT
Festival: Gathering of the Vibes

2000

Lifetime Achievement: B.B. King
Jam: The Disco Biscuits, *Akira* jam, December 31, 1999
Live Set: Phish, December 31, 1999, set I
Live Album: moe., *L*
Studio Album: Percy Hill, *Colour in Bloom*
Release: The Grateful Dead, *So Many Roads*
New Groove: Fat Mama
Fan Web Site: Etree.org
Community Service: Strangers Helping Strangers
Topper Award (industry award for support of the scene): Chris Zahn
Radio Show: "The Music Never Stops," Barry Smolin, KPFK, Los Angeles
Future Jam (musicians' award): Soulive
Home Grown Music Award: Strangefolk, *Lore*
Jambands.com Writer: Jeff Waful

DESITIVELY BONNAROOGLED? THE FESTIVAL SCENE
Not necessarily the Jambands.com news, April 1, 2003:

Another Music Festival to Take Place

Music lovers can take heart in learning that Another Musical Festival will take place. Featuring a roster of artists from the progressive underground grassroots music scene, festival organizers have secured a field. A big field. The promoter comments, "Blah blah blah Bonnaroo. Blah blah blah Bonnaroo. Blah blah branding, blah blah CD/DVD. Blah blah Bonnaroo." The festival organizers also note, "We're working with local authorities to study traffic patterns and maximize existing roadways that we have coming into the venue. When there are particular surges there may be back ups." Confirmed acts include Mofro, Yonder Mountain String Band, and the Roots. [1]

The summer of 2003 affirmed the import (and the perceived import) of festivals to the jamband community. Over every weekend between Memorial Day and Labor Day, Tent Cities (and in many cases, more accurately, Tent Townships) sprouted at farms and fields throughout North America. A flurry of new fests manifested the idea held by promoters (and would-be promoters) that if you build it (or announce your intentions to build it), they will come. This didn't hold true in every instance, as the ubiquity of events mediated their impact (or certainly

BerkFest

their attendance). Nonetheless, despite the diffusion of energy, festivals remain tied to the jam-band scene in a manner that most closely parallels the folk and blues gatherings of the 1960s (and, of course, the major rock fests of that era, though these swiftly became a bit more entwined with mainstream tastes and functioned less to nurture and sustain a musical alternative).

[1] By the way, in addition to this story, we also ran one that played off the fact that a second Bonnaroo event, Bonnaroo NE, had been announced for the week prior to BerkFest. This one, however, carried some unanticipated resonance.

Here is the full text of that April Fools' story:

Bonnaroo NO Announced

The latest installment in the Bonnaroo line of festivals will take place in Japan this October. Bonnaroo NO (North of Osaka) will be held on a concrete slab in downtown Tokyo. Seventy-five thousand music lovers are expected to make the pilgrimage to the city. Although some have expressed concern regarding traffic delays since Tokyo is one of the most congested cities in the world, festival organizers emphasize, "We're working with local authorities to study the traffic patterns and maximize the existing roadways that we have coming into the venue. When there are particular surges there may be back ups." At present, the only confirmed act is Galactic.

Meanwhile, Bonnaroo NE is slated for August 8-10 at Enterprise Park at Calverton Riverhead, New York. The Berkshire Mountain Music Festival (August 15-17 in Great Barrington, MA) is still trying to figure out what happened, commenting, "Bonnaroo NO, hey that's our catchphrase." The granddaddy of them all, the Bonnaroo Music Festival, now in its second year, will take place in Manchester, TN, on June 13-15.

Now, what we didn't appreciate is that Jambands.com has a healthy Japanese readership, much of which has no idea of the culture-specific notion of April Fools' Day. We began to receive frantic e-mails from Japanese music lovers asking for details and expressing some concern about the location of the event. The volume became so steady that two days later News Editor Jeff Waful wrote the following story:

Newsflash: April Fools' Stories Were Jokes; Budnick Apologizes to the People of Japan

Jambands.com wishes to remind readers that this past Tuesday was April Fools' Day. The news posted was intended to reflect the spirit of the day (akin to Philzone.com, which was transformed into a Dr. Phil Tribute page). For instance, Gov't Mule did not announce that Warren Haynes would become the permanent guitarist, as he actually is a founding member of the band. Furthermore, Krusty the Clown has not bought Wetlands Preserve.

We continue to receive a large number of e-mails from confused fans (seriously). The most disturbing letter comes from S. Andoh of Japan, who writes, "Japanese fans are now in panic that we'll have Bonnaroo in Japan... We want to find out if your article is true or false otherwise this issue and controversy will be bigger and bigger. I'd greatly appreciate it if you could conclude our controversy." [News Editor's note: Dean Budnick wrote the Japan story—which, to be abundantly clear, was a "joke"—and wishes to apologize for any confusion.]

Some of the festival fervor of 2003 can be traced to promoters (or putative promoters) hoping to capitalize on the success of the Bonnaroo Music Festival. In the spring of 2002, Superfly Productions and AC Entertainment announced an ambitious event to take place in a field in Manchester, TN, that would bring together many celebrated artists within the jamband realm (Widespread Panic, Phil Lesh & Friends, Trey Anastasio Band, String Cheese Incident, moe., Gov't Mule, Galactic) along with complementary artists (Jack Johnson, Ben Harper, Jurassic 5). The torrent of ticket buyers took even the promoters by surprise, as a lower-priced early bird offer sold out before festival organizers had a chance to announce that the number of these tickets would be capped (leaving some slightly miffed). The event sold out within a matter of days through the direct targeting of concertgoers via the participating bands' e-mail lists, along with minimal advertising. (The promoters initially touted that they had sold out Bonnaroo without the help of a single ad, but between you and me, since I was the one who drafted the text

Phil & Friends at Bonnaroo

for their "What Is Bonnaroo? Find out in X Days" banner on Jambands.com, I'll take a contrary view. At least the second year they modified this claim to "traditional advertising.")

The 70,000 people who migrated to Manchester for what proved to be an extraordinary event did so because it was a case of the right place, right roster, right time (right time in two senses: in terms of the historical moment, as people were ready for a sweeping gesture, and in terms of the time of year, as June is early in the festival season, and folks are particularly hyped to see music outside). Other than the traffic back up—which organizers helped to alleviate the following year partly by creating a temporary exit off the highway—the Bonnaroo promoters really pulled it off, aided by a particularly supportive crowd. Since the event sold out long in advance, those in attendance wanted to be there for the right reasons: music and community. There was little presence from the fringe elements, who carry minimal interest in the long-term vitality of the scene, but rather appear solely to prey on concertgoers.

Some of Bonnaroo's immediate legacy (beyond goosing a mainstream to gape at the music) was a surfeit of fests in 2003. The prevailing idea among certain folks was that as long as they had a farm and/or a field upon which to place a solid roster of bands (which, to their credit, many of these newfangled fests offered), promoters could benefit from the Bonnaroo Bump. The most egregious example is an event called Hobstock that a relative novice attempted to pull off on a 2,000-acre farm in Mississippi, featuring Widespread Panic, the Disco Biscuits, Leftover Salmon, Medeski Martin and Wood, Gov't Mule, and others. When a flood of advance ticket sales did not ensue and bands failed to receive their (inflated) advances, the artists began to pull out, Hobstock never happened, and the attorney general's office ultimately stepped in.

The founders of the inciting fest were Bonnaroogled themselves when, in an effort to "build the brand," Superfly and AC Entertainment's eyes became a bit too big for their stomachs. They decided to hold an event in the Hamptons in August (at the end of a long festival season, amidst the Long Island vacation locale of cranky, litigious Manhattanites). The show was ultimately canceled, the official explanation being that Bonnaroo would not have received sufficient support from local authorities (a previous event on the same site, the Field Day Festival, had to be scaled back and moved), though it is worth noting that ticket sales certainly were not apace with the Tennessee Bonnaroo. Meanwhile, smaller established festivals often found themselves with much lower attendance numbers partly due to the saturation of events, and bands such as the Disco Biscuits, the Recipe, and Leftover Salmon held off on their annual events (as did Walther Productions, which did not hold its Autumn Equinox).

Nonetheless, hundreds of thousands of concertgoers did make the festival rounds during the summer of 2003. This is because these events remain essential to the jamband community, in part for these reasons:

It's no coincidence that the 2002 Other Ones Alpine weekend and The Big Wu's annual festival are both called Family Reunions. These settings provide opportunities for folks to congregate and reconnect, which is all the more important to this scene because many relationships are fostered through the Internet.

Personal engagement with improvisation is at its core a joy of discovery. Festivals offer many such opportunities, not only through hours upon hours of onstage jams, but also through exposure to new artists.

Although the name Woodstock has been tarnished due to the 1999 event, the legacy of the original (and some would say only) Woodstock endures. Some fans relate the bands and happenings of the contemporary jamband circles to the mythos of the psychedelic Sixties.

All-age shows are an important aspect of festivals. While it's true some groups regularly

Phish at Big Cypress

perform in venues without age restrictions, others often play in clubs and bars that have State-imposed age restrictions. The jamband scene is a youthful one, and festival settings give all constituents the chance to take in the action.

Fresh fingers. Guest appearances often animate fans and bands by placing performers in new contexts that yield novel opportunities for improvisation. The guest sit-in has become a celebrated aspect of the festival scene, and many events go so far as to assemble players for one-off improv sets.

There are very few places you can see a band tear it up into the dawn (and in the case of Particle at Bonnaroo, well beyond it). Festival settings offer just that.
Some of the jamband community's denizens are chastised or shunned in their hometowns for their appearance (long hair, style of clothing, etc.). At the fests they can find like-garbed supporters—allowing those freak flags to fly freely.

Laying down (grass) roots. There is pleasure to be found in returning to a site every year with the same crowd even as the artists and other personalities remain in flux.

At times there is a loose, nervous energy to the bands' festival sets that brings out new elements in the music—motivated in part by time limitations, lack of soundchecks, audience numbers, and peers watching from the wings.

Road Trip! With today's limited opportunities to light out for the territories, festivals often provide a destination point for such travels—an excuse to motor.

Self-sufficient, self-selected festivals encourage the populace to care for itself. On occasion this leads to overindulgence, but in general it builds community through mutual respect and support.

Further faves and raves. While many of the groups in this book have crafted memorable studio records, some fans feel they can't fathom the intentions and affinities of a band until they see it live (and a number of the musicians concur). Extended festival bills offer fans the chance to discover new music from artists they've read or heard about, yet never actually heard.

The trade show. To some degree, festivals serve as music conferences and confabs for vendors who can socialize, network, and vent. Similarly, attendees can find a range of gear (and sympathetic merchants) that is not otherwise proximate to their locale.

At few other live events do the boundaries between artist and audience similarly abate. Band members may well be out in the audience or just poking around the site, reveling in the same experiences as their fans.

Tent City. Some folks derive a glee from setting up camp, particularly when it comes with a social component.

Moremoremore music. Occasional charges of excess are levied at the jamband scene, where habitués want new, more, now. Festivals scratch that itch.

For a list of current and impending festivals, your best bet is to pick up the annual issue of *Relix* devoted to this topic or look for the latest online at the Jambands.com festival page: *www.Jambands.com/festivalguide.*

ACKNOWLEDGMENTS

Special thanks to those who inspired, facilitated, provoked, regaled, or otherwise kicked me in the ass along the way: Jan and Al Budnick, Peter Shapiro, Jefferson Waful, Steve Bernstein, Butch Trucks, Kathy Stoddard, Aeve Baldwin, Josh Baron, Jon Schwartz, Sage Litsky, Phyllis Antoniello, Aaron Benor, Ben Bruce, Amy Fodera, Barry Frank and everyone at *Relix*, David Steinberg, Jesse Jarnow, Benjy Eisen, Dan Alford, Paul "Pro" Pearson, John Zinkand, Brian Ferdman, Dan Greenhaus, Phil Simon, Bryan Rodgers, Mike Gruenberg, Patrick Buzby, DNA, Sarah Bruner, Erica Lynn Gruenberg and everyone at Jambands.com, Todd Thomas, Rick Walsh, Chris Russo, Scott Struber, Rick Walsh, Dennis McNally, Matt Fuggi, Jeff Webster, Mick Skidmore, Jon "Topper" Topper, Lee Crumpton, Mike Bouchard, Rick Bucchieri, Cousin Chris, Wildman Steve, Andy Gadiel, Chris Hermann, Bob Makin, Aaron Schimmel, Alexander Gowan, Davis Saslvasky, Ellis Goddard, Rob Turner, Andrew Wagner, Jon and Marsha Zazula, all of the artists who contributed their music to the CD, the many managers, publicists, and agents who make things easy (and some of those who don't), and, above all, the musicians who inspired this work. Extra special thanks to the very patient people at Backbeat Books: Richard Johnston, Nancy Tabor, Nina Lesowitz, Amy Miller, Julie Herrod-Lumsden, Kate Henderson, Kevin Becketti, and the late Jay Kahn.

ABOUT THE AUTHOR

A cultural historian who holds a Ph.D. from Harvard and a J.D. from Columbia, author Dean Budnick is a true jamband fanatic. He founded and edits Jambands.com, the definitive online resource; serves as senior editor of *Relix* magazine; co-hosts the nationally syndicated *Jam Nation* radio program; and is co-founder and producer of the Jammy Awards. He lives in East Greenwich, Rhode Island.

PHOTO CREDITS

Jay Blakesberg: front cover, pages 65, 97 & 227

Dean Budnick: back cover

hilaryphoto.com: page 25

Danny Owen: page 141

Brian Parda: pages 3, 45, 91, 134, 149, 183, 195, 201 & 253

Dave Vann (www.davevann.com): pages 5, 11, 17, 38, 49, 53, 71, 85, 102, 107, 121, 125, 151, 155, 159, 163, 177, 185, 187, 209, 221, 255 & 257

ON THE CD

1. **moe.**, "Moth"; 20:50. This version originally appeared on *L Version 3.1*, the EP that collects three songs the band couldn't quite fit onto *L*, the 2000 Jammy Award winner for Live Release of the Year.

   Vinnie Amico, drums; Rob Derhak, bass and vocals; Chuck Garvey, guitar and vocals; Jim Loughlin, percussion; Al Schnier, vocals and guitar.

2. **The Disco Biscuits**, "7-11"/"Mulberry's Dream"; 18:55. The Biscuits performed these two segued songs during the first set on New Year's Eve 2002 at Philadelphia's Electric Factory. The group later released the pair on *TranceFusionRadio Broadcast 3*.

   Sam Altman, drums; Marc Brownstein, bass and vocals; Jon Gutwillig, vocals and guitar; Aron Magner, keyboards and vocals.

3. **Reid Genauer & the Assembly of Dust**, "Speculator"; 13:35. Recorded on 7/13/02 at the Webster Theater in Hartford, CT, "Speculator" is one of the songs from Genauer's Strangefolk canon that he now performs with AOD, typically animated by Nate Wilson's keys.

   Reid Genauer, vocals and guitar; Andy Herrick, drums; John Leccese, bass and vocals; Nate Wilson, keyboards and vocals; Adam Terrell, guitar and vocals.

4. **Jazz Mandolin Project**, "Nozanina"; 10:57. JMP performed this song on 3/3/03 on the *Jam Nation* radio show, during the outset of a spring tour in which Jamie Masefield expanded his band to a quartet. Jamie explains that this song is adapted from Heitor Villa Lobos's *Chôros No. 3*.

   Danton Boller, bass; Jamie Masefield, mandolin; Matt Shulman, trumpet; Dan Weiss, drums, percussion.

5. **The Motet**, "Cheap Shit"; 9:16. This song opened the Motet's 6/6/03 show at the Fox Theater in its hometown of Boulder, CO. Cochemea "Cheme" Gastelum (Robert Walter's 20th Congress) joined the band on sax for this show and much of its spring and summer tour.

   Mark Donovan, guitar; Cheme Gastelum, sax; Scott Messersmith, percussion; Greg Raymond, keyboards; Garrett Sayers, bass; Dave Watts, drums and percussion.

6. **Keller Williams**, "Breathe"; 5:30. Keller recorded this song as part of his acoustic performance

on *Jam Nation*, 4/21/03. "Breathe" is the title track of Williams's fourth release, in which he is backed by the String Cheese Incident.

Keller Williams, guitar and vocals.

"Moth" written by Al Schnier © Spaz Medicine Music; courtesy of Fatboy Records Inc.

"7-11"/"Mulberry's Dream" written by Jon Gutwillig © Try the Veal, Inc., from *TranceFusionRadio Broadcast 3*, courtesy of Diamond Riggs Records

"Speculator" written by Reid Genauer and Erik Glockler © All Set Guy Publishing

"Nozanina" written by Jamie Masefield © Lenapee Music

"Cheap Shit" written by Dave Watts © The Motet

"Breathe" written by Keller Williams © Basil Leaf Music/ASCAP

For information on recordings and tours:

www.moe.org
www.discobiscuits.com
www.reidgenauer.com
jazzmandolinproject.com
www.themotet.net
www.kellerwilliams.net

INDEX

Note to reader: **Bolded** page numbers refer to the main discussion of a band. *Italicized* page numbers refer to photos.

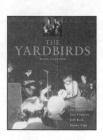